MORE PRAISE FROM ACROSS THE NATION
FOR THE JOBBANK SERIES...

"If you are looking for a job ... before you go to the newspapers and the help-wanted ads, listen to Bob Adams, publisher of *The Metropolitan New York JobBank*."

-Tom Brokaw, *NBC*

"Help on the job hunt ... Anyone who is job-hunting in the New York area can find a lot of useful ideas in a new paperback called *The Metropolitan New York JobBank* ..."

-Angela Taylor, *New York Times*

"For those graduates whose parents are pacing the floor, conspicuously placing circled want ads around the house and typing up resumes, [*The Carolina JobBank*] answers job-search questions."

-*Greensboro News and Record*

"A timely book for Chicago job hunters follows books from the same publisher that were well received in New York and Boston ... [*The Chicago JobBank* is] a fine tool for job hunters ..."

-Clarence Peterson, *Chicago Tribune*

"Because our listing is seen by people across the nation, it generates lots of resumes for us. We encourage unsolicited resumes. We'll always be listed [in *The Chicago JobBank*] as long as I'm in this career."

-Tom Fitzpatrick, Director of Human Resources
Merchandise Mart Properties, Inc.

"*The Florida JobBank* is an invaluable job-search reference tool. It provides the most up-to-date information and contact names available for companies in Florida. I should know -- it worked for me!"

-Rhonda Cody, Human Resources Consultant
Aetna Life and Casualty

"Thanks to our listing in *The Detroit JobBank*, we have received a large number of professional referrals."

-Michael A. Solonika, Human Resources Manager
Prestige Stamping, Inc.

"Through *The Dallas-Fort Worth JobBank,* we've been able to attract high-quality candidates for several positions."

-Rob Bertino, Southern States Sales Manager
CompuServe

"A superior series of job-hunt directories."
                              -Cornell University Career Center's *Where to Start*

"No longer can jobseekers feel secure about finding employment just through want ads. With the tough competition in the job market, particularly in the Boston area, they need much more help. For this reason, *The Boston JobBank* will have a wide and appreciative audience of new graduates, job changers, and people relocating to Boston. It provides a good place to start a search for entry-level professional positions."
                              -Journal of College Placement

"*The Phoenix JobBank* is a first-class publication. The information provided is useful and current."
                              -Lyndon Denton
                              Director of Human Resources and Materials Management
                              Apache Nitrogen Products, Inc.

"*The Seattle JobBank* is an essential resource for job hunters."
                              -Gil Lopez, Staffing Team Manager
                              Battelle Pacific Northwest Laboratories

"I read through the 'Basics of Job Winning' and 'Resumes' sections [in *The Dallas-Fort Worth JobBank*] and found them to be very informative, with some positive tips for the job searcher. I believe the strategies outlined will bring success to any determined candidate."
                              -Camilla Norder, Professional Recruiter
                              Presbyterian Hospital of Dallas

"Packed with helpful contacts, *The Houston JobBank* empowers its reader to launch an effective, strategic job search in the Houston metropolitan area."

                              -Andrew Ceperley, Director
                              College of Communication Career Services
                              The University of Texas at Austin

"[*The Atlanta JobBank* is] one of the best sources for finding a job in Atlanta!"
                              -Luann Miller, Human Resources Manager
                              Prudential Preferred Financial Services

"This well-researched, well-edited, job hunter's aid includes most major businesses and institutional entities in the New York metropolitan area ... [*The Metropolitan New York JobBank* is] highly recommended."
                              -Cheryl Gregory-Pindell, *Library Journal*

What makes the
JobBank series
the nation's premier
line of employment guides?

With vital employment information on thousands of employers across the nation, the JobBank series is the most comprehensive and authoritative set of career directories available today.

Each book in the series provides information on **dozens of different industries** in a given city or area, with the primary employer listings providing contact information, telephone and fax numbers, e-mail addresses, Websites, a summary of the firm's business, internships, and in many cases descriptions of the firm's typical professional job categories.

All of the reference information in the JobBank series is as up-to-date and accurate as possible. Every year, the entire database is thoroughly researched and verified by mail and by telephone. Adams Media Corporation publishes **more local employment guides more often** than any other publisher of career directories.

The JobBank series offers **28 regional titles**, from Minneapolis to Houston, and from Boston to San Francisco as well as **two industry-specific titles**. All of the information is organized geographically, because most people look for jobs in specific areas of the country.

A condensed, but thorough, review of the entire job search process is presented in the chapter **The Basics of Job Winning**, a feature which has received many compliments from career counselors. In addition, each JobBank directory includes a section on **resumes and cover letters** the *New York Times* has acclaimed as "excellent."

The JobBank series gives job hunters the most comprehensive, timely, and accurate career information, organized and indexed to facilitate your job search. An entire career reference library, JobBank books are designed to help you find optimal employment in any market.

Top career publications from Adams Media Corporation

The JobBank Series:
each JobBank book is $16.95

The Atlanta JobBank, 14th Ed.
The Austin/San Antonio JobBank, 3rd Ed.
The Boston JobBank, 19th Ed.
The Carolina JobBank, 6th Ed.
The Chicago JobBank, 18th Ed.
The Colorado JobBank, 13th Ed.
The Connecticut JobBank, 2nd Ed.
The Dallas-Fort Worth JobBank, 13th Ed.
The Detroit JobBank, 9th Ed.
The Florida JobBank, 15th Ed.
The Houston JobBank, 11th Ed.
The Indiana JobBank, 3rd Ed.
The Las Vegas JobBank, 2nd Ed.
The Los Angeles JobBank, 17th Ed.
The Minneapolis-St. Paul JobBank, 11th Ed.
The Missouri JobBank, 3rd Ed.
The New Jersey JobBank, 1st Ed.
The Metropolitan New York JobBank, 18th Ed.
The Ohio JobBank, 10th Ed.
The Greater Philadelphia JobBank, 14th Ed.
The Phoenix JobBank, 8th Ed.
The Pittsburgh JobBank, 2nd Ed.
The Portland JobBank, 3rd Ed.
The San Francisco Bay Area JobBank, 16th Ed.
The Seattle JobBank, 12th Ed.
The Tennessee JobBank, 5th Ed.
The Virginia JobBank, 3rd Ed.
The Metropolitan Washington DC JobBank, 15th Ed.

The JobBank Guide to Computer & High-Tech Companies, 2nd Ed. ($17.95)
The JobBank Guide to Health Care Companies, 2nd Ed. ($17.95)

The National JobBank, 2003 (Covers the entire U.S.: $450.00 hc)

Other Career Titles:
The Adams Cover Letter Almanac ($12.95)
The Adams Internet Job Search Almanac, 6th Ed. ($12.95)
The Adams Executive Recruiters Almanac, 2nd Ed. ($17.95)
The Adams Job Interview Almanac ($12.95)
The Adams Jobs Almanac, 8th Ed. ($16.95)
The Adams Resume Almanac ($10.95)
Business Etiquette in Brief ($7.95)
Campus Free College Degrees, 8th Ed. ($16.95)
Career Tests ($12.95)
Closing Techniques, 2nd Ed. ($8.95)
Cold Calling Techniques, 4th Ed. ($8.95)
College Grad Job Hunter, 4th Ed. ($14.95)
The Complete Resume & Job Search Book for College Students, 2nd Ed. ($12.95)
Cover Letters That Knock 'em Dead, 5th Ed. ($12.95)
Every Woman's Essential Job Hunting & Resume Book ($11.95)
The Everything Cover Letter Book ($12.95)
The Everything Get-A-Job Book ($12.95)
The Everything Hot Careers Book ($12.95)
The Everything Job Interview Book ($12.95)
The Everything Online Business Book ($12.95)
The Everything Online Job Search Book ($12.95)
The Everything Resume Book ($12.95)
The Everything Selling Book ($12.95)
First Time Resume ($7.95)
How to Start and Operate a Successful Business ($9.95)
Knock 'em Dead, 2003 ($14.95)
Knock 'em Dead Business Presentations ($12.95)
Market Yourself and Your Career, 2nd Ed. ($12.95)
The New Professional Image ($12.95)
The 150 Most Profitable Home Businesses for Women ($9.95)
The Resume Handbook, 3rd Ed. ($7.95)
Resumes That Knock 'em Dead, 5th Ed. ($12.95)
The Road to CEO ($20.00 hc)
The 250 Job Interview Questions You'll Most Likely Be Asked ($9.95)
Your Executive Image ($10.95)

17th Edition
THE Los Angeles JobBank

Reference Editor:	Christie L. Barros
Assistant Reference Editor:	Lisa A. Geraghty
Production Manager:	Michelle Roy Kelly

Adams Media Corporation
AVON, MASSACHUSETTS

Published by Adams Media Corporation
57 Littlefield Street, Avon MA 02322. U.S.A.
www.adamsmedia.com

ISBN: 1-58062-819-2
ISSN: 1098-9765
Manufactured in Canada.

*This book is available on standing order
and at quantity discounts for bulk purchases.*

For information, call 800/872-5627 (in Massachusetts, 508/427-7100).

TABLE OF CONTENTS

- *Industrial Vehicles and Moving Equipment*
- *Motor Vehicles and Equipment*
- *Travel Trailers and Campers*

Banking/Savings and Loans/103
Biotechnology, Pharmaceuticals, and Scientific R&D/109
- *Clinical Labs*
- *Lab Equipment Manufacturers*
- *Pharmaceutical Manufacturers and Distributors*

Business Services and Non-Scientific Research/124
- *Adjustment and Collection Services*
- *Cleaning, Maintenance, and Pest Control Services*
- *Credit Reporting Services*
- *Detective, Guard, and Armored Car Services/Security Systems Services*
- *Miscellaneous Equipment Rental and Leasing*
- *Secretarial and Court Reporting Services*

Charities and Social Services/130
- *Job Training and Vocational Rehabilitation Services*

Chemicals/Rubber and Plastics/133
- *Adhesives, Detergents, Inks, Paints, Soaps, Varnishes*
- *Agricultural Chemicals and Fertilizers*
- *Carbon and Graphite Products*
- *Chemical Engineering Firms*
- *Industrial Gases*

Communications: Telecommunications and Broadcasting/140
- *Cable/Pay Television Services*
- *Communications Equipment*
- *Radio and Television Broadcasting Stations*
- *Telephone, Telegraph, and Other Message Communications*

Computer Hardware, Software, and Services/146
- *Computer Components and Hardware Manufacturers*
- *Consultants and Computer Training Companies*
- *Internet and Online Service Providers*
- *Networking and Systems Services*
- *Repair Services/Rental and Leasing*
- *Resellers, Wholesalers, and Distributors*
- *Software Developers/Programming Services*

Educational Services/179
- *Business/Secretarial/Data Processing Schools*
- *Colleges/Universities/Professional Schools*
- *Community Colleges/Technical Schools/Vocational Schools*
- *Elementary and Secondary Schools*
- *Preschool and Child Daycare Services*

Electronic/Industrial Electrical Equipment/185
- *Electronic Machines and Systems*
- *Semiconductor Manufacturers*

Environmental and Waste Management Services/207
- *Environmental Engineering Firms*
- *Sanitary Services*

Fabricated/Primary Metals and Products/213
- *Aluminum and Copper Foundries*
- *Die-Castings*
- *Iron and Steel Foundries/Steel Works, Blast Furnaces, and Rolling Mills*

Financial Services/218
- *Consumer Financing and Credit Agencies*
- *Investment Specialists*
- *Mortgage Bankers and Loan Brokers*
- *Security and Commodity Brokers, Dealers, and Exchanges*

Food and Beverages/Agriculture/226
- Crop Services and Farm Supplies
- Dairy Farms
- Food Manufacturers/Processors and Agricultural Producers
- Tobacco Products

Government/232
- Courts
- Executive, Legislative, and General Government
- Public Agencies (Firefighters, Military, Police)
- United States Postal Service

Health Care: Services, Equipment, and Products/236
- Dental Labs and Equipment
- Home Health Care Agencies
- Hospitals and Medical Centers
- Medical Equipment Manufacturers and Wholesalers
- Offices and Clinics of Health Practitioners
- Residential Treatment Centers/Nursing Homes
- Veterinary Services

Hotels and Restaurants/255
Insurance/262
Legal Services/273
Manufacturing: Miscellaneous Consumer/277
- Art Supplies
- Batteries
- Cosmetics and Related Products
- Household Appliances and Audio/Video Equipment
- Jewelry, Silverware, and Plated Ware
- Miscellaneous Household Furniture and Fixtures
- Musical Instruments
- Tools
- Toys and Sporting Goods

Manufacturing: Miscellaneous Industrial/287
- Ball and Roller Bearings
- Commercial Furniture and Fixtures
- Fans, Blowers, and Purification Equipment
- Industrial Machinery and Equipment
- Motors and Generators/Compressors and Engine Parts
- Vending Machines

Mining/Gas/Petroleum/Energy Related/305
- Anthracite, Coal, and Ore Mining
- Mining Machinery and Equipment
- Oil and Gas Field Services
- Petroleum and Natural Gas

Paper and Wood Products/309
- Forest and Wood Products and Services
- Lumber and Wood Wholesale
- Millwork, Plywood, and Structural Members
- Paper and Wood Mills

Printing and Publishing/311
- Book, Newspaper, and Periodical Publishers
- Commercial Photographers
- Commercial Printing Services
- Graphic Designers

Real Estate/318
- Land Subdividers and Developers
- Real Estate Agents, Managers, and Operators
- Real Estate Investment Trusts

INTRODUCTION

HOW TO USE THIS BOOK

Right now, you hold in your hands one of the most effective job-hunting tools available anywhere. In *The Los Angeles JobBank*, you will find valuable information to help you launch or continue a rewarding career. But before you open to the book's employer listings and start calling about current job openings, take a few minutes to learn how best to use the resources presented in *The Los Angeles JobBank*.

The Los Angeles JobBank will help you to stand out from other jobseekers. While many people looking for a new job rely solely on newspaper help-wanted ads, this book offers you a much more effective job-search method – direct contact. The direct contact method has been proven twice as effective as scanning the help-wanted ads. Instead of waiting for employers to come looking for you, you'll be far more effective going to them. While many of your competitors will use trial and error methods in trying to set up interviews, you'll learn not only how to get interviews, but what to expect once you've got them.

In the next few pages, we'll take you through each section of the book so you'll be prepared to get a jump-start on your competition.

Basics of Job Winning

Preparation. Strategy. Time management. These are three of the most important elements of a successful job search. *Basics of Job Winning* helps you address these and all the other elements needed to find the right job.

One of your first priorities should be to define your personal career objectives. What qualities make a job desirable to you? Creativity? High pay? Prestige? Use *Basics of Job Winning* to weigh these questions. Then use the rest of the chapter to design a strategy to find a job that matches your criteria.

In *Basics of Job Winning*, you'll learn which job-hunting techniques work, and which don't. We've reviewed the pros and cons of mass mailings, help-wanted ads, and direct contact. We'll show you how to develop and approach contacts in your field; how to research a prospective employer; and how to use that information to get an interview and the job.

Also included in *Basics of Job Winning*: interview dress code and etiquette, the "do's and don'ts" of interviewing, sample interview questions, and more. We also deal with some of the unique problems faced by those jobseekers who are currently employed, those who have lost a job, and college students conducting their first job search.

Resumes and Cover Letters

The approach you take to writing your resume and cover letter can often mean the difference between getting an interview and never being noticed. In this section, we discuss different formats, as well as what to put on (and what to leave off) your resume. We review the benefits and drawbacks of professional resume writers, and the importance of a follow-up letter. Also included in this section are sample resumes and cover letters you can use as models.

The Employer Listings

Employers are listed alphabetically by industry. When a company does business under a person's name, like "John Smith & Co.," the company is usually listed by the surname's spelling (in this case "S"). Exceptions occur when a company's name is widely recognized, like "JCPenney" or "Howard Johnson Motor Lodge." In those cases, the company's first name is the key ("J" and "H" respectively).

The Los Angeles JobBank covers a very wide range of industries. Each company profile is assigned to one of the industry chapters listed below.

Accounting and Management Consulting	*Fabricated/Primary Metals and Products*
Advertising, Marketing, and Public Relations	*Financial Services*
Aerospace	*Food and Beverages/Agriculture*
Apparel, Fashion, and Textiles	*Government*
Architecture, Construction, and Engineering	*Health Care: Services, Equipment, and*
Arts, Entertainment, Sports, and Recreation	*Products*
Automotive	*Hotels and Restaurants*
Banking/Savings and Loans	*Insurance*
Biotechnology, Pharmaceuticals, and	*Legal Services*
Scientific R&D	*Manufacturing: Miscellaneous Consumer*
Business Services and Non-Scientific	*Manufacturing: Miscellaneous Industrial*
Research	*Mining/Gas/Petroleum/Energy Related*
Charities and Social Services	*Paper and Wood Products*
Chemicals/Rubber and Plastics	*Printing and Publishing*
Communications: Telecommunications and	*Real Estate*
Broadcasting	*Retail*
Computer Hardware, Software, and Services	*Stone, Clay, Glass, and Concrete Products*
Educational Services	*Transportation/Travel*
Electronic/Industrial Electrical Equipment	*Utilities: Electric/Gas/Water*
Environmental and Waste Management	*Miscellaneous Wholesaling*
Services	

Many of the company listings offer detailed company profiles. In addition to company names, addresses, and phone numbers, these listings also include contact names or hiring departments, and descriptions of each company's products and/or services. Many of these listings also feature a variety of additional information including:

Common positions - A list of job titles that the company commonly fills when it is hiring, organized in alphabetical order from Accountant to X-ray Technician. Note: Keep in mind that *The Los Angeles JobBank* is a directory of major employers in the area, not a directory of openings currently available. Many of the companies listed will be hiring, others will not. However, since most professional job openings are filled without the placement of help-wanted ads, contacting the employers in this book directly is still a more effective method than browsing the Sunday papers.

Special programs - Does the company offer training programs, internships, or apprenticeships? These programs can be important to first time jobseekers and college students looking for practical work experience. Many employer profiles will include information on these programs.

Parent company - If an employer is a subsidiary of a larger company, the name of that parent company will often be listed here. Use this information to supplement your company research before contacting the employer.

Number of employees - The number of workers a company employs.

Company listings may also include information on other U.S. locations and any stock exchanges the firm may be listed on.

A note on all employer listings that appear in *The Los Angeles JobBank*: This book is intended as a starting point. It is not intended to replace any effort that you, the jobseeker, should devote to your job hunt. Keep in mind that while a great deal of effort has been put into collecting and verifying the company profiles provided in this book, addresses and contact names change regularly. Inevitably, some contact names listed herein have changed even before you read this. We recommend you contact a company before mailing your resume to ensure nothing has changed.

Index

The Los Angeles JobBank index is listed alphabetically by industry.

THE JOB SEARCH

THE BASICS OF JOB WINNING: A CONDENSED REVIEW

This chapter is divided into four sections. The first section explains the fundamentals that every jobseeker should know, especially first-time jobseekers. The next three sections deal with special situations faced by specific types of jobseekers: those who are currently employed, those who have lost a job, and college students.

THE BASICS:
Things Everyone Needs to Know

Career Planning

The first step to finding your ideal job is to clearly define your objectives. This is better known as career planning (or life planning if you wish to emphasize the importance of combining the two). Career planning has become a field of study in and of itself.

If you are thinking of choosing or switching careers, we particularly emphasize two things. First, choose a career where you will enjoy most of the day-to-day tasks. This sounds obvious, but most of us have at some point found the idea of a glamour industry or prestigious job title attractive without thinking of the key consideration: Would we enjoy performing the everyday tasks the position entails?

The second key consideration is that you are not merely choosing a career, but also a lifestyle. Career counselors indicate that one of the most common problems people encounter in jobseeking is that they fail to consider how well-suited they are for a particular position or career. For example, some people, attracted to management consulting by good salaries, early responsibility, and high-level corporate exposure, do not adapt well to the long hours, heavy travel demands, and constant pressure to produce. Be sure to ask yourself how you might adapt to the day-to-day duties and working environment that a specific position entails. Then ask yourself how you might adapt to the demands of that career or industry as a whole.

Choosing Your Strategy

Assuming that you've established your career objectives, the next step of the job search is to develop a strategy. If you don't take the time to develop a plan, you may find yourself going in circles after several weeks of randomly searching for opportunities that always seem just beyond your reach.

The most common jobseeking techniques are:

- following up on help-wanted advertisements (in the newspaper or online)
- using employment services
- relying on personal contacts
- contacting employers directly (the Direct Contact method)

Each of these approaches can lead to better jobs. However, the Direct Contact method boasts twice the success rate of the others. So unless you have specific reasons to employ other strategies, Direct Contact should form the foundation of your job search.

If you choose to use other methods as well, try to expend at least half your energy on Direct Contact. Millions of other jobseekers have already proven that Direct Contact has been twice as effective in obtaining employment, so why not follow in their footsteps?

Setting Your Schedule

Okay, so now that you've targeted a strategy it's time to work out the details of your job search. The most important detail is setting up a schedule. Of course, since job searches aren't something most people do regularly, it may be hard to estimate how long each step will take. Nonetheless, it is important to have a plan so that you can monitor your progress.

When outlining your job search schedule, have a realistic time frame in mind. If you will be job-searching full-time, your search could take at least two months or more. If you can only devote part-time effort, it will probably take at least four months.

You probably know a few people who seem to spend their whole lives searching for a better job in their spare time. Don't be one of them. If you are presently working and don't feel like devoting a lot of energy to jobseeking right now, then wait. Focus on enjoying your present position, performing your best on the job, and storing up energy for when you are really ready to begin your job search.

> **The first step in beginning your job search is to clearly define your objectives.**

Those of you who are currently unemployed should remember that *job-hunting is tough work, both physically and emotionally*. It is also intellectually demanding work that requires you to be at your best. So don't tire yourself out by working on your job campaign around the clock. At the same time, be sure to discipline yourself. The most logical way to manage your time while looking for a job is to keep your regular working hours.

If you are searching full-time and have decided to choose several different strategies, we recommend that you divide up each week, designating some time for each method. By trying several approaches at once, you can evaluate how promising each seems and alter your schedule accordingly. Keep in mind that the *majority of openings are filled without being advertised*. Remember also that positions advertised on the Internet are just as likely to already be filled as those found in the newspaper!

If you are searching part-time and decide to try several different contact methods, we recommend that you try them sequentially. You simply won't have enough time to put a meaningful amount of effort into more than one method at once. Estimate the length of your job search, and then allocate so many weeks or months for each contact method, beginning with Direct Contact. The purpose of setting this schedule is not to rush you to your goal but to help you periodically evaluate your progress.

The Direct Contact Method

Once you have scheduled your time, you are ready to begin your search in earnest. Beginning with the Direct Contact method, the first step is to develop a checklist for categorizing the types of firms for which you'd like to work. You might categorize firms by product line, size, customer type (such as industrial or consumer), growth prospects, or geographical location. Keep in mind, the shorter the list the easier it will be to locate a company that is right for you.

Next you will want to use this *JobBank* book to assemble your list of potential employers. Choose firms where *you* are most likely to be able to find a job. Try matching your skills with those that a specific job demands. Consider where your skills might be in demand, the degree of competition for employment, and the employment outlook at each company.

Separate your prospect list into three groups. The first 25 percent will be your primary target group, the next 25 percent will be your secondary group, and the remaining names will be your reserve group.

After you form your prospect list, begin working on your resume. Refer to the Resumes and Cover Letters section following this chapter for more information.

Once your resume is complete, begin researching your first batch of prospective employers. You will want to determine whether you would be happy working at the firms you are researching and to get a better idea of what their employment needs might be. You also need to obtain enough information to sound highly informed about the company during phone conversations and in mail correspondence. But don't go all out on your research yet! You probably won't be able to arrange interviews with some of these firms, so save your big research effort until you start to arrange interviews. Nevertheless, you should plan to spend several hours researching each firm. Do your research in batches to save time and energy. Start with this book, and find out what you can about each of the firms in your primary target group. For answers to specific questions, contact any pertinent professional associations that may be able to help you learn more about an employer. Read industry publications looking for articles on the firm. (Addresses of associations and names of important publications are listed after each section of employer listings in this book.) Then look up the company on the Internet or try additional resources at your local library. Keep organized, and maintain a folder on each firm.

> **The more you know about a company, the more likely you are to catch an interviewer's eye. (You'll also face fewer surprises once you get the job!)**

Information to look for includes: company size; president, CEO, or owner's name; when the company was established; what each division does; and benefits that are important to you. An abundance of company information can now be found electronically, through the World Wide Web or commercial online services. Researching companies online is a convenient means of obtaining information quickly and easily. If you have access to the Internet, you can search from your home at any time of day.

You may search a particular company's Website for current information that may be otherwise unavailable in print. In fact, many companies that maintain a site update their information daily. In addition, you may also search articles written about the company online. Today, most of the nation's largest newspapers, magazines, trade publications, and regional business periodicals have online versions of their publications. To find additional resources, use a search engine like Yahoo! or Alta Vista and type in the keyword "companies" or "employers."

If you discover something that really disturbs you about the firm (they are about to close their only local office), or if you discover that your chances of getting a job there are practically nil (they have just instituted a hiring freeze), then cross them off your prospect list. If possible, supplement your research efforts by contacting individuals who know the firm well. Ideally you should make an informal contact with someone at that particular firm, but often a direct competitor or a major customer will be able to supply you with just as much information. At the very least, try to obtain whatever printed information the company has available – not just annual reports, but product brochures, company profiles, or catalogs. This information is often available on the Internet.

Getting the Interview

Now it is time to make Direct Contact with the goal of arranging interviews. If you have read any books on job-searching, you may have noticed that most of these books tell you to avoid the human resources office like the plague. It is said that the human resources office never hires people; they screen candidates. Unfortunately, this is often the case. If you can identify the appropriate manager with the authority to hire you, you should try to contact that person directly.

The obvious means of initiating Direct Contact are:

- Mail (postal or electronic)
- Phone calls

Mail contact is a good choice if you have not been in the job market for a while. You can take your time to prepare a letter, say exactly what you want, and of course include your resume. Remember that employers receive many resumes every day. Don't be surprised if you do not get a response to your inquiry, *and don't spend weeks waiting for responses that may never come.* If you do send a letter, follow it up (or precede it) with a phone call. This will increase your impact, and because of the initial research you did, will underscore both your familiarity with and your interest in the firm. Bear in mind that your goal is to make your name a familiar one with prospective employers, so that when a position becomes available, your resume will be one of the first the hiring manager seeks out.

DEVELOPING YOUR CONTACTS: NETWORKING

Some career counselors feel that the best route to a better job is through somebody you already know or through somebody to whom you can be introduced. These counselors recommend that you build your contact base beyond your current acquaintances by asking each one to introduce you, or refer you, to additional people in your field of interest.

The theory goes like this: You might start with 15 personal contacts, each of whom introduces you to three additional people, for a total of 45 additional contacts. Then each of these people introduces you to three additional people, which adds 135 additional contacts. Theoretically, you will soon know every person in the industry.

Of course, developing your personal contacts does not work quite as smoothly as the theory suggests because some people will not be able to introduce you to anyone. The further you stray from your initial contact base, the weaker your references may be. So, if you do try developing your own contacts, try to begin with as many people that you know personally as you can. Dig into your personal phone book and your holiday greeting card list and locate old classmates from school. Be particularly sure to approach people who perform your personal business such as your lawyer, accountant, banker, doctor, stockbroker, and insurance agent. These people develop a very broad contact base due to the nature of their professions.

If you send a fax, always follow with a hard copy of your resume and cover letter in the mail. Often, through no fault of your own, a fax will come through illegibly and employers do not often have time to let candidates know.

Another alternative is to make a "cover call." Your cover call should be just like your cover letter: concise. Your first statement should interest the employer in you. Then try to subtly mention your familiarity with the firm. Don't be overbearing; keep your introduction to three sentences or less. Be pleasant, self-confident, and relaxed. This will greatly increase the chances of the person at the other end of the line developing the conversation. But don't press. If you are asked to follow up with "something in the mail," this signals the conversation's natural end. Don't try to prolong the conversation once it has ended, and don't ask what they want to receive in the mail. Always send your resume and a highly personalized follow-up letter, reminding the addressee of the phone conversation. *Always* include a cover letter if you are asked to send a resume, and treat your resume and cover letter as a total package. Gear your letter toward the specific position you are applying for and prove why you would be a "good match" for the position.

> **Always include a cover letter if you are asked to send a resume.**

Unless you are in telephone sales, making smooth and relaxed cover calls will probably not come easily. Practice them on your own, and then with your friends or relatives.

DON'T BOTHER WITH MASS MAILINGS OR BARRAGES OF PHONE CALLS

Direct Contact does not mean burying every firm within a hundred miles with mail and phone calls. Mass mailings rarely work in the job hunt. This also applies to those letters that are personalized -- but dehumanized -- on an automatic typewriter or computer. Don't waste your time or money on such a project; you will fool no one but yourself.

The worst part of sending out mass mailings, or making unplanned phone calls to companies you have not researched, is that you are likely to be remembered as someone with little genuine interest in the firm, who lacks sincerity -- somebody that nobody wants to hire.

If you obtain an interview as a result of a telephone conversation, be sure to send a thank-you note reiterating the points you made during the conversation. You will appear more professional and increase your impact. However, unless specifically requested, don't mail your resume once an interview has been arranged. Take it with you to the interview instead.

You should never show up to seek a professional position without an appointment. Even if you are somehow lucky enough to obtain an interview, you will appear so unprofessional that you will not be seriously considered.

HELP WANTED ADVERTISEMENTS

Only a small fraction of professional job openings are advertised. Yet the majority of jobseekers -- and quite a few people not in the job market -- spend a lot of time studying the help wanted ads. As a result, the competition for advertised openings is often very severe.

A moderate-sized employer told us about their experience advertising in the help wanted section of a major Sunday newspaper:

It was a disaster. We had over 500 responses from this relatively small ad in just one week. We have only two phone lines in this office and one was totally knocked out. We'll never advertise for professional help again.

If you insist on following up on help wanted ads, then research a firm before you reply to an ad. Preliminary research might help to separate you from all of the other professionals responding to that ad, many of whom will have only a passing interest in the opportunity. It will also give you insight about a particular firm, to help you determine if it is potentially a good match. That said, your chances of obtaining a job through the want ads are still much smaller than they are with the Direct Contact method.

Preparing for the Interview

As each interview is arranged, begin your in-depth research. You should arrive at an interview knowing the company upside-down and inside-out. You need to know the company's products, types of customers, subsidiaries, parent company, principal locations, rank in the industry, sales and profit trends, type of ownership, size, current plans, and much more. By this time you have probably narrowed your job search to one industry. Even if you haven't, you should still be familiar with common industry terms, the trends in the firm's industry, the firm's principal competitors and their relative performance, and the direction in which the industry leaders are headed.

Dig into every resource you can! Surf the Internet. Read the company literature, the trade press, the business press, and if the company is public, call your stockbroker (if you have one) and ask for additional information. If possible, speak to someone at the firm before the interview, or if not, speak to someone at a competing firm. The more time you spend, the better. Even if you feel extremely pressed for time, you should set aside several hours for pre-interview research.

> **You should arrive at an interview knowing the company upside-down and inside-out.**

If you have been out of the job market for some time, don't be surprised if you find yourself tense during your first few interviews. It will probably happen every time you re-enter the market, not just when you seek your first job after getting out of school.

Tension is natural during an interview, but knowing you have done a thorough research job should put you more at ease. Make a list of questions that you think might be asked in each interview. Think out your answers carefully and practice them with a friend. Tape record your responses to the problem questions. (See also in this chapter: Informational Interviews.) If you feel particularly unsure of your interviewing skills, arrange your first interviews at firms you are not as interested in. (But remember it is common courtesy to seem enthusiastic about the possibility of working for any firm at which you interview.) Practice again on your own after these first few interviews. Go over the difficult questions that you were asked.

Take some time to really think about how you will convey your work history. Present "bad experiences" as "learning experiences." Instead of saying "I hated my position as a salesperson because I had to bother people on the phone," say "I realized that cold-calling was not my strong suit. Though I love working with people, I decided my talents would be best used in a more face-to-face atmosphere." Always find some sort of lesson from previous jobs, as they all have one.

Interview Attire

How important is the proper dress for a job interview? Buying a complete wardrobe, donning new shoes, and having your hair styled every morning are not enough to guarantee you a career position as an investment banker. But on the other hand, if you can't find a clean, conservative suit or won't take the time to wash your hair, then you are just wasting your time by interviewing at all.

Personal grooming is as important as finding appropriate clothes for a job interview. Careful grooming indicates both a sense of thoroughness and self-confidence. This is not the time to make a statement – take out the extra earrings and avoid any garish hair colors not found in nature. Women should not wear excessive makeup, and both men and women should refrain from wearing any perfume or cologne (it only takes a small spritz to leave an allergic interviewer with a fit of sneezing and a bad impression of your meeting). Men should be freshly shaven, even if the interview is late in the day, and men with long hair should have it pulled back and neat.

Men applying for any professional position should wear a suit, preferably in a conservative color such as navy or charcoal gray. It is easy to get away with wearing the same dark suit to consecutive interviews at the same company; just be sure to wear a different shirt and tie for each interview.

Women should also wear a business suit. Professionalism still dictates a suit with a skirt, rather than slacks, as proper interview garb for women. This is usually true even at companies where pants are acceptable attire for female employees. As much as you may disagree with this guideline, the more prudent time to fight this standard is after you land the job.

The final selection of candidates for a job opening won't be determined by dress, of course. However, inappropriate dress can quickly eliminate a first-round candidate. So while you shouldn't spend a fortune on a new wardrobe, you should be sure that your clothes are adequate. The key is to dress at least as formally or slightly more formally and more conservatively than the position would suggest.

What to Bring

Be complete. Everyone needs a watch, a pen, and a notepad. Finally, a briefcase or a leather-bound folder (containing extra, unfolded, copies of your resume) will help complete the look of professionalism.

Sometimes the interviewer will be running behind schedule. Don't be upset, be sympathetic. There is often pressure to interview a lot of candidates and to quickly fill a demanding position. So be sure to come to your interview with good reading material to keep yourself occupied and relaxed.

The Interview

The very beginning of the interview is the most important part because it determines the tone for the rest of it. Those first few moments are especially crucial. Do you smile when you meet? Do you establish enough eye contact, but not too much? Do you walk into the office with a self-assured and confident stride? Do you shake hands firmly? Do you make small talk easily without being garrulous? It is

---

BE PREPARED:
Some Common Interview Questions

Tell me about yourself.

Why did you leave your last job?

What excites you in your current job?

Where would you like to be in five years?

How much overtime are you willing to work?

What would your previous/present employer tell me about you?

Tell me about a difficult situation that you
faced at your previous/present job.

What are your greatest strengths?

What are your weaknesses?

Describe a work situation where you took initiative
and went beyond your normal responsibilities.

Why should we hire you?

---

human nature to judge people by that first impression, so make sure it is a good one. But most of all, try to be yourself.

Often the interviewer will begin, after the small talk, by telling you about the company, the division, the department, or perhaps, the position. Because of your detailed research, the information about the company should be repetitive for you, and the interviewer would probably like nothing better than to avoid this regurgitation of the company biography. So if you can do so tactfully, indicate to the interviewer that you are very familiar with the firm. If he or she seems intent on providing you with background information, despite your hints, then acquiesce.

But be sure to remain attentive. If you can manage to generate a brief discussion of the company or the industry at this point, without being forceful, great. It will help to further build rapport, underscore your interest, and increase your impact.

> **The interviewer's job is to find a reason to turn you down; your job is to not provide that reason.**
>
> -John L. LaFevre, author,
> *How You Really Get Hired*
>
> Reprinted from the 1989/90 *CPC Annual*, with permission of the National Association of Colleges and Employers (formerly College Placement Council, Inc.), copyright holder.

Soon (if it didn't begin that way) the interviewer will begin the questions, many of which you will have already practiced. This period of the interview usually falls into one of two categories (or somewhere in between): either a structured interview, where the interviewer has a prescribed set of questions to ask; or an unstructured interview, where the interviewer will ask only leading questions to get you to talk about yourself, your experiences, and your goals. Try to sense as quickly as possible in which direction the interviewer wishes to proceed. This will make the interviewer feel more relaxed and in control of the situation.

Remember to keep attuned to the interviewer and make the length of your answers appropriate to the situation. If you are really unsure as to how detailed a response the interviewer is seeking, then ask.

As the interview progresses, the interviewer will probably mention some of the most important responsibilities of the position. If applicable, draw parallels between your experience and the demands of the position as detailed by the interviewer. Describe your past experience in the same manner that you do on your resume: emphasizing results and achievements and not merely describing activities. But don't exaggerate. Be on the level about your abilities.

The first interview is often the toughest, where many candidates are screened out. If you are interviewing for a very competitive position, you will have to make an impression that will last. Focus on a few of your greatest strengths that are relevant to the position. Develop these points carefully, state them again in different words, and then try to summarize them briefly at the end of the interview.

Often the interviewer will pause toward the end and ask if you have any questions. Particularly in a structured interview, this might be the one chance to really show your knowledge of and interest in the firm. Have a list prepared of specific questions that are of real interest to you. Let your questions subtly show your research and your knowledge of the firm's activities. It is wise to have an extensive list of questions, as several of them may be answered during the interview.

Do not turn your opportunity to ask questions into an interrogation. Avoid reading directly from your list of questions, and ask questions that you are fairly certain the interviewer can answer (remember how you feel when you cannot answer a question during an interview).

Even if you are unable to determine the salary range beforehand, do not ask about it during the first interview. You can always ask later. Above all, don't ask about fringe benefits until you have been offered a position. (Then be sure to get all the details.)

Try not to be negative about anything during the interview, particularly any past employer or any previous job. Be cheerful. Everyone likes to work with someone who seems to be happy. Even if you detest your current/former job or manager, do not make disparaging comments. The interviewer may construe this as a sign of a potential attitude problem and not consider you a strong candidate.

Don't let a tough question throw you off base. If you don't know the answer to a question, simply say so -- do not apologize. Just smile. Nobody can answer every question -- particularly some of the questions that are asked in job interviews.

Before your first interview, you may be able to determine how many rounds of interviews there usually are for positions at your level. (Of course it may differ quite a bit even within the different levels of one firm.) Usually you can count on attending at least two or three interviews, although some firms are known to give a minimum of six interviews for all professional positions. While you should be more relaxed as you return for subsequent interviews, the pressure will be on. The more prepared you are, the better.

Depending on what information you are able to obtain, you might want to vary your strategy quite a bit from interview to interview. For instance, if the first interview is a screening interview, then be sure a few of your strengths really stand out. On the other hand, if later interviews are primarily with people who are in a position to veto your hiring, but not to push it forward, then you should primarily focus on building rapport as opposed to reiterating and developing your key strengths.

If it looks as though your skills and background do not match the position the interviewer was hoping to fill, ask him or her if there is another division or subsidiary that perhaps could profit from your talents.

After the Interview

Write a follow-up letter immediately after the interview, while it is still fresh in the interviewer's mind (see the sample follow-up letter format found in the Resumes and Cover Letters chapter). Not only is this a thank-you, but it also gives you the chance to provide the interviewer with any details you may have forgotten (as long as they can be tactfully added in). If you haven't heard back from the interviewer within a week of sending your thank-you letter, call to stress your continued interest in the firm and the position. If you lost any points during the interview for any reason, this letter can help you regain footing. Be polite and make sure to stress your continued interest and competency to fill the position. Just don't forget to proofread it thoroughly. If you are unsure of the spelling of the interviewer's name, call the receptionist and ask.

THE BALANCING ACT:
Looking for a New Job While Currently Employed

For those of you who are still employed, job-searching will be particularly tiring because it must be done in addition to your normal work responsibilities. So don't overwork yourself to the point where you show up to interviews looking exhausted or start to slip behind at your current job. On the other hand, don't be tempted to quit your present job! The long hours are worth it. Searching for a job while you have one puts you in a position of strength.

Making Contact

If you must be at your office during the business day, then you have additional problems to deal with. How can you work interviews into the business day? And if you work in an open office, how can you even call to set up interviews? Obviously, you should keep up the effort and the appearances on your present job. So maximize your use of the lunch hour, early mornings, and late afternoons for calling. If you keep trying, you'll be surprised how often you will be able to reach the executive you are trying to contact during your out-of-office hours. You can catch people as early as 8 a.m. and as late as 6 p.m. on frequent occasions.

Scheduling Interviews

Your inability to interview at any time other than lunch just might work to your advantage. If you can, try to set up as many interviews as possible for your lunch hour. This will go a long way to creating a relaxed atmosphere. But be sure the interviews don't stray too far from the agenda on hand.

Lunchtime interviews are much easier to obtain if you have substantial career experience. People with less experience will often find no alternative to taking time off for interviews. If you have to take time off, you have to take time off. But try to do this as little as possible. Try to take the whole day off in order to avoid being blatantly obvious about your job search, and try to schedule two to three interviews for the same day. (It is very difficult to maintain an optimum level of energy at more than three interviews in one day.) Explain to the interviewer why you might have to juggle your interview schedule; he/she should honor the respect you're showing your current employer by minimizing your days off and will probably appreciate the fact that another prospective employer is interested in you.

> **Try calling as early as 8 a.m. and as late as 6 p.m. You'll be surprised how often you will be able to reach the executive you want during these times of the day.**

References

What do you tell an interviewer who asks for references from your current employer? Just say that while you are happy to have your former employers contacted, you are trying to keep your job search confidential and would rather that your current employer not be contacted until you have been given a firm offer.

IF YOU'RE FIRED OR LAID OFF:
Picking Yourself Up and Dusting Yourself Off

If you've been fired or laid off, you are not the first and will not be the last to go through this traumatic experience. In today's changing economy, thousands of professionals lose their jobs every year. Even if you were terminated with just cause, do not lose heart. Remember, being fired is not a reflection on you as a person. It is usually a reflection of your company's staffing needs and its perception of your recent job performance and attitude. And if you were not performing up to par or enjoying your work, then you will probably be better off at another company anyway.

> **Be prepared for the question "Why were you fired?" during job interviews.**

A thorough job search could take months, so be sure to negotiate a reasonable severance package, if possible, and determine to what benefits, such as health insurance, you are still legally entitled. Also, register for unemployment compensation immediately. Don't be surprised to find other professionals collecting unemployment compensation — it is for everyone who has lost their job.

Don't start your job search with a flurry of unplanned activity. Start by choosing a strategy and working out a plan. Now is not the time for major changes in your life. If possible, remain in the same career and in the same geographical location, at least until you have been working again for a while. On the other hand, if the only industry for which you are trained is leaving, or is severely depressed in your area, then you should give prompt consideration to moving or switching careers.

Avoid mentioning you were fired when arranging interviews, but be prepared for the question "Why were you fired?" during an interview. If you were laid off as a result of downsizing, briefly explain, being sure to reinforce that your job loss was not due to performance. If you were in fact fired, be honest, but try to detail the reason as favorably as possible and portray what you have learned from your mistakes. If you are confident one of your past managers will give you a good reference, tell the interviewer to contact that person. Do not to speak negatively of your past employer and try not to sound particularly worried about your status of being temporarily unemployed.

Finally, don't spend too much time reflecting on why you were let go or how you might have avoided it. Think positively, look to the future, and be sure to follow a careful plan during your job search.

THE COLLEGE STUDENT:
Conducting Your First Job Search

While you will be able to apply many of the basics covered earlier in this chapter to your job search, there are some situations unique to the college student's job search.

THE GPA QUESTION

You are interviewing for the job of your dreams. Everything is going well: You've established a good rapport, the interviewer seems impressed with your qualifications, and you're almost positive the job is yours. Then you're asked about your GPA, which is pitifully low. Do you tell the truth and watch your dream job fly out the window?

Never lie about your GPA (they may request your transcript, and no company will hire a liar). You can, however, explain if there is a reason you don't feel your grades reflect your abilities, and mention any other impressive statistics. For example, if you have a high GPA in your major, or in the last few semesters (as opposed to your cumulative college career), you can use that fact to your advantage.

Perhaps the biggest problem college students face is lack of experience. Many schools have internship programs designed to give students exposure to the field of their choice, as well as the opportunity to make valuable contacts. Check out your school's career services department to see what internships are available. If your school does not have a formal internship program, or if there are no available internships that appeal to you, try contacting local businesses and offering your services. Often, businesses will be more than willing to have an extra pair of hands (especially if those hands are unpaid!) for a day or two each week. Or try contacting school alumni to see if you can "shadow" them for a few days, and see what their daily duties are like.

Informational Interviews

Although many jobseekers do not do this, it can be extremely helpful to arrange an informational interview with a college alumnus or someone else who works in your desired industry. You interview them about their job, their company, and their industry with questions you have prepared in advance. This can be done over the phone but is usually done in person. This will provide you with a contact in the industry who may give you more valuable information -- or perhaps even a job opportunity -- in the future. Always follow up with a thank you letter that includes your contact information.

The goal is to try to begin building experience and establishing contacts as early as possible in your college career.

What do you do if, for whatever reason, you weren't able to get experience directly related to your desired career? First, look at your previous jobs and see if there's anything you can highlight. Did you supervise or train other employees? Did you reorganize the accounting system, or boost productivity in some way? Accomplishments like these demonstrate leadership, responsibility, and innovation -- qualities that most companies look for in employees. And don't forget volunteer activities and school clubs, which can also showcase these traits.

On-Campus Recruiting

Companies will often send recruiters to interview on-site at various colleges. This gives students a chance to interview with companies that may not have interviewed them otherwise. This is particularly true if a company schedules "open" interviews, in which the only screening process is who is first in line at the sign-ups. Of course, since many more applicants gain interviews in this format, this also means that many more people are rejected. The on-campus interview is generally a screening interview, to see if it is worth the company's time to invite you in for a second interview. So do everything possible to make yourself stand out from the crowd.

The first step, of course, is to check out any and all information your school's career center has on the company. If the information seems out of date, check out the company on the Internet or call the company's headquarters and ask for any printed information.

Many companies will host an informational meeting for interviewees, often the evening before interviews are scheduled to take place. DO NOT MISS THIS MEETING. The recruiter will almost certainly ask if you attended. Make an effort to stay after the meeting and talk with the company's representatives. Not only does this give you an opportunity to find out more information about both the company and the position, it also makes you stand out in the recruiter's mind. If there's a particular company that you had your heart set on, but you weren't able to get an interview with them, attend the information session anyway. You may be able to persuade the recruiter to squeeze you into the schedule. (Or you may discover that the company really isn't the right fit for you after all.)

Try to check out the interview site beforehand. Some colleges may conduct "mock" interviews that take place in one of the standard interview rooms. Or you may be able to convince a career counselor (or even a custodian) to let you sneak a peek during off-hours. Either way, having an idea of the room's setup will help you to mentally prepare.

Arrive at least 15 minutes early to the interview. The recruiter may be ahead of schedule, and might meet you early. But don't be surprised if previous interviews have run over, resulting in your 30-minute slot being reduced to 20 minutes (or less). Don't complain or appear anxious; just use the time you do have as efficiently as possible to showcase the reasons *you* are the ideal candidate. Staying calm and composed in these situations will work to your advantage.

LAST WORDS

A parting word of advice. Again and again during your job search you will face rejection. You will be rejected when you apply for interviews. You will be rejected after interviews. For every job offer you finally receive, you probably will have been rejected many times. Don't let rejections slow you down. Keep reminding yourself that the sooner you go out, start your job search, and get those rejections flowing in, the closer you will be to obtaining the job you want.

RESUMES AND COVER LETTERS

When filling a position, an employer will often have 100-plus applicants, but time to interview only a handful of the most promising ones. As a result, he or she will reject most applicants after only briefly skimming their resumes.

Unless you have phoned and talked to the employer -- which you should do whenever you can -- you will be chosen or rejected for an interview entirely on the basis of your resume and cover letter. *Your cover letter must catch the employer's attention, and your resume must hold it.* (But remember -- a resume is no substitute for a job search campaign. *You* must seek a job. Your resume is only one tool, albeit a critical one.)

RESUME FORMAT:
Mechanics of a First Impression

The Basics

Employers dislike long resumes, so unless you have an unusually strong background with many years of experience and a diversity of outstanding achievements, keep your resume length to one page. If you must squeeze in more information than would otherwise fit, try using a smaller typeface or changing the margins. Watch also for "widows" at the end of paragraphs. You can often free up some space if you can shorten the information enough to get rid of those single words taking up an entire line. Another tactic that works with some word processing programs is to decrease the font size of your paragraph returns and changing the spacing between lines.

Print your resume on standard 8 1/2" x 11" paper. Since recruiters often get resumes in batches of hundreds, a smaller-sized resume may be lost in the pile. Oversized resumes are likely to get crumpled at the edges, and won't fit easily in their files.

First impressions matter, so make sure the recruiter's first impression of your resume is a good one. Never hand-write your resume (or cover letter)! Print your resume on quality paper that has weight and texture, in a conservative color such as white, ivory, or pale gray. Good resume paper is easy to find at many stores that sell stationery or office products. It is even available at some drug stores. Use *matching* paper and envelopes for both your resume and cover letter. One hiring manager at a major magazine throws out all resumes that arrive on paper that differs in color from the envelope!

Do not buy paper with images of clouds and rainbows in the background or anything that looks like casual stationery that you would send to your favorite aunt. Do not spray perfume or cologne on your resume. Do not include your picture with your resume unless you have a specific and appropriate reason to do so.

Another tip: Do a test print of your resume (and cover letter), to make sure the watermark is on the same side as the text so that you can read it. Also make sure it is right-side up. As trivial as this may sound, some recruiters check for this! One recruiter at a law firm in New Hampshire sheepishly admitted this is the first thing he checks. *"I open each envelope and check the watermarks on the resume and cover letter. Those candidates that have it wrong go into a different pile."*

Getting it on Paper

Modern photocomposition typesetting gives you the clearest, sharpest image, a wide variety of type styles, and effects such as italics, bold-facing, and book-like justified margins. It is also too expensive for many jobseekers. The quality of today's laser printers means that a computer-generated resume can look just as impressive as one that has been professionally typeset.

A computer with a word processing or desktop publishing program is the most common way to generate your resume. This allows you the flexibility to make changes almost instantly and to store different drafts on disk. Word processing and desktop publishing programs also offer many different fonts to choose from, each taking up different amounts of space. (It is generally best to stay between 9-point and 12-point font size.) Many other options are also available, such as bold-facing or italicizing for emphasis and the ability to change and manipulate spacing. It is generally recommended to leave the right-hand margin unjustified as this keeps the spacing between the text even and therefore easier to read. It is not wrong to justify both margins of text, but if possible try it both ways before you decide.

For a resume on paper, the end result will be largely determined by the quality of the printer you use. Laser printers will generally provide the best quality. Do not use a dot matrix printer.

Many companies now use scanning equipment to screen the resumes they receive, and certain paper, fonts, and other features are more compatible with this technology. White paper is preferable, as well as a standard font such as Courier or Helvetica. You should use at least a 10-point font, and avoid bolding, italics, underlining, borders, boxes, or graphics.

Household typewriters and office typewriters with nylon or other cloth ribbons are *not* good enough for typing your resume. If you don't have access to a quality word processing program, hire a professional with the resources to prepare your resume for you. Keep in mind that businesses such as Kinko's (open 24 hours) provide access to computers with quality printers.

Don't make your copies on an office photocopier. Only the human resources office may see the resume you mail. Everyone else may see only a copy of it, and copies of copies quickly become unreadable. Furthermore, sending photocopies of your resume or cover letter is completely unprofessional. Either print out each copy individually, or take your resume to a professional copy shop, which will generally offer professionally-maintained, extra-high-quality photocopiers and charge fairly reasonable prices. You want your resume to represent you with the look of polished quality.

Proof with Care

Whether you typed it or paid to have it produced professionally, mistakes on resumes are not only embarrassing, but will usually remove you from consideration (particularly if something obvious such as your name is misspelled). No matter how much you paid someone else to type, write, or typeset your resume, *you* lose if there is a mistake. So proofread it as carefully as possible. Get a friend to help you. Read your draft aloud as your friend checks the proof copy. Then have your friend read aloud while you check. Next, read it letter by letter to check spelling and punctuation.

If you are having it typed or typeset by a resume service or a printer, and you don't have time to proof it, pay for it and take it home. Proof it there and bring it back later to get it corrected and printed.

If you wrote your resume with a word processing program, use the built-in spell checker to double-check for spelling errors. Keep in mind that a spell checker will not find errors such as "to" for "two" or "wok" for "work." Many spell check programs do not recognize missing or misused punctuation, nor are they set to check the spelling of capitalized words. It's important that you still proofread your resume to check for grammatical mistakes and other problems, even after it has been spellchecked. If you find mistakes, do not make edits in pen or pencil or use white-out to fix them on the final copy!

Electronic Resumes

As companies rely increasingly on emerging technologies to find qualified candidates for job openings, you may opt to create an electronic resume in order to remain competitive in today's job market. Why is this important? Companies today sometimes request that resumes be submitted by e-mail, and many hiring managers regularly check online resume databases for candidates to fill unadvertised job openings. Other companies enlist the services of electronic employment database services, which charge jobseekers a nominal fee to have their resumes posted to the database to be viewed by potential employers. Still other companies use their own automated applicant tracking systems, in which case your resume is fed through a scanner that sends the image to a computer that "reads" your resume, looking for keywords, and files it accordingly in its database.

Whether you're posting your resume online, e-mailing it directly to an employer, sending it to an electronic employment database, or sending it to a company you suspect uses an automated applicant tracking system, you must create some form of electronic resume to take advantage of the technology. Don't panic! An electronic resume is simply a modified version of your conventional resume. An electronic resume is one that is sparsely formatted, but filled with keywords and important facts.

In order to post your resume to the Internet – either to an online resume database or through direct e-mail to an employer – you will need to change the way your resume is formatted. Instead of a Word, WordPerfect, or other word processing document, save your resume as a plain text, DOS, or ASCII file. These three terms are basically interchangeable, and describe text at its simplest, most basic level, without the formatting such as boldface or italics that most jobseekers use to make their resumes look more interesting. If you use e-mail, you'll notice that all of your messages are written and received in this format. First, you should remove all formatting from your resume including boldface, italics, underlining, bullets, differing font sizes, and graphics. Then, convert and save your resume as a plain text file. Most word processing programs have a "save as" feature that allows you to save files in different formats. Here, you should choose "text only" or "plain text."

Another option is to create a resume in HTML (hypertext markup language), the text formatting language used to publish information on the World Wide Web. However, the real usefulness of HTML resumes is still being explored. Most of the major online databases do not accept HTML resumes, and the vast majority of companies only accept plain text resumes through their e-mail.

Finally, if you simply wish to send your resume to an electronic employment database or a company that uses an automated applicant tracking system, there is no need to convert your resume to a plain text file. The only change you need to make is to organize the information in your resume by keywords. Employers are likely to do keyword searches for information, such as degree held or knowledge of particular types of software. Therefore, using the right keywords or key phrases in your resume is critical to its ultimate success. Keywords are usually nouns or short phrases that the computer searches for which refer to experience, training, skills, and abilities. For example, let's say an employer searches an employment database for a sales representative with the following criteria:

BS/BA
exceeded quota
cold calls
high energy
willing to travel

Even if you have the right qualifications, neglecting to use these keywords would result in the computer passing over your resume. Although there is no way to know for sure which keywords employers are most likely to search for, you can make educated guesses by checking the help-wanted ads or online job postings for your type of job. You should also arrange keywords in a keyword summary, a paragraph listing your qualifications that immediately follows your name and address (see sample letter in this chapter). In addition, choose a nondecorative font with clear, distinct characters, such as Helvetica or Times. It is more difficult for a scanner to accurately pick up the more unusual fonts. Boldface and all capital letters are best used only for major section headings, such as "Experience" and "Education." It is also best to avoid using italics or underlining, since this can cause the letters to bleed into one another.

For more specific information on creating and sending electronic resumes, see *The Adams Internet Job Search Almanac.*

Types of Resumes

The most common resume formats are the functional resume, the chronological resume, and the combination resume. (Examples can be found at the end of this chapter.) A functional resume focuses on skills and de-emphasizes job titles, employers, etc. A functional resume is best if you have been out of the work force for a long time or are changing careers. It is also good if you want to highlight specific skills and strengths, especially if all of your work experience has been at one company. This format can also be a good choice if you are just out of school or have no experience in your desired field.

Choose a chronological format if you are currently working or were working recently, and if your most recent experiences relate to your desired field. Use reverse chronological order and include dates. To a recruiter your last job and your latest schooling are the most important, so put the last first and list the rest going back in time.

A combination resume is perhaps the most common. This resume simply combines elements of the functional and chronological resume formats. This is used by many jobseekers with a solid track record who find elements of both types useful.

Organization

Your name, phone number, e-mail address (if you have one), and a complete mailing address should be at the top of your resume. Try to make your name stand out by using a slightly larger font size or all capital letters. Be sure to spell out everything. Never abbreviate St. for Street or Rd. for Road. If you are a college student, you should also put your home address and phone number at the top.

Change your message on your answering machine if necessary – RUSH blaring in the background or your sorority sisters screaming may not come across well to all recruiters. If you think you may be moving within six months then include a second address and phone number of a trusted friend or relative who can reach you no matter where you are.

Remember that employers will keep your resume on file and may contact you months later if a position opens that fits your qualifications. All too often, candidates are unreachable because they have moved and had not previously provided enough contact options on their resume.

Next, list your experience, then your education. If you are a recent graduate, list your education first, unless your experience is more important than your education. (For example, if you have just graduated from a teaching school, have some business experience, and are applying for a job in business, you would list your business experience first.)

Keep everything easy to find. Put the dates of your employment and education on the left of the page. Put the names of the companies you worked for and the schools you attended a few spaces to the right of the dates. Put the city and state, or the city and country, where you studied or worked to the right of the page.

The important thing is simply to break up the text in some logical way that makes your resume visually attractive and easy to scan, so experiment to see which layout works best for your resume. However you set it up, *stay consistent.* Inconsistencies in fonts, spacing, or tenses will make your resume look sloppy. Also, be sure to use tabs to keep your information vertically lined up, rather than the less precise space bar.

RESUME CONTENT:
Say it with Style
Sell Yourself

You are selling your skills and accomplishments in your resume, so it is important to inventory yourself and know yourself. If you have achieved something, say so. Put it in the best possible light, but avoid subjective statements, such as "I am a hard worker" or "I get along well with my coworkers." Just stick to the facts.

While you shouldn't hold back or be modest, don't exaggerate your achievements to the point of misrepresentation. Be honest. Many companies will immediately drop an applicant from consideration (or fire a current employee) upon discovering inaccurate or untrue information on a resume or other application material.

Write down the important (and pertinent) things you have done, but do it in as few words as possible. Your resume will be scanned, not read, and short, concise phrases are much more effective than long-winded sentences. Avoid the use of "I" when emphasizing your accomplishments. Instead, use brief phrases beginning with action verbs.

While some technical terms will be unavoidable, you should try to avoid excessive "technicalese." Keep in mind that the first person to see your resume may be a human resources person who won't necessarily know all the jargon – and how can they be impressed by something they don't understand?

Keep it Brief

Also, try to hold your paragraphs to six lines or less. If you have more than six lines of information about one job or school, put it in two or more paragraphs. A short resume will be examined more carefully. Remember: Your resume usually has between eight and 45 seconds to catch an employer's eye. So make every second count.

Job Objective

A functional resume may require a job objective to give it focus. One or two sentences describing the job you are seeking can clarify in what capacity your skills will be best put to use. Be sure that your stated objective is in line with the position you're applying for.

Examples:

An entry-level editorial assistant position in the publishing industry.
A senior management position with a telecommunications firm.

Don't include a job objective on a chronological resume unless your previous work experiences are completely unrelated to the position for which you're applying. The presence of an overly specific job objective might eliminate you from consideration for other positions that a recruiter feels are a better match for your qualifications. But even if you don't put an objective on paper, having a career goal in mind as you write can help give your resume a solid sense of direction.

USE ACTION VERBS

How you write your resume is just as important as *what* you write. In describing previous work experiences, the strongest resumes use short phrases beginning with action verbs. Below are a few you may want to use. (This list is not all-inclusive.)

achieved	developed	integrated	purchased
administered	devised	interpreted	reduced
advised	directed	interviewed	regulated
arranged	distributed	launched	represented
assisted	established	managed	resolved
attained	evaluated	marketed	restored
budgeted	examined	mediated	restructured
built	executed	monitored	revised
calculated	expanded	negotiated	scheduled
collaborated	expedited	obtained	selected
collected	facilitated	operated	served
compiled	formulated	ordered	sold
completed	founded	organized	solved
computed	generated	participated	streamlined
conducted	headed	performed	studied
consolidated	identified	planned	supervised
constructed	implemented	prepared	supplied
consulted	improved	presented	supported
controlled	increased	processed	tested
coordinated	initiated	produced	trained
created	installed	proposed	updated
determined	instructed	published	wrote

Some jobseekers may choose to include both "Relevant Experience" and "Additional Experience" sections. This can be useful, as it allows the jobseeker to place more emphasis on certain experiences and to de-emphasize others.

Emphasize continued experience in a particular job area or continued interest in a particular industry. De-emphasize irrelevant positions. It is okay to include one opening line providing a general description of each company you've worked at. Delete positions that you held for less than four months (unless you are a very recent college grad or still in school). Stress your <u>results</u> and your achievements, elaborating on how you contributed in your previous jobs. Did you increase sales, reduce costs, improve a product, implement a new program? Were you promoted? Use specific numbers (i.e., quantities, percentages, dollar amounts) whenever possible.

Education

Keep it brief if you have more than two years of career experience. Elaborate more if you have less experience. If you are a recent college graduate, you may choose to include any high school activities that are directly relevant to your career. If you've been out of school for a while you don't need to list your education prior to college.

Mention degrees received and any honors or special awards. Note individual courses or projects you participated in that might be relevant for employers. For example, if you are an English major applying for a position as a business writer, be sure to mention any business or economics courses. Previous experience such as Editor-in-Chief of the school newspaper would be relevant as well.

If you are uploading your resume to an online job hunting site such as CareerCity.com, action verbs are still important, but the key words or key nouns that a computer would search for become more important. For example, if you're seeking an accounting position, key nouns that a computer would search for such as "Lotus 1-2-3" or "CPA" or "payroll" become very important.

Highlight Impressive Skills

Be sure to mention any computer skills you may have. You may wish to include a section entitled "Additional Skills" or "Computer Skills," in which you list any software programs you know. An additional skills section is also an ideal place to mention fluency in a foreign language.

Personal Data

This section is optional, but if you choose to include it, keep it brief. A one-word mention of hobbies such as fishing, chess, baseball, cooking, etc., can give the person who will interview you a good way to open up the conversation.

Team sports experience is looked at favorably. It doesn't hurt to include activities that are somewhat unusual (fencing, Akido, '70s music) or that somehow relate to the position or the company to which you're applying. For instance, it would be worth noting if you are a member of a professional organization in your industry of interest. Never include information about your age, alias, date of birth, health, physical characteristics, marital status, religious affiliation, or political/moral beliefs.

References

The most that is needed is the sentence "References available upon request" at the bottom of your resume. If you choose to leave it out, that's fine. This line is not really necessary. It is understood that references will most likely be asked for and provided by you later on in the interviewing process. Do not actually send references with your resume and cover letter unless specifically requested.

HIRING A RESUME WRITER:
Is it the Right Choice for You?

If you write reasonably well, it is to your advantage to write your own resume. Writing your resume forces you to review your experiences and figure out how to explain your accomplishments in clear, brief phrases. This will help you when you explain your work to interviewers. It is also easier to tailor your resume to each position you're applying for when you have put it together yourself.

If you write your resume, everything will be in your own words; it will sound like you. It will say what you want it to say. If you are a good writer, know yourself well, and have a good idea of which parts of your background employers are looking for, you should be able to write your own resume better than someone else. If you decide to write your resume yourself, have as many people as possible review and proofread it. Welcome objective opinions and other perspectives.

When to Get Help

If you have difficulty writing in "resume style" (which is quite unlike normal written language), if you are unsure which parts of your background to emphasize, or if you think your resume would make your case better if it did not follow one of the standard forms outlined either here or in a book on resumes, then you should consider having it professionally written.

Even some professional resume writers we know have had their resumes written with the help of fellow professionals. They sought the help of someone who could be objective about their background, as well as provide an experienced sounding board to help focus their thoughts.

If You Hire a Pro

The best way to choose a writer is by reputation: the recommendation of a friend, a personnel director, your school placement officer, or someone else knowledgeable in the field.

Important questions:
- "How long have you been writing resumes?"
- "If I'm not satisfied with what you write, will you go over it with me and change it?"
- "Do you charge by the hour or a flat rate?"

There is no sure relation between price and quality, except that you are unlikely to get a good writer for less than $50 for an uncomplicated resume and you shouldn't have to pay more than $300 unless your experience is very extensive or complicated. There will be additional charges for printing. Assume nothing no matter how much you pay. It is your career at stake if there are mistakes on your resume!

Few resume services will give you a firm price over the phone, simply because some resumes are too complicated and take too long to do for a predetermined price. Some services will quote you a price that applies to almost all of their customers. Once you decide to use a specific writer, you should insist on a firm price quote *before* engaging their services. Also, find out how expensive minor changes will be.

COVER LETTERS:
Quick, Clear, and Concise

Always mail a cover letter with your resume. In a cover letter you can show an interest in the company that you can't show in a resume. You can also point out one or two of your skills or accomplishments the company can put to good use.

Make it Personal

The more personal you can get, the better, so long as you keep it professional. If someone known to the person you are writing has recommended that you contact the company, get permission to include his/her name in the letter. If you can get the name of a person to send the letter to, address it directly to that person (after first calling the company to verify the spelling of the person's name, correct title, and mailing address). Be sure to put the person's name and title on both the letter and the envelope. This will ensure that your letter will get through to the proper person, even if a new person now occupies this position. It will not always be possible to get the name of a person. Always strive to get at least a title.

Be sure to mention something about why you have an interest in the company -- *so many candidates apply for jobs with no apparent knowledge of what the company does!* This conveys the message that they just want any job.

Type cover letters in full. Don't try the cheap and easy ways, like using a computer mail merge program or photocopying the body of your letter and typing in the inside address and salutation. You will give the impression that you are mailing to a host of companies and have no particular interest in any one.

Print your cover letter on the same color and same high-quality paper as your resume.

Cover letter basic format

Paragraph 1: State what the position is that you are seeking. It is not always necessary to state how you found out about the position – often you will apply without knowing that a position is open.

Paragraph 2: Include what you know about the company and why you are interested in working there. Mention any prior contact with the company or someone known to the hiring person if relevant. Briefly state your qualifications and what you can offer. (Do not talk about what you cannot do).

Paragraph 3: Close with your phone number and where/when you can be reached. Make a request for an interview. State when you will follow up by phone (or mail or e-mail if the ad requests no phone calls). Do not wait long – generally five working days. If you say you're going to follow up, then actually do it! This phone call can get your resume noticed when it might otherwise sit in a stack of 225 other resumes.

Cover letter do's and don'ts

- *Do* keep your cover letter brief and to the point.
- *Do* be sure it is error-free.
- *Do* accentuate what you can offer the company, not what you hope to gain.
- *Do* be sure your phone number and address is on your cover letter just in case it gets separated from your resume (this happens!).
- *Do* check the watermark by holding the paper up to a light – be sure it is facing forward so it is readable – on the same side as the text, and right-side up.
- *Do* sign your cover letter (or type your name if you are sending it electronically). Blue or black ink are both fine. Do not use red ink.
- *Don't* just repeat information verbatim from your resume.
- *Don't* overuse the personal pronoun "I."
- *Don't* send a generic cover letter – show your personal knowledge of and interest in that particular company.

THANK YOU LETTERS:
Another Way to Stand Out

As mentioned earlier, *always* send a thank you letter after an interview (see the sample later in this section). So few candidates do this and it is yet another way for you to stand out. Be sure to mention something specific from the interview and restate your interest in the company and the position.

It is generally acceptable to handwrite your thank you letter on a generic thank you card (but *never* a postcard). Make sure handwritten notes are neat and legible. However, if you are in doubt, typing your letter is always the safe bet. If you met with several people it is fine to send them each an individual thank you letter. Call the company if you need to check on the correct spelling of their names.

Remember to:
- Keep it short.
- Proofread it carefully.
- Send it *promptly*.

FUNCTIONAL RESUME

C.J. RAVENCLAW
129 Pennsylvania Avenue
Washington DC 20500
202/555-6652
e-mail: ravenclaw@dcpress.net

Objective
A position as a graphic designer commensurate with my acquired skills and expertise.

Summary
Extensive experience in plate making, separations, color matching, background definition, printing, mechanicals, color corrections, and personnel supervision. A highly motivated manager and effective communicator. Proven ability to:

- **Create Commercial Graphics**
- **Produce Embossed Drawings**
- **Color Separate**

- **Control Quality**
- **Resolve Printing Problems**
- **Analyze Customer Satisfaction**

Qualifications
Printing:
Knowledgeable in black and white as well as color printing. Excellent judgment in determining acceptability of color reproduction through comparison with original. Proficient at producing four- or five-color corrections on all media, as well as restyling previously reproduced four-color artwork.

Customer Relations:
Routinely work closely with customers to ensure specifications are met. Capable of striking a balance between technical printing capabilities and need for customer satisfaction through entire production process.

Specialties:
Practiced at creating silk screen overlays for a multitude of processes including velo bind, GBC bind, and perfect bind. Creative design and timely preparation of posters, flyers, and personalized stationery.

Personnel Supervision:
Skillful at fostering atmosphere that encourages highly talented artists to balance high-level creativity with maximum production. Consistently beat production deadlines. Instruct new employees, apprentices, and students in both artistry and technical operations.

Experience
Graphic Arts Professor, Ohio State University, Columbus OH (1992-1996).
Manager, Design Graphics, Washington DC (1997-present).

Education
Massachusetts Conservatory of Art, Ph.D. 1990
University of Massachusetts, B.A. 1988

CHRONOLOGICAL RESUME

HARRY SEABORN
557 Shoreline Drive
Seattle, WA 98404
(206) 555-6584
e-mail: hseaborn@centco.com

EXPERIENCE

THE CENTER COMPANY   Seattle, WA
Systems Programmer   1996-present
- Develop and maintain customer accounting and order tracking database using a Visual Basic front end and SQL server.
- Plan and implement migration of company wide transition from mainframe-based dumb terminals to a true client server environment using Windows NT Workstation and Server.
- Oversee general local and wide area network administration including the development of a variety of intranet modules to improve internal company communication and planning across divisions.

INFO TECH, INC.   Seattle, WA
Technical Manager   1994-1996

- Designed and managed the implementation of a network providing the legal community with a direct line to Supreme Court cases across the Internet using SQL Server and a variety of Internet tools.
- Developed a system to make the entire library catalog available on line using PERL scripts and SQL.
- Used Visual Basic and Microsoft Access to create a registration system for university registrar.

EDUCATION

SALEM STATE UNIVERSITY   Salem, OR
    M.S. in Computer Science.   1993
    B.S. in Computer Science.   1991

COMPUTER SKILLS

- Programming Languages: Visual Basic, Java, C++, SQL, PERL
- Software: SQL Server, Internet Information Server, Oracle
- Operating Systems: Windows NT, UNIX, Linux

FUNCTIONAL RESUME

Donna Hermione Moss
703 Wizard's Way
Chicago, IL 60601
(312) 555-8841
e-mail: donna@cowfire.com

OBJECTIVE:
To contribute over five years of experience in promotion, communications, and administration to an entry-level position in advertising.

SUMMARY OF QUALIFICATIONS:
- Performed advertising duties for small business.
- Experience in business writing and communications skills.
- General knowledge of office management.
- Demonstrated ability to work well with others, in both supervisory and support staff roles.
- Type 75 words per minute.

SELECTED ACHIEVEMENTS AND RESULTS:
Promotion:
Composing, editing, and proofreading correspondence and public relations materials for own catering service. Large-scale mailings.

Communication:
Instruction; curriculum and lesson planning; student evaluation; parent-teacher conferences; development of educational materials. Training and supervising clerks.

Computer Skills:
Proficient in MS Word, Lotus 1-2-3, Excel, and Filemaker Pro.

Administration:
Record-keeping and file maintenance. Data processing and computer operations, accounts receivable, accounts payable, inventory control, and customer relations. Scheduling, office management, and telephone reception.

PROFESSIONAL HISTORY:
Teacher; Self-Employed (owner of catering service); Floor Manager; Administrative Assistant; Accounting Clerk.

EDUCATION:
Beloit College, Beloit, WI, BA in Education, 1991

CHRONOLOGICAL RESUME

PERCY ZIEGLER
16 Josiah Court
Marlborough CT 06447
203/555-9641 (h)
203/555-8176, x14 (w)

EDUCATION

Keene State College, Keene NH
Bachelor of Arts in Elementary Education, 1998
- Graduated *magna cum laude*
- English minor
- Kappa Delta Pi member, inducted 1996

EXPERIENCE
September 1998-
Present

Elmer T. Thienes Elementary School, Marlborough CT
Part-time Kindergarten Teacher
- Instruct kindergartners in reading, spelling, language arts, and music.
- Participate in the selection of textbooks and learning aids.
- Organize and supervise class field trips and coordinate in-class presentations.

Summers
1995-1997

Keene YMCA, Youth Division, Keene NH
Child-care Counselor
- Oversaw summer program for low-income youth.
- Budgeted and coordinated special events and field trips, working with Program Director to initiate variations in the program.
- Served as Youth Advocate in cooperation with social worker to address the social needs and problems of participants.

Spring 1997

Wheelock Elementary School, Keene NH
Student Teacher
- Taught third-grade class in all elementary subjects.
- Designed and implemented a two-week unit on Native Americans.
- Assisted in revision of third-grade curriculum.

Fall 1996

Child Development Center, Keene NH
Daycare Worker
- Supervised preschool children on the playground and during art activities.
- Created a "Wishbone Corner," where children could quietly look at books or take a voluntary "time-out."

ADDITIONAL INTERESTS
Martial arts, Pokemon, politics, reading, skiing, writing.

ELECTRONIC RESUME

GRIFFIN DORE
69 Dursley Drive
Cambridge, MA 02138
(617) 555-5555

KEYWORD SUMMARY

Senior financial manager with over ten years experience in Accounting and Systems Management, Budgeting, Forecasting, Cost Containment, Financial Reporting, and International Accounting. MBA in Management. Proficient in Lotus, Excel, Solomon, and Windows.

EXPERIENCE

COLWELL CORPORATION, Wellesley, MA
Director of Accounting and Budgets, 1990 to present
    Direct staff of twenty in General Ledger, Accounts Payable, Accounts Receivable, and International Accounting.
    Facilitate month-end closing process with parent company and auditors.
    Implemented team-oriented cross-training program within accounting group, resulting in timely month-end closings and increased productivity of key accounting staff.
    Developed and implemented a strategy for Sales and Use Tax Compliance in all fifty states.
    Prepare monthly financial statements and analyses.

FRANKLIN AND DELANEY COMPANY, Melrose, MA
Senior Accountant, 1987-1990
    Managed Accounts Payable, General Ledger, transaction processing, and financial reporting. Supervised staff of five.

Staff Accountant, 1985-1987
    Managed Accounts Payable, including vouchering, cash disbursements, and bank reconciliation.
    Wrote and issued policies.
    Maintained supporting schedules used during year-end audits.
    Trained new employees.

EDUCATION

MBA in Management, Northeastern University, Boston, MA, 1989
BS in Accounting, Boston College, Boston, MA, 1985

ASSOCIATIONS

National Association of Accountants

GENERAL MODEL
FOR A COVER LETTER

Your mailing address
Date

Contact's name
Contact's title
Company
Company's mailing address

Dear Mr./Ms. _____ :

Immediately explain why your background makes you the best candidate for the position that you are applying for. Describe what prompted you to write (want ad, article you read about the company, networking contact, etc.). Keep the first paragraph short and hard-hitting.

Detail what you could contribute to this company. Show how your qualifications will benefit this firm. Describe your interest in the corporation. Subtly emphasizing your knowledge about this firm and your familiarity with the industry will set you apart from other candidates. Remember to keep this letter short; few recruiters will read a cover letter longer than half a page.

If possible, your closing paragraph should request specific action on the part of the reader. Include your phone number and the hours when you can be reached. Mention that if you do not hear from the reader by a specific date, you will follow up with a phone call. Lastly, thank the reader for their time, consideration, etc.

Sincerely,

(signature)

Your full name (typed)

Enclosure (use this if there are other materials, such as your resume, that are included in the same envelope)

SAMPLE COVER LETTER

16 Josiah Court
Marlborough CT 06447
January 16, 2000

Ms. Leona Malfoy
Assistant Principal
Laningham Elementary School
43 Mayflower Drive
Keene NH 03431

Dear Ms. Malfoy:

Toby Potter recently informed me of a possible opening for a third grade teacher at Laningham Elementary School. With my experience instructing third-graders, both in schools and in summer programs, I feel I would be an ideal candidate for the position. Please accept this letter and the enclosed resume as my application.

Laningham's educational philosophy that every child can learn and succeed interests me, since it mirrors my own. My current position at Elmer T. Thienes Elementary has reinforced this philosophy, heightening my awareness of the different styles and paces of learning and increasing my sensitivity toward special needs children. Furthermore, as a direct result of my student teaching experience at Wheelock Elementary School, I am comfortable, confident, and knowledgeable working with third-graders.

I look forward to discussing the position and my qualifications for it in more detail. I can be reached at 203/555-9641 evenings or 203/555-8176, x14 weekdays. If I do not hear from you before Tuesday of next week, I will call to see if we can schedule a time to meet. Thank you for your time and consideration.

Sincerely,

Percy Ziegler

Percy Ziegler

Enclosure

GENERAL MODEL FOR A
THANK YOU/FOLLOW-UP LETTER

Your mailing address
Date

Contact's name
Contact's title
Company
Company's mailing address

Dear Mr./Ms._____:

Remind the interviewer of the reason (i.e., a specific opening, an informational interview, etc.) you were interviewed, as well as the date. Thank him/her for the interview, and try to personalize your thanks by mentioning some specific aspect of the interview.

Confirm your interest in the organization (and in the opening, if you were interviewing for a particular position). Use specifics to re-emphasize that you have researched the firm in detail and have considered how you would fit into the company and the position. This is a good time to say anything you wish you had said in the initial meeting. Be sure to keep this letter brief; a half page is plenty.

If appropriate, close with a suggestion for further action, such as a desire to have an additional interview, if possible. Mention your phone number and the hours you can be reached. Alternatively, you may prefer to mention that you will follow up with a phone call in several days. Once again, thank the person for meeting with you, and state that you would be happy to provide any additional information about your qualifications.

Sincerely,

(signature)

Your full name (typed)

PRIMARY EMPLOYERS

ACCOUNTING AND MANAGEMENT CONSULTING

You can expect to find the following types of companies in this chapter:

Consulting and Research Firms • Industrial Accounting Firms • Management Services • Public Accounting Firms • Tax Preparation Companies

ARTHUR ANDERSEN
633 West Fifth Street, 24th Floor, Los Angeles CA 90071. 213/614-6500. **Fax:** 213/614-6670. **Contact:** Personnel. **E-mail address:** los.angeles@andersen.com. **World Wide Web address:** http://www.arthurandersen.com. **Description:** One of the largest certified public accounting firms in the world. Arthur Andersen's four key practice areas include Audit and Business Advisory, Tax and Business Advisory, Business Consulting, and Economic and Financial Consulting. **NOTE:** This firm does not accept unsolicited resumes. Please check the Website for available positions. **Corporate headquarters location:** Chicago IL. **Parent company:** Arthur Andersen Worldwide Organization is one of the leading providers of professional services in the world. With over 380 worldwide locations, the global practice of its member firms is conducted through two business units: Arthur Andersen and Andersen Consulting, which provides global management and technology consulting. **Number of employees worldwide:** 91,000.

AON CONSULTING
707 Wilshire Boulevard, Suite 5700, Los Angeles CA 90017. 213/630-2900. **Fax:** 213/627-6155. **Contact:** Human Resources. **World Wide Web address:** http://www.aon.com. **Description:** An international human resources consulting and benefits brokerage firm providing integrated advisory and support services in retirement planning, health care management, organizational effectiveness, compensation, human resources-related communications, and information technologies. The company's organizational effectiveness services include advisory and support services in compensation, strategy development, organizational design, business process redesign, human resources development, management training and development, organizational communications, and information technology applications. Strategic health care services include advisory and support

services in traditional group health and welfare programs, strategic health planning, strategic health care management, quality assurance, flexible benefits and compensation, financial management, data management, vendor oversight, and communications. Strategic retirement planning and educational services include consulting and support services in core actuarial applications, retirement health and welfare benefits, funding and investment strategy, record keeping and administration, employee sensing and communications, personalized retirement modeling, holistic lifestyle and family planning, and database information and proprietary studies. Information technologies services include human resources information systems development (information management strategies, systems, databases, software, and technology advisement) and human resources systems applications (human resources planning, record keeping, communication, and education). **Corporate headquarters location:** Chicago IL. **Listed on:** New York Stock Exchange. **Stock exchange symbol:** AOC.

DELOITTE & TOUCHE
350 South Grand Avenue, Suite 200, Los Angeles CA 90071. 213/688-0800. **Contact:** Human Resources Department. **World Wide Web address:** http://www.us.deloitte.com. **Description:** An international firm of certified public accountants providing professional accounting, auditing, tax, and management consulting services to widely diversified clients. The company has a specialized program consisting of national industry groups and functional groups that cross industry lines. Groups are involved in various disciplines including accounting, auditing, taxation management advisory services, small and growing businesses, mergers and acquisitions, and computer applications.

MERCER HUMAN RESOURCE CONSULTING
777 South Figueroa Street, Suite 2000, Los Angeles CA 90017. 213/346-2200. **Contact:** Human Resources Department. **E-mail address:** careers.west@us.wmmercer.com. **World Wide Web address:** http://www.mercerhr.com. **Description:** One of the world's largest actuarial and human resources management consulting firms, providing advice to organizations on all aspects of employee/management relationships. Services include retirement, health and welfare; performance and rewards; communication; investment; human resources administration; risk finance and insurance; and health care provider consulting. **Corporate headquarters location:** New

York NY. **Listed on:** NASDAQ. **Stock exchange symbol:** MERCS.

MERCER HUMAN RESOURCE CONSULTING
1100 Town & Country Road, Suite 1500, Orange CA 92868. 714/648-3300. **Contact:** Human Resources Department. **World Wide Web address:** http://www.mercerhr.com. **Description:** One of the world's largest actuarial and human resources management consulting firms, providing advice to organizations on all aspects of employee/management relationships. Services include retirement, health and welfare; performance and rewards; communication; investment; human resources administration; risk finance and insurance; and health care provider consulting. **Corporate headquarters location:** New York NY. **Listed on:** NASDAQ. **Stock exchange symbol:** MERCS.

PRICEWATERHOUSECOOPERS
350 South Grand Avenue, Los Angeles CA 90071. 213/356-6000. **Fax:** 213/356-6363. **Contact:** Department of Human Resources. **E-mail address:** westpwcjobs@us.pwcglobal.com. **World Wide Web address:** http://www.pwcglobal.com. **Description:** One of the largest certified public accounting firms in the world. PricewaterhouseCoopers provides public accounting, business advisory, management consulting, and taxation services. **Office hours:** Monday - Friday, 8:00 a.m. - 5:00 p.m. **Corporate headquarters location:** New York NY. **Other U.S. locations:** Nationwide.

PRICEWATERHOUSECOOPERS
400 South Hope Street, 22nd Floor, Los Angeles CA 90071-2889. 213/236-3000. **Contact:** Human Resources Department. **E-mail address:** westpwcjobs@us.pwcglobal.com. **World Wide Web address:** http://www.pwcglobal.com. **Description:** One of the largest certified public accounting firms in the world. PricewaterhouseCoopers provides public accounting, business advisory, management consulting, and taxation services. **Corporate headquarters location:** New York NY. **Other U.S. locations:** Nationwide.

ADVERTISING, MARKETING, AND PUBLIC RELATIONS

You can expect to find the following types of companies in this chapter:

Advertising Agencies • Direct Mail Marketers •
Market Research Firms • Public Relations Firms

BBDO WEST
10960 Wilshire Boulevard, Suite 1600, Los Angeles CA 90024. 310/444-4500. **Fax:** 310/478-7581. **Contact:** Tim Wright, Director of Human Resources Department. **World Wide Web address:** http://www.bbdo.com. **Description:** One location of the worldwide network of advertising agencies with related businesses in public relations, direct marketing, sales promotion, graphic arts, and printing. **Corporate headquarters location:** New York NY. **Other area locations:** San Francisco CA. **Other U.S. locations:** Miami FL; Atlanta GA; Chicago IL; Wellesley MA; Southfield MI. **Parent company:** BBDO Worldwide operates 156 offices in 42 countries and 96 cities. The company operates 83 subsidiaries, affiliates, and associates engaged solely in advertising and related operations.

BDS MARKETING
10 Holland, Irvine CA 92618. 949/472-6700. **Fax:** 949/597-2220. **Contact:** Human Resources. **World Wide Web address:** http://www.bdsmarketing.com. **Description:** Offers a wide variety of marketing services. BDS Marketing provides ideas for sales promotions, product training, and field marketing. **Corporate headquarters location:** This location.

CERRELL ASSOCIATES, INC.
320 North Larchmont Boulevard, Los Angeles CA 90004. 323/466-3445. **Contact:** Human Resources. **World Wide Web address:** http://www.cerrell.com. **Description:** A public relations company specializing in local public affairs, issues management, and political campaigning. **Common positions include:** Account Manager; Secretary. **Special programs:** Internships. **Corporate headquarters location:** This location. **Number of employees at this location:** 30.

DDB NEEDHAM WORLDWIDE, INC.
11601 Wilshire Boulevard, Suite 700, Los Angeles CA 90025. 310/996-5700. **Contact:** Elizabeth Gaudio, Personnel Director. **E-mail address:** elizabeth.gaudio@la.dbb.com. **World Wide Web address:** http://www.ddbn.com. **Description:** A full-

service, international advertising agency. **Common positions include:** Accountant/Auditor; Advertising Clerk; Art Director; Commercial Artist; Computer Programmer; Copywriter; Market Research Analyst; Marketing Specialist; Radio/TV Producer. **Corporate headquarters location:** New York NY. **Other U.S. locations:** Chicago IL. **Parent company:** Omnicom. **Operations at this facility include:** Regional Headquarters. **Listed on:** New York Stock Exchange.

DAILEY & ASSOCIATES ADVERTISING
8687 Melrose Avenue, Suite G300, West Hollywood CA 90069. 310/360-3100. **Contact:** Ms. Jean Anne Hutchinson, Director of Human Resources Administration. **E-mail address:** jhthompson@daileyads.com. **World Wide Web address:** http://www.daileyads.com. **Description:** A full-service advertising agency.

DAVISELEN
865 South Figueroa Street, 12th Floor, Los Angeles CA 90017. 213/688-7000. **Fax:** 213/688-7106. **Contact:** Personnel. **World Wide Web address:** http://www.daviselen.com. **Description:** A full-service advertising agency. **NOTE:** Entry-level positions are offered. **Common positions include:** Administrative Assistant; Advertising Clerk; Buyer; Computer Operator; MIS Specialist. **Special programs:** Internships. **Corporate headquarters location:** This location. **Other U.S. locations:** Phoenix AZ; San Francisco CA; Portland OR. **Listed on:** Privately held.

OGILVY & MATHER
3530 Hayden Avenue, Culver City CA 90232. 310/280-2200xNels. **Contact:** Mary Jensen, Human Resources Director. **World Wide Web address:** http://www.ogilvy.com. **Description:** An advertising agency. **Corporate headquarters location:** This location. **Other U.S. locations:** Nationwide. **Parent company:** WWP Group PLC.

SAATCHI & SAATCHI ADVERTISING
3501 Sepulveda Boulevard, Torrance CA 90505. 310/214-6000. **Contact:** Rose Calhoun, Human Resources. **E-mail address:** rcalhoun@saatchila.com. **World Wide Web address:** http://www.saatchi-saatchi.com. **Description:** A full-service advertising agency. **Corporate headquarters location:** New York NY. **Other U.S. locations:** Nationwide.

VIACOM OUTDOOR
1731 Workman Street, Los Angeles CA 90031. 323/222-7171. **Contact:** Department of Human Resources. **E-mail address:**

humanresources@tdi-usa.com. **World Wide Web address:** http://www.tdiworldwide.com. **Description:** An advertising agency specializing in the design of billboards and posters. **Other U.S. locations:** Nationwide. **Parent company:** Viacom Corporation. **Listed on:** New York Stock Exchange. **Stock exchange symbol:** VIA.

WESTERN INITIATIVE MEDIA CORPORATION
5700 Wilshire Boulevard, Suite 400, Los Angeles CA 90036. 323/370-8000. **Contact:** C. Carranza, Human Resources. **E-mail address:** lajobs@imna.com. **World Wide Web address:** http://www.wimc.com. **Description:** An advertising agency. **Corporate headquarters location:** This location.

AEROSPACE

You can expect to find the following types of companies in this chapter:

Aerospace Products and Services • Aircraft Equipment and Parts

THE AEROSPACE CORPORATION

P.O. Box 92957, MS1/050, Los Angeles CA 90009-2957. 310/336-1614. **Fax:** 310/336-7933. **Contact:** Walter L. Caldwell, Personnel Manager. **E-mail address:** jobs@aero.org. **World Wide Web address:** http://www.aero.org. **Description:** A nonprofit corporation engaged in space systems architecture, engineering, planning, analysis, and research, predominantly for programs managed by the Space and Missile Systems Center (SMC) of the Air Force Material Command. **Common positions include:** Aerospace Engineer; Chemical Engineer; Computer Programmer; Electrical/Electronics Engineer; Industrial Engineer; Mathematician; Mechanical Engineer; Physicist; Software Engineer; Structural Engineer; Systems Analyst. **Corporate headquarters location:** This location. **Other U.S. locations:** Colorado Springs CO; Kennedy Space Center FL; Columbia MD; Albuquerque NM; Houston TX; Crystal City VA; Chantilly VA. **Operations at this facility include:** Research and Development. **Listed on:** Privately held. **Number of employees at this location:** 3,000.

AMETEK AEROSPACE

1644 Whittier Avenue, Costa Mesa CA 92627. 949/642-2400. **Contact:** Gabe Velez, Director of Human Resources. **World Wide Web address:** http://www.ametek.com. **Description:** Manufactures electrical and electronic components, primarily for the defense industry. Products include pressure transducers for flight controls on F-16 aircraft and for engine instrumentation on F-18 and F-20 aircraft. Ametek also provides displacement and pressure transducers for engines used in a variety of military planes. **Common positions include:** Accountant/Auditor; Aerospace Engineer; Blue-Collar Worker Supervisor; Buyer; Chemical Engineer; Computer Programmer; Draftsperson; Electrical/Electronics Engineer; Human Resources Manager; Mechanical Engineer; Operations/Production Manager; Quality Control Supervisor. **Corporate headquarters location:** Buffalo NY. **Listed on:** New York Stock Exchange. **Stock exchange symbol:** AME.

B/E AEROSPACE

3355 East La Palma Avenue, Anaheim CA 92806. 714/630-5150. **Contact:** Debbi Nakamura, Personnel. **World Wide Web address:** http://www.beaerospace.com. **Description:** B/E Aerospace designs, manufactures, sells, and provides global support for one of the industry's broadest lines of commercial aircraft cabin interior products including seating products, passenger entertainment and service systems, galley structures, and inserts. The company is one of the world's largest suppliers of such products, serving most of the world's major airlines and airframe manufacturers. **Corporate headquarters location:** Wellington FL. **Other U.S. locations:** Vista CA; Delray FL; Jacksonville FL; Miami FL; Winston-Salem NC; Arlington WA. **Listed on:** NASDAQ. **Stock exchange symbol:** BEAV. **Annual sales/revenues:** More than $100 million. **Number of employees nationwide:** 3,100.

THE BOEING COMPANY

5301 Bolsa Avenue, Huntington Beach CA 92647-2099. 714/896-3311. **Contact:** Human Resources Department. **E-mail address:** employmentoperations@boeing.com. **World Wide Web address:** http://www.boeing.com. **Description:** A major manufacturer of high-technology aerospace products including military and commercial aircraft. **Corporate headquarters location:** Chicago IL. **Other area locations:** Cypress CA; Long Beach CA. **Other U.S. locations:** Nationwide. **Listed on:** New York Stock Exchange. **Stock exchange symbol:** BA.

C&D AEROSPACE, INC.

5701 Bolsa Avenue, Huntington Beach CA 92647. 714/891-1906. **Contact:** Human Resources Manager. **Description:** Designs and manufactures aircraft interiors for commercial airlines and for various governments. **Common positions include:** Accountant/Auditor; Aerospace Engineer; Blue-Collar Worker Supervisor; Computer Programmer; Designer; Electrical/Electronics Engineer; Human Resources Manager; Mechanical Engineer; Purchasing Agent/Manager; Quality Control Supervisor; Structural Engineer. **Special programs:** Internships. **Corporate headquarters location:** Garden Grove CA. **Other area locations:** La Palma CA; Ontario CA; Santa Maria CA. **Other U.S. locations:** Marysville WA. **Operations at this facility include:** Administration; Manufacturing; Research and Development; Sales. **Listed on:** Privately held. **Facilities Manager:** John Hargreaves. **Number of employees at this location:** 550. **Number of employees nationwide:** 2,500.

J.C. CARTER COMPANY, INC.
671 West 17th Street, Costa Mesa CA 92627-3605. 949/548-3421. **Contact:** Department of Human Resources. **E-mail address:** hr@jccarter.com. **World Wide Web address:** http://www.jccarter.com. **Description:** Designs and manufactures pumps, valves, and pressure regulators used in aircraft fuel systems. **Common positions include:** Accountant/Auditor; Aerospace Engineer; Buyer; Computer Programmer; Draftsperson; Human Resources Manager; Industrial Engineer; Manufacturer's/Wholesaler's Sales Representative; Marketing Specialist; Mechanical Engineer; Operations/Production Manager; Purchasing Agent/Manager; Quality Control Supervisor. **Corporate headquarters location:** This location. **Parent company:** Argo-Tech Corporation.

EMBEE INC.
P.O. Box 15705, Santa Ana CA 92735-0705. 714/546-9842. **Contact:** Personnel. **E-mail address:** embee@embee.com. **World Wide Web address:** http://www.embee.com. **Description:** Manufactures electromagnetic parts for aerospace applications. **Corporate headquarters location: This location.**

FAIRCHILD FASTENERS - U.S.
800 South State College Boulevard, Fullerton CA 92831. 714/871-1550. **Contact:** Personnel Manager. **World Wide Web address:** http://www.fairchildfasteners.com. **Description:** Manufactures and supplies precision fastening systems and components and latching devices for aerospace and industrial applications. Fairchild Fasteners - U.S. was established to collectively manage all of Fairchild's fastener operations in the United States. Fairchild Fasteners - Europe (Germany) is its sister company. **Common positions include:** Aerospace Engineer; Computer Programmer; Customer Service Representative; Draftsperson; Industrial Engineer; Machinist; Mechanical Engineer; Metallurgical Engineer. **Corporate headquarters location:** Dulles VA. **Parent company:** The Fairchild Corporation. **Operations at this facility include:** Administration; Manufacturing; Research and Development; Sales; Service. **Listed on:** New York Stock Exchange. **Stock exchange symbol:** FA. **President/CEO:** Eric Steiner. **Number of employees at this location:** 600.

FAIRCHILD FASTENERS - U.S.
3000 West Lomita Boulevard, Torrance CA 90505. 310/530-2220. **Contact:** Human Resources Manager. **World Wide Web address:** http://www.fairchildfasteners.com. **Description:** Manufactures and supplies precision fastening systems and

components and latching devices for aerospace and industrial applications. Fairchild Fasteners - U.S. was established to collectively manage all of Fairchild's fastener operations in the United States. Fairchild Fasteners - Europe (Germany) is its sister company. **Corporate headquarters location:** Dulles VA. **Listed on:** New York Stock Exchange. **Stock exchange symbol:** FA. **Parent company:** The Fairchild Corporation.

GARRETT AVIATION SERVICES
6201 West Imperial Highway, Los Angeles CA 90045. 310/568-3799. **Toll-free phone:** 800/942-7738. **Fax:** 310/568-3992. **Contact:** Fred Schutz, Manager of Human Resources. **World Wide Web address:** http://www.garrettaviation.com. **Description:** Specializes in the repair and service of corporate aircraft. **Common positions include:** Aircraft Mechanic/Engine Specialist. **Corporate headquarters location:** Tempe AZ. **Other U.S. locations:** IL; NY; TX. **Number of employees at this location:** 140. **Number of employees nationwide:** 700.

GOODRICH AEROSTRUCTURES GROUP
850 Lagoon Drive, Chula Vista CA 91910-2090. 619/691-4111. **Fax:** 619/691-4103. **Contact:** Mary Rose Escobedo, Senior Employment Representative. **E-mail address:** goodrich@rpc.webhire.com. **World Wide Web address:** http://www.rohr.com. **Description:** Designs, integrates, manufactures, sells, and supports aircraft engine nacelle systems and components for large commercial and military aircraft. **Common positions include:** Accountant/Auditor; Aerospace Engineer; Budget Analyst; Buyer; Computer Programmer; Cost Estimator; Designer; Environmental Engineer; Human Resources Manager; Industrial Engineer; Mechanical Engineer; Structural Engineer; Systems Analyst. **Corporate headquarters location:** This location. **Other U.S. locations:** Foley AL; Riverside CA; San Marcos TX. **International locations:** Toulouse, France; Hamburg, Germany. **Parent company:** Goodrich Company. **Listed on:** New York Stock Exchange. **Stock exchange symbol:** GR. **Number of employees at this location:** 2,300. **Number of employees nationwide:** 5,000.

HAMILTON SUNDSTRAND POWER SYSTEMS
P.O. Box 85757, San Diego CA 92186. 858/627-6000. **Contact:** Department of Human Resources. **E-mail address:** professionalstaffing@hamiltonsunstrandcorp.com. **World Wide Web address:** http://www.hamiltonsunstrandcorp.com. **Description:** Manufactures aeronautical and aerospace equipment including auxiliary power systems. **Corporate**

headquarters location: Windsor Locks CT. **Parent company:** United Technologies. **Listed on:** New York Stock Exchange. **Stock exchange symbol:** UTX.

HAMILTON SUNSTRAND SENSOR SYSTEMS
2771 North Garey Avenue, Pomona CA 91767. 909/593-3581. **Contact:** Human Resources Department. **E-mail address:** professionalstaffing@hamiltonsunstrandcorp.com. **World Wide Web address:** http://www.hamiltonsunstrandcorp.com. **Description:** Produces orbiting satellites, small-launch vehicles, and navigational and positioning instruments and provides satellite-based communications systems for industry. **Corporate headquarters location:** Windsor Locks CT. **Parent company:** United Technologies. **Listed on:** New York Stock Exchange. **Stock exchange symbol:** UTX.

HI-SHEAR TECHNOLOGY CORPORATION
2600 Skypark Drive, Torrance CA 90509. 310/326-8110. **Contact:** Manager of Human Resources Department. **E-mail address:** personnel@hstc.com. **World Wide Web address:** http://www.hstc.com. **Description:** Designs, manufactures, and markets a wide range of electronic and ordnance-related products and systems used by the aerospace and defense industries, primarily in space applications, tactical and strategic missile and weapon systems, and advanced fighter aircraft. The company also produces emergency rescue equipment; igniter assemblies for automotive airbag systems; and high-security, electromechanical locks. Aerospace products include microprocessor-based electronic sequencers, power cartridges, electronic and laser firing systems, and mechanical separation devices. **Corporate headquarters location:** Torrance CA. **Parent company:** GFI Industries. **Operations at this facility include:** Administration; Manufacturing; Research and Development; Sales. **Listed on:** American Stock Exchange. **Stock exchange symbol:** HSR. **Number of employees at this location:** 500.

HI-SHEAR TECHNOLOGY CORPORATION
24225 Garnier Street, Torrance CA 90505. 310/784-2100. **Contact:** Department of Human Resources. **World Wide Web address:** http://www.hstc.com. **Description:** Designs, develops, manufactures, and markets a wide range of electronic and ordnance-related products and systems used by the aerospace and defense industries, primarily in space applications, tactical and strategic missile and weapon systems, and advanced fighter aircraft. The company also produces emergency rescue equipment; igniter assemblies for

automotive airbag systems; and high-security, electromechanical locks. Aerospace products include microprocessor-based electronic sequencers, power cartridges, electronic and laser firing systems, and mechanical separation devices. **Corporate headquarters location:** This location. **Parent company:** GFI Industries. **Listed on:** American Stock Exchange. **Stock exchange symbol:** HSR.

HYDRO-AIRE, INC.
P.O. Box 7722, Burbank CA 91510. 818/842-6121. **Physical address:** 3000 Winona Avenue, Burbank CA 91505. **Contact:** Personnel. **E-mail address:** hr@hydroaire.com. **World Wide Web address:** http://www.hydroaire.com. **Description:** Manufactures a variety of components for the commercial and military aircraft markets. Products include microcircuits, servovalves, fuel pumps, and braking control systems. **Common positions include:** Accountant/Auditor; Administrator; Aerospace Engineer; Assembly Worker; Assistant Manager; Buyer; Chemical Engineer; Claim Representative; Computer Operator; Computer Programmer; Contract/Grant Administrator; Cost Estimator; Credit Clerk and Authorizer; Customer Service Representative; Department Manager; Draftsperson; Electrical/Electronics Engineer; Field Engineer; General Manager; Human Resources Manager; Hydraulic Tester; Inspector/Tester/Grader; Licensed Practical Nurse; Licensed Vocational Nurse; Logistics Support Worker; Machine Operator; Machinist; Manufacturer's/Wholesaler's Sales Rep.; Marketing Manager; Mechanical Engineer; Operations/Production Manager; Payroll Clerk; Photographer/Camera Operator; Photographic Process Worker; Precision Assembler; Production Coordinator; Project Planner; Public Relations Specialist; Purchasing Agent/Manager; Quality Control Supervisor; Receptionist; Registered Nurse; Research Technician; Sales Engineer; Scheduler; Secretary; Security Officer; Shipping and Receiving Clerk; Software Engineer; Stock Clerk; Systems Analyst; Technical Writer/Editor; Tool and Die Maker; Truck Driver. **Corporate headquarters location:** This location. **Parent company:** Crane Company. **Listed on:** New York Stock Exchange. **Stock exchange symbol:** CR. **Number of employees at this location:** 500.

ITT INDUSTRIES
GILFILLAN DIVISION
7821 Orion Avenue, Van Nuys CA 91406. 818/988-2600. **Contact:** Mark Casady, Manager of Human Resources Department. **E-mail address:** hr.gilfillan@itt.com. **World Wide Web address:** http://www.gilfillan.itt.com. **Description:**

Develops, manufactures, and services air traffic control (GCA/Landing) and air/coastal defense radar systems, and command/control systems for a wide variety of military and civil applications. **Common positions include:** Accountant/Auditor; Administrative Worker/Clerk; Blue-Collar Worker Supervisor; Buyer; Commercial Artist; Computer Programmer; Credit Manager; Department Manager; Draftsperson; Electrical/Electronics Engineer; Financial Analyst; General Manager; Human Resources Manager; Industrial Designer; Industrial Engineer; Marketing Specialist; Mechanical Engineer; Operations/Production Manager; Physicist; Purchasing Agent/Manager; Quality Control Supervisor; Systems Analyst; Technical Writer/Editor; Transportation/Traffic Specialist. **Corporate headquarters location:** New York NY. **Parent company:** ITT Corporation is a diversified, global enterprise engaged in three major business areas: Financial and Business Services, which includes ITT Hartford, ITT Financial Corporation, and ITT Communications and Information Services, Inc.; Manufactured Products, which includes ITT Automotive, ITT Defense & Electronics, Inc., and ITT Fluid Technology Corporation; and Sheraton Hotels (ITT Sheraton Corporation). **Listed on:** New York Stock Exchange. **Stock exchange symbol:** ITT.

MEGGITT PLC
1915 Voyager Avenue, Simi Valley CA 93063. 805/526-5700. **Contact:** Human Resources Department. **World Wide Web address:** http://www.meggitt.com. **Description:** Develops specialized electric and aerospace technologies. The aerospace unit manufactures systems that measure and process altitude, speed, and engine parameters; ducting systems; control valves; and fire detection/protection systems. The electronics unit manufactures sensors, circuits, and resistors for a variety of industries. **Corporate headquarters location:** This location.

MERCURY AIR GROUP, INC.
5456 McConnell Avenue, Los Angeles CA 90066. 310/827-2737. **Contact:** Steve Antonoff, Director of Human Resources. **World Wide Web address:** http://www.mercuryairgroup.com. **Description:** Engaged primarily in ground support services for passenger and freight air carriers and also in the manufacturing of electronic components. Support services include aircraft refueling and maintenance. Electronic components and parts include resistors, fusing devices, circuit breakers, audio accessories, service accessories, and electrical modules. **Corporate headquarters location:** This location. **Listed on:** American Stock Exchange. **Stock exchange symbol:** MAX.

MONOGRAM SYSTEMS
1300 East Valencia Drive, Fullerton CA 92831. 714/449-3000.
Contact: Department of Human Resources. **World Wide Web
address:** http://www.monogramsystems.com. **Description:**
Manufactures interior aircraft equipment including seats for
passengers and crew, coffee machines, and lavatories.
Corporate headquarters location: Compton CA.

NORTHROP GRUMMAN CORPORATION
One Northrop Avenue, Hawthorne CA 90251. 310/332-1000.
Recorded jobline: 310/335-3000. **Contact:** Human Resources.
World Wide Web address: http://www.northgrum.com.
Description: Manufactures military aircraft, commercial aircraft
parts, and electronic systems. Northrop Grumman develops
the B-2 Spirit Stealth Bomber, parts for the F/A-18 and the
Boeing 747, and radar equipment. Other operations include
computer systems development for management and scientific
applications. **Common positions include:** Accountant/Auditor;
Aerospace Engineer; Buyer; Computer Operator; Computer
Programmer; Electrical/Electronics Engineer; Employment
Interviewer; Industrial Engineer; Mechanical Engineer;
Software Engineer; Structural Engineer; Systems Analyst.
Corporate headquarters location: Los Angeles CA. **Operations
at this facility include:** Manufacturing; Research and
Development. **Listed on:** New York Stock Exchange. **Stock
exchange symbol:** NOC. **Number of employees at this
location:** 25,000.

NORTHROP GRUMMAN CORPORATION
1840 Century Park East, Los Angeles CA 90067. 310/553-
6262. **Contact:** Human Resources Department. **World Wide
Web address:** http://www.northgrum.com. **Description:**
Manufactures military aircraft, commercial aircraft parts, radar
equipment, and electronic systems. Northrop Grumman
develops the B-2 Spirit Stealth Bomber, as well as parts for the
F/A-18 and the Boeing 747. Other operations include
computer systems development for management and scientific
applications. **Corporate headquarters location:** This location.
Other U.S. locations: Nationwide. **Listed on:** New York Stock
Exchange. **Stock exchange symbol:** NOC.

NORTHOP GRUMMAN INFORMATION TECHNOLOGY
3701 Skypark Drive, Suite 200, Torrance CA 90505. 310/331-
1203. **Contact:** Human Resources. **E-mail address:**
northgrumit@hiresystems.com. **World Wide Web address:**
http://www.northopgrummanit.com. **Description:** Develops
state-of-the-art software technology for the U.S. military and

government. **Corporate headquarters location:** Herndon VA. **Other U.S. locations:** Washington DC; Cocoa Beach FL; Indianapolis IN; Omaha NE; Clearfield UT. **Listed on:** New York Stock Exchange Symbol. **Stock exchange symbol:** NOC.

NORTHOP GRUMMAN INFORMATION TECHNOLOGY

222 West Sixth Street, San Pedro CA 90731. 310/831-0611. **Fax:** 310/521-2660. **Contact:** Human Resources. **E-mail address:** northgrumit@hiresystems.com. **World Wide Web address:** http://www.northopgrummanit.com. **Description:** Develops state-of-the-art software and information technology systems for the U.S. military and government. **Common positions include:** Aerospace Engineer; Computer Programmer; Electrical/Electronics Engineer; Software Engineer; Systems Analyst. **Corporate headquarters location:** Herndon VA. **Other U.S. locations:** Washington DC; Cocoa Beach FL; Indianapolis IN; Omaha NE; Clearfield UT. **Operations at this facility include:** Research and Development. **Listed on:** New York Stock Exchange. **Stock exchange symbol:** NOC.

PTI TECHNOLOGIES, INC.

501 Del Norte Boulevard, Oxnard CA 93030. 805/604-3700. **Fax:** 805/604-3772. **Contact:** Human Resources. **E-mail address:** careers@pti-tech.com. **World Wide Web address:** http://www.pti-tech.com. **Description:** Designs, manufactures, and markets filtration and coupling equipment that is used in most commercial, military, and general aviation aircraft. PTI Technologies also produces and markets filters for use in fluid power systems in heavy equipment, industrial machinery, and energy extraction applications. **Common positions include:** Accountant/Auditor; Aerospace Engineer; Blue-Collar Worker Supervisor; Buyer; Computer Programmer; Credit Manager; Draftsperson; Industrial Engineer; Mechanical Engineer; Operations/Production Manager; Purchasing Agent/Manager; Quality Control Supervisor. **Special programs:** Summer Jobs. **Corporate headquarters location:** St. Louis MO. **Parent company:** ESCO Electronics Corporation is a diversified producer of defense systems and commercial products including valves and filters, mobile tactical systems, armament systems, automatic test equipment, utility load management equipment, and anechoic/shielding systems. ESCO's other operating subsidiaries include EMC Test Systems, L.P.; VACCO Industries; Comtrak Technologies, Inc.; Filtertek Inc.; Lindgren RF Enclosures; Distribution Control Systems, Inc.; Rantec Microwave & Electronics. **Listed on:** New York Stock Exchange. **Stock exchange symbol:** ESE.

PACIFIC SCIENTIFIC COMPANY

1800 Highland Avenue, Duarte CA 91010. 626/359-9317. **Contact:** Human Resources Department. **World Wide Web address:** http://www.pacsci.com. **Description:** Manufactures commercial aircraft equipment such as fire extinguishers, industrial gauges, and pressure gauges. **Corporate headquarters location:** Washington DC. **Other U.S. locations:** Silver Spring MD.

PHAOSTRON INSTRUMENT AND ELECTRONIC COMPANY

717 North Coney Avenue, Azusa CA 91702. 626/969-6801. **Fax:** 626/334-8057. **Contact:** Ms. Jackie Cangialosi, Human Resources Department Manager. **World Wide Web address:** http://www.phaostron.com. **Description:** Primarily engaged in the manufacture and sale of panel meters, avionic mechanisms, and edge-lighted plastic panels for a variety of aircraft. **NOTE:** Resumes may be submitted to the above e-mail address. **Common positions include:** Aerospace Engineer; Industrial Engineer; Machinist; Mechanical Engineer; Precision Assembler; Quality Control Supervisor; Receptionist; Tool and Die Maker. **Corporate headquarters location:** This location. **Operations at this facility include:** Manufacturing. **Number of employees at this location:** 50.

SENIOR AEROSPACE

790 Greenfield Drive, El Cajon CA 92021-3101. 619/442-3451. **Contact:** Human Resources Department. **World Wide Web address:** http://www.senioraerospace.com. **Description:** Manufactures aircraft fuselages and related parts. **Common positions include:** Accountant/Auditor; Aerospace Engineer; Blue-Collar Worker Supervisor; Buyer; Computer Programmer; Electrical/Electronics Engineer; Financial Analyst; Mechanical Engineer; Purchasing Agent/Manager; Quality Control Supervisor; Systems Analyst; Technical Writer/Editor. **Corporate headquarters location:** Paoli PA.

SMITH AEROSPACE

1700 Business Center Drive, Duarte CA 91010. 626/359-9211. **Fax:** 626/357-0069. **Contact:** Michelle Crook, Human Resources Representative. **World Wide Web address:** http://www.smithaerospace.com. **Description:** This location manufactures propellers and hydraulic engines. Overall, Smith Aerospace is a diversified manufacturing firm that conducts business in four major industrial segments: Aerospace, Metals, Packaged Products, and Aviation. Aerospace consists of hydraulic and pneumatic valves used in military and commercial fixed-wing aircraft and helicopters, tanks, and the national aerospace program. Metals includes the production of flints and various extruded metals. Packaged Products consists principally of packaged fuels and flints. Aviation includes the chartering, servicing, and sales of helicopters and fixed-wing aircraft. **Common positions include:** Accountant; Buyer; Industrial Engineer; Manufacturing Engineer; Mechanical Engineer; MIS Specialist; Systems Analyst. **Corporate headquarters location:** Sahuarita AZ. **Parent company:** Smiths Group plc. **Listed on:** New York Stock Exchange. **Stock exchange symbol:** SMGKE. **Annual sales/revenues:** More than $100 million. **Number of employees at this location:** 295.

TRW SPACE & ELECTRONICS GROUP
One Space Park, Building E-1, Room 2012, Redondo Beach CA 90278. 310/812-4321. **Contact:** Recruiting Department. **World Wide Web address:** http://www.trw.com. **Description:** Designs and develops sophisticated space systems, microelectronics, and aircraft avionics for worldwide government and commercial use. TRW Space & Electronics Group's technologies are employed in several national security, communications, and science program projects. **Corporate headquarters location:** Cleveland OH. **Parent company:** TRW. **Listed on:** New York Stock Exchange. **Stock exchange symbol:** TRW.

H.R. TEXTRON, INC.
25200 West Rye Canyon Road, Santa Clarita CA 91355-1265. 661/294-6000. **Recorded jobline:** 877/TEXTRON. **Contact:** Employment Specialist. **World Wide Web address:** http://www.textron.com. **Description:** Designs and manufactures components and control systems for major aircraft manufacturers. The manufacturing group designs systems to improve performance and increase safety. **Corporate headquarters location:** Providence RI. **Parent company:** Textron Inc. (Providence RI) is a diversified conglomerate with over 30 separate companies in three primary areas: Aerospace and Defense Technology; Financial Services; and Communications. The company also manufactures automobile parts, outdoor equipment, and specialty fasteners. **Listed on:** New York Stock Exchange. **Stock exchange symbol:** TXT.

THALES IN-FLIGHT SYSTEMS
17481 Red Hill Avenue, Irvine CA 92614. 949/660-7722. **Contact:** Personnel. **E-mail address:** job@thalesgroup.com. **World Wide Web address:** http://www.thalesgroup.com. **Description:** Manufactures passenger video entertainment

systems, cabin video systems, and Passenger Control Units for noise control in airplanes. **Parent company:** Thomson-CSF.

APPAREL, FASHION, AND TEXTILES

You can expect to find the following types of companies in this chapter:
Broadwoven Fabric Mills • Knitting Mills • Curtains and Draperies • Footwear • Nonwoven Fabrics • Textile Goods and Finishing • Yarn and Thread Mills

ACTION EMBROIDERY
1315 West Brooks Street, Ontario CA 91762. 909/983-1359. **Toll-free phone:** 800/638-7223. **Fax:** 909/983-2755. **Contact:** Human Resources Department. **World Wide Web address:** http://www.actionemb.com. **Description:** Manufactures military emblems.

ASHWORTH, INC.
2765 Loker Avenue West, Carlsbad CA 92008. 760/438-6610. **Contact:** Personnel. **E-mail address:** jobs@ashworth.com. **World Wide Web address:** http://www.ashworthinc.com. **Description:** Designs, manufactures, and markets golf apparel including men's and women's cotton shirts, pullovers, vests, sweaters, shorts, pants, and jackets. **Corporate headquarters location:** This location. **Listed on:** NASDAQ. **Stock exchange symbol:** ASHW.

AUTHENTIC FITNESS CORPORATION
6040 Bandini Boulevard, City of Commerce, CA 90040. 323/726-1262. **Contact:** Human Resources Department. **World Wide Web address:** http://www.speedo.com. **Description:** Owns, licenses, and markets activewear worldwide. The company's Speedo division manufactures swimwear and related accessories. Authentic Fitness also designs, sources, and markets a complete selection of skiwear including parkas, ski suits, shells, and ski pants. The company operates Authentic Fitness retail stores, which sell active fitness apparel. **Corporate headquarters location:** Van Nuys CA. **Other U.S. locations:** Nationwide. **International locations:** Canada.

BARCO OF CALIFORNIA
350 West Rosecrans Avenue, Gardena CA 90248. 310/323-7315. **Contact:** Human Resources. **Description:** Manufactures and markets uniforms for health care and fast-food companies. **Corporate headquarters location:** This location. **Number of employees at this location:** 250.

BEACH PATROL INC.
1165 East 230th Street, Carson CA 90745. 310/552-2700. **Contact:** Human Resources Department. **World Wide Web address:** http://www.beachpatrolinc.com. **Description:** Designs swimwear and other apparel. **Corporate headquarters location:** This location. **Other U.S. locations:** Weston FL; Atlanta GA; New York NY; Huntington Valley PA. **International locations:** Australia; Canada; Mexico; New Zealand; Taiwan.

BYER CALIFORNIA
1201 Rio Vista Avenue, Los Angeles CA 90023. 323/266-4561. **Contact:** Letty Hernandez, Human Resources Director. **E-mail address:** clee@byer.com. **World Wide Web address:** http://www.byer.com. **Description:** Manufactures women's sportswear. **Corporate headquarters location:** San Francisco CA.

CHAMBERS BELT
5445 Jillson Street, City of Commerce CA 90040. 323/726-2109. **Contact:** Human Resources Department. **World Wide Web address:** http://www.chambersbelt.com. **Description:** A manufacturer of leather belts for men and women. **Corporate headquarters location:** This location.

DECKERS OUTDOOR CORPORATION
495-A South Fairview Avenue, Goleta CA 93117. 805/967-7611. **Contact:** Human Resources. **World Wide Web address:** http://www.deckers.com. **Description:** Designs, manufactures, and markets footwear developed for high-performance outdoor, recreational, and sports activities, as well as casual wear. Deckers Outdoor's products are sold under the Teva, Simple, Sensi, and Picante brand names, and are marketed through leading outdoor retailers, athletic footwear stores, specialty retailers, and department stores throughout the United States and in select foreign markets. **Corporate headquarters location:** This location.

GUESS? INC.
1444 South Alameda Street, Los Angeles CA 90021. 213/765-3100. **Fax:** 213/744-7832. **Contact:** Human Resources. **E-mail address:** jobs@guess.com. **World Wide Web address:** http://www.guess.com. **Description:** Designs, develops, and markets jeans and other casual wear for men and women. **Corporate headquarters location:** This location. **Listed on:** New York Stock Exchange. **Stock exchange symbol:** GES.

K-SWISS INC.
31248 Oak Crest Drive, Westlake Village CA 91361. 818/706-5100. **Fax:** 818/706-5390. **Contact:** Human Resources. **World Wide Web address:** http://www.kswiss.com. **Description:** Manufactures athletic and casual footwear and apparel. Founded in 1966. **Corporate headquarters location:** This location. **Listed on:** NASDAQ. **Stock exchange symbol:** KSWS.

L.A. GEAR, INC.
5900 Rodeo Road, Los Angeles CA 90016-4313. 310/253-7744. **Fax:** 310/253-7740. **Contact:** Human Resources. **World Wide Web address:** http://www.lagear.com. **Description:** Manufactures athletic/fashion footwear and apparel. **Common positions include:** Accountant/Auditor; Advertising Clerk; Claim Representative; Computer Programmer; Credit Manager; Customer Service Representative; Designer; Human Resources Manager; Paralegal; Public Relations Specialist; Systems Analyst. **Operations at this facility include:** Administration; Divisional Headquarters; Research and Development; Service. **Number of employees at this location:** 200.

LEGGETT & PLATT, INC.
P.O. Box 4956, Whittier CA 90602. 562/945-2641. **Physical address:** 12352 East Whittier Boulevard, Whittier CA 90602. **Contact:** Personnel. **E-mail address:** resumes@leggett.com. **World Wide Web address:** http://www.leggett.com. **Description:** Manufactures and markets a broad line of components for the furniture and bedding industries. Company products also include select lines of commodity fibers and carpet cushioning materials. **Common positions include:** Accountant/Auditor; Branch Manager; Buyer; Customer Service Representative; Environmental Engineer; Industrial Engineer; Manufacturer's/Wholesaler's Sales Rep.; Quality Control Supervisor. **Corporate headquarters location:** Carthage MO. **Other U.S. locations:** Nationwide. **Operations at this facility include:** Administration; Divisional Headquarters; Manufacturing; Sales. **Listed on:** New York Stock Exchange. **Stock exchange symbol:** LEG. **Number of employees at this location:** 250. **Number of employees nationwide:** 16,000.

WORKRITE UNIFORM COMPANY, INC.
P.O. Box 1192, Oxnard CA 93032. 805/483-0175. **Physical address:** 500 East Third Street, Oxnard CA 93030. **Fax:** 805/483-7622. **Contact:** Human Resources. **World Wide Web address:** http://www.workrite.com. **Description:** An apparel manufacturer specializing in flame-retardant garments. Founded in 1973. **NOTE:** Workrite Uniform Company

primarily hires sewing machine operators. Entry-level positions are offered. **Common positions include:** Account Manager; Administrative Assistant; AS400 Programmer Analyst; Chief Financial Officer; Customer Service Representative; Draftsperson; Human Resources Manager; Industrial Designer; Industrial Engineer; Marketing Manager; MIS Specialist; Network/Systems Administrator; Operations Manager; Production Manager; Purchasing Agent/Manager; Quality Assurance Engineer; Quality Control Supervisor; Sales Manager; Typist/Word Processor. **Special programs:** This location also hires seasonally. **Office hours:** Monday - Friday, 7:30 a.m. - 4:00 p.m. **Corporate headquarters location:** This location. **Parent company:** Williamson-Dickie Manufacturing Company. **Operations at this facility include:** Administration; Manufacturing; Sales; Service. **Listed on:** Privately held. **Annual sales/revenues:** $21 - $50 million.

ARCHITECTURE, CONSTRUCTION, AND ENGINEERING

You can expect to find the following types of companies in this chapter:

Architectural and Engineering Services • Civil and Mechanical Engineering Firms • Construction Products, Manufacturers, and Wholesalers • General Contractors/Specialized Trade Contractors

ABS CONSULTING

300 Commerce Drive, Suite 200, Irvine CA 92602. 714/734-4242. **Contact:** Department of Human Resources. **World Wide Web address:** http://www.absconsulting.com. **Description:** Offers engineering consulting for system safety and reliability and provides probable risk assessment to the energy, defense, petrochemical, and manufacturing industries. **Corporate headquarters location:** Houston TX.

ADVANCED FOAM

1745 West 134th Street, Gardena CA 90249. 310/515-0617. **Contact:** Personnel. **Description:** Manufactures specialty sheets of foam for the construction of buildings.

AIR CONDITIONING COMPANY, INC.

6265 San Fernando Road, Glendale CA 91201. 818/244-6571. **Toll-free phone:** 800/998-2226. **Fax:** 818/549-0120. **Contact:** Roberta Kessler, Director of Human Resources Department. **E-mail address:** hrglendale@accoair.com. **World Wide Web address:** http://www.accoair.com. **Description:** A mechanical contracting firm that specializes in the design and construction of HVAC systems. **Common positions include:** Accountant; Buyer; CADD Operator; Design Engineer; Mechanical Engineer; Project Manager. **Corporate headquarters location:** This location. **Other area locations:** Concord CA; Sacramento CA; San Carlos CA; San Diego CA; Tustin CA. **Other U.S. locations:** Orlando FL; Tampa FL; Kent WA. **Operations at this facility include:** Administration; Engineering and Design; Sales; Service. **Listed on:** Privately held. **Annual sales/revenues:** More than $100 million. **Number of employees at this location:** 300. **Number of employees nationwide:** 1,200.

AMELCO CORPORATION
19208 South Vermont Avenue, Gardena CA 90248-4414. 310/327-3070. **Contact:** Human Resources Department. **World Wide Web address:** http://www.amelco.net. **Description:** Provides specialty construction services primarily electrical and mechanical subcontracting. **Corporate headquarters location:** This location. **Other U.S. locations:** Hawaii. **Stock exchange symbol:** AMLC.

ANTHONY AND SYLVAN POOLS
1228 West Shelly Court, Orange CA 92868. 714/628-9600. **Contact:** Human Resources Department. **World Wide Web address:** http://www.anthony-sylvan.com. **Description:** One of the largest builders of residential swimming pools in the United States. **Parent company:** Anthony Industries, Inc. **Operations at this facility include:** Administration; Divisional Headquarters. **Other U.S. locations:** Nationwide. **Listed on:** NASDAQ. **Stock exchange symbol:** SWIM.

BOYLE ENGINEERING CORPORATION
P.O. Box 3030, Newport Beach CA 92660. 949/476-3400. **Physical address:** 1501 Quail Street, Newport Beach CA 92660. **Fax:** 949/721-7142. **Contact:** Personnel Manager. **E-mail address:** recruitingmgr@boyleengineering.com. **World Wide Web address:** http://www.boyleengineering.com. **Description:** Provides comprehensive services ranging from project planning and feasibility studies to design and construction phases. The company specializes in the fields of water resources; water treatment and distribution; wastewater collection, treatment, and reuse; streets, highways, and bridges; light and heavy rail; drainage and flood control; and land planning. **Common positions include:** Agricultural Scientist; Architect; Civil Engineer; Electrical/Electronics Engineer; Mechanical Engineer; Structural Engineer. **Corporate headquarters location:** This location. **Other area locations:** Bakersfield CA; Fresno CA; Lancaster CA; Los Angeles CA; Ontario CA; Orange County CA; Sacramento CA; San Diego CA; San Luis Obispo CA; Santa Rosa CA; Ventura CA. **Other U.S. locations:** CO; FL; NV; NM; TX; VT.

CALPROP CORPORATION
13160 Mindanao Way, Suite 180, Marina Del Rey CA 90292-7903. 310/306-4314. **Contact:** Dori Baron, Personnel Manager. **E-mail address:** info@clpo.com. **World Wide Web address:** http://www.clpo.com. **Description:** Builds and sells single-family homes and condominiums in California. Founded in 1961. **Corporate headquarters location:** This location.

CAPITAL PACIFIC HOLDING
4100 MacArthur Boulevard, Suite 200, Newport Beach CA 92660. 949/622-8400. **Contact:** Human Resources. **World Wide Web address:** http://www.cph-inc.com. **Description:** Builds single-family homes throughout Orange County CA, Las Vegas NV, and Austin TX. **Corporate headquarters location:** This location. **Other U.S. locations:** Mesa AZ; Westminster CO; Austin TX. **Listed on:** American Stock Exchange. **Stock exchange symbol:** CPH.

COAST FOUNDRY AND MANUFACTURING COMPANY
P.O. Box 1788, Pomona CA 91769. 909/596-1883. **Contact:** Human Resources. **Description:** A manufacturer of plumbing supplies. **Common positions include:** Accountant/Auditor; Administrative Manager; Blue-Collar Worker Supervisor; Computer Programmer; Human Resources Manager; Operations/Production Manager; Purchasing Agent/Manager; Quality Control Supervisor. **Corporate headquarters location:** This location. **Number of employees at this location:** 300.

DANIEL, MANN, JOHNSON & MENDENHALL
515 Flower Street, Los Angeles CA 90071. 213/593-8100. **Contact:** Human Resources Recruiter. **E-mail address:** michael.robinson@dmjmhn.com. **World Wide Web address:** http://www.dmjm.com. **Description:** Provides a wide range of architectural/engineering services to the public and private sectors. Operations include transportation, public works, and commercial architecture. **Common positions include:** Architect; Civil Engineer; Electrical/Electronics Engineer; Mechanical Engineer. **Special programs:** Internships. **Corporate headquarters location:** This location. **Other U.S. locations:** San Bernardino CA; San Francisco CA; Santa Monica CA. **Operations at this facility include:** Administration; Divisional Headquarters; Regional Headquarters.

ELIXIR INDUSTRIES
17925 South Broadway, Gardena CA 90247. 310/767-3400. **Toll-free phone:** 800/421-1942. **Contact:** Human Resources. **E-mail address:** elixircorp@elixirind.com. **World Wide Web address:** http://www.elixirind.com. **Description:** Manufactures metal siding, roofing, doors, frame parts, roof vents, roof domes, and related mobile home products. **Corporate headquarters location:** This location.

EXPONENT, INC.
5401 McConnell Avenue, Los Angeles CA 90066. 310/823-2035. **Contact:** Human Resources Department. **E-mail address:**

hr@exponent.com. **World Wide Web address:** http://www.exponent.com. **Description:** Provides accident reconstruction, biomechanics, construction/structural engineering, aviation and marine investigations, environmental assessment, materials and product testing, warnings and labeling issues, accident statistic data analysis, and risk prevention/mitigation. Founded in 1967. **NOTE:** All hiring for Exponent Failure Analysis Associates is conducted through the corporate headquarters. Please mail resumes to Human Resources, 149 Commonwealth Drive, Menlo Park CA 94025. **Corporate headquarters location:** Menlo Park CA. **Listed on:** NASDAQ. **Stock exchange symbol:** EXPO.

FM GLOBAL
P.O. Box 9270, Van Nuys CA 91409. 818/704-1133. **Contact:** Human Resources. **E-mail address:** jobs@fmglobal.com. **World Wide Web address:** http://www.fmglobal.com. **Description:** A loss-control services organization. The company helps owner/company policyholders protect their properties and occupancies against damage from fire, wind, flood, and explosion; from boiler, pressure vessel, and machinery accidents; and from many other insured hazards. **Corporate headquarters location:** Johnston RI. **Other U.S. locations:** Walnut Creek CA; Norwalk CT; Alpharetta GA; Park Ridge IL; Norwood MA; Novi MI; Plymouth MN; St. Louis MO; Charlotte NC; Parsippany NJ; New York NY; North Olmstead OH; Malvern PA; Plano TX; Houston TX; Reston VA; Bellevue WA. **International locations:** Worldwide. **Number of employees worldwide:** 4,000.

FERGUSON ENTERPRISES, INC.
11552 Monarch Street, Garden Grove CA 92841. 714/893-1936. **Contact:** Department of Human Resources. **E-mail address:** resumes@ferguson.com. **World Wide Web address:** http://www.ferguson.com. **Description:** Distributes an extensive variety of building materials throughout the western United States. Major product lines include plumbing supplies, valves and fittings, sprinkler and irrigation products, and solar energy components. Ferguson Enterprises operates over 500 locations in North America. **Corporate headquarters location:** Newport News VA. **Other U.S. locations:** Nationwide. **International locations:** Columbia; Mexico; Puerto Rico.

FLUOR CORPORATION
One Fluor Drive, Aliso Viejo CA 92698. 949/349-2000. **Contact:** Personnel. **E-mail address:** careers@fluor.com. **World Wide Web address:** http://www.fluor.com. **Description:**

Operates within the fields of engineering, global services, coal production, and procurement and construction through four operating groups. Fluor Daniel provides engineering, procurement, and construction services. Fluor Global Services provides a wide range of products and related services including consulting services; equipment rental sales and service; operations; and maintenance services. Fluor Signature Services provides business support services to Fluor Corporation. A.T. Massey Coal Group produces coal for the steel industry. **Common positions include:** Accountant; Architect; Attorney; Buyer; Chemical Engineer; Civil Engineer; Computer Programmer; Draftsperson; Electrical/Electronics Engineer; Financial Analyst; Geologist/Geophysicist; Industrial Engineer; Mechanical Engineer; Purchasing Agent/Manager; Systems Analyst. **Corporate headquarters location:** Aliso Viejo CA. **Listed on:** New York Stock Exchange. **Stock exchange symbol:** FLR.

HOLMES AND NARVER INC.
999 Town & Country Road, Orange CA 92868. 714/567-2567. **Contact:** Pam Cooper, Senior Employment Administrator. **World Wide Web address:** http://www.hninc.com. **Description:** A full-service architectural, engineering, design, and construction company. The company designs and manages the construction of government bases, airports and airfields, remote site camps, bridges, and research laboratories. **Other U.S. locations:** Anchorage AK; Denver CO. **Parent company:** USFilter.

HUNTER DOUGLAS
1818 South Oak Street, Los Angeles CA 90015. 213/749-6333x3205. **Fax:** 213/742-0981. **Contact:** Human Resources. **World Wide World Address:** http://www.hunterdouglas.com. **Description:** A manufacturer of custom-made windows. **Common positions include:** Accountant/Auditor; Adjuster; Blue-Collar Worker Supervisor; Buyer; Clerical Supervisor; Computer Programmer; Credit Manager; Electrician; Human Resources Manager; Industrial Engineer; Management Trainee; Manufacturer's/Wholesaler's Sales Representative; Production Manager; Purchasing Agent/Manager; Quality Control Supervisor; Services Sales Representative; Wholesale and Retail Buyer. **Other U.S. locations:** Augusta GA; Chicago IL. **Parent company:** Hunter Douglas Group. **Operations at this facility include:** Administration; Regional Headquarters; Sales; Service. **Number of employees at this location:** 350. **Number of employees nationwide:** 500.

JACOBS ENGINEERING GROUP INC.

P.O. Box 7084, Pasadena CA 91109-7084. 626/449-2171. **Physical address:** 1111 South Arroyo Parkway, Pasadena CA 91105. **Contact:** Human Resources Department. **World Wide Web address:** http://www.jacobs.com. **Description:** An engineering firm offering a full range of services including environmental studies, feasibility studies, architectural services, engineering/design, procurement, construction, construction management, and construction maintenance. Jacobs Engineering Group is one of the largest engineering and construction companies in the United States. The company specializes in the chemicals and polymers, federal programs, pulp and paper, semiconductor, petroleum refining, facilities and transportation, food and consumer products, and pharmaceuticals and biotechnologies industries. **Corporate headquarters location:** This location. **Common positions include:** Accountant/Auditor; Administrator; Architect; Attorney; Biological Scientist; Blue-Collar Worker Supervisor; Buyer; Chemical Engineer; Chemist; Civil Engineer; Computer Programmer; Draftsperson; Economist; Electrical/Electronics Engineer; Geologist/Geophysicist; Mechanical Engineer; Petroleum Engineer; Physicist; Purchasing Agent/Manager; Quality Control Supervisor; Systems Analyst; Technical Writer/Editor. **Listed on:** New York Stock Exchange. **Stock exchange symbol:** JEC.

JENSEN INDUSTRIES, INC.

1946 East 46th Street, Los Angeles CA 90058. 323/235-6800. **Toll-free phone:** 800/243-2000. **Contact:** Mona M. Mejia, Manager of Human Resources Department. **World Wide Web address:** http://www.jensenindustries.com. **Description:** Primarily engaged in manufacturing building products for residential and commercial industries. The company's products include bath cabinets, vanities, lav-tops, toplights, mailboxes, medicine cabinets, roof vents, range hoods, and monitor panels. **Common positions include:** Accountant/Auditor; Administrator; Blue-Collar Worker Supervisor; Buyer; Computer Programmer; Credit Manager; Customer Service Representative; Department Manager; Draftsperson; General Manager; Human Resources Manager; Industrial Engineer; Manufacturer's/Wholesaler's Sales Rep.; Marketing Specialist; Mechanical Engineer; Operations/Production Manager; Production Manager; Purchasing Agent/Manager. **Corporate headquarters location:** North Haven CT. **Number of employees at this location:** 200.

MATICH CORPORATION

P.O. Box 50000, San Bernardino CA 92412. 909/825-9100. **Fax:** 909/824-2360. **Contact:** Human Resources. **World Wide Web address:** http://www.matichicm.com. **Description:** An asphalt paving and manufacturing company. Matich Corporation is also a highway contractor and construction management firm. Founded in 1918. **Common positions include:** Accountant; Administrative Assistant; Chief Financial Officer; Civil Engineer; Claim Representative; Construction Contractor; Controller; Human Resources Manager; Quality Assurance Engineer; Sales Manager; Sales Representative; Secretary. **Corporate headquarters location:** Colton CA. **Listed on:** Privately held. **Annual sales/revenues:** $21 - $50 million. **Number of employees at this location:** 20. **Number of employees nationwide:** 115.

McELROY METAL INC.

P.O. Box 127, Adelanto CA 92301. 760/246-5545. **Contact:** Human Resources Department. **World Wide Web address:** http://www.mcelroy.com. **Description:** Manufactures metal siding and roofing. **Common positions include:** Account Manager; Account Representative; Administrative Assistant; Administrative Manager; Computer Operator; Customer Service Representative; Sales Manager; Sales Representative. **Corporate headquarters location:** Shreveport LA. **Other U.S. locations:** Nationwide. **Annual sales/revenues:** Less than $5 million. **Number of employees at this location:** 35. **Number of employees nationwide:** 300.

NIELSEN DILLINGHAM BUILDERS

3127 Jefferson Street, San Diego CA 92110. 619/291-6330. **Fax:** 619/291-9940. **Contact:** Karen Canoss, Human Resources. **E-mail address:** hr@ndbi.com. **World Wide Web address:** http://www.nielsendillingham.com. **Description:** A multifaceted construction firm specializing in commercial, industrial, medical/health care, engineering, retail, and hospitality projects. Founded in 1945. **NOTE:** Entry-level positions and part-time jobs are offered. **Company slogan:** Building for the 21st century. **Common positions include:** Accountant; Administrative Assistant; Administrative Manager; AS400 Programmer Analyst; Attorney; Civil Engineer; Computer Support Technician; Computer Technician; Controller; Cost Estimator; Human Resources Manager; Marketing Manager; Mechanical Engineer; MIS Specialist; Operations Manager; Paralegal; Project Manager; Secretary. **Special programs:** Internships. **Office hours:** Monday - Friday, 8:00 a.m. - 5:00 p.m. **Corporate headquarters location:** This location. **Other area locations:** Long Beach CA; Pleasanton CA. **Other U.S. locations:** Las Vegas NV; Portland OR. **Parent company:** Dillingham, Inc. **Listed on:** Privately held. **President:** Larry M. Geiser. **Annual sales/revenues:** More than $100 million. **Number of employees at this location:** 250. **Number of employees nationwide:** 350.

ROEL CONSTRUCTION COMPANY

P.O. Box 80216, San Diego CA 92138. 619/297-4156. **Physical address:** 3366 Kurtz Street, San Diego CA 92110. **Contact:** Human Resources Director. **World Wide Web address:** http://www.roel.com. **Description:** A commercial and residential construction company. Roel Construction also provides tenant improvements, structural concrete construction, construction forensic services, and surety claim services. **Corporate headquarters location:** This location. **Other U.S. locations:** AZ; NV. **President/CEO:** Stephen Roel.

THE RYLAND GROUP, INC.

24025 Park Sorrento, Suite 400, Calabasas CA 91302. 818/223-7500. **Contact:** Human Resources. **World Wide Web address:** http://www.ryland.com. **Description:** One of the nation's largest homebuilders and a leading mortgage finance company. The company builds homes in six regions and more than 25 cities. **Corporate headquarters location:** Los Angeles CA. **Other U.S. locations:** Nationwide. **Subsidiaries include:** Ryland Homes specializes in on-site construction of single-family attached and detached homes. Operating out of 34 retail and four wholesale branches, Ryland Mortgage Company works directly with Ryland Homes. **Listed on:** New York Stock Exchange. **Stock exchange symbol:** RYL. **Number of employees at this location:** 600. **Number of employees nationwide:** 3,200.

SOUTHDOWN CONCRETE PRODUCTS, INC.

2601 Saturn Street, Suite 200, Brea CA 92821. 714/985-4000. **Fax:** 714/985-4064. **Contact:** Human Resources Department Manager. **Description:** Engaged in the production, sale, and delivery of ready-mixed concrete and aggregates. **Common positions include:** Accountant/Auditor; Adjuster; Automotive Mechanic; Blue-Collar Worker Supervisor; Branch Manager; Computer Programmer; Electrician; General Manager; Human Resources Manager; Manufacturer's/Wholesaler's Sales Representative; Metallurgical Engineer; Mining Engineer; Operations/Production Manager. **Corporate headquarters location:** Houston TX. **Parent company:** Southdown, Inc. **Operations at this facility include:** Divisional Headquarters.

Listed on: New York Stock Exchange. **Number of employees at this location:** 360.

STANDARD PACIFIC HOMES

15326 Alton Parkway, Irvine CA 92619. 949/789-1600. **Contact:** Department of Human Resources. **E-mail address:** careers@stanpac.com. **World Wide Web address:** http://www.standardpacifichomes.com. **Description:** Designs, builds, and sells houses for residential use. **Corporate headquarters location:** This location. **Listed on:** New York Stock Exchange. **Stock exchange symbol:** SPF. **Annual sales/revenues:** More than $100 million.

TRANS-PACIFIC CONSULTANTS

27431 Enterprise Circle West, Temecula CA 92590. 909/676-7000. **Fax:** 909/699-7324. **Contact:** Human Resources. **Description:** A full-service consulting company engaged in land planning, civil engineering, and surveying. **Corporate headquarters location:** This location.

ARTS, ENTERTAINMENT, SPORTS, AND RECREATION

You can expect to find the following types of companies in this chapter:

Botanical and Zoological Gardens • Entertainment Groups • Motion Picture and Video Tape Production and Distribution • Museums and Art Galleries • Physical Fitness Facilities • Professional Sports Clubs • Public Golf Courses • Racing and Track Operations • Sporting and Recreational Camps • Theatrical Producers

AIMS MULTIMEDIA

9710 DeSoto Avenue, Chatsworth CA 91311. 818/773-4300. **Toll-free phone:** 800/367-2467. **Fax:** 818/341-6400. **Contact:** Adele Brant, Human Resources Department. **E-mail address:** info@aimsmultimedia.com. **World Wide Web address:** http://www.aims-multimedia.com. **Description:** Engaged in educational video production and distribution. **Corporate headquarters location:** This location.

ARTISAN ENTERTAINMENT

2700 Colorado Avenue, 2nd Floor, Santa Monica CA 90404. 310/449-9200. **Contact:** Human Resources. **World Wide Web address:** http://www.artisanent.com. **Description:** Produces, markets, and distributes motion pictures. **Corporate headquarters location:** This location. **Other U.S. locations:** New York NY. **Listed on:** Privately held. **Annual sales/revenues:** More than $100 million.

BALLY TOTAL FITNESS

P.O. Box 1090, Norwalk CA 90651. 562/484-2000. **Physical address:** 12440 East Imperial Highway, Suite 300, Norwalk CA 90650. **Contact:** Human Resources Department. **E-mail address:** jobs@ballyfitness.com. **World Wide Web address:** http://www.ballyfitness.com. **Description:** One of the world's largest owners and operators of fitness centers. Bally Total Fitness is operated by Bally Health & Tennis Corporation, which, through the subsidiaries it controls, is a nationwide commercial operator of fitness centers in the United States. Bally Health & Tennis operates over 360 fitness centers located in 27 states with approximately 4 million members. The fitness centers operate under the Bally name in conjunction with various others including Holiday Health, Jack LaLanne, Holiday Spa, Chicago Health Clubs, Scandinavian, President's

First Lady, Vic Tanny, Aerobics Plus, and as The Vertical Clubs. **Common positions include:** Customer Service Representative; Management Trainee; Sales Representative. **Special programs:** Internships. **Corporate headquarters location:** Chicago IL. **Other U.S. locations:** Nationwide. **International locations:** Canada. **Parent company:** Bally's Entertainment. **Listed on:** New York Stock Exchange. **Stock exchange symbol:** BFT. **Operations at this facility include:** Divisional Headquarters; Sales; Service.

CASTLE ROCK ENTERTAINMENT
335 North Maple Drive, Suite 135, Beverly Hills CA 90210. 310/285-2300. **Fax:** 310/285-2345. **Contact:** Human Resources Department. **World Wide Web address:** http://www.castle-rock.com. **Description:** A motion picture and video production company. **NOTE:** Warner Brothers handles the hiring for Castle Rock. Please contact WB Human Resources at: 818/954-6000 for more information. **Parent Company:** AOL Time Warner. **Listed on:** New York Stock Exchange. **Stock exchange symbol:** AOL.

COMPOSITE IMAGE SYSTEMS
1144 North Las Palmas Avenue, Hollywood CA 90038. 323/463-8811. **Contact:** Human Resources. **E-mail address:** resumes@cishollywood.com. **World Wide Web address:** http://www.cishollywood.com. **Description:** Provides video post-production services. **Corporate headquarters location:** This location.

CREATIVE ARTISTS AGENCY, INC. (CAA)
9830 Wilshire Boulevard, Beverly Hills CA 90212. 310/288-4545. **Contact:** Human Resources. **World Wide Web address:** http://www.caa.com. **Description:** Manages and represents actors, directors, and writers in the film and television industries. Founded in 1975. **CEO:** Rick Nicita. **Number of employees worldwide:** 400.

DEL MAR THOROUGHBRED CLUB
P.O. Box 700, Del Mar CA 92014. 858/755-1141. **Contact:** Joseph W. Harper, President. **World Wide Web address:** http://www.dmtc.com. **Description:** A horse racing facility. Del Mar Thoroughbred Club is a member of the Thoroughbred Racing Association of North America.

DELUXE LABORATORIES, INC.
1377 North Serrano Avenue, Hollywood CA 90027. 323/462-6171. **Contact:** Human Resources. **World Wide Web address:**

http://www.bydeluxe.com. **Description:** A motion picture film developer. **Parent company:** The Rank Group plc.

DIAMOND ENTERTAINMENT CORPORATION

800 Tucker Lane, Walnut CA 91789. 909/839-1989. **Contact:** Human Resources. **World Wide Web address:** http://www.e-dmec.com. **Description:** A full-service video product duplicating, manufacturing, packaging, and distribution company. Through its Custom Duplication Division, the company duplicates and packages videocassettes on a custom-made basis. Customers for this service include companies and individuals within the multilevel marketing industry who use videocassettes for product information, business recruitment, training, or sales and marketing purposes. The Entertainment Division markets and sells a variety of videocassette titles to the budget home video market. The company's inventory of programs consists of more than 675 titles including children's cartoons, motion pictures, sports highlights, educational, and exercise programs. The feature motion pictures offered by the company include such film classics as *Life with Father* and *It's a Wonderful Life*. **Corporate headquarters location:** This location.

DICK CLARK PRODUCTIONS, INC.

3003 West Olive Avenue, Burbank CA 91505. 818/841-3003. **Fax:** 818/954-8609. **Contact:** Personnel. **World Wide Web address:** http://www.dickclarkproductions.com. **Description:** One of the nation's top entertainment companies. The company primarily produces talk shows, made-for-TV movies, and awards shows such as the Golden Globe Awards. **Special programs:** Internships. **Corporate headquarters location:** This location.

THE WALT DISNEY COMPANY

500 South Buena Vista Street, Burbank CA 91521-7235. 818/560-6335. **Contact:** Staffing Services. **World Wide Web address:** http://disney.go.com. **Description:** One of the nation's top film studios. **Common positions include:** Accountant/Auditor; Budget Analyst; Computer Programmer; Economist; Financial Manager; Market Research Analyst; Marketing Manager; Secretary; Software Engineer; Systems Analyst. **Corporate headquarters location:** This location. **Listed on:** New York Stock Exchange. **Stock exchange symbol:** DIS.

DISNEYLAND

P.O. Box 3232, Anaheim CA 92803. 714/781-1600. **Fax:** 714/781-0065. **Recorded jobline:** 800/766-0888. **Contact:** Professional Staffing Department. **World Wide Web address:** http://www.disney.com. **Description:** One of the largest amusement/theme parks in the world. **Common positions include:** Accountant/Auditor; Buyer; Electrical/Electronics Engineer; Human Resources Manager; Industrial Engineer; Marketing Specialist; Mechanical Engineer; Seasonal Worker; Systems Analyst. **Corporate headquarters location:** Burbank CA. **Parent company:** The Walt Disney Company. **Operations at this facility include:** Resort/Support Functions.

E! ENTERTAINMENT TELEVISION NETWORKS

5750 Wilshire Boulevard, Los Angeles CA 90036. **Recorded jobline:** 323/954-2666. **Contact:** Human Resources. **E-mail address:** hr@eentertainment.com. **World Wide Web address:** http://www.eonline.com. **Description:** Operates a cable network dedicated to the entertainment and fashion industries. **Corporate headquarters location:** This location.

FAMILY FUN CENTERS

1041 North Shepard Street, Anaheim CA 92806. 714/630-7212. **Contact:** Human Resources. **World Wide Web address:** http://www.boomersparks.com. **Description:** An amusement park that features paddle boats, go carts, bumper boats, and a maze that is changed monthly. The park also includes a roller skating rink, arcade, and snack bar. **Corporate headquarters location:** Irvine CA. **Parent company:** Palace Entertainment Company.

FREMANTLE MEDIA

2700 Colorado Avenue, Suite 450, Santa Monica CA 90404. 310/656-1100. **Contact:** Human Resources Department. **World Wide Web address:** http://www.fremantlemedia.com. **Description:** Produces, distributes, markets, and promotes television programs and recorded music both domestically and internationally. The company is a leading distributor of television programming in the first-run syndication and distributes, represents, or owns participations in more than 160 television series, over 250 motion pictures, a variety of children's programming, and live-event specials. **Corporate headquarters location:** This location. **Parent company:** RTL Group. **Number of employees at this location:** 125.

GLOBAL OUTDOORS INC.
GOLD PROSPECTOR'S ASSOCIATION OF AMERICA, INC.
43445 Business Park Drive, Suite 113, Temecula CA 92590. 909/699-4749. **Contact:** Human Resources. **Description:** A leisure and entertainment company that owns and operates The Outdoor Channel, a national television network; Gold Prospector's Association of America, Inc. (also at this location); and the Lost Dutchman's Mining Association, a recreational mining club. **Corporate headquarters location:** This location. **Listed on:** NASDAQ. **Stock exchange symbol:** GLRS.

GOLD'S GYM
4070 Airport Center Drive, Palm Springs CA 92262. 760/322-4653. **Contact:** Manager. **World Wide Web address:** http://www.goldsgym.com. **Description:** A full-service health and fitness club. Each club is complete with weights and cardiovascular equipment, fitness and aerobic classes, tanning, personal training, and childcare facilities. Gold's Gym is one of the world's largest health club chains, with over 550 locations. **NOTE:** Part-time jobs are offered. **Common positions include:** Account Representative; Administrative Manager; Assistant Manager; Child Care Worker; Computer Operator; Customer Service Representative; Fitness Professional; Operations Manager; Sales Representative; Secretary. **Corporate headquarters location:** This location. **Parent company:** Neste Development. **Number of employees at this location:** 40.

GOLD'S GYM
39605 Entrepreneur Lane, Palm Desert CA 92260. 760/360-0565. **Contact:** Manager. **World Wide Web address:** http://www.goldsgym.com. **Description:** A full-service health and fitness club. Each club is complete with weights and cardiovascular equipment, fitness and aerobic classes, tanning, personal training, and childcare facilities. Gold's Gym is one of the world's largest health club chains, with over 550 locations. **NOTE:** Part-time jobs are offered. **Common positions include:** Account Representative; Administrative Manager; Assistant Manager; Child Care Worker; Computer Operator; Customer Service Representative; Fitness Professional; Operations Manager; Sales Representative; Secretary. **Corporate headquarters location:** Palm Springs CA. **Parent company:** Neste Development. **Number of employees at this location:** 40.

GOLD'S GYM
13785 Park Avenue, Victorville CA 92392. 760/243-4653. **Contact:** Manager. **World Wide Web address:** http://www.goldsgym.com. **Description:** A full-service health and fitness club. Each club is complete with weights and cardiovascular equipment, fitness and aerobic classes, tanning, personal training, and childcare facilities. Gold's Gym is one of the world's largest health club chains, with over 550 locations. **NOTE:** Part-time jobs are offered. **Common positions include:** Account Representative; Administrative Manager; Assistant Manager; Child Care Worker; Computer Operator; Customer Service Representative; Fitness Professional; Operations Manager; Sales Representative; Secretary. **Corporate headquarters location:** Palm Springs CA. **Parent company:** Neste Development. **Number of employees at this location:** 40.

GOLD'S GYM
26201 Ynez Road, Suite 1318, Temecula CA 92591. 909/699-5432. **Contact:** Manager. **World Wide Web address:** http://www.goldsgym.com. **Description:** A full-service health and fitness club. Each club is complete with weights and cardiovascular equipment, fitness and aerobic classes, tanning, personal training, and childcare facilities. Gold's Gym is one of the world's largest health club chains, with over 550 locations. **NOTE:** Part-time jobs are offered. **Common positions include:** Account Representative; Administrative Manager; Assistant Manager; Child Care Worker; Computer Operator; Customer Service Representative; Fitness Professional; Operations Manager; Sales Representative; Secretary. **Corporate headquarters location:** Palm Springs CA. **Parent company:** Neste Development. **Number of employees at this location:** 40.

SAMUEL GOLDWYN COMPANY
9570 West Pico Boulevard, Suite 400, Los Angeles CA 90035. 310/860-3100. **Contact:** Human Resources Department. **Description:** Engaged primarily in the financing, production, and distribution of feature-length motion pictures. Samuel Goldwyn Company also finances and distributes television programs intended for licensing to cable and first-run syndication markets, and to U.S. and foreign television networks. **Common positions include:** Accountant/Auditor; Administrative Manager. **Special programs:** Internships. **Corporate headquarters location:** This location. **Other U.S. locations:** New York NY. **Operations at this facility include:** Administration; Regional Headquarters; Research and

Development; Sales. **Number of employees at this location:** 260.

HBO PICTURES

2049 Century Park East, Suite 4100, Los Angeles CA 90067. 310/201-9200. **Contact:** Personnel Department. **World Wide Web address:** http://www.hbo.com. **Description:** Produces original, cable network films. **Parent company:** AOL Time Warner. **Corporate headquarters location:** New York NY.

HOLLYWOOD PARK INC.

P.O. Box 369, Inglewood CA 90306-0369. 310/419-1500. **Physical address:** 1050 South Prairie Avenue, Inglewood CA 90301. **Contact:** Human Resources. **World Wide Web address:** http://www.hollywoodpark.com. **Description:** Owns and operates a horseracing track. **Corporate headquarters location:** This location. **Parent company:** Churchill Downs Inc. **Listed on:** NASDAQ. **Stock exchange symbol:** CHDN.

IMAGE ENTERTAINMENT, INC.

9333 Oso Avenue, Chatsworth CA 91311. 818/407-9100. **Contact:** Human Resources. **World Wide Web address:** http://www.image-entertainment.com. **Description:** One of the largest laser disc licensees and distributors in North America. The company distributes thousands of titles ranging from feature films and music videos to family, documentary, and special interest programming to over 2,500 retail outlets. The company releases exclusive titles from licensers such as Disney's Buena Vista Home Video, New Line Home Video, Orion Home Video, Playboy Home Video, and Turner Home Entertainment. **Corporate headquarters location:** This location. **Listed on:** NASDAQ. **Stock exchange symbol:** DISK.

INTERNATIONAL CREATIVE MANAGEMENT, INC. (ICM)

8942 Wilshire Boulevard, Beverly Hills CA 90211. 310/550-4000. **Fax:** 310/550-4100. **Contact:** Human Resources. **Description:** A talent agency managing film, music, publishing, television, theater, and public affairs clients. The agency also protects intellectual property rights. **Other U.S. locations:** New York NY. **International locations:** London, England; Paris, France; Rome, Italy. **CEO:** Jeff Berg. **Number of employees worldwide:** 500.

IWERKS ENTERTAINMENT, INC.

4520 West Valerio Street, Burbank CA 91505. 818/841-7766. **Contact:** Human Resources. **World Wide Web address:** http://www.iwerks.com. **Description:** Designs, manufactures, installs, and services high-resolution, proprietary motion picture theater attractions in museums, visitor centers, casinos, and newly emerging entertainment venues. The company's attractions are built around a variety of theater systems including fixed and portable simulators, giant screen, 360-degree, and virtual reality theater systems. Business segments include Iwerks Attractions and Technologies, Iwerks Studios, Iwerks Cinetropolis, Iwerks Touring Technologies, and Omni Films International. **NOTE:** Entry-level positions are offered. **Common positions include:** Accountant; Administrative Assistant; Chief Financial Officer; Controller; Electrician; Financial Analyst; Human Resources Manager; Marketing Manager; Public Relations Specialist; Sales Executive; Sales Representative. **Special programs:** Internships. **Corporate headquarters location:** This location. **CEO/President:** Chuck Goldwater. **Sales Manager:** Don Savant. **Number of employees at this location:** 90. **Number of employees nationwide:** 95. **Number of employees worldwide:** 100.

JOSHUA TREE RECREATION
P.O. Box 1245, Joshua Tree CA 92252-0838. 760/366-8415. **Contact:** Human Resources. **Description:** Operates the Joshua Tree Park as well as a community center, and offers a variety of classes and outdoor activity programs.

KNOTT'S BERRY FARM
8039 Beach Boulevard, Buena Park CA 90620. 714/827-1776. **Fax:** 714/220-5150. **Contact:** Staffing. **World Wide Web address:** http://www.knotts.com. **Description:** This location is an amusement park. Overall, Knott's Berry Farm is engaged in the development and management of family restaurants, retail operations, and specialty food products manufacturing. **Common positions include:** Accountant/Auditor; Buyer; Computer Programmer; Food Scientist/Technologist; Restaurant/Food Service Manager; Services Sales Rep.; Store Manager; Systems Analyst. **Special programs:** Internships. **Corporate headquarters location:** This location. **Other area locations:** Irvine CA; Moreno Valley CA; Placentia CA. **Other U.S. locations:** Bloomington MN. **Operations at this facility include:** Administration; Sales.

LASERPACIFIC MEDIA CORPORATION
809 North Cahuenga Boulevard, Hollywood CA 90038. 323/462-6266. **Fax:** 323/464-6005. **Contact:** Personnel. **World Wide Web address:** http://www.laserpacific.com. **Description:** A major supplier of film, videotape, digital sound postproduction, and multimedia services to prime-time

television shows. **Corporate headquarters location:** This location. **Listed on:** NASDAQ. **Stock exchange symbol:** LPAC. **Chairman and CEO:** James R. Parks. **Annual sales/revenues:** $21 - $50 million. **Number of employees nationwide:** 225.

LIBERTY LIVEWIRE
2813 West Alameda Avenue, Burbank CA 91505. 818/840-7000. **Recorded jobline:** 818/840-7378. **Contact:** Human Resources. **World Wide Web address:** http://www.4mc.com. **Description:** Offers television and film production services and satellite transmission uplinking services. **Listed on:** NASDAQ. **Stock exchange symbol:** LWIRA.

LOEWS CINEPLEX ENTERTAINMENT
1925 Century Park East, Suite 300, Los Angeles CA 90067. 310/553-5307. **Contact:** Human Resources Department. **Corporate headquarters location:** jobopps@loewscpx.com. **World Wide Web address:** http://www.loewscineplex.com. **Description:** One of the world's largest movie theater chains. Loews Cineplex Entertainment operates more than 2,925 screens in 385 locations. **Corporate headquarters location:** Toronto, Canada.

LOS ANGELES ATHLETIC CLUB
431 West Seventh Street, Los Angeles CA 90014. 213/625-2211. **Contact:** Stuart Lava, Director of Human Resources. **E-mail address:** laaco.jobs@laac.net. **World Wide Web address:** http://www.laac.com. **Description:** Operates an athletic facility with programs in virtually every sport, as well as concession, banquet, and guest hotel facilities. **Common positions include:** Accountant/Auditor; Assistant Manager; Customer Service Representative. **Corporate headquarters location:** This location. **Other area locations:** Marina del Rey CA; Orange CA. **Operations at this facility include:** Administration; Sales; Service. **Listed on:** Privately held. **Number of employees at this location:** 240. **Number of employees nationwide:** 370.

LOS ANGELES COUNTY MUSEUM OF ART
5905 Wilshire Boulevard, Los Angeles CA 90036. 323/857-6000. **Fax:** 323/857-4720. **Recorded jobline:** 323/857-6069. **Personnel phone:** 323/857-4745. **Contact:** Adam Kaplan, Employment Administrator. **E-mail address:** jobs@lacma.org. **World Wide Web address:** http://www.lacma.org. **Description:** A premier visual arts museum. The museum's collection expresses the creativity of cultures from all over the world. Founded in 1938. **NOTE:** Entry-level positions and part-time jobs are offered. This is a nonprofit company. **Common**

positions include: Accountant; Administrative Assistant; Attorney; Budget Analyst; Chief Financial Officer; Computer Programmer; Computer Support Technician; Computer Technician; Controller; Customer Service Representative; Database Administrator; Editor; Electrician; Event Planner; Financial Analyst; Graphic Artist; Graphic Designer; Help-Desk Technician; Human Resources Manager; Internet Services Manager; Intranet Developer; Librarian; Managing Editor; Marketing Manager; Marketing Specialist; Media Planner; Network Administrator; Operations Manager; Paralegal; Secretary; Systems Analyst; Technical Support Engineer; Telecommunications Manager; Video Production Coordinator; Website Developer. **Office hours:** Monday - Friday, 8:00 a.m. - 5:00 p.m. **Corporate headquarters location:** This location. **Listed on:** Privately held. **President/CEO:** Dr. Andrea Rich. **Facilities Manager:** Donald Battjes. **Information Systems Manager:** Peter Bodell. **Sales Manager:** Keith McKeown. **Annual sales/revenues:** $21 - $50 million.

LOS ANGELES DODGERS

1000 Elysian Park Avenue, Los Angeles CA 90012. 323/224-1500. **Contact:** Human Resources. **World Wide Web address:** http://losangeles.dodgers.mlb.com. **Description:** The offices for the National League baseball team.

LOS ANGELES ZOO

5333 Zoo Drive, Los Angeles CA 90027. 323/666-4650. **Contact:** Human Resources Department. **World Wide Web address:** http://www.lazoo.org. **Description:** A zoo that houses a fully-equipped animal hospital and animal health center, an animal food commissary, and a horticultural section. **NOTE:** For employment information, contact Department of Personnel, Room 100, City Hall South, Los Angeles CA 90012. 213/847-9240. **Number of employees at this location:** 180.

MGM INC.

2500 Broadway Street, Santa Monica CA 90404. 310/449-3560. **Recorded jobline:** 310/449-3569. **Contact:** Human Resources. **World Wide Web address:** http://www.mgm.com. **Description:** A fully-integrated media company providing entertainment through the production and distribution of feature films, television programs, animation, music, and interactive games. **Corporate headquarters location:** New York NY. **Listed on:** New York Stock Exchange. **Stock exchange symbol:** MGM.

PARAMOUNT PICTURES CORPORATION
5555 Melrose Avenue, Los Angeles CA 90038-3197. 323/956-5000. **Fax:** 323/862-1134. **Recorded jobline:** 323/956-5216. **Contact:** Human Resources Department. **World Wide Web address:** http://www.paramount.com. **Description:** Paramount Pictures Corporation is involved in many aspects of the entertainment industry including motion pictures, television, and video production and distribution. Founded in 1905. **Common positions include:** Accountant; Administrative Assistant; Advertising Clerk; Attorney; Budget Analyst; Computer Programmer; Customer Service Representative; Finance Director; Financial Analyst; Graphic Designer; Human Resources Manager; Intellectual Property Lawyer; Market Research Analyst; Marketing Specialist; MIS Specialist; Multimedia Designer; Online Content Specialist; Paralegal; Public Relations Specialist; Secretary; Systems Analyst; Transportation/Traffic Specialist; Typist/Word Processor; Webmaster. **Corporate headquarters location:** New York NY. **Parent company:** Viacom, Inc. Other subsidiaries of Viacom include MTV, Blockbuster, Showtime, Nickelodeon, and Simon & Schuster. **Listed on:** New York Stock Exchange. **Stock exchange symbol:** VIA. **Annual sales/revenues:** More than $100 million. **Number of employees at this location:** 3,000.

PINNACLE ENTERTAINMENT INC.
330 North Brand Boulevard, Suite 1100, Glendale CA 91203. 818/662-5900. **Fax:** 818/662-5901. **Contact:** Human Resources. **World Wide Web address:** http://www.pinnacle-entertainment-inc.com. **Description:** Builds, owns, leases, and operates racetracks and casinos. **Corporate headquarters location:** This location. **Other U.S. locations:** Compton CA; Vevay IN; Harvey LA; Bossier City LA; Biloxi MS; Verdi NV. **International locations:** Neuquen, Argentina. **Listed on:** New York Stock Exchange. **Stock exchange symbol:** PNK. **Annual sales/revenues:** More than $100 million.

SAN DIEGO ZOO
P.O. Box 120551, San Diego CA 92112-0551. 619/231-1515. **Fax:** 619/557-3937. **Recorded jobline:** 619/557-3968. **Contact:** Human Resources Department. **World Wide Web address:** http://www.sandiegozoo.org. **Description:** One of the nation's largest zoos.

SANTA BARBARA LOCATION SERVICES
REAL TALENT/KIDS
1214 Coast Village, Suite 12, Santa Barbara CA 93108. 805/565-1562. **Fax:** 805/969-9595. **Contact:** Ms. Ronnie

Mellen, Owner. **World Wide Web address:** http://www.santabarbara-locations.com. **Description:** Assists the film industry by providing location/production coordination services. Real Talent/Kids (also at this location, 805/969-2222) is a casting company. Founded in 1983. **Common positions include:** Librarian; Operations/Production Manager; Production Assistant; Public Relations Manager; Real Estate Agent. **Number of employees at this location:** 5.

SIX FLAGS MAGIC MOUNTAIN
SIX FLAGS HURRICANE HARBOR
P.O. Box 5500, Valencia CA 91355. 661/255-4100. **Contact:** Alex Hottya, Personnel. **E-mail address:** ahottya@sftp.com. **World Wide Web address:** http://www.sixflags.com. **Description:** An amusement and water theme park. **Other U.S. locations:** Nationwide. **Corporate headquarters location:** New York NY. **Parent company:** Premier Parks (OK) owns and operates 35 theme parks nationwide. **Listed on:** New York Stock Exchange. **Stock exchange symbol:** PKS.

SONY PICTURES ENTERTAINMENT
10202 West Washington Boulevard, Sony Pictures Plaza Building, Suite 3900, Culver City CA 90232. **Contact:** Personnel. **E-mail address:** resumes@spe.sony.com. **World Wide Web address:** http://www.spe.sony.com. **Description:** Sony Pictures is involved in motion pictures, television, theatrical exhibitions, and studio facilities and technology. The motion picture business distributes movies produced by Columbia TriStar Pictures. The television business, which encompasses Columbia TriStar Television, Columbia TriStar Television Distribution, and Columbia TriStar International Television, is involved with numerous cable channels and distributes and syndicates television programs such as *Days of Our Lives*. **Corporate headquarters location:** This location. **Parent company:** Sony Corporation of America. **Operations at this facility include:** Administration; Sales. **Listed on:** New York Stock Exchange. **Stock exchange symbol:** SNE.

SPELLING ENTERTAINMENT INC.
5700 Wilshire Boulevard, Suite 575, Los Angeles CA 90036. 323/965-5700. **Contact:** Human Resources. **Description:** A leading producer and distributor of television, film, and interactive entertainment. The company comprises Spelling Television, which produces made-for-television movies, miniseries, and one-hour series including *Seventh Heaven* and *Sunset Beach*; Big Ticket Television, which produces sitcoms for the broadcast and first-run markets; Spelling Films, which

produces and distributes feature films; Worldwide Vision, which syndicates the Spelling Entertainment library of more than 20,000 hours of television programming and thousands of feature films; Republic Entertainment, a distributor of home videos for the rental and sell-through markets; Virgin Interactive Entertainment, a developer and publisher of interactive games; and Hamilton products, a licensing and merchandising company that handles Spelling Properties. **Office hours:** Monday - Friday, 9:00 a.m. - 6:00 p.m. **Corporate headquarters location:** This location. **Parent company:** Viacom, Inc. **Listed on:** New York Stock Exchange. **Stock exchange symbol:** VIA. **Number of employees worldwide:** 1,000.

THE SPORTS CLUB COMPANY

11100 Santa Monica Boulevard, Suite 300, Los Angeles CA 90025. 310/479-5200. **Fax:** 310/445-9819. **Recorded jobline:** 310/477-6824. **Contact:** Human Resources. **World Wide Web address:** http://www.thesportsclubla.com. **Description:** Owns and operates several health clubs throughout California under the names Sports Club and Spectrum Club. **Corporate headquarters location:** This location. **Listed on:** American Stock Exchange. **Stock exchange symbol:** SCY.

TECHNICOLOR, INC.

4050 Lankershim Boulevard, North Hollywood CA 91608. 818/769-8500. **Contact:** Human Resources Department. **E-mail address:** hrjobs@technicolor.com. **World Wide Web address:** http://www.technicolor.com. **Description:** Engaged in film processing services for the movie industry. **Corporate headquarters location:** Camarillo CA.

UNIVERSAL STUDIOS, INC.

100 Universal City Plaza, Universal City CA 91608. 818/777-1000. **Physical address:** 3900 Lankershim Boulevard, Universal City CA 91604. **Recorded jobline:** 818/777-JOBS. **Contact:** Corporate Workforce Planning & Strategic Staffing. **E-mail address:** jobs@unistudios.com. **World Wide Web address:** http://www.universalstudios.com. **Description:** A diversified entertainment company and a worldwide leader in motion pictures, television, music, and home and location-based themed entertainment. The company's main operating divisions include Universal Studios, Universal Studios Recreation Group, Universal Studios Information Technology, Universal Studios Operations Group, Universal Music Group, Universal Pictures, Universal Networks & Worldwide Television Distribution, Universal Studios Consumer Products

Group, Universal Studios Online, and Spencer Gifts. **NOTE:** Entry-level positions are offered. **Common positions include:** Accountant; Administrative Assistant; Administrative Manager; Architect; Attorney; Auditor; Budget Analyst; Buyer; Chief Financial Officer; Civil Engineer; Computer Animator; Computer Operator; Computer Programmer; Controller; Cost Estimator; Design Engineer; Draftsperson; Editor; Editorial Assistant; Electrical/Electronics Engineer; Electrician; Finance Director; Financial Analyst; General Manager; Graphic Artist; Graphic Designer; Human Resources Manager; Industrial Engineer; Intellectual Property Lawyer; Internet Services Manager; Management Analyst/Consultant; Market Research Analyst; Marketing Manager; Marketing Specialist; Mechanical Engineer; MIS Specialist; Multimedia Designer; Online Content Specialist; Operations Manager; Paralegal; Project Manager; Public Relations Specialist; Purchasing Agent/Manager; Sales Executive; Sales Manager; Sales Representative; Secretary; Systems Analyst; Systems Manager; Technical Writer/Editor; Video Production Coordinator. **Special programs:** Internships; Training; Co-ops; Summer Jobs. **Corporate headquarters location:** This location. **Other U.S. locations:** Orlando FL; New York NY; Memphis TN; Nashville TN; Dallas TX. **International locations:** Worldwide. **Parent company:** The Seagram Co. Ltd. **Stock exchange symbol:** VOX. **Annual sales/revenues:** More than $100 million. **Number of employees worldwide:** 17,000.

WARNER BROS. STUDIOS (WB TELEVISION NETWORK)
4000 Warner Boulevard, Burbank CA 91522. 818/954-6000. **Recorded jobline:** 818/954-5400. **Contact:** Human Resources. **World Wide Web address:** http://www.warnerbros.com. **Description:** An entertainment/film production company. The company also operates a television network with nationwide affiliates. **Common positions include:** Accountant; Architect; Attorney; Budget Analyst; Buyer; Controller; Dietician/Nutritionist; Finance Director; Financial Analyst; Graphic Designer; Human Resources Manager; Secretary. **Corporate headquarters location:** This location. **Parent company:** AOL Time Warner. **Listed on:** New York Stock Exchange. **Stock exchange symbol:** AOL. **Annual sales/revenues:** More than $100 million.

WILLIAM MORRIS AGENCY, INC.
151 El Camino Drive, Beverly Hills CA 90212. 310/859-4000. **Contact:** Human Resources. **World Wide Web address:** http://www.wmaccm.com. **Description:** One of the largest talent and literary agencies in the world. **NOTE:** Entry-level

positions are offered. **Corporate headquarters location:** This location.

AUTOMOTIVE

You can expect to find the following types of companies in this chapter:

Automotive Repair Shops • Automotive Stampings • Industrial Vehicles and Moving Equipment • Motor Vehicles and Equipment • Travel Trailers and Campers

ALFA LEISURE INC.
1612 South Cucamonga Avenue, Ontario CA 91761. 909/628-3265. **Fax:** 909/591-7902. **Contact:** Human Resources. **E-mail address:** info@alfaleisure.com. **World Wide Web address:** http://www.alfaleisure.com. **Description:** Manufactures high-end, fifth-wheel recreation trailers. Founded in 1973. **Common positions include:** Accountant; Administrative Assistant; Blue-Collar Worker Supervisor; Buyer; Chief Financial Officer; Claim Representative; Computer Operator; Computer Programmer; Computer Technician; Customer Service Rep.; Design Engineer; Draftsperson; Industrial Engineer; Industrial Production Manager; Manufacturing Engineer; Marketing Specialist; Mechanical Engineer; Production Manager; Project Manager; Quality Control Supervisor; Sales Executive; Sales Manager; Sales Representative; Typist/Word Processor; Vice President. **Office hours:** Monday - Friday, 8:00 a.m. - 5:00 p.m. **Corporate headquarters location:** This location. **Other U.S. locations:** Worldwide. **Annual sales/revenues:** $21 - $50 million. **Number of employees at this location:** 330.

AMERICAN HONDA MOTOR COMPANY INC.
1919 Torrance Boulevard, Mailstop 100-1C-3A, Torrance CA 90501-2746. 310/783-2000. **Fax:** 310/783-2110. **Contact:** Rex Simpson, Manager of Employment Relations. **World Wide Web address:** http://www.hondacorporate.com. **Description:** Distributes Honda automotive, motorcycle, and power equipment products throughout the United States. Founded in 1959. **Common positions include:** Account Representative; Accountant/Auditor; Administrative Assistant; Administrative Manager; Assistant Manager; Budget Analyst; Buyer; Computer Operator; Credit Manager; Customer Service Representative; Financial Analyst; Management Trainee; Marketing Specialist; Public Relations Specialist; Sales Representative; Systems Analyst; Transportation/Traffic Specialist. **Special programs:** Internships; Training. **Corporate headquarters location:** This location. **Other U.S. locations:** Nationwide. **Subsidiaries include:** American Honda Finance Company. **Parent company:** Honda Motors Ltd. **Operations at this facility**

include: Administration; Research and Development; Sales; Service. **Listed on:** New York Stock Exchange. **Stock exchange symbol:** HMC. **Number of employees at this location:** 1,800. **Number of employees nationwide:** 3,500.

AMERICAN RACING EQUIPMENT
19200 South Reyes Avenue, Rancho Dominguez CA 90221. 310/635-7806. **Contact:** Human Resources Department. **World Wide Web address:** http://www.americanracing.com. **Description:** Manufactures custom wheel parts for automobiles. **Common positions include:** Accountant/Auditor; Administrative Assistant; Auditor; Blue-Collar Worker Supervisor; Buyer; Chemical Engineer; Chemist; Chief Financial Officer; Computer Operator; Computer Programmer; Electrical Engineer; Environmental Engineer; Financial Analyst; General Manager; Graphic Artist; Graphic Designer; Human Resources Manager; Industrial Engineer; Licensed Practical Nurse; Market Research Analyst; Metallurgical Engineer; Operations/Production Manager; Purchasing Agent/Manager; Quality Control Supervisor; Registered Nurse; Sales Executive; Secretary; Systems Analyst. **Corporate headquarters location:** Rancho Dominguez CA. **Other area locations:** Gardena CA. **International locations:** Queretaro, Mexico. **Listed on:** Privately held. **Annual sales/revenues:** More than $100 million. **Number of employees nationwide:** 3,000.

CLAYTON INDUSTRIES
P.O. Box 5530, El Monte CA 91734-1530. 626/443-9381. **Physical address:** 4213 North Temple City Boulevard, El Monte CA 91731. **Fax:** 626/442-3787. **Contact:** Human Resources Department. **World Wide Web address:** http://www.claytonindustries.com. **Description:** Manufactures a broad range of industrial and automotive equipment for a variety of commercial and government customers. Products include steam generators, dynamometers, and a number of automotive diagnostic components. **Common positions include:** Accountant/Auditor; Administrative Manager; Advertising Clerk; Blue-Collar Worker Supervisor; Buyer; Chemical Engineer; Computer Programmer; Customer Service Representative; Designer; Electrical/Electronics Engineer; Financial Analyst; General Manager; Industrial Engineer; Industrial Production Manager; Mechanical Engineer; Operations/Production Manager; Purchasing Agent/Manager; Quality Control Supervisor; Services Sales Representative; Software Engineer; Systems Analyst; Technical Writer/Editor; Transportation/Traffic Specialist. **Special programs:** Internships. **Corporate headquarters location:** This location. **Other U.S.**

locations: Nationwide. **International locations:** Worldwide. **Operations at this facility include:** Administration; Manufacturing; Research and Development; Sales; Service. **Listed on:** Privately held. **Number of employees at this location:** 135.

CONEXANT SYSTEMS INC.

4311 Jamboree Road, Newport Beach CA 92660-3095. 949/483-4600. **Fax:** 949/483-4078. **Contact:** Personnel. **World Wide Web address:** http://www.conexant.com. **Description:** This location manufactures modem chips and semiconductors. Overall, Conexant provides products for the printing, military, automotive, and aerospace industries through its electronics, automotive, and graphics divisions. Products include military and commercial communication equipment, guidance systems, electronics, components for automobiles, and printing presses. **Corporate headquarters location:** This location. **Other U.S. locations:** Austin TX. **Listed on:** NASDAQ. **Stock exchange symbol:** CNXT.

CONEXANT SYSTEMS INC.

9868 Scranton Road, San Diego CA 92121. 858/713-3200. **Contact:** Human Resources Department. **World Wide Web address:** http://www.conexant.com. **Description:** This location manufactures modem chips and semiconductors. Overall, Conexant provides products for the printing, military, automotive, and aerospace industries through its electronics, automotive, and graphics divisions. Products include military and commercial communication equipment, guidance systems, electronics, components for automobiles, and printing presses. **Common positions include:** Computer Programmer; Data Processor; Design Engineer; Electrical/Electronics Engineer; Hardware Engineer; Manager of Information Systems; Software Engineer. **Corporate headquarters location:** This location. **Other U.S. locations:** Austin TX. **Listed on:** NASDAQ. **Stock exchange symbol:** CNXT.

EDELBROCK CORPORATION

2700 California Street, Torrance CA 90503. 310/781-2222. **Fax:** 310/972-2735. **Contact:** Human Resources. **World Wide Web address:** http://www.edelbrock.com. **Description:** Designs, manufactures, distributes, and markets a wide range of high-quality performance products including intake manifolds, carburetors, camshafts, cylinder heads, exhaust systems, and other components designed for most domestic V8 and selected V6 engines. These products are designed to enhance street, off-road, recreational, and competition vehicle performance through increased horsepower, torque, and maneuverability. The company also designs and markets chrome aluminum air cleaners, valve covers, and breathers, which enhance engine and vehicle appearance. **Corporate headquarters location:** This location. **Listed on:** NASDAQ. **Stock exchange symbol:** EDEL.

FLEETWOOD ENTERPRISES, INC.
P.O. Box 7638, Riverside CA 92513-7638. 909/351-3500. **Physical address:** 3125 Myers Street, Riverside CA 92513. **Contact:** Department of Human Resources. **World Wide Web address:** http://www.fleetwood.com. **Description:** Manufactures recreational vehicles with operations worldwide. The company's recreational vehicles are primarily motor homes sold under brand names including American Eagle, Coronado, Bounder, Flair, and PaceArrow. Fleetwood Enterprises also manufactures a variety of trailers and campers and owns subsidiaries that offer financial services and supplies. **Corporate headquarters location:** This location. **Listed on:** New York Stock Exchange. **Stock exchange symbol:** FLE. **Number of employees at this location:** 19,000.

FORD MOTOR COMPANY
4940 Sheila Street, Los Angeles CA 90040. 323/267-6100. **Toll-free phone:** 800/300-7222. **Contact:** Human Resources. **E-mail address:** hireinfo@ford.com. **World Wide Web address:** http://www.ford.com. **Description:** Engaged in the design, development, manufacture, and sale of cars, trucks, tractors, and related components and accessories. Ford Motor Company is also one of the largest providers of financial services in the United States. The company's two core businesses are the Automotive Group and the Financial Services Group (Ford Credit, The Associates, USL Capital, and First Nationwide). Ford is also engaged in other businesses including electronics, glass, electrical and fuel-handling products, plastics, climate-control systems, automotive service and replacement parts, vehicle leasing and rental, and land development. **Corporate headquarters location:** Dearborn MI. **Listed on:** New York Stock Exchange. **Stock exchange symbol:** F. **Number of employees worldwide:** 300,000.

HONEYWELL
3201 West Lomita Boulevard, Torrance CA 90505. 310/530-1981. **Contact:** Human Resources Department. **World Wide Web address:** http://www.honeywell.com. **Description:** This location manufactures turbochargers. Overall, Honeywell is engaged in the research, development, manufacture, and sale

of advanced technology products and services in the fields of chemicals, electronics, automation, and controls. The company's major businesses are home and building automation and control, performance polymers and chemicals, industrial automation and control, space and aviation systems, and defense and marine systems. **Corporate headquarters location:** Plymouth MN. **Listed on:** New York Stock Exchange. **Stock exchange symbol:** HON.

JOHNSON CONTROLS, INC.
1550 East Kimberly Avenue, Fullerton CA 92831. 714/871-7740. **Contact:** Human Resources. **World Wide Web address:** http://www.johnsoncontrols.com. **Description:** Manufactures automotive storage batteries for sale to private labels. **Common positions include:** Accountant/Auditor; Buyer; Customer Service Representative; Industrial Engineer; Mechanical Engineer; Quality Control Supervisor. **Special programs:** Co-ops; Internships. **Corporate headquarters location:** Milwaukee WI. **Other U.S. locations:** Nationwide. **Operations at this facility include:** Manufacturing. **Listed on:** New York Stock Exchange. **Stock exchange symbol:** JCI. **Number of employees at this location:** 300. **Number of employees nationwide:** 35,000.

KAWASAKI MOTORS CORPORATION U.S.A.
P.O. Box 25252, Santa Ana CA 92799-5252. 949/770-0400. **Physical address:** 9950 Jeronimo Road, Irvine CA 92618. **Contact:** Christine Carter, Human Resources Director. **World Wide Web address:** http://www.kawasaki.com. **Description:** Imports and markets a variety of consumer-oriented transportation products and small engines. The company's primary product line is motorcycles, while other interests include gasoline, diesel, and turbine jet engines, as well as jet skis and portable generators. **Corporate headquarters location:** This location.

KIT MANUFACTURING COMPANY
P.O. Box 848, Long Beach CA 90801-0848. 562/595-7451. **Physical address:** 530 East Wardlow Road, Long Beach CA 90807. **Contact:** Human Resources. **World Wide Web address:** http://www.kitmfg.com. **Description:** One of the largest manufacturers of travel trailers and RVs in the United States. **Corporate headquarters location:** This location. **Listed on:** New York Stock Exchange. **Stock exchange symbol:** KIT.

KRACO ENTERPRISES
505 East Euclid Avenue, Compton CA 90224. 310/639-0666. **Toll-free phone:** 800/678-1910 (for submission of new product concepts or prototypes only). **Contact:** Human Resources. **World Wide Web address:** http://www.kraco.com. **Description:** Manufactures a broad range of floor mats for cars, trucks, vans, and SUVs. **Common positions include:** Art Director; Buyer; Chemist; Operations/Production Manager. **Corporate headquarters location:** This location. **Operations at this facility include:** Administration; Manufacturing; Research and Development; Sales. **Number of employees nationwide:** 450.

EARL SCHEIB, INC.
15206 Ventura Boulevard, Suite 200, Sherman Oaks CA 91403. 818/981-9992. **Toll-free phone:** 800/639-3275. **Contact:** Human Resources. **World Wide Web address:** http://www.earlscheib.com. **Description:** Operates a chain of automobile paint centers throughout the United States which offer painting and light body and fender repair services. **Corporate headquarters location:** This location. **Other U.S. locations:** Tampa FL; Evergreen Park IL; Springfield MO. **Operations at this facility include:** Regional Headquarters. **Listed on:** American Stock Exchange. **Stock exchange symbol:** ESH.

SUPERIOR INDUSTRIES INTERNATIONAL
7800 Woodley Avenue, Van Nuys CA 91406. 818/781-4973. **Contact:** Grisdela Padilla, Human Resources Department. **E-mail address:** gpadilla@supind.com. **World Wide Web address:** http://www.supind.com. **Description:** Produces cast aluminum road wheels for original equipment manufacturers and a variety of automotive aftermarket products. **NOTE:** Entry-level positions are offered. **Common positions include:** Accountant/Auditor; Design Engineer; Mechanical Engineer; Systems Analyst. **Corporate headquarters location:** This location. **Other U.S. locations:** AR; KS; TN. **Operations at this facility include:** Administration; Manufacturing. **Annual sales/revenues:** More than $100 million. **Number of employees at this location:** 900. **Number of employees nationwide:** 4,500.

YAMAHA MOTOR CORPORATION U.S.A.
6555 Katella Avenue, Cypress CA 90630. 714/761-7300. **Contact:** Human Resources Department. **World Wide Web address:** http://www.yamaha-motor.com. **Description:** Distributes motorized products including motorcycles, ATVs,

snowmobiles, golf carts, outboards, and power products. **Corporate headquarters location:** This location.

BANKING/SAVINGS AND LOANS

You can expect to find the following types of companies in this chapter:

Banks • Bank Holding Companies and Associations • Lending Firms/Financial Services Institutions

BANK OF AMERICA

345 North Brand Boulevard, Glendale CA 91203. 818/507-6700. **Contact:** Human Resources. **World Wide Web address:** http://www.bankofamerica.com. **Description:** This location is a customer service office. Overall, Bank of America is a full-service banking and financial institution. The company operates through four business segments: Global Corporate and Investment Banking, Principal Investing and Asset Management, Commercial Banking, and Consumer Banking. **Corporate headquarters location:** Charlotte NC. **Other U.S. locations:** Nationwide. **International locations:** Worldwide. **Listed on:** New York Stock Exchange. **Stock exchange symbol:** BAC.

CALIFORNIA BANK AND TRUST

24012 Calle de la Plata, Suite 150, Laguna Hills CA 92653. 949/699-4344. **Contact:** Human Resources Department. **E-mail address:** careers@calbt.com. **World Wide Web address:** http://www.calbanktrust.com. **Description:** California Bank and Trust provides commercial and professional loan and deposit products, SBA loans, and construction financing.

CATHAY BANCORP, INC.
CATHAY BANK

777 North Broadway Street, Los Angeles CA 90012. 213/625-4700. **Contact:** Human Resources. **World Wide Web address:** http://www.cathaybank.com. **Description:** A commercial bank operating through 17 locations. Founded in 1962. **NOTE:** Part-time jobs are offered. **Common positions include:** Bank Teller; Software Engineer. **Corporate headquarters location:** This location. **Other area locations:** Alhambra CA; Cerritos CA; Monterey Park CA; San Gabriel CA; Valley-Stoneman CA; Westminster CA. **Other U.S. locations:** Flushing NY; New York NY; Houston TX. **Operations at this facility include:** Administration. **Listed on:** NASDAQ. **Stock exchange symbol:** CATY. **Number of employees nationwide:** 500.

CITY NATIONAL BANK

400 North Roxbury Drive, Beverly Hills CA 90210. 310/888-6000. **Contact:** Department of Human Resources. **E-mail address:** careers@cnb.com. **World Wide Web address:** http://www.cityntl.com. **Description:** A commercial bank with 50 offices in Northern and Southern California. **NOTE:** Jobseekers should send resumes to Human Resources Division, City National Bank, 633 West Fifth Street, Los Angeles CA 90071. 213/553-8272. **Common positions include:** Accountant/Auditor; Bank Teller; Credit Manager; Customer Service Representative; Management Trainee; Secretary. **Corporate headquarters location:** This location. **Other area locations:** Statewide. **Listed on:** New York Stock Exchange. **Stock exchange symbol:** CYN.

CITY NATIONAL BANK

11 Golden Shore, Long Beach CA 90802. 562/624-8600. **Contact:** Human Resources. **E-mail address:** careers@cnb.com. **World Wide Web address:** http://www.cityntl.com. **Description:** A commercial bank with 50 offices in Northern and Southern California. **NOTE:** Jobseekers should send resumes to Human Resources Division, City National Bank, 633 West Fifth Street, Los Angeles CA 90071. 213/553-8272. **Corporate headquarters location:** Beverly Hills CA. **Other area locations:** Statewide. **Listed on:** New York Stock Exchange. **Stock exchange symbol:** CYN.

COMERICA, INC.

9920 South La Cienega Boulevard, Suite 604, Inglewood CA 90301. 310/417-5600. **Contact:** Vice President. **World Wide Web address:** http://www.comerica.com. **Description:** A multistate financial services provider. **Corporate headquarters location:** Detroit MI. **Listed on:** New York Stock Exchange. **Stock exchange symbol:** CMA.

COMMUNITY BANK

100 East Corson Street, Pasadena CA 91103-3839. 626/568-2067. **Fax:** 626/568-2217. **Contact:** Personnel. **E-mail address:** employment@communitybank-ca.com. **World Wide Web address:** http://www.communitybank-ca.com. **Description:** A commercial bank. **Common positions include:** Accountant/Auditor; Bank Teller; Branch Manager; Customer Service Representative; Financial Analyst; Loan Officer. **Corporate headquarters location:** This location. **Other area locations:** Anaheim CA; Burbank CA; City of Industry CA; Corona CA; Fontana CA; Glendale CA; Huntington Park CA; Inland CA; Irvine CA; Redlands CA; San Bernardino CA; South

Bay CA; Upland CA; Yucaipa CA. **Number of employees at this location:** 370.

DOWNEY SAVINGS AND LOAN ASSOCIATION
3501 Jamboree Road, Newport Beach CA 92660. 949/854-3100. **Contact:** Human Resources. **E-mail address:** humanresources@downeysavings.com. **World Wide Web address:** http://www.downeysavings.com. **Description:** A retail banking and residential real estate loan institution. The association operates through 52 California offices. **Corporate headquarters location:** This location. **Listed on:** New York Stock Exchange. **Stock exchange symbol:** DSL.

FAR EAST NATIONAL BANK
350 South Grand Avenue, 41st Floor, Los Angeles CA 90071. 213/687-1200. **Fax:** 213/617-7838. **Contact:** Personnel. **E-mail address:** hr@fareastnationalbank.com. **World Wide Web address:** http://www.fareastnationalbank.com. **Description:** Offers commercial banking services. **NOTE:** Please submit your application (available to download on company Website) only through postal mail. **Corporate headquarters location:** This location. **Parent company:** Bank SinoPac.

FARMERS AND MERCHANTS BANK
302 Pine Avenue, Long Beach CA 90802. 562/437-0011. **Contact:** Human Resources. **World Wide Web address:** http://www.fmb.com. **Description:** A commercial bank offering a wide range of services through 16 local offices. **Common positions include:** Bank Teller. **Corporate headquarters location:** This location. **Other area locations:** Fullerton CA; Garden Grove CA; Lake Forest CA; Lakewood CA; Orange CA; San Juan Capistrano CA; Santa Ana CA; Seal Beach CA. **Operations at this facility include:** Administration. **Number of employees at this location:** 100.

FIRST FEDERAL BANK OF CALIFORNIA
1610 Colorado Avenue, Santa Monica CA 90404-3820. 310/319-5628. **Contact:** Human Resources Supervisor. **E-mail address:** jobs@firstfedca.com. **World Wide Web address:** http://www.firstfedca.com. **Description:** This location is the human resources and training division. Overall, First Federal Bank of California is a financial services organization comprised of 25 full-service branches and 6 real estate loan production offices located in Southern California. **Common positions include:** Bank Officer/Manager; Bank Teller; Branch Manager; Underwriter/Assistant Underwriter. **Special programs:** Internships. **Corporate headquarters location:** Santa

Monica CA. **Parent company:** FirstFed Financial Corporation. **Number of employees nationwide:** 650. **Listed on:** New York Stock Exchange. **Stock exchange symbol:** FED.

FIRSTFED FINANCIAL CORPORATION
FIRST FEDERAL BANK OF CALIFORNIA
401 Wilshire Boulevard, Santa Monica CA 90401. 310/319-6000. **Contact:** Department of Human Resources. **E-mail address:** jobs@firstfedca.com. **World Wide Web address:** http://www.firstfedca.com. **Description:** A bank holding company. **Corporate headquarters location:** This location. **Subsidiaries include:** First Federal Bank of California (also at this location). **Listed on:** New York Stock Exchange. **Stock exchange symbol:** FED.

FOOTHILL INDEPENDENT BANK
510 South Grand Avenue, Glendora CA 91741-4207. 626/963-8551. **Contact:** Department of Human Resources. **E-mail address:** resume@foothillbank.com. **World Wide Web address:** http://www.foothillbank.com. **Description:** A California state-chartered bank. The bank has 11 full-service offices located throughout the Inland Empire and San Gabriel Valley. Specialized departments include Small Business Administration Lending, Construction Lending, and Asset Based Lending. **Corporate headquarters location:** This location. **Parent company:** Foothill Independent Bancorp. **Listed on:** NASDAQ. **Stock exchange symbol:** FOOT.

MANUFACTURERS BANK
515 South Figueroa Street, 2nd Floor, Los Angeles CA 90071. 213/489-6200. **Contact:** Ted Mergenthaler, Director of Human Resources. **E-mail address:** hr@manubank.com. **World Wide Web address:** http://www.manubank.com. **Description:** A banking institution offering a wide range of services including checking and savings accounts; certificates of deposit; commercial, industrial, real estate, and installment loans; direct and leveraged leases; collections; escrow services; and letters of credit. **Common positions include:** Accountant/Auditor; Bank Officer/Manager; Bank Teller; Customer Service Representative; Loan Officer. **Corporate headquarters location:** This location. **Other area locations:** Beverly Hills CA; Newport Beach CA. **Parent company:** Mitsui Bank, Ltd. **Operations at this facility include:** Administration; Regional Headquarters. **Listed on:** NASDAQ. **Stock exchange symbol:** MITSY.

MERCANTILE NATIONAL BANK

1840 Century Park East, 2nd Floor, Los Angeles CA 90067. 310/277-2265. **Contact:** Human Resources. **E-mail address:** hrdept@mercantileweb.com. **World Wide Web address:** http://www.mercantileweb.com. **Description:** A commercial bank. **Common positions include:** Accountant/Auditor; Customer Service Representative; Loan Officer. **Corporate headquarters location:** This location. **Listed on:** NASDAQ. **Stock exchange symbol:** MBLA.

MIZUHO CORPORATE BANK OF CALIFORNIA

555 West Fifth Street, Los Angeles CA 90013. 213/612-2700. **Contact:** Linda Cormier, Vice President. **World Wide Web address:** http://www.mizuhobank.co.jp/english. **Description:** A full-service commercial bank. Founded in 1974. **NOTE:** Entry-level positions and part-time jobs are offered. **Common positions include:** Accountant; Administrative Assistant; Auditor; Bank Officer/Manager; Branch Manager; Clerical Supervisor; Computer Operator; Customer Service Rep.; Human Resources Manager; Loan Officer; Management Analyst/Consultant; Market Research Analyst; Marketing Specialist; Network/Systems Administrator; Operations Manager; Sales Executive; Secretary; Trust Officer. **Special programs:** Summer Jobs. **Office hours:** Monday - Friday, 8:00 a.m. - 5:00 p.m. **Corporate headquarters location:** This location. **International locations:** Worldwide. **Parent company:** Mizuho Corporate Bank. **President/CEO:** Takuo Yoshida. **Information Systems Manager:** Rick Richardson. **Purchasing Manager:** Stanley Takaki. **Annual sales/revenues:** More than $100 million. **Number of employees at this location:** 90.

UNION BANK OF CALIFORNIA

P.O. Box 85642, San Diego CA 92186-9777. 619/230-4383. **Physical address:** 530 B Street, Suite 1300, San Diego CA 92101. **Contact:** Employment Manager. **E-mail address:** careers05@uboc.com. **World Wide Web address:** http://www.uboc.com. **Description:** A full-service commercial bank providing a broad range of services including retail and small business banking, middle market banking, real estate finance, corporate banking, trade finance, and financial management and trust services. **NOTE:** Union Bank offers management training programs in several areas: community (retail) banking, commercial lending, and business relationships. **Common positions include:** Bank Officer/Manager; Computer Programmer; Financial Analyst; Management Trainee; Systems Analyst. **Corporate**

headquarters location: San Francisco CA. **Subsidiaries include:** U.S. Investment Services, Inc. **Parent company:** UnionBanCal Corporation. **Listed on:** New York Stock Exchange. **Stock exchange symbol:** UB. **Number of employees nationwide:** 10,000.

UNION BANK OF CALIFORNIA

445 South Figueroa, Los Angeles CA 90071. 213/236-7700. **Contact:** Human Resources Department. **E-mail address:** careers05@uboc.com. **World Wide Web address:** http://www.uboc.com. **Description:** A full-service commercial bank providing a broad range of services including retail and small business banking, middle market banking, real estate finance, corporate banking, trade finance, and financial management and trust services. **NOTE:** Union Bank offers management training programs in several areas: community (retail) banking, commercial lending, and business relationships. **Common positions include:** Bank Officer/Manager; Branch Manager; Management Trainee. **Corporate headquarters location:** San Francisco CA. **Subsidiaries include:** U.S. Investment Services, Inc. **Parent company:** UnionBanCal Corporation. **Listed on:** New York Stock Exchange. **Stock exchange symbol:** UB. **Number of employees nationwide:** 10,000.

BIOTECHNOLOGY, PHARMACEUTICALS, AND SCIENTIFIC R&D

You can expect to find the following types of companies in this chapter:

Clinical Labs • Lab Equipment Manufacturers • Pharmaceutical Manufacturers and Distributors

A.P. PHARMA
123 Saginaw Drive, Redwood City CA 94063. 909/624-2594. **Contact:** Shelly Howell, Human Resources Administrator. **E-mail address:** showell@appharma.com. **World Wide Web address:** http://www.appharma.com. **Description:** A developer and marketer of polymer-based delivery systems and related technologies for use in pharmaceuticals, over-the-counter drugs, toiletries, and specialty applications. **Corporate headquarters location:** This location. **Listed on:** NASDAQ. **Stock exchange symbol:** APPA.

ACCUTECH
2641 La Mirada Drive, Vista CA 92083. 760/599-6555. **Contact:** Human Resources Department. **World Wide Web address:** http://www.accutech-llc.com. **Description:** Develops, manufactures, and markets disposable diagnostic tests. **Corporate headquarters location:** This location.

ADVANCED TISSUE SCIENCES
10933 North Torrey Pines Road, La Jolla CA 92037-1005. 858/713-7300. **Fax:** 858/713-7430. **Contact:** Human Resources. **E-mail address:** jobs@advancedtissue.com. **World Wide Web address:** http://www.advancedtissue.com. **Description:** Develops products for tissue and organ replacement by simulating the natural growth conditions that exist in the human body. Advanced Tissue Sciences is able to grow cells that develop and assemble into functional tissue masses. **Corporate headquarters location:** This location. **Listed on:** NASDAQ. **Stock exchange symbol:** ATIS. **Number of employees at this location:** 145.

ALLERGAN, INC.
2525 DuPont Drive, P.O. Box 19534, Irvine CA 92623-9534. 714/246-4500. **Toll-free phone:** 800/347-4500. **Contact:** Human Resources. **E-mail address:** resume@allergan.com. **World Wide Web address:** http://www.allergan.com. **Description:** Develops, manufactures, and distributes prescription and nonprescription pharmaceutical products in

the specialty fields of ophthalmology and dermatology. Allergan, Inc.'s products are designed to treat eye and skin disorders, and to aid contact lens wearers. **Common positions include:** Accountant/Auditor; Biological Scientist; Biomedical Engineer; Buyer; Chemist; Computer Programmer; Customer Service Rep.; Financial Analyst; Manufacturer's/Wholesaler's Sales Rep.; Operations/Production Manager; Quality Control Supervisor. **Corporate headquarters location:** This location. **International locations:** Worldwide. **Listed on:** New York Stock Exchange. **Stock exchange symbol:** AGN. **Operations at this facility include:** Administration; Divisional Headquarters; Manufacturing; Research and Development; Sales.

ALLIANCE PHARMACEUTICAL CORPORATION
3040 Science Park Road, San Diego CA 92121. 858/410-5200. **Fax:** 858/410-5201. **Contact:** Human Resources. **World Wide Web address:** http://www.allp.com. **Description:** Develops, manufactures, and markets pharmaceutical products including Oxygent, a drug used to eliminate the need for blood transfusions during surgery; Liquivent, a drug used to treat acute respiratory illnesses; and Imagent, a diagnostic contrast agent used to enhance ultrasound images. **NOTE:** Alliance Pharmaceutical Corporation hires employees through Alcock & McFadden Employment Consultants, Inc., 3675 Ruffin Road, Suite 225, San Diego CA 92123. 619/505-0303. Fax: 619/505-0445. **Listed on:** NASDAQ. **Stock exchange symbol:** ALLP.

AMERISOURCEBERGEN
4000 Metropolitan Drive, Orange CA 92868. 714/385-4000. **Fax:** 714/385-1442. **Contact:** Recruiting. **E-mail address:** techcareers@bbcjobs.com; careers@bbcjobs.com. **World Wide Web address:** http://www.amerisourcebergen.net. **Description:** Distributes pharmaceuticals and medical-surgical supplies. **Company slogan:** Our people make the difference. **Common positions include:** Accountant; Administrative Assistant; Budget Analyst; Buyer; Computer Programmer; Consultant; Data Entry Clerk; Financial Analyst; Marketing Specialist; Project Manager; Secretary; Systems Analyst; Technical Writer/Editor; Telecommunications Manager; Typist/Word Processor. **Office hours:** Monday - Friday, 7:30 a.m. - 4:30 p.m. **Corporate headquarters location:** This location. **Other U.S. locations:** Valley Forge PA. **Listed on:** New York Stock Exchange. **Stock exchange symbol:** ABC.

AMGEN INC.
One Amgen Center Drive, Thousand Oaks CA 91320-1789. 805/447-1000. **Toll-free phone:** 800/77-AMGEN. **Fax:**

805/447-1985. **Recorded jobline:** 800/446-4007. **Contact:** Human Resources. **E-mail address:** jobs@amgen.com. **World Wide Web address:** http://www.amgen.com. **Description:** Researches, develops, manufactures, and markets human therapeutics based on advanced cellular and molecular biology. Products include EPOGEN (Epoetin Alfa), which counteracts the symptoms of renal failure experienced by kidney dialysis patients; INFERGEN (Interferon alfacon-1); and NEUPOGEN (Filgrastim), which reduces the incidence of infection in cancer patients who receive chemotherapy. When used in conjunction with chemotherapy, NEUPOGEN selectively stimulates the bone marrow to produce neutrophil cells, accelerating the return of the patient's antibacterial defense system. **Common positions include:** Accountant/Auditor; Attorney; Biological Scientist; Buyer; Chemical Engineer; Chemist; Computer Programmer; Customer Service Representative; Financial Analyst; Systems Analyst. **Special programs:** Internships. **Corporate headquarters location:** This location. **Other U.S. locations:** Boulder CO; Longmont CO; Washington D.C.; Louisville KY; Juncos Puerto Rico. **Listed on:** NASDAQ. **Stock exchange symbol:** AMGN. **Annual sales/revenues:** More than $100 million. **Number of employees at this location:** 2,280. **Number of employees worldwide:** 5,600.

AMYLIN PHARMACEUTICALS, INC.

9373 Towne Centre Drive, Suite 250, San Diego CA 92121. 858/552-2200. **Fax:** 858/552-2212. **Contact:** Human Resources. **E-mail address:** jobs@amylin.com. **World Wide Web address:** http://www.amylin.com. **Description:** Researches the hormone amylin, which provides drug strategies for treating juvenile- and maturity-onset diabetes, insulin resistance syndrome, hypertension, and obesity. **NOTE:** If e-mailing resume, please include text version in body of e-mail rather than attaching a separate file. **Corporate headquarters location:** This location. **Number of employees at this location:** 100. **Listed on:** NASDAQ. **Stock exchange symbol:** AMLN.

APPLIED BIOSYSTEMS

850 Lincoln Centre Drive, Foster City CA 94404. 650/570-6667. **Contact:** Personnel Department. **World Wide Web address:** http://www.appliedbiosystems.com. **Description:** Manufactures life science systems and analytical tools for use in such markets as biotechnology, pharmaceuticals, environmental testing, and chemical manufacturing. **Common positions include:** Chemical Engineer; Chemist; Customer

Service Representative; Electrical/Electronics Engineer; Manufacturer's/Wholesaler's Sales Representative; Mechanical Engineer; Technical Writer/Editor. **Corporate headquarters location:** This location. **Operations at this facility include:** Administration; Manufacturing; Research and Development; Sales; Service. **Listed on:** New York Stock Exchange. **Stock exchange symbol:** ABI. **Number of employees nationwide:** 900.

ARETE ASSOCIATES

P.O. Box 6024, Sherman Oaks CA 91413. 818/501-2880x432. **Physical address:** 5000 Van Nuys Boulevard, Suite 400, Sherman Oaks CA 91403. **Fax:** 818/501-2905. **Contact:** Nancy Balbuena, Assistant Manager of Human Resources. **E-mail address:** personnel@arete.com. **World Wide Web address:** http://www.arete.com. **Description:** Provides research and development in the area of signal processing as it applies to atmospheric, oceanographic, and related areas. The company is involved in the mathematical modeling of physical processes, signal and image processing, remote sensing and phenomenology, electro-optics, lidar, radar, and acoustics. Founded in 1976. **NOTE:** U.S. citizenship, a drug test, and a security investigation are required to meet position eligibility. Entry-level positions are offered. **Common positions include:** Electrical/Electronics Engineer; Geologist/Geophysicist; Mathematician; Physicist; Researcher; Scientist; Systems Analyst. **Corporate headquarters location:** This location. **Other U.S. locations:** AZ; FL; VA. **Operations at this facility include:** Administration; Research and Development. **Listed on:** Privately held. **Number of employees at this location:** 90. **Number of employees nationwide:** 125.

BECKMAN COULTER, INC.

200 South Kraemer Boulevard, P.O. Box 8000, Brea CA 92822. 714/993-8584. **Fax:** 714/961-4113. **Contact:** Employment. **E-mail address:** breahr@beckman.com. **World Wide Web address:** http://www.beckman.com. **Description:** Sells and services a diverse range of scientific instruments, reagents, and related equipment. Products include DNA synthesizers, robotic workstations, centrifuges, electrophoresis systems, detection and measurement equipment, data processing software, and specialty chemical and automated general chemical systems. Many of the company's products are used in research and development and diagnostic analysis. **NOTE:** Second and third shifts are offered. **Common positions include:** Accountant; Administrative Assistant; Applications Engineer; Biochemist; Biological Scientist; Chemical Engineer;

Computer Programmer; Computer Support Technician; Customer Service Representative; Database Administrator; Database Manager; Financial Analyst; Librarian; Marketing Specialist; Mechanical Engineer; MIS Specialist; Network/Systems Administrator; Sales Representative; Secretary; Software Engineer. **Other area locations:** Carlsbad CA; Fullerton CA; Palo Alto CA; Porterville CA; San Diego CA. **Other U.S. locations:** Nationwide. **International locations:** Worldwide. **Parent company:** Beckman Instruments, Inc. **Operations at this facility include:** Administration; Manufacturing; Research and Development. **Listed on:** New York Stock Exchange. **Stock exchange symbol:** BEC. **CEO:** Jack Wareham. **Annual sales/revenues:** More than $100 million. **Number of employees worldwide:** 11,000.

BECKMAN COULTER, INC.
2470 Faraday Avenue, Carlsbad CA 92008. 760/438-9151. **Fax:** 760/438-6390. **Contact:** Human Resources. **E-mail address:** clsbdhr@beckman.com. **World Wide Web address:** http://www.beckman.com. **Description:** This location develops monoclonal antibody technology for use in medical diagnostic products. Overall, Beckman Coulter sells and services a diverse range of scientific instruments, reagents, and related equipment. Products include DNA synthesizers, robotic workstations, centrifuges, electrophoresis systems, detection and measurement equipment, data processing software, and specialty chemical and automated general chemical systems. Many of the company's products are used in research and development or diagnostic analysis. **NOTE:** Second and third shifts are offered. **Common positions include:** Accountant; Administrative Assistant; Applications Engineer; Biochemist; Biological Scientist; Chemical Engineer; Computer Programmer; Computer Support Technician; Customer Service Representative; Database Administrator; Database Manager; Financial Analyst; Librarian; Marketing Specialist; Mechanical Engineer; MIS Specialist; Network/Systems Administrator; Sales Representative; Secretary; Software Engineer. **Other area locations:** Brea CA; Fullerton CA; Palo Alto CA; Porterville CA; San Diego CA. **Other U.S. locations:** Nationwide. **International locations:** Worldwide. **Parent company:** Beckman Instruments, Inc. **Listed on:** New York Stock Exchange. **Stock exchange symbol:** BEC.

BIOSOURCE INTERNATIONAL, INC.
542 Flynn Road, Camarillo CA 93012. 805/987-0086. **Toll-free phone:** 800/242-0607. **Fax:** 805/383-5386. **Contact:** Human Resources. **E-mail address:** hr.dept@biosource.com. **World

Wide Web address: http://www.biosource.com. **Description:** Licenses, develops, manufactures, markets, and distributes immunological reagents and enzyme-linked immunosorbent assay (ELISA) test kits used in biomedical research. BioSource International offers over 700 products for the study of cell biology and immunology research. The ELISA test kits are used by researchers and scientists to detect various immunological molecules in biological fluids found in humans, mice, rats, and primates. Founded in 1989. **NOTE:** Entry-level positions and part-time jobs are offered. **Company slogan:** The Art of Science. **Common positions include:** Accountant; Administrative Assistant; Advertising Executive; Biochemist; Biological Scientist; Chemist; Chief Financial Officer; Controller; Customer Service Representative; Financial Analyst; Human Resources Manager; Market Research Analyst; Marketing Manager; Marketing Specialist; MIS Specialist; Network/Systems Administrator; Purchasing Agent/Manager; Quality Control Supervisor; Sales Executive; Sales Manager; Sales Representative. **Office hours:** Monday - Friday, 7:00 a.m. - 5:00 p.m. **Corporate headquarters location:** This location. **Other area locations:** Foster City CA. **Other U.S. locations:** Hopkinton MA; Rockville MD. **International locations:** Belgium, Germany, the Netherlands. **Listed on:** NASDAQ. **Stock exchange symbol:** BIOI. **President/CEO:** Leonard Hendrickson. **Annual sales/revenues:** $21 - $50 million. **Number of employees at this location:** 75. **Number of employees nationwide:** 145. **Number of employees worldwide:** 190.

B. BRAUN/McGAW INC.
P.O. Box 19791, Irvine CA 92623-9791. 949/660-2000. **Fax:** 949/660-2821. **Recorded jobline:** 949/660-2272. **Contact:** Personnel. **E-mail address:** hr.irvine@bbraun.com. **World Wide Web address:** http://www.bbraunusa.com. **Description:** Manufactures intravenous systems and solutions. The company also offers IV accessories, critical care products, and epidural anesthesia and pharmaceutical devices. **Other U.S. locations:** Cherry Hill NJ; Allentown PA; Bethlehem PA; Carrollton TX.

CORTEX PHARMACEUTICALS INCORPORATED
15241 Barranca Parkway, Irvine CA 92618. 949/727-3157. **Contact:** Human Resources. **World Wide Web address:** http://www.cortexpharm.com. **Description:** Researches and develops neuropharmaceuticals including the brand name AMPALEX which interacts with AMPA receptors and may increase certain types of memory. **Corporate headquarters**

location: This location. **Listed on:** American Stock Exchange. **Stock exchange symbol:** COR.

COSMODYNE INC.

2920 Columbia Street, Torrance CA 90503. 310/320-5650. **Contact:** Human Resources Department. **World Wide Web address:** http://www.cosmodyne.com. **Description:** Involved in cryogenics research and applications. **Common positions include:** Chemical Engineer; Designer; Draftsperson; Electrical Engineer; Mechanical Engineer. **Corporate headquarters location:** This location. **Parent company:** Cryogenic Group. **Operations at this facility include:** Manufacturing. **Listed on:** Privately held. **Number of employees at this location:** 85.

DIAGNOSTIC PRODUCTS CORPORATION

5700 West 96th Street, Los Angeles CA 90045. 310/645-8200. **Toll-free phone:** 800/372-1782. **Contact:** Personnel Department. **E-mail address:** info@dpconline.com. **World Wide Web address:** http://www.dpcweb.com. **Description:** Manufactures medical immunodiagnostic test kits that are used to diagnose and treat a variety of medical conditions such as allergies, anemia, cancer, diabetes, infectious diseases, reproductive disorders, thyroid disorders, and veterinary applications. **Common positions include:** Biological Scientist; Chemist; Clinical Lab Technician. **Corporate headquarters location:** This location. **Operations at this facility include:** Administration; Manufacturing; Research and Development; Sales; Service. **Listed on:** New York Stock Exchange. **Stock exchange symbol:** DP. **Number of employees at this location:** 430.

ELAN PHARMACEUTICALS, INC.

7475 Lusk Boulevard, San Diego CA 92121. 858/457-2553. **Fax:** 858/457-4823. **Contact:** Human Resources Department. **World Wide Web address:** http://www.elan.com. **Description:** A research-based pharmaceutical company with a focus on drug delivery systems and specializing in neurology, cancer, pain management, and infectious diseases. **Common positions include:** Account Manager; Account Representative; Accountant; Administrative Assistant; Attorney; Biochemist; Biological Scientist; Biomedical Engineer; Budget Analyst; Buyer; Chemist; Chief Financial Officer; Clinical Lab Technician; Computer Engineer; Computer Support Technician; Computer Technician; Construction Contractor; Controller; Customer Service Representative; Database Administrator; Database Manager; Desktop Publishing Specialist; Draftsperson; Editor; Editorial Assistant;

Electrical/Electronics Engineer; Electrician; Finance Director; Financial Analyst; Graphic Designer; Human Resources Manager; Intellectual Property Lawyer; Internet Services Manager; Librarian; Market Research Analyst; Marketing Manager; Marketing Specialist; MIS Specialist; Network/Systems Administrator; Occupational Therapist; Pharmacist; Physician; Purchasing Agent/Manager; Registered Nurse; Sales Executive; Sales Manager; Sales Rep.; Secretary; Statistician; Systems Manager; Technical Writer/Editor; Typist/Word Processor; Webmaster. **Corporate headquarters location:** Dublin, Ireland. **Parent company:** Elan Corporation. **Listed on:** New York Stock Exchange. **Stock exchange symbol:** ELN. **Annual sales/revenues:** More than $100 million.

HEMACARE CORPORATION
4954 Van Nuys Boulevard, Sherman Oaks CA 91403. 818/986-3883. **Fax:** 818/251-5300. **Contact:** Personnel. **World Wide Web address:** http://www.hemacare.com. **Description:** Provides blood management systems such as plasma exchange and bone marrow transplantation. The company also operates a donor center. **Corporate headquarters location:** This location. **Subsidiaries include:** HemaBiologics, Inc. conducts research on anti-HIV pharmaceuticals.

HYCOR BIOMEDICAL INC.
7272 Chapman Avenue, Garden Grove CA 92841. 714/895-9558. **Contact:** Human Resources Department. **World Wide Web address:** http://www.hycorbiomedical.com. **Description:** Develops, produces, and markets a broad range of diagnostic and medical products. The company's focus is on allergy diagnostics and therapy, microscopic urinalysis, specialized immunodiagnostics, and laboratory controls. **Corporate headquarters location:** This location. **Listed on:** NASDAQ. **Stock exchange symbol:** HYBD.

I-FLOW CORPORATION
20202 Windrow Drive, Lake Forest CA 92630. 949/553-0888. **Contact:** Human Resources Department. **E-mail address:** hr@i-flowcorp.com. **World Wide Web address:** http://www.i-flowcorp.com. **Description:** Manufactures drug delivery systems. The company is also engaged in epidural, chronic, and wound site pain management. **Corporate headquarters location:** This location. **Listed on:** NASDAQ. **Stock exchange symbol:** IFLO.

IDEC PHARMACEUTICALS CORPORATION
3030 Callan Road, San Diego CA 92121. 858/431-8500. **Contact:** Personnel. **E-mail address:** hr info@idecpharm.com. **World Wide Web address:** http://www.idecpharm.com. **Description:** Manufactures chemotherapeutic pharmaceuticals for the treatment of lymphoma. The company is also in the clinical trial phase of drug development for diseases such as arthritis. **Corporate headquarters location:** This location. **Listed on:** NASDAQ. **Stock exchange symbol:** IDPH.

IMMUNE RESPONSE CORPORATION
5935 Darwin Court, Carlsbad CA 92008. 760/431-7080. **Contact:** Human Resources. **World Wide Web address:** http://www.imnr.com. **Description:** Develops treatments in three distinct proprietary technologies, which are treatment for HIV-infected patients, autoimmune disease treatment, and gene therapy treatment. **Subsidiaries include:** TargeTech, Inc. **Corporate headquarters location:** This location.

INAMED CORPORATION
5540 Ekwill Street, Suite D, Santa Barbara CA 93111. 805/692-5400. **Contact:** Human Resources. **World Wide Web address:** http://www.inamed.com. **Description:** INAMED Corporation is a medical products company with 23 subsidiaries across the United States and Europe. The company develops, manufactures, and markets implantable products including mammary prostheses, tissue expanders, and facial implants; develops, produces, and distributes premium products for dermatology, wound care, and burn treatment; and packages and sterilizes medical grade components for other medical device companies. **Corporate headquarters location:** This location. **Subsidiaries include:** Bioenterics Corporation (Carpinteria CA); McGhan Medical Corporation (Santa Barbara CA); McGhan, Ltd. (Arklow, Ireland). **Listed on:** NASDAQ. **Stock exchange symbol:** IMDC.

INTERNATIONAL REMOTE IMAGING SYSTEMS, INC. (IRIS)
9162 Eton Avenue, Chatsworth CA 91311. 818/709-1244. **Contact:** Human Resources. **E-mail address:** hr@proiris.com. **World Wide Web address:** http://www.proiris.com. **Description:** Manufactures and markets The Yellow IRIS, an automated urinalysis workstation. The workstation uses its patented slideless Automated Intelligent Microscopy (AIM) technology and other technology to automate the manipulative steps in routine urinalyses performed by hospital and reference clinical laboratories, including counting and classifying microscopic particles found in urine specimens. Other

laboratory products manufactured by IRIS are used for blood collection, blood coagulation, and genetic analysis. **Corporate headquarters location:** This location. **Listed on:** American Stock Exchange. **Stock exchange symbol:** IRI. **Number of employees nationwide:** 65.

IRWIN NATURALS FOR HEALTH
NATURE'S SECRET
5310 Beethoven Street, Los Angeles CA 90066. 310/253-5305. **Toll-free phone:** 866/54IRWIN. **Contact:** Human Resources. **World Wide Web address:** http://www.irwinnaturals.com. **Description:** Develops herbal remedies and nutritional products. Nature's Secret is the brand name of the company's line of vitamins. **Common positions include:** Sales Executive; Sales Representative. **Parent company:** OMNI Neutraceuticals. **Annual sales/revenues:** $21 - $50 million.

ISIS PHARMACEUTICALS, INC.
Carlsbad Research Center, 2292 Faraday Avenue, Carlsbad CA 92008. 760/931-9200. **Fax:** 760/603-2700. **Recorded jobline:** 760/603-3858. **Contact:** Department of Human Resources. **E-mail address:** resume@isisph.com. **World Wide Web address:** http://www.isip.com. **Description:** Develops antisense technology drugs and combinatorial drugs to combat cancer and infectious or inflammatory diseases. **Corporate headquarters location:** This location. **Listed on:** NASDAQ. **Stock exchange symbol:** ISIP.

JAYCOR
3394 Carmel Mountain Road, San Diego CA 92121. 858/720-4000. **Fax:** 858/720-4137. **Contact:** Phyllis Stuart, Human Resources Administrator. **E-mail address:** jobs@jaycor.com. **World Wide Web address:** http://www.jaycor.com. **Description:** Provides scientific, high-tech research and development for public and private companies as well as the U.S. Department of Defense. The company specializes in civil engineering, communications, and biological defense systems. **NOTE:** Entry-level positions are offered. **Common positions include:** Accountant/Auditor; Computer Programmer; Electrical/Electronics Engineer; Physicist; Secretary; Technical Writer/Editor. **Special programs:** Internships. **Corporate headquarters location:** This location. **Other U.S. locations:** Nationwide. **Parent company:** Titan Corporation. **Operations at this facility include:** Administration; Research and Development. **Listed on:** New York Stock Exchange. **Stock exchange symbol:** TTN. **Number of employees at this location:** 120. **Number of employees nationwide:** 500.

LA JOLLA PHARMACEUTICAL COMPANY (LJP)

6455 Nancy Ridge Drive, San Diego CA 92121. 858/452-6600. **Fax:** 858/625-0155. **Contact:** Human Resources. **E-mail address:** jobs@ljpc.com. **World Wide Web address:** http://www.ljpc.com. **Description:** La Jolla Pharmaceutical Company (LJP) develops highly specific therapeutics to treat antibody-mediated and inflammatory diseases. The company is a leader in B-cell tolerance for treatment of antibody-mediated diseases and conducts Phase II clinical trials for the treatment of lupus. LJP also develops therapeutics for recurrent fetal loss, autoimmune stroke, Rh hemolytic disease of the newborn, myasthenia gravis, and Graves' disease. The company also develops compounds that control inflammation. **Corporate headquarters location:** This location. **Listed on:** NASDAQ. **Stock exchange symbol:** LJPC.

LABORATORY CORPORATION OF AMERICA (LABCORP)

5601 Oberlin Drive, Suite 100, San Diego CA 92121. 858/455-1221. **Contact:** Personnel. **World Wide Web address:** http://www.labcorp.com. **Description:** One of the nation's leading clinical laboratory companies, providing services primarily to physicians, hospitals, clinics, nursing homes, and other clinical labs nationwide. LabCorp performs tests on blood, urine, and other body fluids and tissue, aiding the diagnosis of disease. **Corporate headquarters location:** Burlington NC. **Listed on:** New York Stock Exchange. **Stock exchange symbol:** LH.

LIGAND PHARMACEUTICALS INC.

10275 Science Center Drive, San Diego CA 92121. 858/550-7500. **Contact:** Department of Human Resources. **E-mail address:** jobs@ligand.com. **World Wide Web address:** http://www.ligand.com. **Description:** A biopharmaceutical company that researches, develops, and markets small molecule pharmaceutical products that address the medical needs of patients with cancer, cardiovascular and inflammatory diseases, osteoporosis, and metabolic disorders. **Corporate headquarters location:** This location. **Listed on:** NASDAQ. **Stock exchange symbol:** LGND.

MERCK RESEARCH LABORATORIES

3535 General Atomics Court, San Diego CA 92121. 858/202-5000. **Contact:** Human Resources Department. **World Wide Web address:** http://www.merck.com. **Description:** A biochemistry laboratory involved in neuroscience research. **Corporate headquarters location:** This location.

NEXELL THERAPEUTICS

9 Parker, Irvine CA 92618. 949/470-9011. **Contact:** Human Resources Department. **World Wide Web address:** http://www.nexellinc.com. **Description:** Develops and sells diagnostics and cell therapies for autoimmune, genetic, and metabolic diseases, and cancer. Nexell Therapeutics' products include the Isolex Cell Selection System, Cryocyte, and Lifecell. **Corporate headquarters location:** This location. **Listed on:** NASDAQ. **Stock exchange symbol:** NEXL.

PSYCHEMEDICS CORPORATION

5832 Uplander Way, Culver City CA 90230. 310/216-7776. **Toll-free phone:** 800/628-8073. **Contact:** Personnel. **World Wide Web address:** http://www.psychemedics.com. **Description:** A biotechnology company concentrating on diagnostics through the detection and measurement of substances in the body by using hair samples. The first commercial product, a testing service for the detection of abused substances, is provided principally to private sector companies. This drug test detects cocaine, marijuana, opiates, methamphetamine, and PCP. A test for methadone is used in the treatment industry. Psychemedics Corporation's testing methods use a patented technology for performing immunoassays on enzymatically dissolved hair samples with confirmation testing by gas chromatography/mass spectrometry. **Corporate headquarters location:** Cambridge MA. **Listed on:** American Stock Exchange. **Stock exchange symbol:** PMD. **Number of employees nationwide:** 95.

QUEST DIAGNOSTICS

7600 Tyrone Avenue, Van Nuys CA 91405. 818/989-2520. **Contact:** Human Resources Department. **World Wide Web address:** http://www.questdiagnostics.com. **Description:** One of the largest clinical laboratories in North America. The company provides a broad range of clinical laboratory services to health care clients such as physicians, hospitals, clinics, dialysis centers, pharmaceutical companies, and corporations. The company offers and performs tests on blood, urine, and other bodily fluids and tissues to provide information for health and well-being. **Corporate headquarters location:** Teterboro NJ. **Listed on:** New York Stock Exchange. **Stock exchange symbol:** DGX.

QUEST DIAGNOSTICS AT NICHOLS INSTITUTE

33608 Ortega Highway, San Juan Capistrano CA 92690-6130. 949/728-4000. **Fax:** 949/728-4781. **Recorded jobline:** 949/728-4526. **Contact:** Human Resources. **World Wide Web**

address: http://www.questdiagnostics.com. **Description:** One of the largest clinical laboratories in North America, providing a broad range of clinical laboratory services to health care clients such as physicians, hospitals, clinics, dialysis centers, pharmaceutical companies, and corporations. The company offers and performs tests on blood, urine, and other bodily fluids and tissues to provide information for health and well-being. **Corporate headquarters location:** Teterboro NJ. **Other U.S. locations:** Nationwide. **Listed on:** New York Stock Exchange. **Stock exchange symbol:** DGX.

QUESTCOR PHARMACEUTICALS CORPORATION
2714 Loker Avenue West, Carlsbad CA 92008. 760/929-9500. **Contact:** Human Resources. **E-mail address:** hr@questcor.com. **World Wide Web address:** http://www.questcor.com. **Description:** An integrated specialty pharmaceutical company that researches, develops, and markets a variety of pharmaceuticals to the health care industry. The company's products include Emitasol, Ethamolin, Inulin, Glofil-125, and NeoFlo. **NOTE:** Interested jobseekers should send their resumes to Questcor Pharmaceuticals Corporation, Human Resources Department, 26118 Research Road, Hayward CA 94545. **Corporate headquarters location:** Union City CA. **Listed on:** American Stock Exchange. **Stock exchange symbol:** QSC.

QUIDEL CORPORATION
10165 McKellar Court, San Diego CA 92121. 858/552-1100. **Toll-free phone:** 800/874-1517. **Fax:** 858/453-4338. **Contact:** Human Resources. **E-mail address:** hr@quidel.com. **World Wide Web address:** http://www.quidel.com. **Description:** Engaged in the research, development, and manufacture of immunodiagnostic products designed to provide accurate testing for acute and chronic human illnesses. Customers include physicians, clinical laboratories, and consumers. **Office hours:** Monday - Friday, 8:00 a.m. - 5:00 p.m. **Corporate headquarters location:** This location. **Subsidiaries include:** VHA Inc. **Listed on:** NASDAQ. **Stock exchange symbol:** QDEL. **President/CEO:** Andre de Bruin.

SHAKLEE CORPORATION
4747 Willow Road, Pleasanton CA 90623. 714/670-5602. **Contact:** Roseanne Jennings, Personnel Manager. **World Wide Web address:** http://www.shaklee.com. **Description:** Manufactures and markets vitamins, minerals, protein powders, and other nutritional products.

SKYEPHARMA
10450 Science Center Drive, San Diego CA 92121. 858/625-2424. **Fax:** 858/678-3999. **Contact:** Human Resources. **E-mail address:** jobs@skyepharma.com. **World Wide Web address:** http://www.skyepharma.com. **Description:** Develops proprietary, injectable material that can encapsulate a wide variety of drugs to provide sustained and controlled delivery. **Corporate headquarters location:** This location. **Listed on:** NASDAQ. **Stock exchange symbol:** SKYE. **Number of employees at this location:** 60.

SYNCOR INTERNATIONAL CORPORATION
6464 Canoga Avenue, Woodland Hills CA 91367-2407. 818/737-4000. **Toll-free phone:** 800/678-6779. **Contact:** Human Resources Department. **World Wide Web address:** http://www.syncor.com. **Description:** Compounds, dispenses, and distributes patient-specific intravenous drugs and solutions for use in diagnostic imaging and offers a complete range of pharmacy services. **Common positions include:** Account Manager; Accountant/Auditor; Administrative Manager; Computer Programmer; Human Resources Manager; Marketing Manager; Pharmacist; Sales Manager. **Corporate headquarters location:** This location. **Operations at this facility include:** Administration. **Listed on:** NASDAQ. **Stock exchange symbol:** SCOR. **Number of employees at this location:** 175. **Number of employees nationwide:** 2,200.

TANABE RESEARCH LABORATORIES USA, INC.
4540 Towne Center Court, San Diego CA 92121. 858/622-7000. **Contact:** Personnel. **E-mail address:** jobs@trlusa.com. **World Wide Web address:** http://www.trlusa.com. **Description:** Researches allergies, rheumatism, asthma, and arthritis. **Corporate headquarters location:** Osaka, Japan. **Parent company:** Tanabe Seiyaku Corporation, Ltd.

UNILAB CORPORATION
18408 Oxnard Street, Tarzana CA 91356-1504. 818/996-7300. **Recorded jobline:** 818/758-6680. **Contact:** Human Resources. **E-mail address:** hrtarzana@unilab.com. **World Wide Web address:** http://www.unilab.com. **Description:** A clinical laboratory that analyzes a wide variety of medical tests. Unilab also performs drug testing. **NOTE:** At time of publication, Quest Diagnostics announced plans to acquire Unilab Corporation. Please see Web site for more details. **Corporate headquarters location:** This location. **Listed on:** NASDAQ. **Stock exchange symbol:** ULAB.

VICAL INC.

9373 Towne Centre Drive, Suite 100, San Diego CA 92121. 858/453-9900. **Contact:** Human Resources. **World Wide Web address:** http://www.vical.com. **Description:** Provides research and development services for DNA, gene therapy, cancer, AIDS, and malaria. **Corporate headquarters location:** This location. **Listed on:** NASDAQ. **Stock exchange symbol:** VICL.

WATSON PHARMACEUTICALS, INC.

311 Bonnie Circle, Corona CA 92880. 909/270-1400. **Contact:** Human Resources Department. **World Wide Web address:** http://www.watsonpharm.com. **Description:** Produces and distributes off-patent and proprietary pharmaceuticals such as analgesics, dermatological, primary care, antihypertensive, hormonal, generic, and central nervous system treatments. **Common positions include:** Budget Analyst; Computer Programmer; Intellectual Property Lawyer; Manufacturing Engineer; Paralegal; Quality Assurance Engineer; Quality Control Supervisor. **Corporate headquarters location:** This location. **Subsidiaries include:** Circa Pharmaceuticals, Inc.; Oclassen Pharmaceuticals, Inc.; Watson Laboratories, Inc. **Listed on:** New York Stock Exchange. **Stock exchange symbol:** WPI. **CEO:** Dr. Allen Chao. **Facilities Manager:** Bill Liberty. **Information Systems Manager:** Frank Chen. **Purchasing Manager:** Linda Childs. **Sales Manager:** Jesse Childs.

BUSINESS SERVICES AND NON-SCIENTIFIC RESEARCH

You can expect to find the following types of companies in this chapter:

Adjustment and Collection Services • Cleaning, Maintenance, and Pest Control Services • Credit Reporting • Detective, Guard, and Armored Car Services • Miscellaneous Equipment Rental and Leasing • Secretarial and Court Reporting Services

ABM INDUSTRIES INCORPORATED

5200 Southeastern Avenue, Los Angeles CA 90040. 323/720-4020. **Contact:** Personnel. **World Wide Web address:** http://www.abm.com. **Description:** A national contract maintenance firm providing janitorial and related services in over 60 metropolitan areas through more than 200 branch offices. **Corporate headquarters location:** San Francisco CA. **Listed on:** New York Stock Exchange. **Stock exchange symbol:** ABM. **Number of employees nationwide:** 57,000.

ADT SECURITY SERVICES

5400 West Rosecrans Avenue, Hawthorne CA 90250. 310/725-2978. **Fax:** 310/725-2973. **Contact:** Human Resources Representative. **World Wide Web address:** http://www.adtsecurityservices.com. **Description:** Designs, programs, markets, and installs protective systems to safeguard life and property from hazards such as burglary, hold-up, and fire. ADT Security Services has over 180,000 customers in the United States, Canada, and Western Europe. **Common positions include:** Accountant/Auditor; Credit Manager; Customer Service Representative; Draftsperson; Financial Analyst; Human Resources Manager; MIS Specialist; Paralegal; Services Sales Representative. **Corporate headquarters location:** Boca Raton FL. **Other area locations:** Brea CA; Foster City CA; Sacramento CA; San Diego CA; Van Nuys CA. **Operations at this facility include:** Administration; Sales; Service. **Listed on:** New York Stock Exchange. **Number of employees at this location:** 370.

ACADEMY TENT & CANVAS

5035 Gifford Avenue, Los Angeles CA 90058. 323/277-8368. **Toll-free phone:** 800/228-3687. **Contact:** Human Resources. **World Wide Web address:** http://www.academytent.com. **Description:** Sets up a wide variety of tents and structures for various special occasions. **Other U.S. locations:** Shelbyville KY.

ARAMARK UNIFORM SERVICES

P.O. Box 7891, Burbank CA 91510. 818/973-3700. **Physical address:** 115 North First Street, Burbank CA 91502. **Toll-free phone:** 800/ARAMARK. **Contact:** Human Resources. **World Wide Web address:** http://www.aramark-uniform.com. **Description:** One of America's largest uniform providers with over 400,000 customers. The company offers uniforms to reinforce corporate identities or to meet specialized demands for static control and flame resistance and provides a variety of products including walk-off mats, cleaning cloths, disposable towels, and other environmental control items. **Common positions include:** Accountant/Auditor; Computer Programmer; District Manager; General Manager; Services Sales Representative. **Corporate headquarters:** This location. **Parent company:** ARAMARK (Philadelphia PA) is one of the world's leading providers of managed services. The company operates in all 50 states and 10 foreign countries, offering a broad range of services to businesses of all sizes including most *Fortune* 500 companies and thousands of universities, hospitals, and municipal, state, and federal government facilities. The company is employee-owned. ARAMARK's businesses include Food, Leisure, and Support Services including Campus Dining Services, School Nutrition Services, Leisure Services, Business Dining Services, International Services, Healthcare Support Services, Conference Center Management, and Refreshment Services; Facility Services; Correctional Services; Industrial Services; Uniform Services, which includes Uniform Services and Wearguard, a direct marketer of work clothing; Health and Education Services including Spectrum Healthcare Services and Children's World Learning Centers; and Book and Magazine Services. **Listed on:** New York Stock Exchange. **Stock exchange symbol:** RMK. **Number of employees nationwide:** 150,000.

AUTOMATIC DATA PROCESSING (ADP)

5355 Orangethorpe Avenue, La Palma CA 90623. 714/739-6240. **Contact:** Human Resources Department. **World Wide Web address:** http://www.adp.com. **Description:** Engaged in payroll processing services including unemployment claims management and local, state, and federal tax filing. **Corporate headquarters location:** Roseland NJ. **Listed on:** New York Stock Exchange. **Stock exchange symbol:** ADP. **Number of employees nationwide:** 20,000.

BURNS INTERNATIONAL SECURITY SERVICES

3333 Wilshire Boulevard, Suite 615, Los Angeles CA 90010. 213/480-1907. **Contact:** Personnel. **Description:** Offers a wide range of protective services and contract security guard programs to businesses and government. Burns International Security Services also provides electronic security systems and security planning consultations. **Common positions include:** Security Officer. **Parent company:** Borg-Warner Protective Services. **Number of employees nationwide:** 20,000.

COMPUTER HORIZONS CORPORATION

1411 West 190th Street, Suite 470, Gardena CA 90248-4324. 310/771-0770. **Toll-free phone:** 800/711-2421. **Fax:** 310/771-0777. **Contact:** Human Resources. **World Wide Web address:** http://www.computerhorizons.com. **Description:** A full-service technology solutions company offering contract staffing, outsourcing, re-engineering, data migration, downsizing support, and network management. The company has a worldwide network of 43 offices. Founded in 1969. **Corporate headquarters location:** Mountain Lakes NJ. **International locations:** Canada; England. **Listed on:** NASDAQ. **Stock exchange symbol:** CHRZ.

ELECTRO RENT CORPORATION

6060 Sepulveda Boulevard, Van Nuys CA 91411-2525. 818/787-2100. **Toll-free phone:** 800/688-1111. **Fax:** 818/786-1602. **Contact:** Human Resources. **World Wide Web address:** http://www.electrorent.com. **Description:** Rents and leases electronic equipment including test and measurement instruments, workstations, personal computers, and data communication products. **Common positions include:** Account Manager; Administrative Assistant; Advertising Clerk; Computer Operator; Customer Service Representative; Electronics Technician; Secretary. **Corporate headquarters location:** This location. **Other U.S. locations:** Nationwide. **Listed on:** NASDAQ. **Stock exchange symbol:** ELRC. **Annual sales/revenues:** More than $100 million. **Number of employees at this location:** 200. **Number of employees nationwide:** 500.

ELECTRONIC CLEARING HOUSE, INC. (ECHO)

28001 Dorothy Drive, Agoura Hills CA 91301-2697. 818/706-8999. **Fax:** 818/991-5973. **Contact:** Anita Baxter, Human Resources. **E-mail address:** hr@echo-inc.com. **World Wide Web address:** http://www.echo-inc.com. **Description:** A holding company. **Subsidiaries include:** National Credit Card Reserve Corporation, which provides electronic credit card authorizations, fund transfers, and deposits for merchants, banks, and other customers; XpressCheX, Inc., which provides check guarantee services; ECHO Payment Services, Inc., which leases, rents, and sells point of sale terminals and related equipment; and Computer Based Controls, Inc., which designs, manufactures, and sells terminals and related equipment. **Listed on:** NASDAQ. **Stock exchange symbol:** ECHO.

IN A WORD
811 West Seventh Street, Suite 204, Los Angeles CA 90017. 213/688-6200. **Toll-free phone:** 800/805-WORD. **Fax:** 213/688-6201. **Contact:** Stella Fridman Hayes, Director of Language Services. **E-mail address:** stellaf@inaword.net. **World Wide Web address:** http://www.inaword.net. **Description:** Offers language translation services on documents including patents, legal documents, product labels, manuals and user guides, advertising copy, and Web material. The company also provides interpreters for meetings and training seminars and electronic publishing services. **Corporate headquarters location:** This location.

PINKERTON SECURITY & INVESTIGATION SERVICES
1540 East First Street, #244, Santa Ana CA 92701. 714/245-9200. **Contact:** Human Resources Department. **E-mail address:** hr@usa.pinkertons.com. **World Wide Web address:** http://www.pinkertons.com. **Description:** One of the world's largest suppliers of global, total security solutions. The company provides a broad array of security-related services to address the protection needs of more than 20,000 customers through 220 offices in the United States, Canada, Mexico, Europe, and Asia. Pinkerton counts approximately half of the *Fortune* 500 companies as its clients. Founded in 1850. **NOTE:** Hiring is conducted through the corporate headquarters. Please send resumes to 4330 Park Terrace Drive, Westlake Village CA 91361. **Common positions include:** Branch Manager; Customer Service Representative; Department Manager; General Manager; Human Resources Manager; Management Trainee; Marketing Specialist; Operations/Production Manager; Quality Control Supervisor; Services Sales Representative. **Special programs:** Internships. **Corporate headquarters location:** Chicago IL. **Other U.S. locations:** Nationwide. **Operations at this facility include:** Regional Headquarters.

PITNEY BOWES MANAGEMENT SERVICES
1149 South Broadway, Suite 100, Los Angeles CA 90015. 213/765-3700. **Contact:** Department of Human Resources. **E-mail address:** staffing@pb.com. **World Wide Web address:**

http://www.pb.com. **Description:** A facility management company specializing in reprographics, facsimiles, mailroom, supply room, file room, and other related office services. **Common positions include:** Accountant/Auditor; Assistant Manager; Chemist; Customer Service Representative; Department Manager; Employment Interviewer; Financial Manager; General Manager; Human Resources Manager; Management Trainee; Market Research Analyst; Purchasing Agent/Manager; Receptionist; Secretary; Services Sales Representative; Site Representative; Supervisor; Systems Analyst; Typist/Word Processor. **Special programs:** Internships. **Corporate headquarters location:** Stamford CT. **Other U.S. locations:** Chicago IL; New York NY; Dallas TX. **Parent company:** Pitney Bowes Inc. **Operations at this facility include:** Administration; Divisional Headquarters; Regional Headquarters; Sales. **Number of employees at this location:** 6,000.

PRUDENTIAL OVERALL SUPPLY
P.O. Box 11210, Santa Ana CA 92711. 949/250-4855. **Physical address:** 1661 Alton Parkway, Irvine CA 92606. **Toll-free phone:** 800/767-5536. **Fax:** 949/261-1947. **Contact:** Human Resources Manager. **E-mail address:** hrjobs@pos-clean.com. **World Wide Web address:** http://www.pos-clean.com. **Description:** An industrial laundry service. Founded in 1932. **NOTE:** Entry-level positions are offered. **Common positions include:** Blue-Collar Worker Supervisor; Management Trainee; Services Sales Representative. **Corporate headquarters location:** This location. **Other U.S. locations:** Phoenix AZ; Tucson AZ; Fresno CA; Los Angeles CA; San Diego CA; San Jose CA. **Operations at this facility include:** Administration; Manufacturing; Sales; Service. **Listed on:** Privately held. **Annual sales/revenues:** More than $100 million. **Number of employees at this location:** 100. **Number of employees nationwide:** 2,000.

SOURCECORP
20500 Belshaw Avenue, Carson CA 90746. 310/763-7575. **Fax:** 310/763-7211. **Contact:** Human Resources. **E-mail address:** careers@srcp.com. **World Wide Web address:** http://www.srcp.com. **Description:** Provides full-service records management for businesses through data storage and imaging services. Data is stored on both disk and microfilm. **Corporate headquarters location:** Dallas TX. **Listed on:** NASDAQ. **Stock exchange symbol:** SRCP.

WESTERN OILFIELDS SUPPLY COMPANY
dba RAIN FOR RENT
P.O. Box 581, Riverside CA 92502. 909/653-2171. **Physical address:** 6400 Fischer Road, Riverside CA 92507. **Toll-free phone:** 800/742-7246. **Contact:** Human Resources. **World Wide Web address:** http://www.rainforrent.com. **Description:** Engaged in the rental, sale, and installation of liquid handling systems, pumps, tanks, and irrigation systems to industrial and agricultural customers. **Corporate headquarters location:** Bakersfield CA. **Other U.S. locations:** Nationwide. **International locations:** Mexico. **Number of employees nationwide:** 435.

WESTERN OILFIELDS SUPPLY COMPANY
dba RAIN FOR RENT
P.O. Box 2248, Bakersfield CA 93303. 661/399-9124. **Fax:** 661/399-1086. **Contact:** Kim Strasner, Director of Human Resources Department. **World Wide Web address:** http://www.rainforrent.com. **Description:** Engaged in the rental, sale, and installation of liquid handling systems, pumps, tanks, and irrigation systems to industrial and agricultural customers. Founded in 1934. **Office hours:** Monday - Friday, 8:00 a.m. - 5:00 p.m. **Corporate headquarters location:** This location. **Other area locations:** Riverside CA. **Other U.S. locations:** Nationwide. **International locations:** Mexico. **Number of employees at this location:** 150. **Number of employees nationwide:** 435.

CHARITIES AND SOCIAL SERVICES

You can expect to find the following types of organizations in this chapter:

Social and Human Service Agencies • Job Training and Vocational Rehabilitation Services • Nonprofit Organizations

AMERICAN CANCER SOCIETY

1523 California Avenue, Bakersfield CA 93304. 661/327-2424. **Contact:** Human Resources Department. **World Wide Web address:** http://www.cancer.org. **Description:** A nationwide, community-based, nonprofit, voluntary health organization dedicated to eliminating cancer as a major health problem by funding cancer research and public education. The society helps patients directly by offering services including transportation to treatment and rehabilitation services. **Corporate headquarters location:** Atlanta GA. Other U.S. locations: Nationwide.

AMERICAN CANCER SOCIETY

8560 Vineyard Avenue, Suite 108, Rancho Cucamonga CA 91730. 909/949-6115. **Fax:** 909/949-6115. **Contact:** Human Resources. **World Wide Web address:** http://www.cancer.org. **Description:** A nationwide, community-based, nonprofit, voluntary health organization dedicated to eliminating cancer as a major health problem by funding cancer research and public education. The society helps patients directly by offering services including transportation to treatment and rehabilitation services. **Corporate headquarters location:** Atlanta GA. **Other U.S. locations:** Nationwide.

AMERICAN RED CROSS

3650 Fifth Avenue, San Diego CA 92103. 619/542-7400. **Contact:** Cindy DiPiero, Director of Human Resources. **World Wide Web address:** http://www.redcross.org. **Description:** A humanitarian organization that aids disaster victims, gathers blood for crisis distribution, trains individuals to respond to emergencies, educates individuals on various diseases, and raises funds for other charitable establishments. **Corporate headquarters location:** Washington DC. **Other U.S. locations:** Nationwide.

AMERICAN RED CROSS

2700 Wilshire Boulevard, Los Angeles CA 90057. 213/739-5200. **Contact:** Jennie Braun, Director of Personnel. **World Wide Web address:** http://www.redcross.org. **Description:** A humanitarian organization that aids disaster victims, gathers blood for crisis distribution, trains individuals to respond to emergencies, educates individuals on various diseases, and raises funds for other charitable establishments. **Corporate headquarters location:** Washington DC. **Other U.S. locations:** Nationwide.

BIENVENIDOS CHILDREN'S CENTER
205 East Palms Street, Altadena CA 91001. 626/798-7222. **Fax:** 626/798-84444. **Contact:** Human Resources. **World Wide Web address:** http://www.bienvenidos.org. **Description:** Runs a group residential home for children who are placed by the courts and a foster family agency. Bienvenidos Children's Center also provides outpatient mental health services to children aged birth to 21 years.

EXCEPTIONAL CHILDREN'S FOUNDATION
3750 West Martin Luther King, Jr. Boulevard, Los Angeles CA 90008. 323/290-2000. **Contact:** Human Resources Department. **E-mail address:** hrecf@aol.com. **World Wide Web address:** http://www.ecf-la.org. **Description:** A nonprofit, educational service that provides schooling for children and adults with developmental disabilities.

GOODWILL INDUSTRIES OF SOUTHERN CALIFORNIA
342 North San Fernando Road, Los Angeles CA 90031. 323/223-1211. **Contact:** Human Resources. **World Wide Web address:** http://www.lagoodwill.org. **Description:** Besides operating 1,400 thrift stores nationwide, Goodwill is a nonprofit provider of employment training for the disabled and the poor. **Corporate headquarters location:** Bethesda MD. **Other U.S. locations:** Nationwide.

ORANGE COUNTY ASSOCIATION FOR RETARDED CITIZENS
225 West Carl Karcher Way, Anaheim CA 92801-2499. 714/744-5301. **Contact:** Human Resources. **Description:** A supported employment program where adults with mental disabilities provide product packaging and assembly. **Corporate headquarters location:** This location.

REGIONAL CENTER OF ORANGE COUNTY
P.O. Box 22010, Santa Ana CA 92702-2010. 714/796-5100. **Contact:** Human Resources Department. **World Wide Web address:** http://www.rcocdd.com. **Description:** A nonprofit organization dedicated to helping individuals with all types of

learning disabilities ranging from mental retardation to cerebral palsy. **Common positions include:** Social Worker. **Corporate headquarters location:** This location. **Operations at this facility include:** Administration; Service. **Listed on:** Privately held. **Number of employees at this location:** 200.

CHEMICALS/RUBBER AND PLASTICS

You can expect to find the following types of companies in this chapter:

Adhesives, Detergents, Inks, Paints, Soaps, Varnishes •
Agricultural Chemicals and Fertilizers • Carbon and Graphite
Products • Chemical Engineering Firms• Industrial Gases

AMERICAN VANGUARD CORPORATION

4100 East Washington Boulevard, Los Angeles CA 90023. 323/264-3910. **Toll-free phone:** 888/462-6822. **Fax:** 323/269-4668. **Contact:** Human Resources. **World Wide Web address:** http://www.american-vanguard.com. **Description:** A holding company. **Corporate headquarters location:** This location. **Subsidiaries include:** AMVAC manufactures and formulates chemicals for crop, human, and animal health protection. These chemicals, which include insecticides, fungicides, plant growth regulators, and soil fumigants, are marketed in liquid, powder, and granular forms. **Listed on:** American Stock Exchange. **Stock exchange symbol:** AVD.

AMERON INTERNATIONAL

P.O. Box 7007, Pasadena CA 91109. 626/683-4000. **Physical address:** 245 South Los Robles Avenue, Pasadena CA 91101. **Fax:** 626/683-4020. **Contact:** Human Resources. **World Wide Web address:** http://www.ameron.com. **Description:** Manufactures and supplies goods and services to the industrial, utility, marine, and construction markets. The business is divided into four groups: The Protective Coatings Group develops, manufactures, and markets high-performance coatings and surface systems on a worldwide basis. These products are utilized for the preservation of major structures such as metallic and concrete facilities and equipment to prevent their decomposition by corrosion, abrasion, marine fouling, and other forms of chemical and physical attack; The Fiberglass Pipe Group develops, manufactures, and markets filament-wound and molded fiberglass pipe fittings; The Concrete and Steel Pipe Group offers products and services used in the construction of pipeline facilities for various utilities. Eight plants manufacture concrete cylinder pipe, prestressed concrete cylinder pipe, steel pipe, and reinforced concrete pipe for water transmission, and storm and industrial wastewater and sewage collection; The Construction & Allied Products Group includes the HC&D Division, which supplies ready-mix concrete, crushed and sized basaltic aggregates, dune sand, concrete pipe, and box culverts, primarily to the construction industry in Hawaii. **Corporate headquarters location:** This location. **Listed on:** New York Stock Exchange. **Stock exchange symbol:** AMN.

AMERON INTERNATIONAL
201 North Berry Street, Brea CA 92821. 714/529-1951. **Toll-free phone:** 800/9-AMERON. **Contact:** Personnel. **World Wide Web address:** http://www.ameron.com. **Description:** This location develops, manufactures, and markets proprietary, high-performance protective coatings for the offshore, chemical processing, refining, rail, power, bridge, water and waste treatment, pulp and paper, and light industrial/commercial markets. Overall, Ameron International manufactures and supplies goods and services to the industrial, utility, marine, and construction markets. The business of the company is divided into three other groups. The Fiberglass Pipe Group develops, manufactures, and markets filament-wound and molded fiberglass pipe fittings. The Construction & Allied Products Group includes the HC&D Division, which supplies ready-mix concrete, crushed and sized basaltic aggregates, dune sand, concrete pipe, and box culverts, primarily to the construction industry in Hawaii. The Concrete and Steel Pipe Group supplies products and services used in the construction of pipeline facilities for various utilities. Products include concrete cylinder pipe, prestressed concrete cylinder pipe, steel pipe, and reinforced concrete pipe for water transmission, storm and industrial wastewater, and sewage collection. **Corporate headquarters location:** Pasadena CA. **Listed on:** New York Stock Exchange. **Stock exchange symbol:** AMN.

ARRK PRODUCT DEVELOPMENT GROUP
8880 Rehco Road, San Diego CA 92121. 858/552-1587. **Toll-free phone:** 800/735-ARRK. **Fax:** 858/626-2379. **Contact:** Human Resources. **E-mail address:** hr@arrk.com. **World Wide Web address:** http://www.arrk.com. **Description:** Manufactures plastic prototypes for a variety of industries including health care. **Corporate headquarters location:** This location. **Other area locations:** Los Angeles CA; San Francisco CA. **Other U.S. locations:** Atlanta GA; Detroit MI; Waxhaw NC; New York NY; Portland OR; Dallas TX. **International locations:** Australia; Canada; France; Hungary; Italy; Japan; Korea; Thailand; United Kingdom.

CALBIOCHEM-NOVABIOCHEM
10394 Pacific Center Court, San Diego CA 92121. 858/450-9600. **Contact:** Ms. Mary O'Mally, Director of Human

Resources Department. **E-mail address:** jobs@cnbi.com. **World Wide Web address:** http://www.calbiochem.com. **Description:** Manufactures fine chemicals for the research, biochemical, and pharmaceutical industries. **Common positions include:** Biological Scientist; Chemist. **Corporate headquarters location:** This location. **Parent company:** CN Biosciences, Inc. **Operations at this facility include:** Production; Warehouse/Distribution.

COAST PACKAGING
P.O. Box 248, Miraloma CA 91752. 909/681-0666. **Contact:** Human Resources. **Description:** Distributes polystyrene insulation board and packaging trays. **Common positions include:** Accountant/Auditor; Blue-Collar Worker Supervisor; Chemical Engineer; Customer Service Representative; General Manager; Human Resources Manager; Inspector/Tester/Grader; Mechanical Engineer; Payroll Clerk; Production Manager; Receptionist; Transportation/Traffic Specialist; Truck Driver. **Corporate headquarters location:** Lake Forest IL. **Operations at this facility include:** Manufacturing.

GOODYEAR TIRE & RUBBER COMPANY
19200 South Main Street, Gardena CA 90248. 323/770-0456. **Contact:** Human Resources Department. **World Wide Web address:** http://www.goodyear.com. **Description:** Develops, manufactures, distributes, and sells tires. Goodyear Tire & Rubber Company also manufactures and sells a broad spectrum of rubber products and rubber-related chemicals for various industrial and consumer markets and provides auto repair services. The company operates 32 plants in the United States, 42 plants in 29 other countries, and more than 1,800 retail tire and service centers and other distribution facilities around the globe. Strategic business units of Goodyear Tire & Rubber include North American Tire, Kelly-Springfield, Goodyear Europe, Goodyear Latin America, Goodyear Asia, Engineered Products, Chemicals, Celeron, and Goodyear Racing. **Common positions include:** Department Manager; Management Trainee; Marketing Specialist; Retail Sales Worker. **Corporate headquarters location:** Akron OH. **Operations at this facility include:** Divisional Headquarters; Regional Headquarters; Sales. **Listed on:** New York Stock Exchange. **Stock exchange symbol:** GT.

HENKEL INC.
P.O. Box 1282, City of Industry CA 91749-1282. 626/968-6511. **Fax:** 626/336-0526. **Contact:** Human Resources. **World Wide Web address:** http://www.henkel.com. **Description:**

Manufactures coating powders and high-performance liquid encapsulates for use in the electronics industry. **Common positions include:** Accountant/Auditor; Blue-Collar Worker Supervisor; Buyer; Chemist; Customer Service Representative; General Manager; Operations/Production Manager; Quality Control Supervisor; Systems Analyst. **Special programs:** Internships. **Corporate headquarters location:** Windsor Locks CT. **Other U.S. locations:** Nationwide. **Operations at this facility include:** Administration; Divisional Headquarters; Manufacturing; Research and Development; Sales.

HONEYWELL

3201 West Lomita Boulevard, Torrance CA 90505. 310/530-1981. **Contact:** Human Resources Department. **World Wide Web address:** http://www.honeywell.com. **Description:** This location manufactures turbochargers. Overall, Honeywell is engaged in the research, development, manufacture, and sale of advanced technology products and services in the fields of chemicals, electronics, automation, and controls. The company's major businesses are home and building automation and control, performance polymers and chemicals, industrial automation and control, space and aviation systems, and defense and marine systems. **Corporate headquarters location:** Plymouth MN. **Listed on:** New York Stock Exchange. **Stock exchange symbol:** HON.

HUTCHINSON SEAL CORPORATION
NATIONAL O-RING DIVISION

11634 Patton Road, Downey CA 90241-5295. 562/862-8163. **Fax:** 562/862-4596. **Contact:** Personnel. **World Wide Web address:** http://www.hutchinsonrubber.com. **Description:** Engaged in various distribution and manufacturing operations. **Corporate headquarters location:** This location. **Subsidiaries include:** National O-Ring, which manufactures and distributes a full-range of standard-size, low-cost, synthetic rubber o-ring sealing devices for use in automotive and industrial applications.

INTESYS TECHNOLOGIES

265 Briggs Avenue, Costa Mesa CA 92626. 714/546-4460. **Fax:** 714/556-6955. **Contact:** Human Resources Department. **E-mail address:** resumes@intesys.com. **World Wide Web address:** http://www.intesys.com. **Description:** A major developer and manufacturer of high-performance plastic components for commercial, industrial, and medical uses. The company also custom formulates and compounds reinforced thermoplastic materials. InteSys produces engineered parts and

subassemblies that are key components for computer equipment, printers, data cartridges, telecommunication devices, business machines, electronic products, commercial irrigation, automobile, and plumbing systems. **Common positions include:** Accountant/Auditor; Adjuster; Administrative Manager; Advertising Clerk; Blue-Collar Worker Supervisor; Buyer; Chemical Engineer; Clerical Supervisor; Computer Programmer; Cost Estimator; Customer Service Representative; Draftsperson; Electrical/Electronics Engineer; Electrician; General Manager; Industrial Engineer; Industrial Production Manager; Mechanical Engineer; Purchasing Agent/Manager; Quality Control Supervisor; Systems Analyst. **Corporate headquarters location:** Gilbert AZ. **Other U.S. locations:** NV; NC. **Operations at this facility include:** Administration; Divisional Headquarters; Manufacturing; Regional Headquarters; Sales; Service. **Number of employees at this location:** 600. **Number of employees nationwide:** 700.

PACTIV CORPORATION
14505 Proctor Avenue, City of Industry CA 91746. 626/968-3801. **Contact:** Charles Daniel, Personnel Manager. **World Wide Web address:** http://www.pactiv.com. **Description:** Manufactures proprietary products made entirely or partially of plastics. Major product lines include food packaging, apparel hangers, internally-illuminated signs, recreational vehicle components, and swimming pool products. **Corporate headquarters location:** Lake Forest IL. **Listed on:** New York Stock Exchange. **Stock exchange symbol:** PTV.

PLASTIC DRESS-UP COMPANY
11077 East Rush Street, South El Monte CA 91733. 626/442-7711. **Contact:** Human Resources. **World Wide Web address:** http://www.pdu.com. **Description:** Manufactures plastic trophy components. **Corporate headquarters location:** This location.

ROPAK CORPORATION
660 South State College Boulevard, Fullerton CA 92831. 714/870-9757. **Toll-free phone:** 800/367-3779. **Contact:** Manager of Human Resources. **World Wide Web address:** http://www.ropakcorp.com. **Description:** Manufactures plastic containers for a wide range of uses. **Corporate headquarters location:** This location. **Parent company:** LINPAC Group.

SHIPLEY RONAL
27021 Puerta Real, Suite 270, Mission Viejo CA 92691. 949/347-2040. **Contact:** Personnel Department. **World Wide Web address:** http://www.shipley.com. **Description:** An

international supplier of specialty chemicals for applications in the production of printed circuit boards and semiconductors. Shipley Ronal is also engaged in research and development, manufacturing, and sales of photoresistors and other related products. **Common positions include:** Accountant/Auditor; Chemist; Manufacturer's/Wholesaler's Sales Rep. **Special programs:** Internships. **Corporate headquarters location:** Lansing IL. **Parent company:** Morton International is a diversified manufacturer. Product lines of Morton International include salt, automotive airbags, and specialty chemicals. **Operations at this facility include:** Administration; Research and Development; Sales. **Listed on:** New York Stock Exchange. **Stock exchange symbol:** ROH.

SUMMA INDUSTRIES
21250 Hawthorne Boulevard, Suite 500, Torrance CA 90503. 310/792-7024. **Contact:** Miriam Rivera, Human Resources. **E-mail address:** mrivera@summaindustries.com. **World Wide Web address:** http://www.summaindustries.com. **Description:** Manufactures plastic components for a variety of commercial and industrial markets. Products include optical components, conveyor belts, fittings, valves, coil forms, and tubing. **NOTE:** Jobseekers should send resumes to Summa Human Resources, 1101 California Avenue, Suite 100, Corona CA 92881. Fax: 801/749-6952. **Corporate headquarters location:** This location. **Other U.S. locations:** FL; IL; MI; MS; OK; TN. **Listed on:** NASDAQ. **Stock exchange symbol:** SUMX. **Annual sales/revenues:** More than $100 million.

TRICOR REFINING LLC
P.O. Box 5877, Bakersfield CA 93308. 310/277-4511. **Contact:** Personnel. **Description:** Produces a wide range of special-purpose chemical and petroleum products as well as engineered materials and parts for industrial and consumer use.

U.S. BORAX INC.
P.O. Box 926, Valencia CA 91355. 661/287-5400. **Physical address:** 26877 Tourney Road, Valencia CA 91355. **Contact:** Deborah Stevens, Human Resources Specialist. **World Wide Web address:** http://www.borax.xom. **Description:** Produces borax, boric acid, and other boron compounds. **Common positions include:** Account Manager; Accountant; Administrative Assistant; Budget Analyst; Chemist; Credit Manager; Customer Service Representative; Financial Analyst; Geologist/Geophysicist; Human Resources Manager; Librarian; Marketing Manager; Marketing Specialist; Sales Manager; Sales

Rep.; Secretary; Systems Analyst; Telecommunications Analyst; Transportation/Traffic Specialist. **Special programs:** Training. **Corporate headquarters location:** This location. **Parent company:** Rio Tinto PLC. **Listed on:** New York Stock Exchange. **Stock exchange symbol:** RTP. **Number of employees at this location:** 175. **Number of employees nationwide:** 1,000.

UNITED PLASTICS GROUP
3125 East Coronado Street, Anaheim CA 92806. 714/630-6411. **Contact:** Personnel Department. **World Wide Web address:** http://www.unitedplasticsgroup.com. **Description:** Manufactures custom injection-molded plastic products. **Corporate headquarters location:** Westmont IL. **Other U.S. locations:** Nationwide. **International locations:** Worldwide. **Number of employees at this location:** 500.

WD-40 COMPANY
1061 Cudahy Place, San Diego CA 92110. 619/275-1400. **Fax:** 619/275-5823. **Contact:** Human Resources. **World Wide Web address:** http://www.wd40.com. **Description:** Manufactures and markets WD-40, a petroleum-based industrial lubricant spray. WD-40 is also a rust preventative, a penetrant, and a moisture displacer. **Corporate headquarters location:** This location. **Listed on:** NASDAQ. **Stock exchange symbol:** WDFC. **Number of employees at this location:** 140.

COMMUNICATIONS: TELECOMMUNICATIONS AND BROADCASTING

You can expect to find the following types of companies in this chapter:

Cable/Pay Television Services • Communications Equipment• Radio and Television Broadcasting Systems • Telephone, Telegraph, and other Message Communications

ABC FAMILY
10960 Wilshire Boulevard, Los Angeles CA 90024. 310/235-5100. **Contact:** Human Resources. **World Wide Web address:** http://www.abcfamily.go.com. **Description:** Produces, exhibits, and distributes entertainment and informational programming as well as related products targeted at families worldwide. **Other U.S. locations:** Nationwide.

ABC, INC.
4151 Prospect Avenue, Los Angeles, CA 90067. 310/557-7777. **Contact:** Human Resources Department Representative. **E-mail address:** hr.mail@dig.com. **World Wide Web address:** http://www.abctelevision.com. **Description:** A diversified communications organization. The company is engaged in television and radio broadcasting, provides cable television service to subscribers, and publishes newspapers and other specialized publications. Broadcasting operations include ABC Television Network Group, the Broadcast Group, the Cable and International Broadcast Group, and the Multimedia Group. In addition to its network operations, the broadcasting segment consists of 8 network-affiliated television stations, 10 radio stations, cable television systems providing service to subscribers in 16 states, and the developing multimedia video-by-wire business. Publishing operations consist of 8 daily newspapers, 78 weekly newspapers, 63 shopping guides, and several other business and specialized publications.

ADC TELECOMMUNICATIONS, INC.
WIRELINE SYSTEMS DIVISON
14402 Franklin Avenue, Tustin CA 92780-7013. 714/832-9922. **Toll-free phone:** 800/366-3891. **Fax:** 714/832-9924. **Contact:** Human Resources. **World Wide Web address:** http://www.adc.com. **Description:** A major supplier of High-bit-rate Digital Subscriber Line (HDSL)-based and HDSL2-based products and systems. ADC's CopperOptics allows transmission of fiber-optic quality communications over

copper cable. ADC's Solutions give end users instant access to digital services including LAN internetworking and video conferencing. Founded in 1988. **Corporate headquarters location:** Minneapolis MN. **Other U.S. locations:** Nationwide. **International locations:** Worldwide. **Listed on** NASDAQ. **Stock exchange symbol:** ADCT.

ADAPTIVE BROADBAND
111 Castilian Drive, Santa Barbara CA 93117. 805/968-9621. **Fax:** 805/968-0791. **Contact:** Personnel. **World Wide Web address:** http://www.adaptivebroadband.com. **Description:** Provides a wireless access network for data, Internet, video, and voice applications. **Corporate headquarters location:** This location. **Other U.S. locations:** Rochester NY. **International locations:** London, England; Beijing, China.

CBS CORPORATION
6121 Sunset Boulevard, Los Angeles CA 90028. 323/460-3000. **Contact:** CBS Placement. **World Wide Web address:** http://www.cbsnews.com. **Description:** Houses the offices of CBS-2 News and KNX Radio News. **Special programs:** Internships. **Parent company:** Viacom Inc.

COX COMMUNICATIONS, INC.
5159 Federal Boulevard, San Diego CA 92105. 619/263-9251. **Contact:** Human Resources. **World Wide Web address:** http://www.cox.com. **Description:** A local franchise of the nationwide cable television distributor. Cox Communications provides service to over 6 million customers. **Common positions include:** Customer Service Representative; Services Sales Representative. **Corporate headquarters location:** Atlanta GA. **Parent company:** Cox Enterprises, Inc. **Listed on:** New York Stock Exchange. **Stock exchange symbol:** COX.

DMX MUSIC LLC
11400 West Olympic Boulevard, Suite 1100, Los Angeles CA 90064. 310/444-1744. **Toll-free phone:** 800/700-4412. **Fax:** 310/477-0724. **Contact:** Department of Human Resources. **E-mail address:** jobs@dmxmusic.com. **World Wide Web address:** http://www.dmxmusic.com. **Description:** Programs, distributes, and markets a premium digital music service, Digital Music Express, which provides continuous, commercial-free, CD-quality music programming. DMX is delivered by two methods: for a monthly, per-subscriber license fee, it is sent direct to cable operators by C-Band satellite for distribution to residential and commercial cable subscribers; for a monthly, per-subscriber fee, it is distributed

by KuBand direct broadcast satellite (DBS) to small satellite dishes that connect through a specially designed DMX tuner to a commercial subscriber's stereo system. **Corporate headquarters location:** This location. **Parent company:** Liberty Media, Inc.

DISCOVERY COMMUNICATIONS INC.
10100 Santa Monica Boulevard, Suite 1500, Los Angeles CA 90067. 310/551-1611. **Contact:** Human Resources. **E-mail address:** explore_careers@discovery.com. **World Wide Web address:** http://www.discovery.com. **Description:** Produces the Discovery Channel, a cable television network dedicated to providing information about nature, science and technology, history, and world exploration. **Corporate headquarters location:** Bethesda MD.

FOX TELEVISION
KTTV-FOX 11
1999 South Bundy Drive, Los Angeles CA 90025. 310/584-2000. **Contact:** Human Resources. **World Wide Web address:** http://www.fox11a.com. **Description:** A national television broadcasting network. **Special programs:** Internships. **Internship information:** All internships are unpaid and are offered during summer, fall, and spring semesters. Internships in the newsroom, sports, publicity, and community relations are offered. The program requires a 12- to 15-hour-per-week commitment, and preference is given to juniors and seniors in college. Resumes should be addressed to the attention of the Internship Coordinator. **Corporate headquarters location:** Los Angeles CA. **Parent company:** Twentieth Century Fox. **Listed on:** New York Stock Exchange. **Stock exchange symbol:** FOX.

FREEDOM COMMUNICATIONS INC.
P.O. Box 19549, Irvine CA 92623. 949/553-9292. **Physical address:** 17666 Fitch, Irvine CA 92614. **World Wide Web address:** http://www.freedom.com. **Contact:** Human Resources Department. **Description:** Owns the *Orange County Register* and 26 other daily newspapers, as well as 25 weekly newspapers and five television stations.

HARRIS CORPORATION
809 Calle Plano, Camarillo CA 93012. 805/987-9511. **Contact:** David Cunningham, Human Resources Department Manager. **World Wide Web address:** http://www.harris.com. **Description:** A communications equipment company that provides broadcast, network, government, and wireless support products and systems. Founded in 1895. **Common**

positions include: Accountant/Auditor; Administrator; Blue-Collar Worker Supervisor; Buyer; Computer Programmer; Customer Service Rep.; Electrical/Electronics Engineer; Financial Analyst; Industrial Engineer; Mechanical Engineer; Operations/Production Manager; Production Manager; Quality Control Supervisor. **Special programs:** Internships. **Corporate headquarters location:** Melbourne FL. **Other U.S. locations:** Nationwide. **International locations:** Worldwide. **Operations at this facility include:** Administration; Manufacturing; Research and Development; Sales. **Listed on:** New York Stock Exchange. **Stock exchange symbol:** HRS. **Annual sales/revenues:** More than $100 million. **Number of employees nationwide:** 10,500.

L3 COMMUNICATIONS, INC.

9020 Balboa Avenue, San Diego CA 92123. 858/279-0411. **Fax:** 858/571-1259. **Contact:** Department of Human Resources. **E-mail address:** cooljobs@l-3com.com. **World Wide Web address:** http://www.l-3com.com. **Description:** Designs and manufactures integrated microwave antenna subassemblies and low-radar, cross-section antenna designs and measurements. **Common positions include:** Accountant/Auditor; Aerospace Engineer; Buyer; Computer Programmer; Cost Estimator; Department Manager; Human Resources Manager; Mechanical Engineer; Microwave Engineer; Operations/Production Manager; Purchasing Agent/Manager; Quality Control Supervisor; Support Personnel; Systems Analyst. **Corporate headquarters location:** New York NY. **Listed on:** New York Stock Exchange. **Stock exchange symbol:** LLL.

NLYNX SYSTEMS

4615 Industrial Street, Suite 1A, Simi Valley CA 93063. 805/527-2300. **Contact:** Department of Human Resources. **E-mail address:** job@decisiondata.com. **World Wide Web address:** http://www.nlynx.com. **Description:** Manufactures telecommunications equipment including Earth station satellite, cellular, and microwave antennas, towers, shelters, cables, and associated equipment. **Corporate headquarters location:** Austin TX. **Subsidiaries include:** Decision Data.

QUALCOMM INCORPORATED

5775 Morehouse Drive, San Diego CA 92191. 858/587-1121. **Recorded jobline:** 858/658-JOBS. **Contact:** Human Resources Department. **E-mail address:** resumes@qualcomm.com. **World Wide Web address:** http://www.qualcomm.com. **Description:** This location houses the corporate headquarters as well as

CDMA University, the company's training facility. Overall, QUALCOMM Incorporated designs and manufactures CDMA (Code Division Multiple Access) wireless products. These products include digital cellular portable phones that use microprocessors, allowing good voice quality, low power requirements, and a wide coverage area. The company manufactures a wide variety of communications products from desktop phones to the OmniTRACS satellite communications system, all using CDMA technology. QUALCOMM Incorporated also designs and manufactures network planning software to help design wireless networks; and indoor or outdoor base stations for cellular and wireless local loop systems. The company also offers wireless network planning and deployment services. **Company slogan:** We're building the wireless world. **Special programs:** Training. **Corporate headquarters location:** This location. **Other U.S. locations:** Boulder CO. **International locations:** Argentina; Brazil; Canada; China; India. **Listed on:** NASDAQ. **Stock exchange symbol:** QCOM. **Annual sales/revenues:** More than $100 million.

UNISYS PULSEPOINT COMMUNICATIONS
6307 Carpinteria Avenue, Carpinteria CA 93013. 805/566-2000. **Contact:** Human Resources. **World Wide Web address:** http://www.unisys.com. **Description:** Designs, manufactures, and markets information processing systems that deliver unified messaging. The company's products enable service providers and large corporations to offer a wide variety of services to end users including basic voicemail, automated attendant, fax mail, and fax overflow (guaranteed fax). **Listed on:** New York Stock Exchange. **Stock exchange symbol:** UIS.

VERIZON COMMUNICATIONS
One Verizon Way, Thousand Oaks CA 91362-3811. 805/372-6000. **Contact:** Human Resources Department. **World Wide Web address:** http://www.verizon.com. **Description:** A full-service communications services provider. Verizon offers residential local and long distance telephone services and Internet access; wireless service plans, cellular phones, and data services; a full-line of business services including Internet access, data services, and telecommunications equipment and services; and government network solutions including Internet access, data services, telecommunications equipment and services, and enhanced communications services. **Corporate headquarters location:** New York NY. **Other U.S. locations:** Nationwide. **Listed on:** New York Stock Exchange. **Stock exchange symbol:** VZ.

WESTWOOD ONE INC.
9540 Washington Boulevard, Culver City CA 90232. 310/840-4000. **Contact:** Human Resources Department. **World Wide Web address:** http://www.westwoodone.com. **Description:** A radio broadcasting network that produces and distributes syndicated radio shows. **Corporate headquarters location:** Valencia CA. **Other U.S. locations:** Chicago IL; Detroit MI; New York NY; Arlington VA. **Corporate headquarters location:** Valencia CA.

COMPUTER HARDWARE, SOFTWARE, AND SERVICES

You can expect to find the following types of companies in this chapter:

Computer Components and Hardware Manufacturers • Consultants and Computer Training Companies • Internet and Online Service Providers • Networking and Systems Services • Repair Services/Rental and Leasing • Resellers, Wholesalers, and Distributors • Software Developers/Programming Services • Web Technologies

ASD SOFTWARE
4650 Arrow Highway, Suite E6, Montclair CA 91763. 909/624-2594. **Contact:** Human Resources. **World Wide Web address:** http://www.asdsoft.com. **Description:** Manufactures and markets utility program software for Macintosh operating systems. **Corporate headquarters location:** This location.

ACCENTURE
2101 Rosecrans Avenue, Suite 3300, El Segundo CA 90245. 310/726-2700. **Fax:** 310/726-2950. **Contact:** Human Resources Department Manager. **World Wide Web address:** http://www.accenture.com. **Description:** A management and technology consulting firm. Accenture offers a wide range of services including business re-engineering, customer service system consulting, data system design and implementation, Internet sales systems research and design, and strategic planning. **Corporate headquarters location:** Chicago IL. **Other U.S. locations:** Nationwide. **International locations:** Worldwide. **Listed on:** New York Stock Exchange. **Stock exchange symbol:** ASN.

ACMA COMPUTERS
1565 Reliance Way, Fremont CA 94539. 510/623-1212. **Toll-free phone:** 800/786-6888. **Fax:** 510/623-0818. **Contact:** Human Resources Department. **World Wide Web address:** http://www.acma.com. **Description:** Manufactures personal computers. **Office hours:** Monday - Friday, 8:30 a.m. - 5:30 p.m. **Corporate headquarters location:** This location.

ACOM SOLUTIONS INC.
2850 East 29th Street, Long Beach CA 90806-2313. 562/424-7899. **Contact:** Human Resources. **World Wide Web address:** http://www.acom.com. **Description:** Resells laser printers and

distributes software to various businesses. **Other U.S. locations:** Los Angeles CA; Duluth GA; St. Paul MN.

ACTEL CORPORATION
6 Venture Street, Suite 100, Irvine CA 92692. 949/727-0470. **Contact:** Human Resources. **World Wide Web address:** http://www.actel.com. **Description:** Designs, manufactures, and markets programmable integrated circuits used in computers, peripherals, telecommunications devices, and consumer electronics. GateField Corporation also develops the software used for its products. **Corporate headquarters location:** Sunnyvale CA.

ADVANCED COMPUTER SOLUTIONS
12675 Danielson Court, Suite 407, Poway CA 92064. 858/748-6800. **Contact:** Human Resources. **World Wide Web address:** http://www.acsolutions.com. **Description:** Designs and manufactures hardware including flat-panel display systems, embedded systems, and motherboards for various industries.

AJILON SERVICES INC.
1960 East Grand Avenue, Suite 555, El Segundo CA 90245. 310/335-4800. **Contact:** Human Resources Department. **E-mail address:** info@ajilon.com. **World Wide Web address:** http://www.ajilon.com. **Description:** Offers computer consulting services, project support, and end user services. **Corporate headquarters location:** Towson MD. **Other U.S. locations:** Nationwide. **Parent company:** Adecco.

AMDAHL CORPORATION
770 The City Drive South, Suite 4000, Orange CA 92868. 714/740-0440. **Contact:** Human Resources Department. **E-mail address:** jobs@amdahl.com. **World Wide Web address:** http://www.amdahl.com. **Description:** This location is engaged in sales and services. Overall, Amdahl designs, develops, manufactures, markets, and services large-scale, high-performance, general-purpose computer systems including both hardware and software. Customers are primarily large corporations, government agencies, and large universities with high-volume data-processing requirements. Amdahl markets more than 470 different systems. **Corporate headquarters location:** Sunnyvale CA. **Other U.S. locations:** Nationwide. **International locations:** Worldwide. **Parent company:** Fujitsu, Ltd. **Listed on:** NASDAQ. **Stock exchange symbol:** FJTSY. **Number of employees nationwide:** 6,000. **Number of employees worldwide:** 9,500.

ANACOMP, INC.

12365 Crosthwaite Circle, Poway CA 92064. 858/679-9797. **Contact:** Human Resources Department. **World Wide Web address:** http://www.anacomp.com. **Description:** Provides document storage solutions; manufactures computer hardware and software; and develops customized financial software. **Common positions include:** Accountant/Auditor; Computer Programmer; Customer Service Rep.; Electrical/Electronics Engineer; Financial Analyst; Human Resources Manager; Industrial Engineer; Manufacturer's/Wholesaler's Sales Rep.; Mechanical Engineer; Operations/Production Manager; Purchasing Agent/Manager; Quality Control Supervisor; Systems Analyst; Technical Writer/Editor. **Corporate headquarters location:** This location. **Other U.S. locations:** Nationwide. **International locations:** Austria; France; Germany; Italy; Netherlands; Sweden; Switzerland; United Kingdom. **Operations at this facility include:** Administration; Engineering and Design; Manufacturing; Marketing; Research and Development; Sales.

AONIX

5040 Shoreham Place, Suite 100, San Diego CA 92122. 858/457-2700. **Toll-free phone:** 800/97-AONIX. **Fax:** 858/824-0212 **Contact:** Department of Human Resources. **E-mail address:** resume@aonix.com. **World Wide Web address:** http://www.aonix.com. **Description:** Develops and markets computer-aided software engineering (CASE) products that allow a network of minicomputers to interact. **Corporate headquarters location:** This location. **International locations:** France; Germany; Sweden; United Kingdom.

AUTO-GRAPHICS, INC.

3201 Temple Avenue, Pomona CA 91768-3200. 909/595-7204. **Toll-free phone:** 800/776-6939. **Fax:** 909/595-5190. **Contact:** Human Resources. **E-mail address:** info@auto-graphics.com. **World Wide Web address:** http://www.auto-graphics.com. **Description:** Provides software and processing services to database and information publishers. Services include the computerized preparation and processing of customer-supplied information to be published in various formats including print, microform, CD-ROM, and/or online computer access. In addition, the company markets CD-ROM hardware and software packages for access to computer generated information. **Corporate headquarters location:** This location. **Subsidiaries include:** A-G Canada; Datacat; Dataquad; LibraryCard. **Number of employees at this location:** 115.

AUTOLOGIC INFORMATION INTERNATIONAL INC.

1050 Rancho Conejo Boulevard, Thousand Oaks CA 91320. 805/498-9611. **Fax:** 805/376-5003. **Recorded jobline:** 805/376-5400. **Contact:** Gina Cody, Human Resources. **E-mail address:** gcody@autologic.com. **World Wide Web address:** http://www.autoiii.com. **Description:** Develops, assembles, and markets computer-based systems that automate the functions of prepress production for the publishing and printing industries. Products can be separated into three categories: Automated Workflow Solutions includes servers, plateroom management tracking systems, and output file managers; Document Distribution Systems provides electronic document distribution and other communication services; and Integrated Products includes drum and flatbed scanners, and drum and computer-to-plate imagers. **Common positions include:** Administrative Manager; Computer Operator; Electronics Technician; Software Engineer. **programs:** Internships. **Corporate headquarters location:** This location. **Other U.S. locations:** Nationwide. **International locations:** Worldwide. **Number of employees nationwide:** 335. **Number of employees worldwide:** 385.

BEST SOFTWARE, INC.

56 Technology Drive, Irvine CA 92618. 949/753-1222. **Contact:** Human Resources. **World Wide Web address:** http://www.bestsoftware.com. **Description:** Develops, markets, and supports high-end microcomputer accounting software. **Corporate headquarters location:** This location.

CCH INC.

21250 Hawthorne Boulevard, Torrance CA 90503. 310/543-6200. **Toll-free phone:** 800/PFX-9998. **Fax:** 310/543-6544. **Contact:** Human Resources. **World Wide Web address:** http://www.cch.com. **Description:** One of the nation's largest developers of income tax processing software. The company markets its software products to tax attorneys, tax accountants, and CPAs. **Common positions include:** Computer Programmer; Customer Service Representative; Systems Analyst; Tax Specialist; Technical Support Representative; Technical Writer/Editor. **Corporate headquarters location:** Riverwoods IL. **Other U.S. locations:** Chatsworth CA; Washington DC; Chicago IL; St. Cloud MN. **Parent company:** Wolters Kluwer. **Number of employees at this location:** 400.

CI DESIGN

4320 East Miraloma Avenue, Anaheim CA 92807. 714/646-0111. **Fax:** 714/646-0268. **Contact:** Human Resources. **E-mail**

address: kj@cidesign.com. **World Wide Web address:** http://www.ci-design.com. **Description:** Designs and manufactures computer hardware and peripherals including storage and disk drive systems. **Corporate headquarters location:** This location. **Other U.S. locations:** Nationwide. **International locations:** The Netherlands; Taiwan.

CABLE & COMPUTER TECHNOLOGY
1555 South Sinclair Street, Anaheim CA 92806. 714/937-1341. **Fax:** 714/937-1225. **World Wide Web address:** http://www.c2t.com. **Contact:** Department of Human Resources. **Description:** Manufactures computer emulation hardware for the U.S. government. **Corporate headquarters location:** This location.

CAM COMMERCE SOLUTIONS
17075 Newhope Street, Fountain Valley CA 92708. 714/241-9241. **Contact:** Human Resources. **World Wide Web address:** http://www.camcommerce.com. **Description:** Designs, manufactures, markets, and services inventory management, point-of-sale, order entry, and accounting software systems for small to medium-sized retailers and wholesalers. CAM provides its products and services on a direct basis only. The company also offers after-sale services including phone support, nationwide hardware and software service, database conversions, and regular program enhancements. Founded in 1983. **Corporate headquarters location:** This location. **Other U.S. locations:** Burlingame CA; Aurora CO; Altamonte Springs FL; Hopkinton MA; St. Louis MO; Saddle River NJ; Henderson NV; Dallas TX. **Listed on:** NASDAQ. **Stock exchange symbol:** CADA. **Chairman and CEO:** Geoff Knapp. **Number of employees at this location:** 115.

CANDLE CORPORATION
201 North Douglas Street, El Segundo CA 90245. 310/535-3600. **Contact:** Human Resources. **World Wide Web address:** http://www.candle.com. **Description:** Develops and markets systems software. **Common positions include:** Computer Programmer; Computer Scientist; Design Engineer; Electrical/Electronics Engineer; Manufacturing Engineer; Software Engineer. **Corporate headquarters location:** This location. **Other area locations:** Agoura Hills CA. **Other U.S. locations:** AZ; CO; DC; GA; IL; ME; MA; MI; MN; NY; OH; TX. **International locations:** Worldwide.

CANON BUSINESS MACHINES, INC.

3191 Red Hill Avenue, Costa Mesa CA 92626. 714/556-4700. **Fax:** 714/433-8103. **Contact:** Human Resources Department. **E-mail address:** resumes@cbm.canon.com. **World Wide Web address:** http://www.cbm.canon.com. **Description:** This location is a research and development facility. Operations at this facility focus on the bubble-jet printer development and image processing technology. Overall, Canon Business Machines manufactures bubble-jet printer consumables, copier toner and drums, and operates a product recycling facility. Founded in 1974. **Company slogan:** Think again, think Canon. **Common positions include:** Accountant; Buyer; Chemical Engineer; Computer Programmer; Computer Support Technician; Design Engineer; Electrical/Electronics Engineer; Mechanical Engineer; Network/Systems Administrator; Software Engineer. **Special programs:** Internships. **Office hours:** Monday - Friday, 8:00 a.m. - 5:00 p.m. **Corporate headquarters location:** This location. **Other area locations:** Irvine CA; Santa Clara CA. **Other U.S. locations:** Washington DC; Atlanta GA; Chicago IL; Jamesburg NJ; Dallas TX. **Parent company:** Canon, Inc. (Japan). **Listed on:** New York Stock Exchange. **Stock exchange symbol:** CAJ. **Annual sales/revenues:** More than $100 million.

CHARTERHOUSE SOFTWARE CORPORATION

2801 Townsgate Road, Suite 212, Westlake Village CA 91361. 805/494-5191. **Contact:** Human Resources. **World Wide Web address:** http://www.chsoft.com. **Description:** Manufactures and markets accounting software, sells business forms, and offers related consulting services.

COMPAQ COMPUTER CORPORATION

22 Executive Park, Irvine CA 92614-6790. 949/261-4300. **Contact:** Human Resources. **World Wide Web address:** http://www.compaq.com. **Description:** Compaq Computer Corporation is a manufacturer of electronic computer systems and peripherals, including laptop and desktop personal computers, PC-based client servers, notebook computers, and tower systems. Compaq Computer Corporation sells its products through retail stores, warehouses, resellers, mail-order catalogs, and telemarketers. The company conducts business in more than 90 countries. **NOTE:** Compaq merged with Hewlett Packard in April 2002. Resumes should be sent to: P.O. Box 692000, Houston TX 97269. **Corporate headquarters location:** Houston TX. **Other U.S. locations:** Nationwide. **International locations:** Worldwide. **Listed on:** New York Stock Exchange. **Stock exchange symbol:** CPQ.

COMPUTER ASSOCIATES INTERNATIONAL, INC.
9740 Scranton Road, Suite 200, San Diego CA 92121. 858/452-0170. **Contact:** Personnel. **World Wide Web address:** http://www.ca.com. **Description:** This location develops software. Overall, Computer Associates International is one of the world's leading developers of client/server and distributed computing software. The company develops, markets, and supports enterprise management, database and applications development, business applications, and consumer software products for a broad range of mainframe, midrange, and desktop computers. Computer Associates International serves major business, government, research, and educational organizations. Founded in 1976. **Corporate headquarters location:** Islandia NY. **Other U.S. locations:** Nationwide. **International locations:** Worldwide. **Listed on:** New York Stock Exchange. **Stock exchange symbol:** CA. **Annual sales/revenues:** More than $100 million. **Number of employees nationwide:** 5,000. **Number of employees worldwide:** 11,000.

COMPUTER ASSOCIATES INTERNATIONAL, INC.
8511 Fallbrook Avenue, Suite 200, West Hills CA 91304. 818/593-0300. **Contact:** Human Resources. **World Wide Web address:** http://www.ca.com. **Description:** One of the world's leading developers of client/server and distributed computing software. The company develops, markets, and supports enterprise management, database and applications development, business applications, and consumer software products for a broad range of mainframe, midrange, and desktop computers. Computer Associates International serves major business, government, research, and educational organizations. **Corporate headquarters location:** Islandia NY. **Other U.S. locations:** Nationwide. **International locations:** Worldwide. **Listed on:** New York Stock Exchange. **Stock exchange symbol:** CA. **Number of employees nationwide:** 5,000. **Number of employees worldwide:** 11,000.

COMPUTER HORIZONS CORPORATION
1411 West 190th Street, Suite 470, Gardena CA 90248-4324. 310/771-0770. **Toll-free phone:** 800/711-2421. **Fax:** 310/771-0777. **Contact:** Human Resources. **World Wide Web address:** http://www.computerhorizons.com. **Description:** A full-service technology solutions company offering contract staffing, outsourcing, re-engineering, data migration, downsizing support, and network management. The company has a worldwide network of 43 offices. Founded in 1969. **Corporate headquarters location:** Mountain Lakes NJ. **International**

locations: Canada; England. **Listed on:** NASDAQ. **Stock exchange symbol:** CHRZ.

COMPUTER SCIENCES CORPORATION

2100 East Grand Avenue, El Segundo CA 90245. 310/615-0311. **Contact:** Fred Vollrath, Vice President of Corporate Personnel. **World Wide Web address:** http://www.csc.com. **Description:** This location primarily serves the U.S. government. Overall, Computer Sciences Corporation helps clients in industry and government use information technology to achieve strategic and operational objectives. The company tailors solutions from a broad suite of integrated service and technology offerings including e-business strategies and technologies; management and IT consulting; systems development and integration; application software; and IT and business process outsourcing. **Common positions include:** Business Analyst; Computer Scientist; Economist; Engineer; Geologist/Geophysicist; Mathematician; Operations Research Analyst; Physicist; Statistician. **Corporate headquarters location:** This location. **International locations:** Canada; Germany; Japan; the Netherlands; Saudi Arabia; South Korea; Spain; United Kingdom. **Listed on:** New York Stock Exchange. **Stock exchange symbol:** CSC. **Number of employees nationwide:** 20,000. **Number of employees worldwide:** 68,000.

COMPUTER SCIENCES CORPORATION

4845 Hancock Street, San Diego CA 92110-5164. 619/225-8401. **Contact:** Manager of Human Resources. **World Wide Web address:** http://www.csc.com. **Description:** This location is engaged in research and development for the U.S. Navy. Overall, Computer Sciences Corporation is comprised of four sectors: the Systems Group Division designs, engineers, and integrates computer-based systems and communications systems, providing all of the hardware, software, training, and related elements necessary to operate such a system; the Consulting Division includes consulting and technical services in the development of computer and communication systems to nonfederal organizations; the Industry Services Group provides service to the health care, insurance, and financial services industries, as well as providing large-scale claim processing and other insurance-related services; CSC Health Care markets business systems and services to the managed health care industry, clinics, and physicians; CSC Enterprises provides consumer credit reports and account management services to credit grantors. **Corporate headquarters location:** El Segundo CA. **International locations:** Canada; Germany;

Japan; the Netherlands; Saudi Arabia; South Korea; Spain; United Kingdom. **Listed on:** New York Stock Exchange. **Stock exchange symbol:** CSC. **Number of employees nationwide:** 20,000. **Number of employees worldwide:** 68,000.

CONVERA
1801 Aston Avenue, Suite 290, Carlsbad CA 92008. 760/438-7900. **Fax:** 703/761-1986. **Contact:** Human Resources. **E-mail address:** recruit@convera.com. **World Wide Web address:** http://www.convera.com. **Description:** Designs, develops, markets, and supports computer software products used for the document imaging and multimedia information retrieval marketplaces. The company also offers consulting, training, maintenance, and systems integration services. In addition, the company performs research and development under contract and licenses proprietary software products for use in office, identification, and multimedia information retrieval systems. The company distributes its products through direct sales, distributors, select resellers, and vertical market suppliers. **Corporate headquarters location:** Vienna VA. **Listed on:** NASDAQ. **Stock exchange symbol:** CNVR.

CREATIVE COMPUTER APPLICATIONS, INC.
26115-A Mureau Road, Calabasas CA 91302. 818/880-6700. **Contact:** Human Resources. **E-mail address:** jobs@ccainc.com. **World Wide Web address:** http://www.ccainc.com. **Description:** Designs and manufactures computer-based, clinical information systems and products that automate the acquisition and management of clinical data for the health care industry. The company sells its products and systems to hospitals, clinics, reference laboratories, veterinarians, other health care institutions, and original equipment manufacturers. **Corporate headquarters location:** This location.

D-LINK SYSTEMS, INC.
53 Discovery Drive, Irvine CA 92618. 949/788-0805. **Contact:** Human Resources Department. **E-mail address:** hr@dlink.com. **World Wide Web address:** http://www.dlink.com. **Description:** Manufactures networking, connectivity, and data communications products. The company's product line includes adapters, hubs, switches, routers, and print servers. **Corporate headquarters location:** This location.

DTC COMPUTER SUPPLIES
P.O. Box 2834, Rancho Cucamonga CA 91729-2834. 909/466-7680. **Toll-free phone:** 800/700-7683. **Contact:** Human Resources Department. **World Wide Web address:**

http://www.dtc1.com. **Description:** Distributes computer supplies. DTC also manufactures magnetic computer tape. **Corporate headquarters location:** This location.

DTK COMPUTERS
770 Epperson Drive, City of Industry CA 91748. 626/810-0098. **Contact:** Human Resources. **World Wide Web address:** http://www.dtkcomputer.com. **Description:** A computer wholesaler. **Office hours:** Monday - Friday, 8:30 a.m. - 5:30 p.m.

EDS PLM SOLUTIONS
10824 Hope Street, Cypress CA 90630. 714/952-0311. **Contact:** Recruiter. **E-mail address:** careers@eds.com. **World Wide Web address:** http://www.eds.com. **Description:** Provides integrated hardware, software, and network solutions to *Fortune* 500 companies. EDS PLM Solutions focuses primarily on international corporations in the service, wholesale, distribution, and transportation industries. **Corporate headquarters location:** Plano TX. **Listed on:** New York Stock Exchange. **Stock exchange symbol:** EDS.

ELECTRO RENT CORPORATION
6060 Sepulveda Boulevard, Van Nuys CA 91411-2525. 818/787-2100. **Toll-free phone:** 800/688-1111. **Fax:** 818/786-1602. **Contact:** Human Resources. **World Wide Web address:** http://www.electrorent.com. **Description:** Rents and leases electronic equipment including test and measurement instruments, workstations, personal computers, and data communication products. **Common positions include:** Account Manager; Administrative Assistant; Advertising Clerk; Computer Operator; Customer Service Representative; Electronics Technician; Secretary. **Corporate headquarters location:** This location. **Other U.S. locations:** Nationwide. **Listed on:** NASDAQ. **Stock exchange symbol:** ELRC. **Annual sales/revenues:** More than $100 million. **Number of employees at this location:** 200. **Number of employees nationwide:** 500.

EMULEX CORPORATION
3535 Harbor Boulevard, Costa Mesa CA 92626. 714/662-5600. **Toll-free phone:** 800/EMULEX-1. **Contact:** Sadie Herrera, Director of Human Resources Department. **E-mail address:** hr@emulex.com. **World Wide Web address:** http://www.emulex.com. **Description:** Emulex Corporation specializes in intelligent interface technology for the computer industry. Emulex designs, manufactures, and markets data

storage and network connectivity products, as well as advanced integrated circuits. **Corporate headquarters location:** This location. **Listed on:** NASDAQ. **Stock exchange symbol:** EMLX.

ENCAD, INC.
6059 Cornerstone Court West, San Diego CA 92121. 858/452-0882. **Toll-free phone:** 800/45-ENCAD. **Fax:** 858/457-5831. **Contact:** Department of Human Resources. **E-mail address:** jobs1@encad.com. **World Wide Web address:** http://www.encad.com. **Description:** ENCAD, Inc. designs, develops, manufactures, and markets wide-format, color ink-jet printers and plotters. Typical users are in industries utilizing computer-aided design; architectural, engineering, and construction design; geographic information systems such as surveying and mapping; and graphic arts such as digital photo imaging and editing, sign-making, three-dimensional renderings, and presentation graphics. **Corporate headquarters location:** This location.

EPICOR SOFTWARE CORPORATION
195 Technology Drive, Irvine CA 92618. 949/585-4000. **Fax:** 949/585-4093. **Contact:** Human Resources Department. **E-mail address:** careers@epicor.com. **World Wide Web address:** http://www.epicor.com. **Description:** Develops financial and manufacturing software for use in a client/server environment. Epicor Software focuses exclusively on mid-market companies. Founded in 1984. **Common positions include:** Account Manager; Account Representative; Accountant; Administrative Assistant; Applications Engineer; Attorney; Buyer; Chief Financial Officer; Computer Programmer; Computer Support Technician; Controller; Credit Manager; Customer Service Representative; Database Administrator; Database Manager; Event Planner; Finance Director; Financial Analyst; Human Resources Manager; Market Research Analyst; Marketing Manager; MIS Specialist; Network Engineer; Network/Systems Administrator; Public Relations Specialist; Purchasing Agent/Manager; Sales Executive; Sales Manager; Sales Representative; Software Engineer; SQL Programmer; Systems Analyst; Webmaster. **Office hours:** Monday - Friday, 8:00 a.m. - 5:00 p.m. **Corporate headquarters location:** This location. **Other U.S. locations:** Nationwide. **International locations:** Worldwide. **Listed on:** NASDAQ. **Stock exchange symbol:** EPIC. **Annual sales/revenues:** $51 - $100 million. **Number of employees at this location:** 400. **Number of employees nationwide:** 1,300. **Number of employees worldwide:** 1,700.

EXECUTIVE SOFTWARE INTERNATIONAL

7590 North Glen Oaks Boulevard, Burbank CA 91504. 818/547-2050. **Contact:** Director of Personnel. **World Wide Web address:** http://www.execsoft.com. **Description:** Develops and markets systems software and applications for the Windows NT operating system. **Common positions include:** Applications Engineer; Computer Programmer; Systems Manager; Technical Writer/Editor. **Corporate headquarters location:** This location. **Listed on:** Privately held. **Annual sales/revenues:** $21 - $50 million. **Number of employees at this location:** 100.

FILENET CORPORATION

3565 Harbor Boulevard, Costa Mesa CA 92626. 714/327-3400. **Contact:** Kenneth Ross, Employment Manager. **World Wide Web address:** http://www.filenet.com. **Description:** FileNET develops and markets electronic content management software and e-business solutions. Products and services are used to help corporations and organizations build intranets, create electronic portals to streamline information management, and to create, process, edit, organize, and store all forms of digital content for Internet applications. **Common positions include:** Accountant/Auditor; Computer Programmer; Customer Service Representative; Financial Analyst; Human Resources Manager; Management Analyst/Consultant; Software Developer; Systems Analyst; Teacher/Professor; Technical Writer/Editor. **Special programs:** Internships. **Corporate headquarters location:** This location. **Other U.S. locations:** Nationwide. **Listed on:** NASDAQ. **Stock exchange symbol:** FILE. **Number of employees at this location:** 800. **Number of employees worldwide:** 1,700.

GRC INTERNATIONAL, INC.

5383 Hollister Avenue, Suite 200, Santa Barbara CA 93111. 805/964-7724. **Fax:** 805/964-9834. **Contact:** Carol Mulkern, Technical Recruiter. **World Wide Web address:** http://www.grci.com. **Description:** This location is a research and development facility. Overall, GRC International creates large-scale, decision-support systems and software engineering environments; applies operations research and mathematical modeling to business and management systems; and implements advanced database technology. GRC International also provides studies and analysis capabilities for policy development and planning; modeling and simulation of hardware and software used in real-time testing of sensor, weapon, and battlefield management command, control, and communication systems; and testing and evaluation. GRC

International's services are offered primarily to government and commercial customers. **Common positions include:** Computer Programmer; Database Manager; Design Engineer; Marketing Specialist; Operations/Production Manager; Sales Engineer; Software Engineer; Systems Analyst; Systems Manager; Telecommunications Manager. **Special programs:** Internships. **Corporate headquarters location:** Vienna VA. **Other U.S. locations:** Nationwide. **Parent company:** AT&T Corporation. **Operations at this facility include:** Regional Headquarters. **Listed on:** New York Stock Exchange. **Stock exchange symbol:** T. **Number of employees at this location:** 120. **Number of employees worldwide:** 1,300.

GEAC COMPUTER
15621 Red Hill Avenue, Suite 100, Tustin CA 92780. 714/258-5800. **Contact:** Human Resources. **World Wide Web address:** http://www.geac.com. **Description:** This location is a customer support center. Overall, Geac Computer develops and markets business applications software in the areas of human resources, materials, management, manufacturing, health care, and higher education. Products include the SmartStream series of financial software. **Corporate headquarters location:** This location.

GENERAL AUTOMATION INC.
17731 Mitchell North, Irvine CA 92614. 949/250-4800. **Fax:** 949/752-6772. **Contact:** Human Resources. **World Wide Web address:** http://www.genauto.com. **Description:** Engaged in systems and software integration services. **Corporate headquarters location:** This location.

GOLDEN RAM
8 Whatney, Irvine CA 92618. 949/460-9000. **Toll-free phone:** 800/222-8861. **Contact:** Human Resources Department. **E-mail address:** jobs@goldenram.com. **World Wide Web address:** http://www.goldenram.com. **Description:** Manufactures third-party memory modules for computers to increase RAM. **Corporate headquarters location:** This location.

GRECO SYSTEMS
372 Coogan Way, El Cajon CA 92020. 619/442-0205. **Toll-free phone:** 800/234-7326. **Fax:** 619/447-8982. **Contact:** Human Resources. **E-mail address:** hrweb@grecosystems.com. **World Wide Web address:** http://www.grecosystems.com. **Description:** Manufactures industrial computer software and hardware systems for communication and storage in factory automation facilities. **Common positions include:** Sales

Representative; Software Engineer. **Corporate headquarters location:** This location. **Listed on:** Privately held. **Annual sales/revenues:** $5 - $10 million. **Number of employees at this location:** 60.

HNC SOFTWARE INC.

5935 Cornerstone Court West, San Diego CA 92121-3728. 858/546-8877. **Contact:** Human Resources. **World Wide Web address:** http://www.hnc.com. **Description:** Develops and markets advanced decision software for the financial services, retail, educational publishing, insurance information, Internet commerce, and market research industries. **NOTE:** Resumes should be sent to the Resume Processing Center, P.O. Box 828, Burlington MA 01803. **Office hours:** Monday - Friday, 8:00 a.m. - 5:00 p.m. **Corporate headquarters location:** This location. **Listed on:** NASDAQ. **Stock exchange symbol:** HNCS. **President/CEO:** Robert L. North.

HEWLETT-PACKARD COMPANY

16399 West Bernardo Drive, San Diego CA 92127. 858/655-4100. **Contact:** Human Resources. **World Wide Web address:** http://www.hp.com. **Description:** This location manufactures printers. Overall, Hewlett-Packard is engaged in the design and manufacture of measurement and computation products and systems used in business, industry, engineering, science, health care, and education. Principal products include integrated instrument and computer systems such as hardware and software, peripheral products, and medical electronic equipment and systems. **NOTE:** Hewlett Packard merged with Compaq in April 2002. See the Website for more information. Jobseekers should send resumes to: Employment Response Center, Hewlett-Packard Company, Mail Stop 20-APP, 3000 Hanover Street, Palo Alto CA 94304. **Common positions include:** Computer Programmer; Electrical/Electronics Engineer; Financial Analyst; Marketing Specialist. **Corporate headquarters location:** Palo Alto CA. **Other U.S. locations:** Nationwide. **Listed on:** New York Stock Exchange. **Stock exchange symbol:** HPQ. **Number of employees nationwide:** 93,000.

HEWLETT-PACKARD COMPANY

4995 Murphy Canyon Road, Suite 301, San Diego CA 92123-4366. 858/279-3200. **Contact:** Human Resources. **World Wide Web address:** http://www.hp.com. **Description:** This location is a sales office. Overall, Hewlett-Packard is engaged in the design and manufacture of measurement and computation products and systems used in business, industry, engineering, science, health care, and education. The company's principal products are integrated instrument and computer systems such as hardware and software, peripheral products, and medical electronic equipment and systems. **NOTE:** Hewlett Packard merged with Compaq in April 2002. See the Website for more information. Jobseekers should send resumes to the Employment Response Center, Hewlett-Packard Company, Mail Stop 20-APP, 3000 Hanover Street, Palo Alto CA 94304. **Common positions include:** Computer Programmer; Electrical/Electronics Engineer; Financial Analyst; Marketing Specialist. **Corporate headquarters location:** Palo Alto CA. **Other U.S. locations:** Nationwide. **Listed on:** New York Stock Exchange. **Stock exchange symbol:** HPQ. **Number of employees at this location:** 150. **Number of employees nationwide:** 93,000.

HITACHI KOKI IMAGING SOLUTIONS

1757 Tapo Canyon Road, Suite 209, Simi Valley CA 93063. 805/578-4000. **Fax:** 805/578-4009. **Contact:** Personnel. **World Wide Web address:** http://www.hitachi-hkis.com. **Description:** Develops, manufactures, and markets data handling and output equipment. The company's products include printers and digital communications equipment. **Common positions include:** Electrical/Electronics Engineer; Mechanical Engineer. **Corporate headquarters location:** This location. **Parent company:** Hitachi Ltd. **Operations at this facility include:** Administration; Manufacturing; Research and Development; Sales; Service. **Listed on:** New York Stock Exchange. **Stock exchange symbol:** HIT.

HOSTING.COM

8913 Complex Drive, San Diego CA 92123. 858/637-3600. **Fax:** 858/450-3216. **Contact:** Kelly Conley, Human Resources. **E-mail address:** jobs@hosting.com. **World Wide Web address:** http://www.hosting.com. **Description:** Provides Internet access for businesses, supports World Wide Web home pages, and offers colocation services. Founded in 1995. **NOTE:** Entry-level positions are offered. **Common positions include:** Controller; Human Resources Manager; Internet Services Manager; Marketing Manager; Marketing Specialist; MIS Manager; Sales Executive; Sales Manager; Sales Representative; Systems Manager. **Special programs:** Internships; Co-ops; Summer Jobs. **Corporate headquarters location:** Boston MA. **Parent company:** Allegiance Telecom Hosting Company. **Listed on:** NASDAQ. **Stock exchange symbol:** ALGX.

IMAGE MICRO SYSTEMS, INC.
6301 Chalet Drive, Commerce CA 90040. 562/776-3333. **Fax:** 562/776-3322. **Contact:** Human Resources. **World Wide Web address:** http://www.imagemicro.com. **Description:** A reseller of computer hardware and software. **Corporate headquarters location:** This location.

IMATION CORPORATION
330 South Lewis Road, Camarillo CA 93012-8485. 805/482-1911. **Contact:** Cynthia Batastini, Human Resources. **World Wide Web address:** http://www.imation.com. **Description:** Develops data storage products, medical imaging and photo products, printing and publishing systems, and customer support technologies and document imaging, and markets them under the trademark names Dry View laser imagers, Matchprint and Rainbow color proofing systems, Travan data cartridges, and LS-120 diskette technology. **Corporate headquarters location:** Oakdale MN. **Listed on:** New York Stock Exchange. **Stock exchange symbol:** IMN.

INFONET SERVICES CORPORATION
2160 East Grand Avenue, El Segundo CA 90245. 310/335-1073. **Fax:** 310/335-2679. **Contact:** Ken Montgomery, Human Resources. **E-mail address:** ken_montgomery@infonet.com. **World Wide Web address:** http://www.infonet.com. **Description:** Provides networking services to international corporations. Founded in 1970. **Corporate headquarters location:** This location. **Listed on:** New York Stock Exchange. **Stock exchange symbol:** IN.

INGRAM MICRO
1600 East Saint Andrew Place, Santa Ana CA 92705. 714/566-1000. **Contact:** Human Resources Department. **World Wide Web address:** http://www.ingrammicro.com. **Description:** Distributes microcomputer products including desktop and notebook PCs, servers, CD-Rom drives, printers, and software. **Corporate headquarters location:** This location. **Listed on:** New York Stock Exchange. **Stock exchange symbol:** IM.

INSIGHT ELECTRONICS, INC.
9980 Huennekens Street, San Diego CA 92121. 858/677-3111. **Contact:** Human Resources. **World Wide Web address:** http://www.insight-electronics.com. **Description:** Distributes computers and semiconductors. **Corporate headquarters location:** This location. **Parent company:** Memec.

INTUIT, INC.
6220 Greenwich Drive, San Diego CA 92122. 858/784-4000. **Contact:** Human Resources. **World Wide Web address:** http://www.intuit.com. **Description:** Develops and markets personal finance and small business accounting software and also offers support services. Products include Quicken, which allows users to organize and manage personal finances. **Corporate headquarters location:** Mountain View CA. **Listed on:** NASDAQ. **Stock exchange symbol:** INTU. **Number of employees nationwide:** 500.

KAY COMPUTERS
722 Genevieve Street, Suite N, Solana Beach CA 92075. 858/481-0225. **Contact:** Human Resources. **World Wide Web address:** http://www.kaycomputers.com. **Description:** Manufactures personal computers. **Corporate headquarters location:** This location.

KEANE, INC.
133 Technology Drive, Suite 200, Irvine CA 92618. 949/450-4601. **Toll-free phone:** 800/315-8306. **Fax:** 949/450-4658. **Contact:** Edith Tarter, Human Resources Department. **E-mail address:** careers@keane.com. **World Wide Web address:** http://www.keane.com. **Description:** A software development and consulting firm providing systems and software applications to the transportation, finance, health care, and insurance industries. **Common positions include:** Account Manager; Accountant; Administrative Assistant; Advertising Executive; Chief Financial Officer; Computer Engineer; Computer Support Technician; Controller; Database Administrator; Database Manager; Desktop Publishing Specialist; Event Planner; Financial Analyst; Graphic Artist; Graphic Designer; Help-Desk Technician; Human Resources Manager; Internet Services Manager; Market Research Analyst; Marketing Manager; Marketing Specialist; MIS Specialist; Network Engineer; Network/Systems Administrator; Operations Manager; Project Manager; Public Relations Specialist; Purchasing Agent/Manager; Sales Executive; Sales Manager; Sales Representative; Secretary; Software Engineer; Systems Analyst; Systems Manager; Technical Writer/Editor; Typist/Word Processor; Webmaster. **Office hours:** Monday - Friday, 8:00 a.m. - 5:00 p.m. **Corporate headquarters location:** Boston MA. **Listed on:** American Stock Exchange. **Stock exchange symbol:** KEA.

KINGSTON TECHNOLOGY

17600 Newhope Street, Fountain Valley CA 92708. 714/435-2600. **Toll-free phone:** 877/KINGSTON. **Fax:** 714/427-3555. **Contact:** Department of Human Resources. **E-mail address:** jobs@kingston.com. **World Wide Web address:** http://www.kingston.com. **Description:** A leading independent manufacturer of more than 2,000 memory, processor, and other peripheral products. Founded in 1987. **NOTE:** Entry-level positions are offered. **Common positions include:** Account Manager; Account Representative; Accountant; Administrative Assistant; AS400 Programmer Analyst; Buyer; Chief Financial Officer; Computer Engineer; Computer Operator; Computer Programmer; Computer Support Technician; Controller; Credit Manager; Customer Service Representative; Database Administrator; Database Manager; Electrical/Electronics Engineer; Financial Analyst; Graphic Designer; Human Resources Manager; Internet Services Manager; Manufacturing Engineer; Market Research Analyst; Marketing Manager; Marketing Specialist; Mechanical Engineer; MIS Specialist; Network/Systems Administrator; Operations/Production Manager; Production Manager; Public Relations Specialist; Purchasing Agent/Manager; Quality Assurance Engineer; Quality Control Supervisor; Sales Manager; Sales Representative; Software Engineer; SQL Programmer; Systems Analyst; Systems Manager; Technical Writer/Editor; Webmaster. **Corporate headquarters location:** This location. **International locations:** France; Germany; Ireland; Taiwan; United Kingdom. **Listed on:** Privately held. **Annual sales/revenues:** More than $100 million. **Number of employees worldwide:** 1,200.

KONTRON AMERICA

6260 Sequence Drive, San Diego CA 92121. 858/677-0877. **Contact:** Human Resources. **World Wide Web address:** http://www.kontron.com. **Description:** A manufacturer of ruggedized PC chassis and a reseller of computer hardware. **Corporate headquarters location:** Eching, Germany.

LMS CORPORATION

2205 South Wright Street, Santa Ana CA 92705. 714/549-2688. **Toll-free phone:** 800/240-8721. **Contact:** Human Resources Department. **World Wide Web address:** http://www.lmsservice.com. **Description:** Distributes computer printers, accessories, supplies, and enclosures. **Corporate headquarters location:** This location.

LANTRONIX
15353 Barranca Parkway, Irvine CA 92618. 949/453-3990. **Fax:** 949/453-7165. **Contact:** Linda Duffy, Director of Human Resources. **E-mail address:** webhr@lantronix.com. **World Wide Web address:** http://www.lantronix.com. **Description:** Provides network-enabling technology that allows for configuring and communicating over the Internet and shared networks. **Corporate headquarters location:** This location. **Annual sales/revenues:** $21 - $50 million. **Listed on:** NASDAQ. **Stock exchange symbol:** LTRX.

LEGACY COMMUNICATIONS
3868 Carson Street, Suite 205, Torrance CA 90503. 310/792-0844. **Contact:** Lisa Wiggins, Human Resources. **E-mail address:** lisawiggins@legacycomm.com. **World Wide Web address:** http://www.legacycomm.com. **Description:** Designs, programs, manufactures, markets, and services LAN-to-LAN routers. **Common positions include:** Accountant/Auditor; Administrator; Buyer; Computer Programmer; Credit Manager; Customer Service Representative; Department Manager; Draftsperson; Electrical/Electronics Engineer; Human Resources Manager; Operations/Production Manager; Purchasing Agent/Manager; Quality Control Supervisor. **Corporate headquarters location:** This location.

MAI SYSTEMS CORPORATION
HOTEL INFORMATION SYSTEMS
9601 Jeronimo Road, Irvine CA 92618. 949/598-6000. **Fax:** 949/598-6415. **Contact:** Human Resources Department. **World Wide Web address:** http://www.maisystems.com. **Description:** A worldwide provider of total information systems solutions software for the hospitality industry and mid-size manufacturers and distributors. **Common positions include:** Accountant/Auditor; Administrative Assistant; Applications Engineer; Attorney; Buyer; Chief Financial Officer; Computer Operator; Computer Programmer; Controller; Customer Service Representative; Design Engineer; Finance Director; Financial Analyst; Human Resources Manager; Marketing Manager; Marketing Specialist; MIS Specialist; Paralegal; Project Manager; Public Relations Specialist; Purchasing Agent/Manager; Quality Control Supervisor; Sales Representative; Secretary; Software Engineer; Systems Analyst; Systems Manager; Technical Writer/Editor. **Corporate headquarters location:** This location. **Operations at this facility include:** Administration; Manufacturing; Research and Development; Sales; Service. **Listed on:** American Stock Exchange. **Stock exchange symbol:** NOW. **Number of**

employees at this location: 225. **Number of employees nationwide:** 365. **Number of employees worldwide:** 575.

MSC SOFTWARE CORPORATION

2 MacArthur Place, Santa Ana CA 92707. 323/258-9111. **Contact:** Human Resources Department. **E-mail address:** msc.jobs@mscsoftware.com. **World Wide Web address:** http://www.mscsoftware.com. **Description:** Develops, markets, and supports software for computer-aided engineering. **Corporate headquarters location:** This location. **Listed on:** New York Stock Exchange. **Stock exchange symbol:** MNS.

MTI TECHNOLOGIES CORPORATION

4905 East La Palma Avenue, Anaheim CA 92807. 714/970-0300. **Contact:** Kathy Pate, Assistant Director of Human Resources Department. **E-mail address:** jobs@mti.com. **World Wide Web address:** http://www.mti.com. **Description:** Designs, manufactures, markets, and services high-performance storage solutions for the DEC, IBM, and open UNIX systems computing environments. These storage solutions integrate MTI's proprietary application and embedded software with its advanced servers and industry standard storage peripherals. Products include NetBacker client/server application software, Infinity Automated Tape Library Series, and other systems and related application software. **Corporate headquarters location:** This location.

MANUGISTICS

26707 Agoura Road, Suite 200, Calabasas CA 91302. 818/880-0800. **Contact:** Department of Human Resources. **E-mail address:** jobs@manu.com. **World Wide Web address:** http://www.westdata.com. **Description:** Manugistics develops defense systems software. **Corporate headquarters location:** Rockville MD. **Listed on:** NASDAQ. **Stock exchange symbol:** MANU.

MERISEL, INC.

200 Continental Boulevard, El Segundo CA 90245. 310/615-3080. **Toll-free phone:** 800/201-1322. **Contact:** Personnel. **E-mail address:** hr.elsegundo@merisel.com. **World Wide Web address:** http://www.merisel.com. **Description:** A wholesaler of computer hardware and software products. Merisel distributes the products to computer resellers throughout the United States and Canada. **Common positions include:** Accountant; Claim Representative; Marketing Manager; Sales Representative. **Office hours:** Monday - Friday, 8:30 a.m. - 5:30 p.m. **Corporate headquarters location:** This location.

166/The Los Angeles JobBank

Other U.S. locations: Marlborough MA; Cary NC. **International locations:** Canada. **Listed on:** NASDAQ. **Stock exchange symbol:** MSEL. **Annual sales/revenues:** More than $100 million. **Number of employees at this location:** 800. **Number of employees nationwide:** 1,500. **Number of employees worldwide:** 2,500.

MICRO 2000, INC.
1100 East Broadway, Suite 301, Glendale CA 91205. 818/547-0125. **Toll-free phone:** 800/864-8008. **World Wide Web address:** http://www.micro2000.com. **Description:** Develops and markets computer diagnostic products for troubleshooting. Founded in 1990. **Common positions include:** Customer Service Representative; Sales Executive; Software Engineer; Technical Support Representative. **Corporate headquarters location:** This location. **International locations:** Australia; Germany; Holland; United Kingdom. **Listed on:** Privately held. **Annual sales/revenues:** $5 - $10 million. **Number of employees at this location:** 45.

MICROSOFT CORPORATION
3 Park Plaza, Suite 1800, Irvine CA 92614. 949/263-0200. **Contact:** Human Resources Department. **E-mail address:** jobs@microsoft.com. **World Wide Web address:** http://www.microsoft.com. **Description:** This location is a district sales office. Overall, Microsoft designs, sells, and supports a product line of microcomputer software for business, home, and professional use. Microsoft also produces related books and hardware products. Software products include spreadsheets, desktop publishing, project management, graphics, word processing, and database applications, as well as operating systems and programming languages. **Corporate headquarters location:** Redmond WA. **Listed on:** NASDAQ. **Stock exchange symbol:** MSFT.

MITCHELL INTERNATIONAL
9889 Willow Creek Road, San Diego CA 92131. 858/578-6550. **Toll-free phone:** 800/854-7030. **Fax:** 858/530-4636. **Contact:** Department of Human Resources. **E-mail address:** web.resume@mitchell.com. **World Wide Web address:** http://www.mitchell.com. **Description:** Provides printed information and electronic software products for the automotive industry. **Common positions include:** Accountant/Auditor; Adjuster; Administrative Manager; Automotive Mechanic; Budget Analyst; Computer Programmer; Building Inspector; Construction Contractor; Credit Manager; Customer Service Representative; Economist;

Editor; Financial Analyst; Human Resources Manager; Human Service Worker; Insurance Agent/Broker; Librarian; Public Relations Specialist; Purchasing Agent/Manager; Quality Control Supervisor; Services Sales Representative; Software Engineer; Systems Analyst; Technical Writer/Editor. **Special programs:** Internships. **Corporate headquarters location:** Stamford CT. **Other U.S. locations:** Chicago IL; Detroit MI; McLean VA; Milwaukee WI. **Subsidiaries include:** EH Boeckh (Milwaukee WI); Mitchell-Medical (VA); NAG's (Detroit MI). **Parent company:** Thomson Corporation. **Number of employees at this location:** 500. **Number of employees nationwide:** 730.

MUSITEK
410 Bryant Circle, Suite K, Ojai CA 93023. 805/646-8051. **Toll-free phone:** 800/676-8055. **Contact:** Personnel. **World Wide Web address:** http://www.musitek.com. **Description:** Develops music software including MIDISCAN, which converts printed sheet music into multitrack MIDI files. **Corporate headquarters location:** This location.

NEW HORIZONS WORLDWIDE
1990 South State College Boulevard, Anaheim CA 92806. 714/556-1220. **Fax:** 714/938-6004. **Contact:** Personnel. **E-mail address:** career.corp@newhorizons.com. **World Wide Web address:** http://www.newhorizons.com. **Description:** Offers computer training classes to individuals and businesses. New Horizons Worldwide operates over 240 centers worldwide. Founded in 1982. **Corporate headquarters location:** This location. **Other U.S. locations:** Nationwide. **International locations:** Worldwide. **Listed on:** NASDAQ. **Stock exchange symbol:** NEWH. **Annual sales/revenues:** More than $100 million.

NORTEL NETWORKS
4640 Admiralty Way, 6th Floor, Marina Del Ray CA 90292. 310/827-8000. **Contact:** Human Resources Department. **E-mail address:** work@nortelnetworks.com. **World Wide Web address:** http://www.nortelnetworks.com. **Description:** Designs, produces, and supports multimedia access devices for use in building corporate, public, and Internet networks. The primary focus of the company's services is the consolidation of voice, fax, video, and data and multimedia traffic into a single network link. **Company slogan:** How the world shares ideas. **Common positions include:** Accountant; Administrative Assistant; Customer Service Rep.; Electrical Engineer; Finance Director; Help-Desk Technician; Manufacturing Engineer;

Marketing Specialist; Multimedia Designer. **Office hours:** Monday - Friday, 8:00 a.m. - 5:00 p.m. **Corporate headquarters location:** Ontario, Canada. **Other U.S. locations:** Nationwide. **International locations:** Worldwide. **Parent company:** Nortel. **Listed on:** New York Stock Exchange. **Stock exchange symbol:** NT. **President/CEO:** John Roth. **Information Systems Manager:** Orville Beach. **Annual sales/revenues:** More than $100 million. **Number of employees at this location:** 400. **Number of employees worldwide:** 70,000.

OPTIMAL SYSTEMS SERVICES
2722 South Fairview Street, Santa Ana CA 92704-5947. 714/957-8500. **Toll-free phone:** 800/253-3434. **Fax:** 714/957-8705. **Contact:** Human Resources. **World Wide Web address:** http://www.oss.opmr.com. **Description:** Provides consulting, networking, software support, and maintenance services. **Corporate headquarters location:** This location. **Parent company:** Optimal Robotics Inc.

PCMALL
2555 West 190th Street, Torrance CA 90504. 310/366-6900. **Toll-free phone:** 800/863-3282. **Contact:** Human Resources. **E-mail address:** salesrecruit@pcmall.com **World Wide Web address:** http://www.pcmall.com. **Description:** A leading reseller of computer products to businesses, governmental and educational institutions, and consumers. Founded in 1987. **Corporate headquarters location:** This location. **Listed on:** NASDAQ. **Stock exchange symbol:** MALL. **Annual sales/revenues:** More than $100 million.

PARASOFT CORPORATION
2031 South Myrtle Avenue, Monrovia CA 91016. 626/305-0041. **Fax:** 626/305-3036. **Contact:** Human Resources. **E-mail address:** jobs@parasoft.com. **World Wide Web address:** http://www.parasoft.com. **Description:** Develops software using C and C++. **Corporate headquarters location:** This location.

PHOENIX TECHNOLOGIES LTD.
135 Technology Drive, Irvine CA 92618. 949/790-2000. **Fax:** 949/790-2001. **Contact:** Human Resources. **World Wide Web address:** http://www.phoenix.com. **Description:** This location is a supplier of standards-based system software and semiconductor IP for PCs and information appliances. Overall, Phoenix Technologies designs, develops, and markets systems software and end user software products. The Peripherals Division designs, develops, and supplies printer emulation

software, page distribution languages, and controller hardware designs for the printing industry. The PhoenixPage imaging software architecture enables printer manufacturers to offer products that are compatible with the PostScript language, the PCL printer language, and other imaging standards. Phoenix Technologies' PC Division works with leading vendors and standards committees to ensure that Phoenix products enable manufacturers to develop and deploy next-generation PCs quickly and cost-effectively. The company's Package Products Division is a single-source publisher of MS-DOS, Windows, and other software packages. **NOTE:** Entry-level positions are offered. **Common positions include:** Applications Engineer; Software Engineer. **Special programs:** Internships. **Corporate headquarters location:** San Jose CA. **International locations:** Worldwide. **Listed on:** NASDAQ. **Stock exchange symbol:** PTEC. **Annual sales/revenues:** More than $100 million. **Number of employees at this location:** 140. **Number of employees worldwide:** 800.

PREVIO INC.
12636 High Bluff Drive, Suite 400, San Diego CA 92130. 858/794-4300. **Contact:** Human Resources Department. **E-mail address:** jobs@previo.com. **World Wide Web address:** http://www.previo.com. **Description:** Develops business systems recovery software. **Corporate headquarters location:** This location. **Listed on:** NASDAQ. **Stock exchange symbol:** PRVO.

PRINTRONIX INC.
14600 Myford Road, Irvine CA 92606. 949/863-1900. **Contact:** Julie Holder, Human Resources Department. **E-mail address:** employment@printronix.com. **World Wide Web address:** http://www.printronix.com. **Description:** Designs, manufactures, and markets impact line printers and laser printers for use with minicomputers, microcomputers, and other computer systems. **Common positions include:** Accountant/Auditor; Computer Programmer; Customer Service Representative; Draftsperson; Electrical Engineer; Financial Analyst; Mechanical Engineer; Operations/Production Manager; Quality Control Supervisor; Technical Writer/Editor. **Corporate headquarters location:** This location. **Operations at this facility include:** Administration; Manufacturing; Research and Development; Sales; Service. **Listed on:** NASDAQ. **Stock exchange symbol:** PTNX.

QAD INC.
6450 Via Real, Carpinteria CA 93013. 805/684-6614. **Fax:** 805/566-6091. **Contact:** Human Resources. **World Wide Web address:** http://www.qad.com. **Description:** This location houses administrative offices. Overall, QAD develops software including MFG/PRO, a software package designed to aid in supply and distribution management for large companies. **Corporate headquarters location:** This location. **Listed on:** NASDAQ. **Stock exchange symbol:** QADI.

QLOGIC CORPORATION
26600 Laguna Hills Drive, Aliso Viejo CA 92656. 949/389-6000. **Toll-free phone:** 800/662-4471. **Fax:** 949/389-6009. **Contact:** Human Resources. **E-mail address:** hr@qlogic.com. **World Wide Web address:** http://www.qlogic.com. **Description:** Develops, manufactures, and markets network connectivity components. Founded in 1985. **Corporate headquarters location:** This location. **Listed on:** NASDAQ. **Stock exchange symbol:** QLGC. **Annual sales/revenues:** More than $100 million.

QUALITY SYSTEMS, INC.
17822 East 17th Street, Suite 210, Tustin CA 92780. 714/731-7171. **Toll-free phone:** 800/888-7955. **Fax:** 714/731-9494. **Contact:** Denise Allen, Manager of Human Resources. **E-mail address:** hr@qsii.com. **World Wide Web address:** http://www.qsii.com. **Description:** Develops and markets computerized information processing systems primarily to group dental and medical practices. The systems provide advanced computer-based automation in various aspects of group practice management including the retention of patient information, treatment planning, appointment scheduling, billing, insurance claims processing, electronic insurance claims submission, allocation of income among group professionals, managed care reporting, word processing, and accounting. Founded in 1973. **NOTE:** Entry-level positions are offered. **Common positions include:** Account Manager; Account Representative; Applications Engineer; Internet Services Manager; Project Manager; Sales Representative; Software Engineer; Technical Writer/Editor. **Special programs:** Internships. **Corporate headquarters location:** This location. **Listed on:** NASDAQ. **Stock exchange symbol:** QSII. **Annual sales/revenues:** $11 - $20 million. **Number of employees at this location:** 160.

RAINBOW TECHNOLOGIES
50 Technology Drive West, Irvine CA 92618. 949/450-7300. **Contact:** Human Resources. **E-mail address:** hr@rainbow.com. **World Wide Web address:** http://www.rainbow.com. **Description:** Develops security-related technology such as secure Web servers and Virtual Pirate Network acceleration boards, Internet software distribution solutions, data, voice, and satellite security systems, and smart card readers. **Corporate headquarters location:** This location. **Listed on:** NASDAQ. **Stock exchange symbol:** RBOW.

RAINING DATA CORPORATION
17500 Cartwright Road, Irvine CA 92614. 949/442-4400. **Contact:** Human Resources Department. **World Wide Web address:** http://www.rainingdata.com. **Description:** Develops, markets, and supports software products for the development and deployment of applications for accessing multiuser databases in workgroup and enterprisewide client/server computing environments. The company's products are used by corporations, system integrators, small businesses, and independent consultants to deliver custom information management applications for a wide range of uses including financial management, decision support, executive information, sales and marketing, and multimedia authoring systems. In addition to these products, Raining Data provides consulting, technical support, and training to help plan, analyze, implement, and maintain applications software based on the company's technology. **Corporate headquarters location:** This location. **Listed on:** NASDAQ. **Stock exchange symbol:** RDTA.

SMS TECHNOLOGIES, INC.
9877 Waples Street, San Diego CA 92121. 858/587-6900. **Fax:** 858/450-0218. **Contact:** Deborah Reinhard, Human Resources Manager. **E-mail address:** jobs@smstech.com. **World Wide Web address:** http://www.smstech.com. **Description:** Provides turnkey electronic manufacturing services to the telecommunications, medical electronics, computer, and industrial equipment industries. **NOTE:** Second and third shift positions are offered. **Common positions include:** Account Manager; Accountant; Administrative Assistant; Administrative Manager; Buyer; Computer Operator; Controller; Cost Estimator; Draftsperson; Electrical/Electronics Engineer; Human Resources Manager; Industrial Engineer; Manufacturing Engineer; Mechanical Engineer; MIS Specialist; Operations Manager; Production Manager; Quality Assurance Engineer; Quality Control Supervisor; Sales Representative; Secretary;

Systems Manager; Webmaster. **Special programs:** Training. **Corporate headquarters location:** This location. **Operations at this facility include:** Administration; Divisional Headquarters; Manufacturing; Research and Development. **Listed on:** Privately held. **CEO:** Robert L. Blumberg. **Sales Manager:** Elliot Shev. **Annual sales/revenues:** $21 - $50 million. **Number of employees at this location:** 200.

SCIENCE APPLICATIONS INTERNATIONAL CORPORATION
10260 Campus Point Drive, San Diego CA 92121. 858/826-7624. **Contact:** Department of Human Resources. **E-mail address:** jobs@saic.com. **World Wide Web address:** http://www.saic.com. **Description:** Offers technology development, computer system integration, and technology support services. Founded in 1969. **Common positions include:** Account Manager; Business Analyst; Systems Manager. **Special programs:** Internships. **Corporate headquarters location:** This location. **Subsidiaries include:** AMSEC; Carreker-Antinori; Danet; GSC; Global Integrity Corp.; Hicks & Assoc.; INTESA; Leadership 2000; Network Solutions, Inc.; PAI. **Annual sales/revenues:** More than $100 million. **Number of employees worldwide:** 36,000.

SEAGATE TAPE
1650 Sunflower Avenue, Costa Mesa CA 92626. 714/641-0279. **Contact:** Stephen Shoda, Personnel Manager. **World Wide Web address:** http://www.seagate.com. **Description:** Manufactures disc drives, magnetic discs, read-write heads, and tape drives. Seagate Tape also develops business intelligence software. **Corporate headquarters location:** Scotts Valley CA. **Parent company:** Seagate Technology.

SEEBEYOND
404 East Huntington Drive, Monrovia CA 91016. 626/471-6000. **Fax:** 626/478-3275. **Contact:** Human Resources. **World Wide Web address:** http://www.stc.com. **Description:** Develops data interface engines and database software for enterprisewide solutions. Products include e*Gate, an enterprise integration program. **Corporate headquarters location:** This location. **Listed on:** NASDAQ. **Stock exchange symbol:** SBYN.

SIEMENS MEDICAL SOLUTIONS HEALTH SERVICES
3010 Old Ranch Parkway, Suite 450, Seal Beach CA 90740. 562/596-4554. **Contact:** Recruiter. **World Wide Web address:** http://www.smed.com. **Description:** This location is a technical support office. Overall, Siemens Medical Solutions is

a leading provider of health care information systems and service solutions to hospitals, multi-entity health care corporations, integrated health networks, physician groups, and other health care providers in North America and Europe. Siemens Medical Solutions also provides a full complement of solutions for the newly emerging community health information networks, which includes payers and employers as well as providers. The company offers a comprehensive line of health care information systems including clinical, financial, administrative, ambulatory, and decision support systems, for both the public and private health care sectors. These systems are offered on computers operating at the customer site, at the Siemens Information Services Center, or as part of a distributed network. The company also provides a portfolio of professional services including systems installation, support, and education. In addition, the company provides specialized consulting services for the design and integration of software and networks, facilities management, information systems planning, and systems-related process reengineering. **NOTE:** Please contact the corporate Human Resources Department for employment information: 601/219-6300. **Common positions include:** Computer Programmer; Database Manager; MIS Specialist; Systems Analyst; Systems Manager; Technical Writer/Editor. **Corporate headquarters location:** Malvern PA. **Other U.S. locations:** Nationwide. **Listed on:** New York Stock Exchange. **Stock exchange symbol:** SI. **Annual sales/revenues:** More than $100 million. **Number of employees at this location:** 150. **Number of employees worldwide:** 5,000.

SIMPLE TECHNOLOGY INC.
3001 Daimler Street, Santa Ana CA 92705. 949/260-8372. **Toll-free phone:** 800/367-7330. **Fax:** 949/476-0852. **Contact:** Human Resources. **E-mail address:** jobs@simpletech.com. **World Wide Web address:** http://www.simpletech.com. **Description:** Designs and manufactures computer memory products, portable storage devices, and PC cards. Founded in 1990. **NOTE:** Second and third shifts are offered. **Common positions include:** Accountant; Applications Engineer; Manufacturing Engineer; Process Engineer; Purchasing Agent/Manager; Sales Engineer; Sales Manager; Sales Representative; Software Engineer; Technical Writer/Editor; Test Engineer. **Corporate headquarters location:** This location. **International locations:** Canada; Scotland. **Listed on:** NASDAQ. **Stock exchange symbol:** STEC. **Annual sales/revenues:** More than $100 million. **Number of employees at this location:** 300. **Number of employees nationwide:** 350.

SMITH MICRO SOFTWARE, INC.
51 Columbia Street, Suite 200, Aliso Viejo CA 92656. 949/362-5800. **Contact:** Human Resources Department. **E-mail address:** jobs@smithmicro.com. **World Wide Web address:** http://www.smithmicro.com. **Description:** A computer consulting firm. **Corporate headquarters location:** This location. **Other U.S. locations:** Boulder CO. **Listed on:** NASDAQ. **Stock exchange symbol:** SMSI.

SOLID OAK SOFTWARE, INC.
P.O. Box 6826, Santa Barbara CA 93160. 805/967-9853. **Fax:** 805/967-1614. **Contact:** Human Resources Department. **World Wide Web address:** http://www.solidoak.com. **Description:** Develops access-control software. **Corporate headquarters location:** This location.

SPESCOM SOFTWARE
9339 Carroll Park Drive, San Diego CA 92121. 858/625-3000. **Fax:** 858/546-7671. **Contact:** Sylvia Govender, Human Resources Department Manager. **E-mail address:** sgovender@spescom.com. **World Wide Web address:** http://www.spescom.com. **Description:** Designs, develops, integrates, and markets electronic document management software for industrial, utility, commercial, and government applications. **Corporate headquarters location:** South Africa. **International locations:** England. **Number of employees at this location:** 85.

SUNGARD FINANCIAL SYSTEMS INC.
23975 Park Sorrento, 4th Floor, Calabasas CA 91302. 818/884-5515. **Contact:** Department of Human Resources. **E-mail address:** jobs@sungard.com. **World Wide Web address:** http://www.sungard.com. **Description:** Develops and sells investment portfolio software for financial institutions. **Parent company:** SunGard Data Systems provides specialized computer services, mainly proprietary investment support systems for the financial services industry and disaster recovery services. The company's disaster recovery services include alternate-site backup, testing, and recovery services for IBM, DEC, Prime, Stratus, Tandem, and Unisys computer installations. The company's computer service unit provides remote-access IBM computer processing, direct marketing, and automated mailing services. **Listed on:** New York Stock Exchange. **Stock exchange symbol:** SDS.

3COM CORPORATION

575 Anton Boulevard, Suite 300, Costa Mesa CA 92626. 714/432-6588. **Contact:** Professional Staffing. **World Wide Web address:** http://www.3com.com. **Description:** 3Com is a *Fortune* 500 company delivering global data networking solutions to organizations around the world. 3Com designs, manufactures, markets, and supports a broad range of ISO 9000-compliant global data networking solutions including routers, hubs, remote access servers, switches, and adapters for Ethernet, Token Ring, and high-speed networks. These products enable computers to communicate at high speeds and share resources including printers, disk drives, modems, and minicomputers. **Common positions include:** Accountant/Auditor; Administrator; Buyer; Customer Service Representative; Electrical/Electronics Engineer; Financial Analyst; Human Resources Manager; Marketing Specialist; Operations/Production Manager; Sales Representative; Software Engineer; Systems Analyst. **Special programs:** Internships. **Corporate headquarters location:** Santa Clara CA. **Other U.S. locations:** North Billerica MA. **Operations at this facility include:** Administration; Manufacturing; Research and Development; Sales; Service. **Listed on:** NASDAQ. **Stock exchange symbol:** COMS. **Annual sales/revenues:** More than $100 million. **Number of employees nationwide:** 5,000.

TITAN SYSTEMS

10636 Scripps Summit Court, Suite 101, San Diego CA 92131. 858/457-2111. **Contact:** Personnel. **World Wide Web address:** http://www.titansystemscorp.com. **Description:** Develops real-time video and image processing boards targeting medical, machine vision, security, and surveillance applications. Founded in 1988. **NOTE:** Entry-level positions are offered. **Common positions include:** Computer Engineer; Computer Programmer; Computer Scientist; Electrical/Electronics Engineer. **Corporate headquarters location:** 3033 Science Park Road, San Diego CA 92121. **Parent company:** The Titan Corporation. **Listed on:** New York Stock Exchange. **Stock exchange symbol:** TTN. **Annual sales/revenues:** $21 - $50 million. **Number of employees at this location:** 200. **Number of employees nationwide:** 330.

TOSHIBA AMERICA INFORMATION SYSTEMS INC.

9740 Irvine Boulevard, Irvine CA 92718. 949/583-3000. **Contact:** Human Resources Department. **E-mail address:** ccrecruiter@tais.toshiba.com. **World Wide Web address:** http://www.toshiba.com. **Description:** Develops, markets, and supports computers, printers, fax machines, security imaging systems, industrial video products, voice processing systems, and medical and PC cameras. **Corporate headquarters location:** New York NY. **Parent company:** Toshiba America Inc.

UNISYS CORPORATION

10850 Via Frontera, San Diego CA 92127. 858/451-3000. **Contact:** Human Resources Manager. **World Wide Web address:** http://www.unisys.com. **Description:** This location is a manufacturing facility. Overall, Unisys Corporation provides information services, technology, and software. Unisys specializes in developing critical business solutions based on open information networks. The company's Enabling Software Team creates a variety of software projects that facilitate the building of user applications and the management of distributed systems. The company's Platforms Group is responsible for UNIX Operating Systems running across a wide range of multiple processor server platforms including all peripheral and communication drivers. The Unisys Commercial Parallel Processing Team develops microkernel-based operating systems, I/O device drivers, ATM hardware, diagnostics, and system architectures. The System Management Group is in charge of the overall management of development programs for UNIX desktop and entry-server products. **Corporate headquarters location:** Blue Bell PA. **Other U.S. locations:** Nationwide. **Listed on:** New York Stock Exchange. **Stock exchange symbol:** UIS. **Number of employees worldwide:** 49,000.

UNISYS CORPORATION

2049 Century Park East, Suite 310, Century City CA 90067. 310/208-1511. **Contact:** Human Resources Department. **World Wide Web address:** http://www.unisys.com. **Description:** Provides information services, technology, and software. Unisys Corporation specializes in developing critical business solutions based on open information networks. The company's Enabling Software Team creates a variety of software projects that facilitate the building of user applications and the management of distributed systems. The company's Platforms Group is responsible for UNIX Operating Systems running across a wide range of multiple processor server platforms including all peripheral and communication drivers. The Unisys Commercial Parallel Processing Team develops microkernel-based operating systems, I/O device drivers, ATM hardware, diagnostics, and system architectures. The System Management Group is in charge of the overall management of development programs for UNIX desktop and entry-server products. **Corporate headquarters location:** Blue Bell PA. **Other U.S. locations:** Nationwide. **Listed on:** New York Stock Exchange. **Stock exchange symbol:** UIS. **Number of employees worldwide:** 49,000.

UNISYS CORPORATION
25725 Jeronimo Road, Mission Viejo CA 92691. 949/380-5000. **Contact:** Human Resources. **World Wide Web address:** http://www.unisys.com. **Description:** This location is an engineering office. Overall, Unisys Corporation provides information services, technology, and software. Unisys specializes in developing critical business solutions based on open information networks. The company's Enabling Software Team creates a variety of software projects that facilitate the building of user applications and the management of distributed systems. The company's Platforms Group is responsible for UNIX Operating Systems running across a wide range of multiple processor server platforms including all peripheral and communication drivers. The Unisys Commercial Parallel Processing Team develops microkernel-based operating systems, I/O device drivers, ATM hardware, diagnostics, and system architectures. The System Management Group is in charge of the overall management of development programs for UNIX desktop and entry-server products. **Corporate headquarters location:** Blue Bell PA. **Other U.S. locations:** Nationwide. **Listed on:** New York Stock Exchange. **Stock exchange symbol:** UIS. **Number of employees worldwide:** 49,000.

VIEWSONIC CORPORATION
381 Brea Canyon Road, Walnut CA 91789. 909/468-1252. **Fax:** 909/468-1252. **Contact:** Human Resources. **World Wide Web address:** http://www.viewsonic.com. **Description:** Manufactures computer monitors, flat-panel displays, and projectors for the business, education, entertainment, and professional markets. **Corporate headquarters location:** This location. **Office hours:** Monday - Friday, 7:00 a.m. - 6:00 p.m. **CEO:** James Chu.

VIVENDI UNIVERSAL GAMES
6080 Center Drive, 10th Floor, Los Angeles CA 90045. 310/793-0600. **Contact:** Corporate Recruiter. **World Wide Web address:** http://www.vivendiuniversal.com. **Description:** A publisher and distributor of multimedia educational and entertainment software for both the home and school markets. **Corporate headquarters location:** This location. **Listed on:** New York Stock Exchange. **Stock exchange symbol:** VE.

WONDERWARE CORPORATION

26561 Rancho Parkway South, Lake Forest CA 92630. 949/727-3200. **Contact:** Human Resources. **E-mail address:** employment@wonderware.com. **World Wide Web address:** http://www.wonderware.com. **Description:** A developer of industrial applications software. **Corporate headquarters location:** This location.

XIRCOM, INC.

2300 Corporate Center Drive, Thousand Oaks CA 91320. 805/376-9300. **Contact:** Human Resources. **World Wide Web address:** http://www.xircom.com. **Description:** Develops modems and networking adaptors. Founded in 1988. **Parent company:** Intel. **Listed on:** NASDAQ. **Stock exchange symbol:** INTC. **President/CEO:** Dirk Gates.

ZYXEL COMMUNICATIONS INC.

1650 East Miraloma Avenue, Placentia CA 92870-6622. 714/632-0882. **Contact:** Human Resources. **World Wide Web address:** http://www.zyxel.com. **Description:** ZyXEL is a manufacturer of computer modems, routers, and ISDN terminal adapters. **Corporate headquarters location:** Taiwan.

EDUCATIONAL SERVICES

You can expect to find the following types of facilities in this chapter:
*Business/Secretarial/Data Processing Schools •
Colleges/Universities/Professional Schools • Community
Colleges/Technical Schools/Vocational Schools • Elementary
and Secondary Schools • Preschool and Child Daycare
Services*

ALLIANT INTERNATIONAL UNIVERSITY
1000 South Fremont Avenue, Alhambra CA 91803. 415/346-4500. **Contact:** Human Resources Department. **E-mail address:** jobs@alliant.edu. **World Wide Web address:** http://www.alliant.edu. **Description:** Offers undergraduate and graduate degree programs in liberal arts, education, business, and behavioral and social sciences. **Common positions include:** Accountant/Auditor; Administrative Manager; Administrative Worker/Clerk; Admissions Officer; Computer Programmer; Contract/Grant Administrator; Department Manager; Financial Aid Officer; Human Resources Manager; Marketing Specialist; Public Relations Specialist; Systems Analyst. **Corporate headquarters location:** This location. **Other area locations:** Fresno CA; Irvine CA; Los Angeles CA; Sacramento CA; San Diego CA; San Francisco CA. **International locations:** Nairobi, Kenya; Mexico City, Mexico. **Number of employees at this location:** 30. **Number of employees nationwide:** 1,100.

CALIFORNIA POLYTECHNIC STATE UNIVERSITY
One Grand Avenue, Administration Building, Room 110, San Luis Obispo CA 93407. 805/756-2236. **Fax:** 805/756-5483. **Recorded jobline:** 805/756-1533. **Contact:** Human Resources. **E-mail address:** hree@calpoly.edu (for inquiries only). **World Wide Web address:** http://www.calpoly.edu. **Description:** A university specializing in the field of engineering.

CALIFORNIA STATE UNIVERSITY, FULLERTON
P.O. Box 34080, Fullerton CA 92834-9480. 714/278-2011. **Physical address:** 800 North State College Boulevard, Fullerton CA 92831-3599. **Fax:** 714/278-2425. **Recorded jobline:** 714/278-3385. **Contact:** Employment Coordinator. **E-mail address:** csuf-hr@fullerton.edu. **World Wide Web address:** http://www.fullerton.edu. **Description:** A four-year state university with an enrollment of over 25,000 students. **NOTE:**

Send completed application to: 2600 East Nutwood Avenue, Suite 700, Fullerton CA 92834-6806 by 5:00 PM on the final filing date for that position. **Common positions include:** Accountant/Auditor; Buyer; Clerical Supervisor; Clinical Lab Technician; Computer Programmer; Counselor; Draftsperson; Editor; Education Administrator; Electrician; Human Resources Manager; Librarian; Pharmacist; Physical Therapist; Physician; Public Relations Specialist; Purchasing Agent/Manager; Registered Nurse; Sociologist; Speech-Language Pathologist; Systems Analyst; Teacher/Professor. **Parent company:** California State University System. **Operations at this facility include:** Administration. **Number of employees at this location:** 2,100.

CALIFORNIA TEACHERS ASSOCIATION
P.O. Box 2153, Santa Fe Springs CA 90670-0018. 562/942-7979. **Physical address:** 11745 East Telegraph Road, Santa Fe Springs CA 90670. **Contact:** Human Resources Department. **E-mail address:** employment@cta.org. **World Wide Web address:** http://www.cta.org. **Description:** An affiliate of the National Education Association, California Teachers Association represents over 175,000 public school teachers throughout the state of California. **Corporate headquarters location:** Burlingame CA. **Other area locations:** Citrus Heights CA; Orange CA.

COLLEGE OF THE DESERT
43-500 Monterey Avenue, Palm Desert CA 92260-2412. 760/346-8041. **Contact:** Human Resources. **E-mail address:** humanresources@dccd.cc.ca.us. **World Wide Web address:** http://www.desert.cc.ca.us. **Description:** A community college offering degrees in over 70 majors.

EAST LOS ANGELES COLLEGE
1301 Cesar Chavez Avenue, Monterey Park CA 91754. 323/265-8650. **Contact:** Human Resources Department. **World Wide Web address:** http://www.elac.cc.ca.us. **Description:** A two-year, community college. **Common positions include:** Accountant/Auditor; Electrician; Financial Analyst; Human Service Worker; Librarian; Management Trainee; Mathematician; Teacher/Professor. **Corporate headquarters location:** Los Angeles CA. **Operations at this facility include:** Divisional Headquarters. **Number of employees at this location:** 600.

GLENDALE COMMUNITY COLLEGE
1500 North Verdugo Road, Glendale CA 91208. 818/240-1000. **Contact:** Human Resources. **World Wide Web address:** http://www.glendale.cc.ca.us. **Description:** A two-year community college with an enrollment of over 20,000 students.

THE LOS ANGELES COMMUNITY COLLEGES DISTRICT OFFICE
770 Wilshire Boulevard, Los Angeles CA 90017. 213/891-2000. **Fax:** 213/891-2411. **Contact:** Human Resources. **E-mail address:** jobs@laccd.cc.ca.us. **World Wide Web address:** http://www.laccd.edu. **Description:** Encompasses nine community colleges.

LOYOLA MARYMOUNT UNIVERSITY
One LMU Drive, Los Angeles CA 90045. 310/338-2700. **Contact:** Human Resources. **World Wide Web address:** http://www.lmu.edu. **Description:** A private, four-year college offering certificates, bachelor's degrees, and master's degrees including a Master's in Business Administration. Approximately 3,800 undergraduate and 1,000 graduate students attend Loyola Marymount University.

POMONA COLLEGE
550 North College Avenue, Claremont CA 91711-6318. 909/621-8175. **Contact:** Anne Johnson, Personnel. **E-mail address:** anne.johnson@pomona.edu. **World Wide Web address:** http://www.pomona.edu. **Description:** A private, four-year, liberal arts college.

RANCHO SANTIAGO COMMUNITY COLLEGE DISTRICT
2323 North Broadway, 4th Floor, Santa Ana CA 92706. 714/480-7484. **Recorded jobline:** 714/480-7499. **Contact:** Elouise Marasigan, Human Resources Coordinator. **World Wide Web address:** http://www.rancho.cc.ca.us. **Description:** A college district comprised of Santa Ana College and Santiago Canyon College. Located in central Orange County, the community college district's service area includes Santa Ana, Orange, Villa Park, and portions of Garden Grove and Anaheim Hills. **NOTE:** Entry-level positions and second and third shifts are offered. **Common positions include:** Accountant; Computer Operator; Computer Programmer; Counselor; Database Manager; Education Administrator; ESL Teacher; Librarian; Secretary; Systems Analyst; Teacher. **Office hours:** Monday - Friday, 8:00 a.m. - 5:00 p.m. **Corporate**

headquarters location: This location. **Number of employees at this location:** 675.

SAN DIEGO COMMUNITY COLLEGE DISTRICT
3375 Camino Del Rio South, Suite 330, San Diego CA 92108. 619/584-6579. **Fax:** 619/388-6897. **Contact:** Beverly Dean, Employment Manager. **World Wide Web address:** http://www.sdccd.cc.ca.us. **Description:** A community college district comprised of San Diego City College, San Diego Mesa College, and San Diego Miramar College. **Common positions include:** Accountant/Auditor; Budget Analyst; Buyer; Clerical Supervisor; Clinical Lab Technician; Construction and Building Inspector; Financial Analyst; Human Resources Manager; Librarian; Registered Nurse; Teacher Aide; Veterinarian. **Operations at this facility include:** Administration. **Number of employees at this location:** 5,000.

SAN DIEGO STATE UNIVERSITY
5500 Campanile Drive, Mail Code 1625, San Diego CA 92182. 619/594-5200. **Contact:** Sue Blair, Director of Personnel. **E-mail address:** employ@mail.sdsu.edu. **World Wide Web address:** http://www.sdsu.edu. **Description:** An undergraduate and graduate state university.

UNIVERSITY OF CALIFORNIA, IRVINE
Berkeley Place, Suite 2500, Irvine CA 92697-4600. 949/824-5205. **Contact:** Department of Human Resources. **World Wide Web address:** http://www.uci.edu. **Description:** A research university that is part of the University of California system. University of California, Irvine offers bachelor's, master's, and doctoral degrees. **NOTE:** Part-time positions are offered. **Common positions include:** Accountant; Administrative Assistant; Administrative Manager; Architect; AS400 Programmer Analyst; Assistant Manager; Auditor; Biochemist; Biological Scientist; Budget Analyst; Certified Occupational Therapy Assistant; Civil Engineer; Claim Representative; Clinical Lab Technician; Computer Operator; Computer Programmer; Computer Support Technician; Computer Technician; Construction Contractor; Counselor; Database Administrator; Database Manager; Desktop Publishing Specialist; Dietician/Nutritionist; Editor; EEG Technologist; EKG Technician; Electrician; Finance Director; Financial Analyst; Industrial Engineer; Internet Services Manager; Librarian; Medical Assistant; Medical Records Technician; MIS Specialist; Network/Systems Administrator; Nurse Practitioner; Occupational Therapist; Pharmacist; Physical Therapist; Physical Therapy Assistant; Physician; Preschool Worker;

Project Manager; Public Relations Specialist; Purchasing Agent/Manager; Radiological Technologist; Registered Nurse; Respiratory Therapist; Social Worker; Speech-Language Pathologist; SQL Programmer; Systems Analyst; Systems Manager; Technical Writer/Editor; Telecommunications Manager; Webmaster. **Special programs:** Summer Jobs. **Operations at this facility include:** Administration; Research and Development; Service. **Number of employees at this location:** 5,000.

UNIVERSITY OF CALIFORNIA, LOS ANGELES
10920 Wilshire Boulevard, Suite 205, Los Angeles CA 90024. 310/794-0890. **Fax:** 310/794-0895. **Recorded jobline:** 310/825-9151. **Contact:** Virginia Oaxaca, Staff Employment Division. **E-mail address:** jobs@ucla.edu. **World Wide Web address:** http://www.chr.ucla.edu. **Description:** A campus of the state university system offering undergraduate and graduate degree programs. **NOTE:** Part-time positions are offered. **Company slogan:** UCLA - The University of Big Ideas. **Common positions include:** Account Manager; Accountant; Administrative Assistant; Administrative Manager; Applications Engineer; Architect; AS400 Programmer Analyst; Auditor; Biochemist; Budget Analyst; Buyer; Chemist; Chief Financial Officer; Clerical Supervisor; Clinical Lab Technician; Computer Engineer; Computer Programmer; Computer Support Technician; Computer Technician; Construction Contractor; Controller; Database Administrator; Database Manager; Design Engineer; Desktop Publishing Specialist; Editor; EEG Technologist; EKG Technician; Electrician; Emergency Medical Technician; Environmental Engineer; Financial Analyst; Fund Manager; Graphic Artist; Home Health Aide; Internet Services Manager; Librarian; Licensed Practical Nurse; Market Research Analyst; Medical Assistant; MIS Specialist; Multimedia Designer; Network/Systems Administrator; Nurse Practitioner; Paralegal; Pharmacist; Physical Therapist; Quality Assurance Engineer; Registered Nurse; Secretary; Social Worker; Software Engineer; SQL Programmer; Statistician; Systems Analyst; Systems Manager; Technical Writer/Editor; Underwriter/Assistant Underwriter; Webmaster. **Special programs:** Internships. **Corporate headquarters location:** This location. **Number of employees at this location:** 18,000.

UNIVERSITY OF CALIFORNIA, RIVERSIDE
1160 University Avenue, Suite C, Riverside CA 92521. 909/787-3127. **Contact:** Sheila Morris, Director of Academic Personnel. **E-mail address:** smorris@admin.ucr.edu. **World Wide Web address:** http://www.ucr.edu. **Description:** A

campus of the state university system. **Common positions include:** Administrator; Computer Programmer; Customer Service Representative; Department Manager; General Manager; Researcher. **Special programs:** Internships. **Operations at this facility include:** Research and Development; Service.

UNIVERSITY OF CALIFORNIA, SAN DIEGO
9500 Gilman Drive, Mail Code 0922, La Jolla CA 92093-0922. 858/534-2230. **Contact:** Human Resources. **World Wide Web address:** http://www.ucsd.edu. **Description:** A campus of the state university system offering undergraduate and graduate programs.

UNIVERSITY OF CALIFORNIA, SANTA BARBARA
Human Resources/Employment, Room 3101 SAASB, Santa Barbara CA 93106-3160. 805/893-3166. **Fax:** 805/893-8269. **Contact:** Employment Manager. **E-mail address:** hr.webcontact@hr.ucsb.edu. **World Wide Web address:** http://www.ucsb.edu. **Description:** A campus of the state university system offering undergraduate and graduate degree programs. **NOTE:** The above email address may be used to request an employment application only. This institution does not accepted resumes submitted through e-mail.

UNIVERSITY OF SOUTHERN CALIFORNIA
3535 South Figueroa Street, Los Angeles CA 90089-1260. 213/740-7252. **Contact:** Employment Manager. **World Wide Web address:** http://www.usc.edu/jobs. **Description:** A private university offering bachelor's, master's, doctoral, and professional degrees to approximately 28,000 students. **NOTE:** UCSC accepts only resumes submitted through electronic mail. **Common positions include:** Accountant/Auditor; Administrative Worker/Clerk; Administrator; Attorney; Buyer; Civil Engineer; Computer Programmer; Electrical/Electronics Engineer; Financial Analyst; Human Resources Manager; Mechanical Engineer; Project Planner; Purchasing Agent/Manager; Secretary; Student Services Specialist; Technical Writer/Editor. **Corporate headquarters location:** This location. **Operations at this facility include:** Administration; Research and Development; Service.

ELECTRONIC/INDUSTRIAL ELECTRICAL EQUIPMENT

You can expect to find the following types of companies in this chapter:
Electronic Machines and Systems • Semiconductor Manufacturers

ADVANCED PHOTONIX, INC.
1240 Avenida Acaso, Camarillo CA 93012. 805/987-0146. **Fax:** 805/484-9935. **Contact:** Human Resources Manager. **E-mail address:** hr@adavancedphotonix.com. **World Wide Web address:** http://www.advancedphotonix.com. **Description:** Advanced Photonix, Inc., with its subsidiary, Silicon Detector Corporation, develops, markets, and manufactures proprietary, advanced, solid-state silicon photodetection devices that utilize Avalanche Photodetection (APD) technology. These devices are designed to detect and amplify signals from light and radiant energy sources and convert them into electrical impulses or signals. Products are used for measurement, control, monitoring, and other functions in industrial, medical, military, scientific, and other commercial applications. Such applications include medical diagnostic imaging, airport security detection, fiber-optic communications, and nuclear radiation monitoring and detection systems. **Corporate headquarters location:** This location. **Listed on:** American Stock Exchange. **Stock exchange symbol:** API. **Number of employees at this location:** 95.

AMISTAR CORPORATION
237 Via Vera Cruz, San Marcos CA 92069. 760/471-1700. **Fax:** 760/761-9065. **Contact:** Human Resources. **World Wide Web address:** http://www.amistar.com. **Description:** Amistar designs, develops, manufactures, markets, and services a broad variety of automatic and semi-automatic equipment for assembling electronic components to be placed in printed circuit boards. The company is also a contract assembler of printed circuit boards. **Corporate headquarters location:** This location. **Number of employees at this location:** 170. **Listed on:** NASDAQ. **Stock exchange symbol:** AMTA.

ASTEC AMERICA
5810 Van Allen Way, Carlsbad CA 92008. 760/757-1880. **Toll-free phone:** 800/41-ASTEC. **Fax:** 760/930-0698. **Contact:** Ms. Rita Soza, Vice President of Human Resources. **E-mail address:** hr@astec.com. **World Wide Web address:**

http://www.astecpoer.com. **Description:** Manufactures switch mode power supplies. **Common positions include:** Manufacturer's/Wholesaler's Sales Rep. **Parent company:** Emerson Electric. **International locations:** France; Germany; Hong Kong; Italy; Japan; The Netherlands, United Kingdom.

AVNET, INC.
9800 La Cienga, Inglewood CA 90301. 310/665-2600. **Contact:** Human Resources Department. **E-mail address:** www-human-resources@avnet.com. **World Wide Web address:** http://www.avnet.com. **Description:** Distributes electronic components and computer products for industrial and military customers. The company also produces and distributes other electronic, electrical, and video communications products. **Corporate headquarters location:** Phoenix AZ. **U.S. locations:** Nationwide. **International locations:** Worldwide. **Listed on:** New York Stock Exchange. **Stock exchange symbol:** AVT.

BAE SYSTEMS
600 East Bonita Avenue, Pomona CA 91767. 909/624-8021. **Contact:** Personnel. **E-mail address:** careers@baesystems.com. **World Wide Web address:** http://www.baesystems.com. **Description:** Manufactures microwave frequency generation and control devices, microwave integrated assemblies, and specialized semiconductors. **NOTE:** Formerly was known as Sanders, a subsidiary of Lockheed Martin.

BEI TECHNOLOGIES
13100 Telfair Avenue, Sylmar CA 91342. 818/362-7151. **Contact:** Human Resources Department. **World Wide Web address:** http://www.bei-tech.com. **Description:** Manufactures encoders that provide shaft angle positions that interface with digital computer circuitry or computers in military, industrial, and commercial systems. **Other area locations:** Concord CA; Goleta CA; San Marcos CA; San Francisco CA; Tustin CA. **Other U.S. locations:** Maumelle AR. **Listed on:** NASDAQ. **Stock exchange symbol:** BEIQ.

BABCOCK, INC.
14930 East Alondra Boulevard, La Mirada CA 90638-5752. 714/994-6500. **Fax:** 714/994-0967. **Contact:** Personnel. **E-mail address:** personnel@babcockinc.com. **World Wide Web address:** http://www.babcockinc.com. **Description:** Designs and manufactures electronic components including switch mode power supplies for satellites and military and aerospace applications, gas plasma and vacuum fluorescent displays, and

electromagnetic relays for high-reliability aerospace applications. **Common positions include:** Accountant; Administrative Assistant; Chemist; Chief Financial Officer; Computer Programmer; Computer Support Technician; Controller; Customer Service Representative; Database Administrator; General Manager; Human Resources Manager; Marketing Manager; Production Manager; Purchasing Agent/Manager; Quality Control Supervisor; Sales Manager; Secretary. **Corporate headquarters location:** This location. **Parent company:** Electro-Module. **Listed on:** Privately held. **Annual sales/revenues:** $21 - $50 million. **Number of employees at this location:** 250.

BOURNS, INC.
1200 Columbia Avenue, Riverside CA 92507. 909/781-5690. **Toll-free phone:** 877/426-8767. **Contact:** Charles McBeth, Human Resources Department. **E-mail address:** bournshr.riv@bourns.com. **World Wide Web address:** http://www.bourns.com. **Description:** A manufacturer of electronic components and high-technology equipment. Products include semiconductor devices, aerial reconnaissance cameras, and potentiometers. **Corporate headquarters location:** This location. **Other U.S. locations:** Barrington IL; Logan UT. **International locations:** China; Costa Rica; Ireland; Japan; Mexico; Switzerland; Taiwan; United Kingdom.

CALIFORNIA AMPLIFIER INC.
460 Calle San Pablo, Camarillo CA 93012. 805/987-9000. **Fax:** 805/987-2655. **E-mail address:** resume@calamp.com. **Contact:** Human Resources Department. **World Wide Web address:** http://www.calamp.com. **Description:** California Amplifier Inc. designs, develops, manufactures, and markets microwave and radio frequency components and integrated subsystems. Products include amplifiers, oscillators, phase and filters for use in electronic warfare, radar, communication, navigation; and ground support systems for the military and defense industries. **Corporate headquarters location:** This location. **Number of employees at this location:** 335. **Listed on:** NASDAQ. **Stock exchange symbol:** CAMP.

COHU, INC.
3912 Calle Fortunada, San Diego CA 92123-1827. 858/277-6700. **Contact:** Human Resources Department. **E-mail address:** hr@cohu.com (no attachments, please). **World Wide Web address:** http://www.cohu-cameras.com. **Description:** Supplies television camera equipment for use in such fields as area surveillance, teleconferencing, and industrial process control.

Corporate headquarters location: This location. **Listed on:** NASDAQ. **Stock exchange symbol:** COHU.

CONEXANT SYSTEMS INC.
4311 Jamboree Road, Newport Beach CA 92660-3095. 949/483-4600. **Fax:** 949/483-4078. **Contact:** Personnel. **World Wide Web address:** http://www.conexant.com. **Description:** This location manufactures modem chips and semiconductors. Overall, Conexant provides products for the printing, military, automotive, and aerospace industries through its electronics, automotive, and graphics divisions. Products include military and commercial communication equipment, guidance systems, electronics, components for automobiles, and printing presses. **Corporate headquarters location:** This location. **Other U.S. locations:** Austin TX. **Listed on:** NASDAQ. **Stock exchange symbol:** CNXT.

CONEXANT SYSTEMS INC.
9868 Scranton Road, San Diego CA 92121. 858/713-3200. **Contact:** Human Resources Department. **World Wide Web address:** http://www.conexant.com. **Description:** This location manufactures modem chips and semiconductors. Overall, Conexant provides products for the printing, military, automotive, and aerospace industries through its electronics, automotive, and graphics divisions. Products include military and commercial communication equipment, guidance systems, electronics, components for automobiles, and printing presses. **Common positions include:** Computer Programmer; Data Processor; Design Engineer; Electrical/Electronics Engineer; Hardware Engineer; Manager of Information Systems; Software Engineer. **Corporate headquarters location:** This location. **Other U.S. locations:** Austin TX. **Listed on:** NASDAQ. **Stock exchange symbol:** CNXT.

CUBIC CORPORATION
P.O. Box 85587, San Diego CA 92186-5587. 858/277-6780. **Fax:** 858/505-1524. **Recorded jobline:** 858/505-1540. **Contact:** Human Resources. **E-mail address:** jobs@cubic.com. **World Wide Web address:** http://www.cubic.com. **Description:** Cubic Corporation operates through two major segments: the Cubic Transportation Systems Group and the Cubic Defense Group. The Cubic Transportation Systems Group designs and manufactures automatic revenue collection systems throughout the world for public mass transit including railroads, buses, bridges, tunnels, toll roads, and parking lots. The Cubic Defense Group provides instrumented training systems for the U.S. Army, Air Force, and Navy, as well as avionics, data links,

aerospace systems, and logistical product support. The Defense Group also provides battle command training, radio communication systems, and field service operation and maintenance. Founded in 1951. **Corporate headquarters location:** This location. **Number of employees nationwide:** 2,650. **Listed on:** American Stock Exchange. **Stock exchange symbol:** CUB.

CUSTOM CONTROL SENSORS, INC.
P.O. Box 2516, Chatsworth CA 91313. 818/341-4610. **Physical address:** 21111 Plummer Street, Chatsworth CA 91313. **Contact:** Marsha Beach, Human Resources Coordinator. **E-mail address:** mbeach@ccsdualsnap.com. **World Wide Web address:** http://www.ccsdualsnap.com. **Description:** Manufactures pressure, flow, and temperature switches for industrial and airborne applications. **Corporate headquarters location:** This location.

DPAC TECHNOLOGIES
7321 Lincoln Way, Garden Grove CA 92841. 714/898-0007. **Fax:** 714/899-7558. **Contact:** Human Resources. **E-mail address:** hr@dpactech.com. **World Wide Web address:** http://www.dpactech.com. **Description:** Designs, develops, manufactures, and markets a broad line of standard and custom monolithic memories and memory/logic/analog modules and subsystems. The company's products are used in a variety of military, industrial, and commercial applications where high-density, high-performance, and high-reliability standards are required. Typical product applications are in the areas of communications, medical instrumentation, missiles, avionics, and space satellites. **Corporate headquarters location:** This location. **Listed on:** NASDAQ. **Stock exchange symbol:** DPAC.

DIODES INC.
3050 East Hillcrest Drive, Suite 200, Westlake Village CA 91362. 805/446-4800. **Contact:** Human Resources. **E-mail address:** resumes@didodes.com. **World Wide Web address:** http://www.diodes.com. **Description:** This location is a distribution and sales office. Overall, Diodes is a producer and distributor of electronic diodes primarily used in the semiconductor industry. **Corporate headquarters location:** This location. **Listed on:** NASDAQ. **Stock exchange symbol:** DIOD.

ELGAR ELECTRONICS CORPORATION

9250 Brown Deer Road, San Diego CA 92121-2294. 858/458-0201. **Toll-free phone:** 800/733-5427. **Fax:** 858/458-0257. **Contact:** Tom Erickson, Vice President of Human Resources. **E-mail address:** admin@elgar.com. **World Wide Web address:** http://www.elgar.com. **Description:** Manufactures power electronics equipment including AC/DC programmable power supplies for test and measurement purposes and power conditioning/back-up systems for special applications such as harsh environments. **Common positions include:** Accountant/Auditor; Buyer; Computer Programmer; Customer Service Representative; Designer; Draftsperson; Electrical/Electronics Engineer; Financial Analyst; General Manager; Mechanical Engineer; Purchasing Agent/Manager; Quality Control Supervisor; Software Engineer; Systems Analyst. **Corporate headquarters location:** This location. **Operations at this facility include:** Administration; Manufacturing; Research and Development; Sales; Service. **Number of employees at this location:** 400.

ELPAC ELECTRONICS INC.

1562 Reynolds Avenue, Irvine CA 92614. 949/476-6070. **Toll-free phone:** 888/ELPAC80. **Fax:** 949/476-6080. **Contact:** Human Resources. **E-mail address:** engr@elpac.com. **World Wide Web address:** http://www.elpac.com. **Description:** Manufactures power supplies, capacitors, and filters. **Common positions include:** Accountant/Auditor; Blue-Collar Worker Supervisor; Buyer; Credit Manager; Customer Service Representative; Designer; Draftsperson; Electrical/Electronics Engineer; Industrial Engineer; Manufacturer's/Wholesaler's Sales Rep.; Operations/Production Manager; Purchasing Agent/Manager; Quality Control Supervisor; Systems Analyst; Technician. **Corporate headquarters location:** This location. **Operations at this facility include:** Manufacturing.

ENDEVCO CORPORATION

30700 Rancho Viejo Road, San Juan Capistrano CA 92675. 949/493-8181. **Toll-free phone:** 800/982-6732. **Contact:** Jack Marieta, Personnel Administrator. **E-mail address:** jobs@endevco.com. **World Wide Web address:** http://www.endevco.com. **Description:** Manufactures electronic instrumentation systems that measure vibration, shock, motion, and pressure. **Common positions include:** Computer Programmer; Electrical/Electronics Engineer; Mechanical Engineer; Metallurgical Engineer. **Corporate headquarters location:** This location. **Parent company:** Meggitt PLC. **Operations at this facility include:**

Administration; Manufacturing; Research and Development; Sales; Service.

ENOVATION GRAPHIC SYSTEMS INC.
4425 Sheila Street, Los Angeles CA 90023. 323/268-9500. **Contact:** Human Resource Department. **World Wide Web address:** http://www.enovationgraphics.com. **Description:** A wholesaler of electronic components. **Common positions include:** Accountant/Auditor; Computer Programmer; Credit Manager; Electrical/Electronics Engineer; Human Resources Manager; Manufacturer's/Wholesaler's Sales Representative; MIS Specialist; Purchasing Agent/Manager; Systems Analyst. **Corporate headquarters location:** This location. **Other U.S. locations:** Nationwide. **Operations at this facility include:** Administration; Regional Headquarters; Sales. **Annual sales/revenues:** More than $100 million. **Number of employees at this location:** 200. **Number of employees nationwide:** 1,500.

GLENAIR INC.
1211 Air Way, Glendale CA 91201. 818/247-6000. **Contact:** Orlando Bernal, Personnel Director. **World Wide Web address:** http://www.glenair.com. **Description:** Manufactures electrical connector accessories and other electrical products. **Corporate headquarters location:** This location.

GRAYBAR ELECTRIC INC.
383 South Cheryl Lane, City of Industry CA 91789. 323/265-7000. **Toll-free phone:** 800/GRAYBAR. **Contact:** Human Resources Department Manager. **E-mail address:** opportunities@graybaronline.com. **World Wide Web address:** http://www.graybar.com. **Description:** Engaged in the national wholesale distribution of electrical equipment, supplies, and appliances, primarily to electrical contractors, industrial plants, communications companies, power utilities, government agencies, and consumer products dealers. **Corporate headquarters location:** New York NY.

HRL LABORATORIES, LLC
3011 Malibu Canyon Road, Malibu CA 90265. 310/317-5000. **Contact:** Lynn W. Ross, Human Resources Department. **E-mail address:** staffing@hrl.com. **World Wide Web address:** http://www.hrl.com. **Description:** Researches and develops lasers, fiber optic devices and systems, computational electromagnetics, optoelectronics, and radar. **Special programs:** Summer internships. **Corporate headquarters location:** This location. **Parent company:** HRL Laboratories is

jointly owned by Hughes Electronics Corporation and Raytheon Company.

HEWLETT-PACKARD COMPANY
16399 West Bernardo Drive, San Diego CA 92127. 858/655-4100. **Contact:** Human Resources. **World Wide Web address:** http://www.hp.com. **Description:** This location manufactures printers. Overall, Hewlett-Packard is engaged in the design and manufacture of measurement and computation products and systems used in business, industry, engineering, science, health care, and education. Principal products include integrated instrument and computer systems such as hardware and software, peripheral products, and medical electronic equipment and systems. **NOTE:** Hewlett Packard merged with Compaq in April 2002. See the Website for more information. Jobseekers should send resumes to: Employment Response Center, Hewlett-Packard Company, Mail Stop 20-APP, 3000 Hanover Street, Palo Alto CA 94304. **Common positions include:** Computer Programmer; Electrical/Electronics Engineer; Financial Analyst; Marketing Specialist. **Corporate headquarters location:** Palo Alto CA. **Other U.S. locations:** Nationwide. **Listed on:** New York Stock Exchange. **Stock exchange symbol:** HPQ. **Number of employees nationwide:** 93,000.

HEWLETT-PACKARD COMPANY
4995 Murphy Canyon Road, Suite 301, San Diego CA 92123-4366. 858/279-3200. **Contact:** Human Resources. **World Wide Web address:** http://www.hp.com. **Description:** This location is a sales office. Overall, Hewlett-Packard is engaged in the design and manufacture of measurement and computation products and systems used in business, industry, engineering, science, health care, and education. The company's principal products are integrated instrument and computer systems such as hardware and software, peripheral products, and medical electronic equipment and systems. **NOTE:** Hewlett Packard merged with Compaq in April 2002. See the Website for more information. Jobseekers should send resumes to the Employment Response Center, Hewlett-Packard Company, Mail Stop 20-APP, 3000 Hanover Street, Palo Alto CA 94304. **Common positions include:** Computer Programmer; Electrical/Electronics Engineer; Financial Analyst; Marketing Specialist. **Corporate headquarters location:** Palo Alto CA. **Other U.S. locations:** Nationwide. **Listed on:** New York Stock Exchange. **Stock exchange symbol:** HPQ. **Number of employees at this location:** 150. **Number of employees nationwide:** 93,000.

HIROSE ELECTRIC USA, INC.

2688 Westhills Court, Simi Valley CA 93065-6235. 805/522-7958. **Fax:** 805/522-0208. **Contact:** Human Resources. **World Wide Web address:** http://www.hirose.com. **Description:** Manufactures and distributes electric, electronic, and optical connections. **Common positions include:** Accountant/Auditor; Buyer; Customer Service Representative; Electrical/Electronics Engineer; Human Resources Manager; Mechanical Engineer; Services Sales Representative. **Corporate headquarters location:** Tokyo, Japan. **Other U.S. locations:** IL; MA; TX. **Operations at this facility include:** Administration; Divisional Headquarters; Manufacturing; Sales; Service. **Number of employees at this location:** 60.

HONEYWELL

3201 West Lomita Boulevard, Torrance CA 90505. 310/530-1981. **Contact:** Human Resources Department. **World Wide Web address:** http://www.honeywell.com. **Description:** This location manufactures turbochargers. Overall, Honeywell is engaged in the research, development, manufacture, and sale of advanced technology products and services in the fields of chemicals, electronics, automation, and controls. The company's major businesses are home and building automation and control, performance polymers and chemicals, industrial automation and control, space and aviation systems, and defense and marine systems. **Corporate headquarters location:** Plymouth MN. **Listed on:** New York Stock Exchange. **Stock exchange symbol:** HON.

ITT CANNON

666 East Dyer Road, Santa Ana CA 92705. 714/557-4700. **Contact:** Human Resources. **World Wide Web address:** http://www.ittcannon.com. **Description:** Engaged in the development and manufacture of electrical interconnecting devices. Products are used in commercial, military/aerospace, and micro applications. The company's production functions are die casting, stamping, molding, plating, and machining. ITT Cannon is an operating unit of ITT Defense & Electronics, Inc. **Common positions include:** Financial Analyst; Industrial Engineer; Manufacturing Engineer; Mechanical Engineer. **Corporate headquarters location:** White Plains NY. **Parent company:** ITT Corporation is a diversified, global enterprise engaged in three major business areas: Financial and Business Services, which includes ITT Hartford, ITT Financial Corporation, and ITT Communications and Information Services, Inc.; Manufactured Products, which includes ITT Automotive, ITT Defense & Electronics, Inc., and ITT Fluid

Technology Corporation; and Sheraton Hotels (ITT Sheraton Corporation). **Operations at this facility include:** Divisional Headquarters; Manufacturing. **Listed on:** New York Stock Exchange. **Stock exchange symbol:** ITT.

INTERLINK ELECTRONICS

546 Flynn Road, Camarillo CA 93012. 805/484-8855. **Fax:** 805/484-5560. **Contact:** Patrice Poleto, Personnel. **E-mail address:** ppoleto@interlinkelectronics.com. **World Wide Web address:** http://www.interlinkelectronics.com. **Description:** Interlink's force-sensing technology transforms physical pressure applied to a sensor into a corresponding electronic response. Products incorporating a sensor using the company's force-sensing resistor (FSR) devices can react to pressure when applied by any means such as through human touch, a mechanical device, a fluid, or a gas. With supporting electronics, an FSR sensor can start, stop, intensify, select, direct, detect, or measure a desired response. **Corporate headquarters location:** This location. **Listed on:** NASDAQ. **Stock exchange symbol:** LINK.

INTERSTATE ELECTRONICS CORPORATION

P.O. Box 3117, Anaheim CA 92803-3117. 714/758-0500. **Physical address:** 602 East Vermont Avenue, Anaheim CA 92805. **Toll-free phone:** 800/854-6979. **Contact:** Personnel. **E-mail address:** iecresumes@L-3com.com. **World Wide Web address:** http://www.iechome.com. **Description:** Manufactures and markets advanced electronic systems for both military and industrial markets. **Common positions include:** Accountant/Auditor; Buyer; Electrical/Electronics Engineer; Systems Analyst. **Corporate headquarters location:** This location.

INVENSYS CLIMATE CONTROLS

100 West Victoria Street, Long Beach CA 90805. 310/638-6111. **Contact:** Personnel. **World Wide Web address:** http://www.invensys.com. **Description:** A manufacturer of control instrumentation. Products include automatic controls used in homes, commercial buildings, and industrial applications to conserve energy and to enable machinery to work efficiently and automatically; level controls such as RF/microprocessor-based level controls and precision level controls; vibration detectors including monitor and control; recorders and controllers; accessories; diaphragm-actuated control valves; self-actuated temperature regulators; and control systems including system components. The company also produces Sylphon-formed bellows and assemblies,

automobile thermostats, caps, water outlet housings, and heater control valves. **Corporate headquarters location:** This location.

JMAR PRECISION SYSTEMS, INC.
9207 Eton Avenue, Chatsworth CA 91311. 818/700-8977. **Fax:** 818/700-8984. **Contact:** Human Resources. **World Wide Web address:** http://www.jmar-psi.com. **Description:** Specializes in the manufacture and integration of measurement and material processing systems based on submicron motion control and optical measurement technology. **Parent company:** JMAR Technologies, Inc. develops, manufactures, and sells high-reliability precision manufacturing and measurement systems to improve productivity in the microelectronics and biomedical industries. In addition to JMAR Precision Systems, Inc., it also conducts its business through JMAR Research, Inc., a research and development organization specializing in the development of new products using its advanced electro-optical/laser technology base. One of JMAR Research's major projects is the development of a patented process for point source X-ray lithography to enable the semiconductor industry to make computer chips that operate much faster and have substantially more memory than today's products. A substantial portion of products incorporate JMAR Technologies' advanced laser systems for performing a wide variety of welding, measurement, cutting, or drilling operations during the manufacture of precision electronics and/or medical products. **Corporate headquarters location:** Carlsbad CA. **Listed on:** NASDAQ. **Stock exchange symbol:** JMAR.

JMAR TECHNOLOGIES, INC.
3956 Sorrento Valley Boulevard, San Diego CA 92121. 858/535-1706. **Contact:** Human Resources. **World Wide Web address:** http://www.jmar.com. **Description:** Develops, manufactures, and sells cost-effective, high-reliability precision manufacturing and measurement systems to improve productivity in the microelectronics and biomedical industries. A substantial portion of the company's products incorporate advanced laser systems for performing a wide variety of welding, measurement, cutting, or drilling operations during the manufacture of precision electronics and/or medical products. **Corporate headquarters location:** This location. **Subsidiaries include:** JMAR Precision Systems, Inc. specializes in the manufacture and integration of measurement and material processing systems based on its proprietary submicron motion control and optical measurement technology; JMAR Research, Inc. is a research and development organization

specializing in the development of new products using its advanced electro-optical/laser technology base. One of JMAR Research's major projects is the development of a patented process for point source X-ray lithography to enable the semiconductor industry to make computer chips that operate much faster and have substantially more memory than today's products. **Listed on:** NASDAQ. **Stock exchange symbol:** JMAR.

JOSLYN SUNBANK COMPANY, LLC

1740 Commerce Way, Paso Robles CA 93446. 805/238-2840. **Contact:** Licia Blackburn, Manager of Human Resources. **World Wide Web address:** http://www.sunbankcorp.com. **Description:** Manufactures electrical connector accessories (backshells) and flexible conduit cabling systems. **Common positions include:** Accountant/Auditor; Blue-Collar Worker Supervisor; Buyer; Computer Programmer; Cost Estimator; Credit Manager; Draftsperson; Environmental Engineer; Financial Analyst; Human Resources Manager; Machinist; Mechanical Engineer; Operations/Production Manager; Purchasing Agent/Manager; Quality Control Supervisor; Systems Analyst. **Corporate headquarters location:** This location. **Parent company:** Danaher Corporation. **Operations at this facility include:** Administration; Divisional Headquarters; Manufacturing; Research and Development; Sales; Service. **Listed on:** New York Stock Exchange. **Stock exchange symbol:** DHR. **Number of employees at this location:** 200.

KIMBALL MICROELECTRONICS, INC.

28575 Livingston Avenue, Valencia CA 91355. 818/768-7400. **Toll-free phone:** 800/634-9497. **Contact:** Human Resources. **World Wide Web address:** http://www.kegroup.com. **Description:** Processes, screens, and tests semiconductor die, manufactures packaging products, and offers testing services. **Common positions include:** Accountant/Auditor; Administrator; Aerospace Engineer; Blue-Collar Worker Supervisor; Buyer; Computer Programmer; Customer Service Rep.; Department Manager; Electrical/Electronics Engineer; Human Resources Manager; Manufacturer's/Wholesaler's Sales Representative; Marketing Specialist; Metallurgical Engineer; Operations/Production Manager; Purchasing Agent/Manager; Quality Control Supervisor; Systems Analyst; Technical Writer/Editor. **Corporate headquarters location:** This location. **Parent company:** Kimball Electronics Group.

KYOCERA AMERICA, INC.
8611 Balboa Avenue, San Diego CA 92123. 858/576-2600. **Fax:** 858/268-3035. **Contact:** Human Resources. **E-mail address:** kai.hr@kyocera.com. **World Wide Web address:** http://www.kyocera.com/kai. **Description:** Manufactures a broad line of products for the electronics industry including integrated circuit packages, chip capacitors, industrial ceramics, and insulator parts. Other operations include the manufacturing of such consumer and office products as cameras, jewelry, copiers, and portable and personal computers. **NOTE:** Entry-level positions are offered. **Common positions include:** Accountant/Auditor; Computer Programmer; Credit Manager; Industrial Engineer; Manufacturing Engineer; Operations/Production Manager; Sales Engineer; Systems Analyst. **Special programs:** Internships; Training. **Corporate headquarters location:** This location. **Parent company:** Kyocera International, Inc. **Operations at this facility include:** Administration; Manufacturing; Research and Development. **Listed on:** New York Stock Exchange. **Stock exchange symbol:** KYO. **Annual sales/revenues:** More than $100 million. **Number of employees at this location:** 1,000.

L3 COMMUNICATIONS, INC.
9020 Balboa Avenue, San Diego CA 92123. 858/279-0411. **Fax:** 858/571-1259. **Contact:** Human Resources Department. **E-mail address:** cooljobs@l-3com.com. **World Wide Web address:** http://www.l-3com.com. **Description:** Designs and manufactures integrated microwave antenna subassemblies and low-radar, cross-section antenna designs and measurements. **Common positions include:** Accountant; Aerospace Engineer; Buyer; Computer Programmer; Cost Estimator; Department Manager; Human Resources Manager; Mechanical Engineer; Microwave Engineer; Operations/Production Manager; Purchasing Agent/Manager; Quality Control Supervisor; Support Personnel; Systems Analyst. **Corporate headquarters location:** New York NY. **Listed on:** New York Stock Exchange. **Stock exchange symbol:** LLL.

LASER POWER OPTICS
36570 Briggs Road, Murrieta CA 92563. 909/926-7646. **Contact:** Human Resources. **World Wide Web address:** http://www.laserpower.com. **Description:** A manufacturer of optics for high-power lasers. **Common positions include:** Accountant/Auditor; Administrator; Assistant Manager; Blue-Collar Worker Supervisor; Customer Service Representative; Manufacturer's/Wholesaler's Sales Rep.; Mechanical Engineer;

Operations/Production Manager; Optical Engineer. **Corporate headquarters location:** This location. **Operations at this facility include:** Administration; Manufacturing; Research and Development; Sales; Service. **Number of employees at this location:** 100.

LEACH INTERNATIONAL
6900 Orangethorpe Avenue, Buena Park CA 90622-5032. 714/739-0770. **Contact:** Human Resources Department. **E-mail address:** jobs@leachintl.com. **World Wide Web address:** http://www.leachintl.com. **Description:** Manufactures electronic and electrical relays for industrial customers. **Corporate headquarters location:** New York NY.

LITTON INDUSTRIES, INC.
21240 Burbank Boulevard, Woodland Hills CA 91367. 818/598-5000. **Contact:** Personnel. **World Wide Web address:** http://www.littoncorp.com. **Description:** A leader in defense and commercial electronics, shipbuilding, and information technology. Litton is involved in the electronic warfare and command, navigation, and guidance and control markets. Litton also designs, repairs, and modernizes ships. Founded in 1953. **Corporate headquarters location:** This location. **International locations:** Canada; Germany; Italy. **Stock exchange symbol:** LIT. **Annual sales/revenues:** More than $100 million.

LOCKHEED MARTIN
1121 West Reeves Avenue, Ridgecrest CA 93555. 760/446-1700. **Contact:** Department of Human Resources. **E-mail address:** jobslmc@lmco.com. **World Wide Web address:** http://www.lmco.com. **Description:** This location develops threat simulation training equipment for various government agencies. Overall, Lockheed Martin is an aerospace and technology company engaged in the design, manufacture, and management of systems and products in the fields of space, defense, electronics, communications, information management, energy, and materials. **Corporate headquarters location:** Bethesda MD. **Listed on:** New York Stock Exchange. **Stock exchange symbol:** LMT.

MEGGITT PLC
1915 Voyager Avenue, Simi Valley CA 93063. 805/526-5700. **Contact:** Human Resources. **World Wide Web address:** http://www.meggitt.com. **Description:** Develops specialized electric and aerospace technologies. The aerospace unit manufactures systems that measure and process altitude,

speed, and engine parameters; ducting systems; control valves; and fire detection/protection systems. The electronics unit manufactures sensors, circuits, and resistors for a variety of industries. **Corporate headquarters location:** This location.

MICRON IMAGING DESIGN CENTER
135 North Los Robles Avenue, 7th Floor, Pasadena CA 91101. 626/685-5100. **Contact:** Human Resources. **World Wide Web address:** http://www.micron.com. **Description:** Manufactures electronic imaging sensors, cameras, and systems. The company is a leader in CMOS Imaging Technology. Founded in 1995. **Corporate headquarters location:** San Jose CA. **Parent company:** Micron Technology Inc. **Listed on:** New York Stock Exchange. **Stock exchange symbol:** MU.

ORINCON INDUSTRIES
9363 Towne Centre Drive, San Diego CA 92121. 858/455-5530. **Fax:** 858/453-9274. **Contact:** Doreen Bortos, Human Resources. **E-mail address:** resumes@orincon.com. **World Wide Web address:** http://www.orincon.com. **Description:** Engaged in the design, development, and evaluation of signal processing communications, navigation, artificial intelligence, and tracking systems for U.S. Department of Defense applications, as well as for the transportation, biotechnology, and financial markets. **NOTE:** Entry-level positions are offered. **Common positions include:** Software Engineer. **Corporate headquarters location:** This location. **Annual sales/revenues:** $11 - $20 million. **Number of employees at this location:** 100.

POWER-ONE, INC.
740 Calle Plano, Camarillo CA 93012. 805/987-8741. **Toll-free phone:** 800/678-9445. **Fax:** 805/389-8911. **Contact:** Melissa Dugan, Personnel Director. **E-mail address:** melissadugan@power-one.com. **World Wide Web address:** http://www.power-one.com. **Description:** Engaged in the manufacturing of DC power supplies. The company's product line includes linears, switchers, and hi-power to three kilowatts. Founded in 1973. **Common positions include:** Computer Programmer; Customer Service Representative; Design Engineer; Draftsperson; Electrical/Electronics Engineer; Purchasing Agent/Manager; Quality Control Supervisor; Software Engineer. **Corporate headquarters location:** This location. **Operations at this facility include:** Administration; Manufacturing; Research and Development; Sales; Service. **Listed on:** NASDAQ. **Stock exchange symbol:** PWER. **Annual sales/revenues:** $51 - $100 million. **Number of employees at this location:** 250. **Number of employees worldwide:** 1,800.

PULSE ENGINEERING INC.

12220 World Trade Drive, San Diego CA 92127. 858/674-8100. **Fax:** 858/674-8292. **Contact:** Sheila Ricks, Personnel Director. **E-mail address:** resume@pulseeng.com. **World Wide Web address:** http://www.pulseeng.com. **Description:** Designs, manufactures, and markets a variety of electronic components and modules for original equipment manufacturers in the data processing, telecommunications networking, and power supply markets. **Common positions include:** Accountant/Auditor; Customer Service Representative; Designer; Electrical/Electronics Engineer; Financial Analyst; Manufacturer's/Wholesaler's Sales Rep.; Mechanical Engineer. **Special programs:** Internships. **Corporate headquarters location:** This location. **Other U.S. locations:** Wesson MI. **Parent company:** Technitrol. **Operations at this facility include:** Administration; Research and Development; Sales; Service. **Listed on:** New York Stock Exchange. **Stock exchange symbol:** TNL. **Number of employees at this location:** 170. **Number of employees nationwide:** 4,000.

PYXIS CORPORATION

3750 Torrey View Court, San Diego CA 92130. 858/480-6000. **Contact:** Human Resources. **World Wide Web address:** http://www.pyxis.com. **Description:** A manufacturer of automated point-of-use systems. Products are used in hospitals for distribution management and control of supplies and medicines. **Corporate headquarters location:** This location. **Parent company:** Cardinal Health, Inc. **Listed on:** New York Stock Exchange. **Stock exchange symbol:** CAH. **Annual sales/revenues:** More than $100 million.

RACAL INSTRUMENTS

4 Goodyear Street, Irvine CA 92618. 949/859-8999. **Toll-free phone:** 800/722-2528. **Fax:** 949/859-7328. **Contact:** Human Resources. **E-mail address:** resume@racalinstruments.com. **World Wide Web address:** http://www.racalinst.com. **Description:** Manufactures specialized electronic systems, instrumentation, and software for the test and measurement, recording, and electronic design automation markets. Products include high-end VXIbus instruments, digital word generators, subsystems for automatic test equipment, and signal-switching and routing systems. The company also produces professional recording equipment including telemetry, voice logging, and physical research systems. **Corporate headquarters location:** Sunrise FL. **Parent company:** The Racal Corporation.

RAYTHEON SYSTEMS COMPANY

2000 East El Segundo Boulevard, El Segundo CA 90245. 310/364-6000. **Contact:** Human Resources Department. **E-mail address:** join-rayrecruiter@ls.rayjobs.com. (Use this e-mail address to request monthly news about Raytheon and upcoming recruiting events). **World Wide Web address:** http://www.raytheon.com. **Description:** Raytheon Systems Company is a leader in the design of military tactical communications, electronic combat, command and control, and antisubmarine warfare products and systems for the armed forces of the United States and allied nations. **Parent company:** Raytheon Company. **Listed on:** New York Stock Exchange. **Stock exchange symbol:** RTN.

REMEC, INC.

9404 Chesapeake Drive, San Diego CA 92123. 858/560-1301. **Fax:** 858/569-7111. **Contact:** Lillian Turman, Personnel Manager. **E-mail address:** careers@remec.com. **World Wide Web address:** http://www.remec.com. **Description:** An electronics company engaged in the design, development, and manufacture of custom RF and microwave products. **Common positions include:** Accountant/Auditor; Draftsperson; Electrical/Electronics Engineer; Human Resources Manager; Mechanical Engineer; Software Engineer. **Corporate headquarters location:** This location. **Subsidiaries include:** Humphrey, Inc. manufactures motion sensor devices. **Operations at this facility include:** Administration; Manufacturing; Research and Development. **Listed on:** NASDAQ. **Stock exchange symbol:** RMEC. **Number of employees at this location:** 525. **Number of employees nationwide:** 750.

REXEL CALCON

2 Morgan Street, Irvine CA 92618. 949/855-4242. **Contact:** Human Resources. **E-mail address:** job@rexel.com. **World Wide Web address:** http://www.rexel.com. **Description:** Distributes electrical supplies, wire, cable, switchboards, and light fixtures to small businesses, electrical contractors, and industrial customers. **Common positions include:** Branch Manager; Manufacturer's/Wholesaler's Sales Rep.; Operations/Production Manager; Purchasing Agent/Manager. **Corporate headquarters location:** Dallas TX.

SANMINA-SCI CORPORATION

2945 Airway Avenue, Costa Mesa CA 92626. 949/623-3800. **Fax:** 714/371-2834. **Contact:** Human Resources Department. **World Wide Web address:** http://www.sanmina.com.

Description: Manufactures custom-designed backpanel assemblies and subassemblies; multilayer, high-density printed circuit boards; and surface mount technology assemblies used in sophisticated electronics equipment. The company serves original equipment manufacturers in the telecommunication, data communication, industrial/medical, computer systems, and contract assembly business sectors. **Common positions include:** Accountant/Auditor; Administrative Worker/Clerk; Buyer; Human Resources Manager; MIS Specialist; Operations/Production Manager; Production Operator; Production/Material Planner; Quality Control Supervisor; Stock Clerk. **International locations:** Canada; France; Ireland; Mexico; Scotland; Singapore; Thailand. **Listed on:** NASDAQ. **Stock exchange symbol:** SANM. **Annual sales/revenues:** More than $100 million.

SCANTRON CORPORATION
1361 Valencia Avenue, Tustin CA 92780. 714/247-2700. **Fax:** 714/247-0010. **Contact:** Sherre McKaig, Director of Human Resources. **E-mail address:** jobs@scantron.com. **World Wide Web address:** http://www.scantron.com. **Description:** Manufactures and markets optical mark reader, test scoring, and data entry equipment. **Common positions include:** Electrical/Electronics Engineer; Human Service Worker; Mechanical Engineer; Services Sales Representative. **Corporate headquarters location:** This location. **Other U.S. locations:** Nationwide. **Parent company:** J.H. Harland. **Listed on:** New York Stock Exchange. **Stock exchange symbol:** JH. **Number of employees at this location:** 600.

SEMICOA SEMICONDUCTORS, INC.
333 McCormick Avenue, Costa Mesa CA 92626. 714/979-1900. **Fax:** 714/557-4541. **Contact:** Gerri Gibb, Personnel Manager. **E-mail address:** ggibb@semicoa.com. **World Wide Web address:** http://www.semicoa.com. **Description:** A custom manufacturer of small signal RF, discrete, bipolar transistors and photodiodes. Founded in 1968. **NOTE:** Entry-level positions and second and third shifts are offered. **Common positions include:** Accountant/Auditor; Administrative Assistant; Applications Engineer; Assistant Manager; Blue-Collar Worker Supervisor; Buyer; Chemical Engineer; Clerical Supervisor; Computer Programmer; Customer Service Representative; Database Manager; Electrical/Electronics Engineer; Manufacturing Engineer; Marketing Manager; Mechanical Engineer; Metallurgical Engineer; MIS Specialist; Production Manager; Purchasing Agent/Manager; Quality Control Supervisor; Sales Engineer;

Sales Executive; Sales Manager; Sales Representative; Secretary; Systems Analyst. **Special programs:** Training. **Corporate headquarters location:** This location. **Listed on:** Privately held. **Annual sales/revenues:** $5 - $10 million. **Number of employees at this location:** 90.

SQUARE D COMPANY

21680 Gateway Center Drive, Suite 300,Diamond Bar CA 91765-2435. 909/612-5400. **Contact:** Human Resources. **E-mail address:** uwb@schneiderelectricjobs.com. **World Wide Web address:** http://www.squared.com. **Description:** A manufacturer of electrical distribution products for the construction industry. Products are used in commercial and residential construction, industrial facilities, and machinery and original equipment manufacturers' products. Residential building products feature circuit breakers with an exclusive quick-open mechanism that isolates potential dangers quickly; and a complete home wiring system connecting multiple telephone lines, audio signals, and VCR, cable, or closed circuit television. In office developments, hotels and restaurants, retail shops, and other businesses, Square D provides products ranging from parking lot gate controls and uninterrupted power systems for personal computers to space-saving remote-controlled lighting and custom circuit breaker panel boards. Square D also equips public buildings such as schools, stadiums, museums, hospitals, prisons, military bases, and wastewater treatment plants with electrical distribution systems. **Common positions include:** Electrical/Electronics Engineer; Industrial Engineer; Mechanical Engineer; Sales and Marketing Manager. **Corporate headquarters location:** Palatine IL. **Parent company:** Schneider Electric. **Operations at this facility include:** Regional Headquarters; Sales. **Listed on:** Privately held.

TAITRON COMPONENTS INCORPORATED

28040 West Harrison Parkway, Valencia CA 91355. 661/257-6060. **Contact:** Human Resources. **World Wide Web address:** http://www.taitroncomponents.com. **Description:** Distributes electronic components including discretes, optos, and passives. **Corporate headquarters location:** This location. **Listed on:** NASDAQ. **Stock exchange symbol:** TAIT.

TERADYNE, INC.
SEMICONDUCTOR TEST DIVISION

30801 Agoura Road, Agoura Hills CA 91301. 818/991-2900. **Contact:** Personnel. **E-mail address:** resume@teradyne.com. **World Wide Web address:** http://www.teradyne.com.

Description: This location of Teradyne manufactures semiconductor testers. Overall, Teradyne manufactures in-circuit testers, automated inspection systems (optical), and probe testers for printed circuit board manufacturers. **Corporate headquarters location:** Boston MA. **Listed on:** New York Stock Exchange. **Stock exchange symbol:** TER. **Number of employees nationwide:** 5,000.

TRIKON TECHNOLOGIES, INC.

10540 Talbert Avenue, Suite 100, Fountain Valley CA 92708. 800/727-5585. **Contact:** Human Resources Department. **E-mail address:** website.mail@trikon.com. **World Wide Web address:** http://www.trikon.com. **Description:** Manufactures etch and deposition equipment using Etch, CVD, and PVD technologies that are necessary for semiconductor manufacturing. Trikon has three divisions: Etch, Deposition, and Global Sales and Field Operations. The Deposition Division (Newport, South Wales) houses all operations involving the Forcefill PVD and Flowfill CVD product lines. **Corporate headquarters location:** This location. **Listed on:** NASDAQ. **Stock exchange symbol:** TRKN.

TRIPOINT GLOBAL

3111 Fujita Street, Torrance CA 90505. 310/539-6704. **Contact:** Human Resources. **World Wide Web address:** http://www.tripointglobal.com. **Description:** A supplier of microwave transmission line components and networks for the telecommunications, space, and defense industries. Tripoint Global's products include a variety of standard antenna feed components in addition to custom-designed and fabricated components. **Corporate headquarters location:** Newton NC.

UNIVERSAL ELECTRONICS INC.

6101 Gateway Drive, Cypress CA 90630-4841. 714/820-1000. **Fax:** 714/820-1010. **Contact:** Department of Human Resources. **E-mail address:** hr@ueic.com. **World Wide Web address:** http://www.universalelectronicsus.com. **Description:** Develops, designs, engineers, and markets preprogrammed universal remote controls for use with home video and audio entertainment equipment. Universal Electronics also produces home safety and automation equipment. **Corporate headquarters location:** This location. **Office hours:** Monday - Friday, 7:00 a.m. - 5:00 p.m. **Number of employees at this location:** 90.

VISHAY INTERTECHNOLOGY
4051 Greystone Drive, Ontario CA 91761. 909/923-3313. **Contact:** Personnel Department. **World Wide Web address:** http://www.vishay.com. **Description:** Manufactures a variety of electronic components including sensors. **Corporate headquarters location:** Columbus OH. **Listed on:** New York Stock Exchange. **Stock exchange symbol:** VSH.

WEMS ELECTRONICS INC.
P.O. Box 528, Hawthorne CA 90251. 310/644-0251. **Physical address:** 4650 West Rosecrans Avenue, Hawthorne CA 90250. **Fax:** 310/644-5334. **Contact:** Theresa Sunbury, Personnel Manager. **World Wide Web address:** http://www.wems.com. **Description:** Specializes in box-build turnkey manufacturing. Current programs include electrical, electro-mechanical, pneumatic, hydraulic, and mechanical components as well as high-level electronics. Founded in 1960. **Common positions include:** Accountant; Administrative Assistant; Buyer; Controller; Customer Service Representative; Design Engineer; Draftsperson; Electrical/Electronics Engineer; Human Resources Manager; Mechanical Engineer; Network/Systems Administrator; Operations Manager; Production Manager; Quality Control Supervisor; Sales Executive. **Office hours:** Monday - Friday, 8:00 a.m. - 5:00 p.m. **Corporate headquarters location:** This location. **Other U.S. locations:** Danvers MA. **Operations at this facility include:** Administration; Manufacturing; Sales. **Listed on:** Privately held. **President:** Ronald Hood. **Facilities Manager:** Mel Hughes. **Sales Manager:** Carroll Whitney. **Annual sales/revenues:** $11 - $20 million. **Number of employees at this location:** 120.

WESTERN DIGITAL CORPORATION
20511 Lake Forest Drive, Lake Forest CA 92630. 949/672-7000. **Contact:** Director of Compensation. **E-mail address:** employment@westerndigital.com. **World Wide Web address:** http://www.westerndigital.com. **Description:** Engaged in information storage management. Western Digital is a leader in manufacturing hard-disk drives for servers, workstations, and individual computers. **Corporate headquarters location:** This location. **Listed on:** New York Stock Exchange. **Stock exchange symbol:** WDC.

XONTECH, INC.
6862 Hayvenhurst Avenue, Van Nuys CA 91406. 818/787-7380. **Fax:** 818/904-9440. **Contact:** Human Resources. **E-mail address:** human_resources@xenotech.com. **World Wide Web address:** http://www.xontech.com. **Description:** A research

and development firm specializing in the development of advanced concepts, technologies, and systems to support defense programs. Xontech is engaged in the fields of radar and communications, missile and sensor phenomenology, flight test data analysis, and applied physics. The company also deals in state-of-the-art software applications and algorithm development. **Common positions include:** Computer Programmer; Mathematician; Software Engineer. **Corporate headquarters location:** This location. **Other area locations:** Santa Clara CA; Huntington Beach CA; Los Angeles CA; Walnut Creek CA. **Other U.S. locations:** Huntsville AL; Colorado Springs CO; Washington DC. **Listed on:** Privately held. **Number of employees at this location:** 130.

ENVIRONMENTAL AND WASTE MANAGEMENT SERVICES

You can expect to find the following types of companies in this chapter:

Environmental Engineering Firms • Sanitary Services

ARCADIS

1400 North Harbor Boulevard, Suite 700, Fullerton CA 92835. 714/278-0992. **Fax:** 714/278-0051. **Contact:** Human Resources Department. **E-mail address:** arcadisgm@arcadis-us.com. **World Wide Web address:** http://www.arcadis-us.com. **Description:** A consulting firm that provides environmental and engineering services. The company focuses on the environmental, building, and infrastructure markets. Founded in 1888. **Corporate headquarters:** Highlands Ranch CO. **Other U.S. locations:** Nationwide. **International locations:** The Netherlands; United Kingdom. **Subsidiaries include:** JSA Environmental Inc. (Long Beach CA) provides environmental assessment and analysis services. **Listed on:** NASDAQ. **Stock exchange symbol:** ARCAF. **Number of employees worldwide:** 6,700.

BROWNING-FERRIS INDUSTRIES, INC. (BFI)

9200 Glenoaks Boulevard, Sun Valley CA 91352. 818/790-5410. **Contact:** Personnel. **World Wide Web address:** http://www.bfi.com. **Description:** Engaged primarily in the collection and disposal of solid waste for commercial, industrial, and residential customers. Services provided by Browning-Ferris Industries, Inc. include landfill services, waste-to-energy programs, hazardous waste removal, and liquid waste removal. The company has worldwide operations at more than 500 facilities. **Common positions include:** Accountant/Auditor; Administrator; Blue-Collar Worker Supervisor; Branch Manager; Credit Manager; Customer Service Representative; Human Resources Manager; Marketing Specialist; Operations/Production Manager; Services Sales Representative. **Corporate headquarters location:** Houston TX. **Parent company:** Allied Waste Industries. **Listed on:** New York Stock Exchange. **Stock exchange symbol:** AW.

ENSR INTERNATIONAL

2850 South Red Hill Avenue, Suite 110, Santa Ana CA 92705. 949/756-2667. **Toll-free phone:** 800/722-2440. **Fax:** 949/756-8461. **Contact:** Personnel. **E-mail address:** hrwest@ensr.com. **World Wide Web address:** http://www.ensr.com. **Description:**

A full-service environmental consulting firm specializing in regulatory compliance management, risk assessment, and remediation. **NOTE:** Jobseekers who send resumes should specify the department in which they seek employment. **Common positions include:** Chemical Engineer; Civil Engineer; Construction Contractor; Draftsperson; Environmental Engineer; Geologist/Geophysicist; Science Technologist. **Corporate headquarters location:** Westford MA. **Other U.S. locations:** Nationwide.

ENVIRON CORPORATION
2010 Main Street, Suite 900, Irvine CA 92614. 949/261-5151. **Fax:** 949/261-6202. **Contact:** Human Resources. **World Wide Web address:** http://www.environcorp.com. **Description:** A multidisciplinary environmental and health sciences consulting firm that provides a broad range of services relating to the presence of hazardous substances in the environment, consumer products, and the workplace. Services provided by ENVIRON are concentrated on the assessment and management of chemical risk. **Corporate headquarters location:** Arlington VA. **Other area locations:** Emeryville CA; Novato CA. **Other U.S. locations:** Princeton NJ; Houston TX. **Parent company:** Applied BioScience International Inc.

INTERNATIONAL TECHNOLOGY CORPORATION (IT)
3347 Michelson Drive, Suite 200, Irvine CA 92612. 949/261-6441. **Contact:** Recruiting Department. **E-mail address:** jobswest@theitgroup.com; collegerecruiting@theitgroup.com. **World Wide Web address:** http://www.theitgroup.com. **Description:** Applies engineering, analytical, remediation, and pollution control expertise to meet the environmental needs of its clients from site assessment to remediation. **Common positions include:** Chemical Engineer; Chemist; Civil Engineer; Customer Service Rep.; General Manager; Geological Engineer; Geologist/Geophysicist; Geotechnical Engineer; Hardware Engineer; Hydrogeologist; Operations/Production Manager; Services Sales Representative; Technical Writer/Editor. **Corporate headquarters location:** Monroeville PA. **Other area locations:** Cerritos CA; Martinez CA; San Diego CA; San Jose CA; Wilmington CA. **Operations at this facility include:** Regional Headquarters. **Number of employees worldwide:** 4,000.

MONTGOMERY WATSON
555 East Walnut Street, Pasadena CA 91101. 626/568-6400. **Contact:** Corporate Human Resources. **World Wide Web address:** http://www.mwlaboratories.com. **Description:** Offers

engineering consulting services for water, wastewater, and hazardous waste facilities. **Common positions include:** Accountant/Auditor; Architect; Chemist; Civil Engineer; Computer Programmer; Draftsperson; Electrical/Electronics Engineer; Environmental Engineer; Hydrogeologist; Mechanical Engineer; Microbiologist; Sanitary Engineer; Software Engineer; Structural Engineer. **Special programs:** Internships. **Corporate headquarters location:** This location. **Other U.S. locations:** Nationwide. **Operations at this facility include:** Administration; Divisional Headquarters; Research and Development. **Listed on:** Privately held. **Annual sales/revenues:** More than $100 million. **Number of employees at this location:** 300. **Number of employees nationwide:** 2,000. **Number of employees worldwide:** 3,500.

PARSONS CORPORATION
100 West Walnut Street, Pasadena CA 91124. 626/440-2000. **Fax:** 626/440-2630. **Contact:** Staffing Department. **World Wide Web address:** http://www.parsons.com. **Job page:** http://www.parsonsjobs.com. **Description:** This location is an environmental engineering firm that provides consulting, design, construction, and program management services. Overall, Parsons Corporation provides engineering, planning, design, project management, and related services for a variety of projects including rail systems, highways, bridges, hazardous waste management, aviation facilities, environmental engineering, resorts, power generation and delivery systems, natural resources development, defense systems, industrial and institutional facilities, and community planning and development. **NOTE:** All jobseekers should express a geographic preference when applying for a position. **Common positions include:** Biological Scientist; Chemical Engineer; Civil Engineer; Environmental Engineer; Geologist/Geophysicist. **Corporate headquarters location:** This location. **Other U.S. locations:** Nationwide. **Number of employees nationwide:** 2,000.

SAFETY-KLEEN CORPORATION
10651 Hickson Street, El Monte CA 91731. 626/575-4685. **Contact:** Human Resources. **World Wide Web address:** http://www.safetykleen.com. **Description:** A chemical waste recycler. **Corporate headquarters location:** Columbia SC.

SEVERN TRENT LABORATORIES, INC.
1721 South Grand Avenue, Santa Ana CA 92705. 714/258-8610. **Contact:** Human Resources. **World Wide Web address:** http://www.stl-inc.com. **Description:** Provides a complete

range of environmental testing services to private industry, engineering consultants, and government agencies in support of federal and state environmental regulations. The company also possesses analytical capabilities in the fields of air toxins, field analytical services, radiochemistry/mixed waste, and advanced technology. **Corporate headquarters location:** North Canton OH. **Other U.S. locations:** FL; MO; NC; OH; TN; TX; WA.

J.F. SHEA COMPANY, INC.
P.O. Box 489, Walnut CA 91788. 909/982-8803. **Fax:** 909/444-4268. **Contact:** John Boland, Chief Estimator. **World Wide Web address:** http://www.jfshea.com. **Description:** Engaged in the construction of water resource, water, and wastewater treatment systems. **Common positions include:** Civil Engineer; Cost Estimator. **Parent company:** Zurn Industries, Inc. (Erie PA) also has operations in three other industry segments. The Power Systems segment designs, constructs, and operates small to medium-sized alternate energy and combined-cycle power plants; designs steam generators and waste heat energy recovery and incineration systems; and produces equipment and fans to control emissions of solid particulate and gaseous pollutants. The Mechanical Power Transmission segment manufactures and markets clutches, couplings, and universal joints in the United States and Europe. The last segment, Lynx Golf, manufactures golf clubs in Nevada, which are finished and assembled in California, Mexico, and Scotland for distribution worldwide. **Operations at this facility include:** Administration; Divisional Headquarters. **Listed on:** New York Stock Exchange. **Annual sales/revenues:** $51 - $100 million. **Number of employees at this location:** 250.

SMITH-EMERY COMPANY
791 East Washington Boulevard, Los Angeles CA 90021. 213/749-3411. **Contact:** Human Resources. **World Wide Webb address:** http://www.smithemery.com. **Description:** A testing and inspection laboratory for concrete, soil, and chemical samples. **Corporate headquarters location:** This location.

TETRA TECH, INC.
670 North Rosemead Boulevard, Pasadena CA 91107-2101. 626/351-4664. **Fax:** 626/351-8725. **Contact:** Rachel Breitbach, Human Resources Department Manager. **E-mail address:** jobs@tetratech.com. **World Wide Web address:** http://www.tetratech.com. **Description:** Tetra Tech is a leading

provider of specialized management consulting and technical services in resource management, infrastructure, and communications. Founded in 1966. **NOTE:** Entry-level positions and part-time jobs are offered. **Common positions include:** Accountant; Administrative Assistant; Architect; Chemical Engineer; Chief Financial Officer; Civil Engineer; Computer Programmer; Controller; Design Engineer; Environmental Engineer; Financial Analyst; Geologist/Geophysicist; Human Resources Manager; Landscape Architect; Marketing Specialist; Network/Systems Administrator; Project Manager; Secretary; Systems Analyst; Systems Manager; Website Developer. **Office hours:** Monday - Friday, 8:00 a.m. - 5:00 p.m. **Corporate headquarters location:** This location. **Other U.S. locations:** Nationwide. **Subsidiaries include:** Environmental Management, Inc.; FLO Engineering; HSI GeoTrans; IWA Engineers; KCM Inc.; Simons, Li & Associates. **Listed on:** NASDAQ. **Stock exchange symbol:** TTEK. **President:** Dr. Hwang. **Number of employees at this location:** 95. **Number of employees nationwide:** 5,615.

URS CORPORATION
911 Wilshire Boulevard, Suite 800, Los Angeles CA 90017. 213/683-0471. **Fax:** 213/996-2515. **Contact:** Personnel. **World Wide Web address:** http://www.urscorp.com. **Description:** An architectural, engineering, and environmental consulting firm that specializes in air transportation, environmental solutions, surface transportation, and industrial environmental and engineering concerns. **Corporate headquarters location:** San Francisco CA. **Listed on:** New York Stock Exchange. **Stock exchange symbol:** URS.

USA BIOMASS CORPORATION
7314 Scout Avenue, Bell Gardens CA 90201. 562/928-9900. **Contact:** Human Resources Department. **Description:** This location houses administrative offices. Overall, USA Biomass provides waste removal and recycling services for green waste. The company is a vertically integrated green waste management business that services both corporate customers and municipalities. **Common positions include:** Accountant/Auditor; Administrative Manager; Clerical Supervisor; Typist/Word Processor. **Corporate headquarters location:** This location. **Operations at this facility include:** Administration. **Annual sales/revenues:** $11 - $20 million. **Number of employees at this location:** 10.

WASTE MANAGEMENT, INC.
1970 East 213th Street, Long Beach CA 90801. 310/222-8700. **Contact:** Personnel. **E-mail address:** careers@wm.com. **World Wide Web address:** http://www.wastemanagement.com. **Description:** Engaged in commercial and residential refuse removal. **Corporate headquarters location:** Oak Brook IL. **Other U.S. locations:** Nationwide. **Listed on:** New York Stock Exchange. **Stock exchange symbol:** WMI.

FABRICATED/PRIMARY METALS AND PRODUCTS

You can expect to find the following types of companies in this chapter:

Aluminum and Copper Foundries • Die-Castings • Iron and Steel Foundries • Steel Works, Blast Furnaces, and Rolling Mills

AGI (ATHANOR GROUP, INC.)

921 East California Avenue, Ontario CA 91761. 909/467-1205. **Contact:** Personnel Manager. **World Wide Web address:** http://www.athanorgroupinc.com. **Description:** Manufactures screw machine products (nonproprietary metal components) produced in large quantities to customer specifications. Founded in 1958. **Corporate headquarters location:** This location. **Subsidiaries include:** Alger Manufacturing Company, Inc.

ACCURIDE INTERNATIONAL INC.

12311 South Shoemaker Avenue, Santa Fe Springs CA 90670. 562/903-0200. **Fax:** 562/903-0403. **Contact:** Lois Crum, Corporate Recruiting Manager. **World Wide Web address:** http://www.accuride.com. **Description:** A metals manufacturing company. Products include ball bearing slides for office furniture, copiers, computers, and tool chests. Founded in 1966. **Common positions include:** Accountant/Auditor; Blue-Collar Worker Supervisor; Buyer; Computer-Aided Designer; Customer Service Representative; Department Manager; Industrial Engineer; Management Trainee; Manufacturer's/Wholesaler's Sales Rep.; Mechanical Engineer; Purchasing Agent/Manager; Quality Control Supervisor. **Corporate headquarters location:** This location. **Other U.S. locations:** South Bend IN; Charlotte NC. **International locations:** Germany; Japan; Switzerland, United Kingdom. **Listed on:** Privately held. **Number of employees at this location:** 400. **Number of employees nationwide:** 700.

CARPENTER SPECIAL PRODUCTS CORPORATION

P.O. Box 609036, San Diego CA 92160-9036. 619/448-1000. **Contact:** Department of Human Resources. **E-mail address:** employment@cartech.com. **World Wide Web address:** http://www.cartech.com. **Description:** Manufactures, fabricates, and markets a wide range of specialty metals for a variety of end use markets. The company also produces stainless steel, tool steel, high-temperature and electronic alloys, and other special purpose metals. **Common positions**

include: Accountant/Auditor; Blue-Collar Worker Supervisor; Buyer; Computer Programmer; Designer; Electrical/Electronics Engineer; Electrician; General Manager; Mechanical Engineer; Nuclear Engineer; Quality Control Supervisor; Systems Analyst. **Corporate headquarters location:** Wyomissing PA. **Other U.S. locations:** Atlanta GA; Fryeburg ME; Orangeburg SC; Dallas TX. **Parent company:** Carpenter Technology Corporation. **Listed on:** New York Stock Exchange. **Stock exchange symbol:** CRS. **Number of employees at this location:** 130. **Number of employees nationwide:** 3,750.

A.M. CASTLE & COMPANY
14001 Orange Avenue, Paramount CA 90723. 562/630-1400. **Contact:** Personnel. **E-mail address:** jobs@amcastle.com. **World Wide Web address:** http://www.amcastle.com. **Description:** Distributes a large variety of metals to industrial companies. Metals distributed include nickel alloys, brass and copper, titanium, stainless steels, and aluminum. **Corporate headquarters location:** Franklin Park IL. **Other U.S. locations:** Nationwide. **Subsidiaries include:** Castle UK; Keystone Honing; Keystone Tube Company; Oliver Steel Plate; Total Plastics. **Listed on:** American Stock Exchange. **Stock exchange symbol:** CAS.

CERRO METAL PRODUCTS
104900 Garfield Avenue, Paramount CA 90723. 562/602-6200. **Contact:** Lorraine Carter, Personnel Director. **World Wide Web address:** http://www.pmpa.org/mem/pmpanw.htm. **Description:** A manufacturer of brass rods. **Corporate headquarters location:** Bellefonte PA. **Other U.S. locations:** Shenandoah VA; Weyers Cave VA. **Operations at this facility include:** Manufacturing; Sales.

CROWN CITY PLATING COMPANY
4350 Temple City Boulevard, El Monte CA 91731. 626/444-9291. **Fax:** 626/448-6915. **Contact:** Personnel Director. **E-mail address:** jobs@crown-city-plating.com. **World Wide Web address:** http://www.crown-city-plating.com. **Description:** Engaged in the metal finishing and plating for industrial customers. **Corporate headquarters location:** This location.

DAVIS WIRE CORPORATION
P.O. Box 2145, Irwindale CA 91706. 626/969-7651. **Toll-free phone:** 877/328-4748. **Contact:** Laura Oravec, Director of Human Resources Department. **World Wide Web address:** http://www.daviswire.com. **Description:** Manufactures wire and related products. **Common positions include:**

Accountant/Auditor; Blue-Collar Worker Supervisor; Customer Service Representative; Metallurgical Engineer. **Corporate headquarters location:** San Ramon CA. **Other U.S. locations:** Hayward CA; Kent WA. **Parent company:** Heico. **Operations at this facility include:** Administration; Divisional Headquarters; Manufacturing; Sales. **Listed on:** Privately held. **Number of employees at this location:** 200. **Number of employees nationwide:** 550.

E.M.J.
P.O. Box 2315, Brea CA 92822-2315. 714/579-8823. **Physical address:** 3050 East Birch Street, Brea CA 92821. **Contact:** Human Resources Department. **World Wide Web address:** http://www.emjmetals.com. **Description:** A nationwide distributor and processor of steel and aluminum products. Products include alloy, carbon, stainless, tool, and specialty steels. **Corporate headquarters location:** This location.

GENERAL DYNAMICS ORDNANCE AND TACTICAL SYSTEMS
9236 East Hall Road, Downey CA 90241. 562/904-7500. **Fax:** 562/904-7524. **Contact:** Sheri Silva, Human Resources Department Representative. **World Wide Web address:** http://www.gd-ots.com. **Description:** This location is engaged in the research, design, development, and manufacture of medium-caliber ammunition for the military. **Common positions include:** Accountant; Administrative Assistant; Chemical Engineer; Computer Programmer; Controller; Electrical/Electronics Engineer; Electrician; Environmental Engineer; Financial Analyst; Human Resources Manager; Manufacturing Engineer; Mechanical Engineer; MIS Specialist; Operations Manager; Quality Control Supervisor; Secretary. **Corporate headquarters location:** St. Petersburg FL. **Parent company:** General Dynamics Corporation. **Operations at this facility include:** Administration; Manufacturing; Research and Development. **Listed on:** New York Stock Exchange. **Stock exchange symbol:** GD. **Annual sales/revenues:** More than $100 million. **Number of employees at this location:** 155.

A.L. JOHNSON COMPANY
4671 Calle Carga, Camarillo CA 93012. 805/389-4631. **Fax:** 805/389-4632. **Contact:** Human Resources Department. **E-mail address:** aljcat@ix.netcom.com. **World Wide Web address:** http://www.aljcast.com. **Description:** Manufactures aluminum and zinc castings including machining and finishing operations. Founded in 1954. **Corporate headquarters location:** This location.

MADISON INDUSTRIES, INC.
1900 East 64th Street, Los Angeles CA 90001. 323/583-4061. **Fax:** 323/582-1015. **Contact:** Human Resources. **World Wide Web address:** http://www.madisonind.com. **Description:** A construction company involved in maintenance, installations, manufacturing, engineering, and design. Madison's manufacturing facilities provide the various metal components needed to complete its building projects. **Corporate headquarters location:** This location.

P.A.C. FOUNDRIES
705 Industrial Avenue, Port Hueneme CA 93041. 805/488-6451. **Contact:** Maria De La Torre, Director of Human Resources Department. **World Wide Web address:** http://www.pacfoundries.com. **Description:** Manufactures steel and aluminum investment castings. **Common positions include:** Accountant/Auditor; Computer Programmer; Customer Service Representative; Manufacturer's/Wholesaler's Sales Rep.; Metallurgical Engineer; Purchasing Agent/Manager; Quality Control Supervisor. **Corporate headquarters location:** This location. **Number of employees at this location:** 240.

RELIANCE STEEL & ALUMINUM COMPANY
2550 East 25th Street, Los Angeles CA 90058. 213/687-7700. **Contact:** Donna Newton, Vice President of Human Resources. **World Wide Web address:** http://www.rsac.com. **Description:** One of the largest Western-based metals service center companies in the United States. Through a network of 20 metals service centers, the company distributes a full line of ferrous and nonferrous metal products including galvanized, hot-rolled and cold-finished steel, stainless steel, aluminum, brass, copper, and alloy steel. The company sells metal products from locations in nine states and to more than 30,000 customers engaged in a wide variety of industries. Some of these metals service centers provide processing services for specialty metals only. **Corporate headquarters location:** This location. **Subsidiaries include:** Valex Corporation manufactures and sells electropolished stainless steel tubing and fittings for use in the semiconductor, biotech, and pharmaceutical industries. **Listed on:** New York Stock Exchange. **Stock exchange symbol:** RS.

TW METALS
2211 Tubeway Avenue, Commerce CA 90040. 323/728-9101. **Contact:** Sharon Gonzalez, Personnel Director. **World Wide Web address:** http://www.twmetals.com. **Description:** Stores and distributes steel and nickel alloy products. Provides a wide

range of products to the aerospace, automotive, chemical processing, utilities, and machine industries. **Corporate headquarters location:** Exton PA.

FINANCIAL SERVICES

You can expect to find the following types of companies in this chapter:
Consumer Finance and Credit Agencies • Investment Specialists • Mortgage Bankers and Loan Brokers • Security and Commodity Brokers, Dealers, and Exchanges

AFSA DATA CORPORATION
2277 East 220th Street, Long Beach CA 90810. 310/513-2700. **Contact:** Human Resources. **World Wide Web address:** http://www.afsa.com. **Description:** Administers, bills, and processes student loans acquired by individuals attending higher education institutions. **Corporate headquarters:** This location. **Parent Company:** FleetBoston Financial.

AAMES FINANCIAL CORPORATION
3731 Wilshire Boulevard, Suite 630, Los Angeles CA 90010. 213/388-9044. **Toll-free phone:** 800/851-8538. **Contact:** Human Resources Department. **World Wide Web address:** http://www.aamesfinancial.com. **Description:** Offers mortgage loans to homeowners. Aames Financial Corporation also functions as an insurance agent and mortgage trustee through some of its subsidiaries. Services include originating (brokering and funding), purchasing, selling, and servicing first and junior trust deed loans primarily for single-family residences in the western United States. **NOTE:** Please send resumes to Human Resources, 350 South Grand Avenue, 51st Floor, Los Angeles CA 90071. 323/210-5300. **Corporate headquarters location:** This location. **Other U.S. locations:** Nationwide.

AMERICAN GENERAL FINANCE
400 South Citrus Avenue, Covina CA 91723-2927. 626/966-0501. **Contact:** Ms. Teresa Molina, Manager. **World Wide Web address:** http://www.agfinance.com. **Description:** American General Finance offers wholesale and retail financing to business and industry, as well as direct consumer loans to individuals through 1,600 offices. **Corporate headquarters location:** Evansville IN. **Other U.S. locations:** Nationwide.

BEAR, STEARNS & COMPANY, INC.
1999 Avenue of the Stars, 32nd Floor, Los Angeles CA 90067-6100. 310/201-2600. **Contact:** Human Resources. **E-mail address:** hresources_internet@bear.com. **World Wide Web address:** http://www.bearstearns.com. **Description:** Bear,

Stearns & Company, Inc. is a leading worldwide investment banking, securities trading, and brokerage firm. The firm's business includes corporate finance, mergers and acquisitions, public finance, institutional equities, fixed-income sales and trading, private client services, foreign exchange, future sales and trading, derivatives, and asset management. **Corporate headquarters location:** New York NY. **Other U.S. locations:** Nationwide. **International locations:** Worldwide. **Parent company:** The Bear Stearns Companies Inc. other subsidiaries include Bear, Stearns Securities Corporation, providing professional and correspondent clearing services including securities lending, and Custodial Trust Company, providing master trust, custody, and government securities services. **Listed on:** New York Stock Exchange. **Stock exchange symbol:** BSC. **Annual sales/revenues:** More than $100 million. **Number of employees nationwide:** 7,800.

CALIFORNIA FIRST LEASING CORPORATION

5 Hutton Centre Drive, Suite 250, Santa Ana CA 92707. 714/751-7551. **Toll-free phone:** 800/496-4640. **Fax:** 714/436-6541. **Contact:** Barbara Bumblis, Human Resources. **World Wide Web address:** http://www.calfirstbankcorp.com. **Description:** A lessor of capital assets including high-technology equipment and systems. Founded in 1977. **Corporate headquarters location:** This location. **Parent company:** California First Bank Corporation. **Listed on:** NASDAQ. **Stock exchange symbol:** CFNB.

THE CAPITAL GROUP COMPANIES
AMERICAN FUNDS DISTRIBUTORS

11100 Santa Monica Boulevard, Los Angeles CA 90025. 310/996-6000. **Contact:** Recruiting Department. **World Wide Web address:** http://www.capgroup.com. **Description:** An investment management company with 15 mutual funds and 10 companies. American Funds Distributors (http://www.americanfunds.com) is also at this location. The company provides financial advisement services including 28 mutual funds, variable annuities, and retirement planning. **Common positions include:** Accountant; Administrative Manager; Attorney; Computer Programmer; Customer Service Representative; Economist; Financial Analyst; Statistician; Systems Analyst. **Corporate headquarters location:** This location. **Other area locations:** Brea CA; San Francisco CA. **Other U.S. locations:** Washington DC; Atlanta GA; Chicago IL; Indianapolis IN; New York NY; Reno NV; San Antonio TX. **International locations:** Canada; England; Hong Kong; Japan; Singapore.

COMMONWEALTH FINANCIAL CORPORATION

524 Escondido Avenue, Vista CA 92084. 760/945-9891. **Toll-free phone:** 800/780-4560. **Fax:** 760/945-4991. **Contact:** Human Resources. **E-mail address:** info@cfchomeloan.com. **World Wide Web address:** http://www.cfchomeloan.com. **Description:** Provides a wide range of mortgages, home loans, and debt consolidation services. **Corporate headquarters location:** This location.

CONSUMER PORTFOLIO SERVICES, INC.

13655 Laguna Canyon Road, Irvine CA 92618. 949/753-6800. **Contact:** Human Resources Department. **E-mail address:** hr@consumerportfolio.com. **World Wide Web address:** http://www.consumerportfolio.com. **Description:** Consumer Portfolio Services, Inc. and its subsidiaries purchase, sell, and service retail automobile installment sales contracts originated by dealers located primarily in California. The company purchases contracts to resell them to institutional investors either as bulk sales or in the form of securities backed by the contracts. **Corporate headquarters location:** This location. **Number of employees at this location:** 65.

COUNTRYWIDE CREDIT INDUSTRIES

4500 Park Granada, Calabasas CA 91302. 818/225-3000. **Recorded jobline:** 888/470-JOBS. **Contact:** Human Resources. **World Wide Web address:** http://www.countrywide.com. **Description:** A holding company. **Common positions include:** Accountant/Auditor; Administrative Manager; Advertising Clerk; Attorney; Bank Officer/Manager; Branch Manager; Budget Analyst; Buyer; Clerical Supervisor; Computer Programmer; Customer Service Representative; Economist; Financial Analyst; Financial Services Sales Representative; Human Resources Manager; Librarian; Management Analyst/Consultant; Operations/Production Manager; Paralegal; Property and Real Estate Manager; Purchasing Agent/Manager; Quality Control Supervisor; Securities Sales Representative; Services Sales Representative; Software Engineer; Statistician; Systems Analyst; Underwriter/Assistant Underwriter. **Special programs:** Internships. **Corporate headquarters location:** This location. **Subsidiaries include:** Countrywide Funding Corporation originates, purchases, sells, and services mortgage loans. The company's mortgage loans are principally first-lien loans secured by single-family residences. **Listed on:** New York Stock Exchange. **Stock exchange symbol:** CCR.

COUNTRYWIDE CREDIT INDUSTRIES

35 North Lake Avenue, Pasadena CA 91101. 626/304-8400. **Recorded jobline:** 888/470-JOBS. **Contact:** Human Resources. **World Wide Web address:** http://www.countrywide.com. **Description:** A holding company. **Common positions include:** Accountant/Auditor; Administrative Manager; Advertising Clerk; Attorney; Bank Officer/Manager; Branch Manager; Budget Analyst; Buyer; Clerical Supervisor; Computer Programmer; Customer Service Representative; Economist; Financial Analyst; Financial Services Sales Representative; Human Resources Manager; Librarian; Management Analyst/Consultant; Operations/Production Manager; Paralegal; Property and Real Estate Manager; Purchasing Agent/Manager; Quality Control Supervisor; Securities Sales Representative; Services Sales Representative; Software Engineer; Statistician; Systems Analyst; Underwriter/Assistant Underwriter. **Special programs:** Internships. **Corporate headquarters location:** Calabasas CA. **Other U.S. locations:** Nationwide. **Subsidiaries include:** Countrywide Funding Corporation originates, purchases, sells, and services mortgage loans. The company's mortgage loans are principally first-lien loans secured by single-family residences. **Operations at this facility include:** Administration; Divisional Headquarters; Regional Headquarters; Sales; Service. **Listed on:** New York Stock Exchange. **Stock exchange symbol:** CCR. **Number of employees at this location:** 1,200. **Number of employees nationwide:** 3,500.

DVI, INC.

4041 MacArthur Boulevard, Suite 401, Newport Beach CA 92660. 949/474-5800. **Toll-free phone:** 800/665-4384. **Contact:** Human Resources. **E-mail address:** careers@dvi-inc.com. **World Wide Web address:** http://www.dvifs.com. **Description:** Provides equipment financing and related services for the users of diagnostic imaging, radiation therapy, and other medical technologies. The company's customer base consists principally of outpatient health care providers, physician groups, and hospitals. **Corporate headquarters location:** Jamison PA. **Number of employees at this location:** 90. **Listed on:** New York Stock Exchange. **Stock exchange symbol:** DVI.

GEORGE ELKINS MORTGAGE BANKING COMPANY

12100 Wilshire Boulevard, Suite 300, Los Angeles CA 90025. 310/207-3456. **Contact:** Human Resources Department. **Description:** Provides mortgage and loan services to individuals and commercial clients. **Common positions**

include: Accountant/Auditor; Computer Programmer; Department Manager; Insurance Agent/Broker; Property and Real Estate Manager; Underwriter/Assistant Underwriter. **Corporate headquarters location:** This location. **Number of employees at this location:** 50.

FIRST AMERICAN TITLE COMPANY

520 North Central Avenue, Glendale CA 91203. 626/912-3664. **Contact:** Human Resources. **World Wide Web address:** http://www.firstam.com. **Description:** Provides escrow and mortgage services for real estate transactions. **Corporate headquarters location:** Santa Ana CA. **Listed on:** New York Stock Exchange. **Stock exchange symbol:** FAF.

FIRST MORTGAGE CORPORATION

3230 Fallow Field Drive, Diamond Bar CA 91765. 909/595-1996. **Contact:** Human Resources Department. **World Wide Web address:** http://www.firstmortgage.com. **Description:** Originates, purchases, sells, and services first deed of trust loans (mortgage loans) for the purchase or refinance of owner-occupied one- to four-family residences. Founded in 1975. **Corporate headquarters location:** This location. **Other U.S. locations:** NV; OR; WA.

THE FOOTHILL GROUP, INC.

2450 Colorado Avenue, Suite 300W, Santa Monica CA 90404. 310/996-7000. **Toll-free phone:** 800/535-1811. **Contact:** Tracey Tigges, Human Resources. **World Wide Web address:** http://www.foothillcapital.com. **Description:** The Foothill Group is one of the largest publicly-owned commercial lenders in the nation. The company operates two businesses: commercial lending and money management. **Corporate headquarters location:** This location. **Subsidiaries include:** Foothill Capital Corporation provides asset-based financing to businesses throughout the United States and engages in money management for institutional investors through two limited partnerships.

GE CAPITAL CORPORATION

2400 East Katella Avenue, Suite 800, Anaheim CA 92806. 714/456-9400. **Contact:** Christen Watson, Personnel. **World Wide Web address:** http://www.gecapital.com. **Description:** This location finances commercial equipment. Overall, GE Capital Corporation is one of the largest leasing companies in the United States and Canada, providing fleet financing and related management services to corporate clients through 27 divisions. **NOTE:** Please send resumes to Human Resources,

GE Capital Corporation, 2929 West Airfield Drive, Dallas TX 75261. **Common positions include:** Accountant/Auditor; Administrator; Attorney; Computer Programmer; Credit Manager; Customer Service Representative; Department Manager; Retail Sales Worker; Systems Analyst. **Corporate headquarters location:** Danbury CT. **Parent company:** General Electric Company operates in the following areas: aircraft engines (jet engines, replacement parts, and repair services for commercial, military, executive, and commuter aircraft); appliances; broadcasting (NBC); industrial (lighting products, electrical distribution and control equipment, transportation systems products, electric motors and related products, a broad range of electrical and electronic industrial automation products, and a network of electrical supply houses); materials (plastics, ABS resins, silicones, superabrasives, and laminates); power systems (products for the generation, transmission, and distribution of electricity); technical products and systems (medical systems and equipment, as well as a full range of computer-based information and data interchange services for both internal use and external commercial and industrial customers); and capital services (consumer services, financing, and specialty insurance). **Listed on:** New York Stock Exchange. **Stock exchange symbol:** GE.

IMPAC COMPANIES
1401 Dove Street, Suite 100, Newport Beach CA 92660. 714/556-0122. **Contact:** Human Resources. **World Wide Web address:** http://www.impaccompanies.com. **Description:** Provides mortgage banking services. **Corporate headquarters location:** This location. **Listed on:** American Stock Exchange. **Stock exchange symbol:** IMH.

IMPERIAL CREDIT INDUSTRIES, INC.
23530 Hawthorne Boulevard, Building One, Suite 230, Torrance CA 90505. 310/373-1704. **Contact:** Cindy Rosenbush, Human Resources Department. **E-mail address:** crosenbush@icii.com. **World Wide Web address:** http://www.icii.com. **Description:** Offers business and consumer financing through five divisions: Business Finance Lending, Consumer Lending, Commercial Mortgage Lending, Franchise Lending, and Investment/Asset Management Services. **Corporate headquarters location:** This location. **Subsidiaries include:** Auto Marketing Network, Inc. (Boca Raton FL); Franchise Mortgage Acceptance Company, LLC (Greenwich CT); Imperial Business Credit, Inc. (San Diego CA); Imperial Credit Advisors, Inc. (Santa Ana Heights CA);

Southern Pacific Thrift and Loan Association (Los Angeles CA). **Listed on:** NASDAQ. **Stock exchange symbol:** ICII.

JEFFERIES & COMPANY, INC.
11100 Santa Monica Boulevard, 11th Floor, Los Angeles CA 90025. 310/445-1199. **Contact:** Dee Dee Bird, Recruiting Coordinator. **E-mail address:** dbird@jefco.com. **World Wide Web address:** http://www.jefco.com. **Description:** Jefferies & Company is engaged in equity, convertible debt and taxable fixed income securities brokerage and trading, and corporate finance. Jefferies & Company is one of the leading national firms engaged in the distribution and trading of blocks of equity securities primarily in the third market. Founded in 1962. **Corporate headquarters location:** This location. **Parent company:** Jefferies Group, Inc. is a holding company that, through Investment Technology Group, Inc., Jeffries & Company, Inc., Jefferies International Limited, and Jefferies Pacific Limited, is engaged in securities brokerage and trading, corporate finance, and other financial services. **Listed on:** New York Stock Exchange. **Stock exchange symbol:** JEF.

PACIFIC LIFE INSURANCE
700 Newport Center Drive, Newport Beach CA 92660. 949/640-3011. **Contact:** Human Resources. **E-mail address:** plemploy@pacificlife.com. **World Wide Web address:** http://www.pacificlife.com. **Description:** Provides insurance services including group health, life, and pensions. Pacific Life Insurance also provides financial services including annuities, mutual funds, and investments. **Corporate headquarters location:** This location.

PROMINENT USA
777 South Figueroa Street, Suite 3050, Los Angeles CA 90017. 213/623-4001. **Contact:** Human Resources. **Description:** An international, multibusiness trading and investment company. Prominent USA specializes in developing and sponsoring profitable opportunities in international and domestic commerce, industry, and finance, either as a principal or as an agent. **Corporate headquarters location:** New York NY.

SUNAMERICA INC.
One SunAmerica Center, Century City, Los Angeles CA 90067-6022. 310/772-6000. **Contact:** Human Resources Department. **World Wide Web address:** http://www.sunamerica.com. **Description:** SunAmerica Inc. is a large financial services company specializing in long-term, tax-deferred, investment-oriented savings products. **Common positions include:**

Accountant/Auditor; Actuary; Attorney; Computer Programmer; Customer Service Representative; Financial Analyst; Human Resources Manager; Manufacturer's/Wholesaler's Sales Rep.; Paralegal; Public Relations Specialist; Securities Sales Representative; Systems Analyst. **Corporate headquarters location:** This location. **Operations at this facility include:** Administration; Divisional Headquarters; Service. **Number of employees at this location:** 450. **Number of employees nationwide:** 1,000.

WFS FINANCIAL
23 Pasteur Road, Irvine CA 92618-3820. 949/727-1000. **Contact:** Human Resources Department. **E-mail address:** employment@wfsfinancial.com. **World Wide Web address:** http://www.wfb.com. **Description:** A financial services holding company that operates throughout the West Coast. **Corporate headquarters location:** This location. **Parent company:** Westcorp. **Listed on:** NASDAQ. **Stock exchange symbol:** WFSI. **Number of employees at this location:** 350. **Number of employees nationwide:** 1,200.

WEDBUSH MORGAN SECURITIES
P.O. Box 30014, Los Angeles CA 90030. 213/688-8000. **Physical address:** 1000 Wilshire Boulevard, 9th Floor, Los Angeles CA 90017. **Contact:** Human Resources. **E-mail address:** hrd@wedbush.com. **World Wide Web address:** http://www.wedbush.com. **Description:** An investment banking securities brokerage. **Common positions include:** Accountant/Auditor; Branch Manager; Brokerage Clerk; Computer Programmer; Credit Manager; Customer Service Representative; Human Resources Manager; Marketing Manager; Purchasing Agent/Manager; Services Sales Representative. **Special programs:** Internships. **Corporate headquarters location:** This location. **Operations at this facility include:** Administration; Banking; Research and Development; Sales; Service. **Listed on:** Privately held. **Number of employees at this location:** 270. **Number of employees nationwide:** 510.

FOOD AND BEVERAGES/ AGRICULTURE

You can expect to find the following types of companies in this chapter:
Crop Services and Farm Supplies • Dairy Farms • Food Manufacturers/Processors and Agricultural Producers • Tobacco Products

ADAMS & BROOKS INC.
P.O. Box 7303, Los Angeles CA, 90007. 213/749-3226. **Physical address:** 1915 South Hoover Street, Los Angeles CA 90007. **Fax:** 213/746-7614. **Contact:** Mrs. Tempe Brooks, Personnel Director. **E-mail address:** info@adams-brooks.com. **World Wide Web address:** http://www.adams-brooks.com. **Description:** Manufactures candy including P-Nuttles toffee coated peanuts, Coffee Rio caramel candy, Cup-O-Gold chocolate cups, specialty lollipops, and Fairtime Taffy. Founded in 1932. **Common positions include:** Food Scientist/Technologist; Industrial Engineer; Science Technologist; Services Sales Representative. **Corporate headquarters location:** This location. **Listed on:** Privately held.

ALTA DENA CERTIFIED DAIRY
17637 East Valley Boulevard, City of Industry CA 91744. 626/964-6401. **Contact:** Personnel. **World Wide Web address:** http://www.altadenadairy.com. **Description:** Specializes in the production of a full line of dairy products. **Corporate headquarters location:** This location.

BAKER COMMODITIES
4020 Bandini Boulevard, Los Angeles CA 90023. 323/268-2801. **Contact:** Maxine Taylor, Human Resources Director. **Description:** Manufactures animal oils, proteins, and prepared feeds. **President:** James Andreoli.

BASKIN-ROBBINS, INC.
600 North Brand Boulevard, 6th Floor, Glendale CA 91203. 818/956-0031. **Contact:** Director of Human Resources. **Description:** An ice cream manufacturer that also operates retail locations. **NOTE:** Please send resumes to: Human Resources Department, 14 Pacella Park Drive, Randolph MA 02368. **Corporate headquarters location:** Randolph MA. **International locations:** Worldwide. **Parent company:** Allied

Domecq Quick Service Restaurants. **Number of employees nationwide:** 875.

BRIDGFORD FOODS CORPORATION

1308 North Patt Street, Anaheim CA 92801. 714/526-5533. **Toll-free phone:** 800/527-2105. **Contact:** Personnel Director. **E-mail address:** info@bridgford.com. **World Wide Web address:** http://www.bridgford.com. **Description:** Manufactures and distributes refrigerated, frozen, and snack food products. The company markets its products throughout the United States and sells through retail and wholesale outlets, restaurants, institutions, and retail food stores. **Corporate headquarters location:** This location. **Other U.S. locations:** Chicago IL; Statesville NC; Dallas TX.

CHALONE WINE GROUP, LTD.

621 Airpark Road, Napa CA 94558-6272. 707/254-4200. **Fax:** 707/254-4207. **Contact:** Human Resources. **World Wide Web address:** http://www.chalonewinegroup.com. **Description:** Chalone Wine Group, Ltd. produces, markets, and sells premium white and red varietal table wines, primarily Chardonnay, Pinot Noir, Cabernet Sauvignon, and Sauvignon Blanc. **Corporate headquarters location:** This location. **Listed on:** NASDAQ. **Stock exchange symbol:** CHLN.

DANONE WATERS OF NORTH AMERICA

3280 East Foothill Boulevard, Suite 400, Pasadena CA 91107. 626/585-1000. **Contact:** Human Resources. **World Wide Web address:** http://www.danone.com. **Description:** Produces bottled water under the names Evian, Ferrarelle, and Volvic. **Special programs:** Internships.

DOLE FOOD COMPANY, INC.

One Dole Drive, Westlake Village CA 91362-7300. 818/879-6600. **Contact:** Human Resources Department. **E-mail address:** dole@rpc.webhire.com. **World Wide Web address:** http://www.dole.com. **Description:** Processes canned fruits. Founded in 1851. **Corporate headquarters location:** This location. **Listed on:** New York Stock Exchange. **Stock exchange symbol:** DOL. **Number of employees nationwide:** 44,000.

FARMER JOHN MEATS COMPANY

3049 East Vernon Avenue, Los Angeles CA 90058. 323/583-4621. **Contact:** Anthony Clougherty, Personnel Director. **E-mail address:** farmerjohn@farmerjohn.com. **World Wide Web address:** http://www.farmerjohn.com. **Description:** Processes and packs meat products. **Corporate headquarters location:** This location.

FISHKING PROCESSORS
1320 Newton Street, Los Angeles CA 90021. 213/746-1307. **Contact:** Personnel Director. **Description:** Processes and sells fresh and frozen fish products.

FRITO-LAY, INC.
9535 Archibald Avenue, Rancho Cucamonga CA 91730. 909/948-3600. **Contact:** Human Resources. **World Wide Web address:** http://www.fritolay.com. **Description:** A worldwide manufacturer and wholesaler of snack products including the brand names Fritos Corn Chips, Doritos Tortilla Chips, Lays Potato Chips, and Smartfood Popcorn. **Corporate headquarters location:** Plano TX. **Parent company:** PepsiCo, Inc. (Purchase NY) consists of Frito-Lay, Inc., Pepsi-Cola Company, and Tropicana Products, Inc. **Listed on:** New York Stock Exchange. **Stock exchange symbol:** PEP. **Number of employees nationwide:** 29,000.

GALLO WINE COMPANY
2700 South Eastern Avenue, Commerce CA 90040. 323/869-6435. **Toll-free phone:** 800/499-1761. **Fax:** 323/869-6460. **Contact:** Recruiting. **E-mail address:** jobs@ejgallo.com. **World Wide Web address:** http://www.gallo.com. **Description:** Produces, markets, and distributes premium wines and brandy. Founded in 1933. **Common positions include:** Sales Representative. **Corporate headquarters location:** Modesto CA. **Other U.S. locations:** Nationwide. **International locations:** Worldwide. **Parent company:** E&J Gallo Winery. **Operations at this facility include:** Divisional Headquarters; Sales. **Listed on:** Privately held. **Annual sales/revenues:** More than $100 million. **Number of employees at this location:** 450.

GLACIER WATER SERVICES, INC.
2651 La Mirada, Suite 100, Vista CA 760/560-1111. **Fax:** 760/560-0226. **Contact:** Human Resources Department. **E-mail address:** jobs@glacierwater.com. **World Wide Web address:** http://www.glacierwater.com. **Description:** A leading provider of drinking water dispensed to consumers through coin-operated, self-service vending machines. **Corporate headquarters location:** This location.

HUNT-WESSON INC.

3353 Michaelson Drive, Irvine CA 92612. 949/437-1000. **Contact:** Human Resources. **World Wide Web address:** http://www.hunt-wesson.com. **Description:** This location is a tomato cannery. Overall, Hunt-Wesson is an integrated food, vegetable, and convenience food manufacturer, and is one of the nation's largest producers of tomato-based products. **Corporate headquarters location:** Fullerton CA. **Parent company:** ConAgra, Inc. **Listed on:** New York Stock Exchange. **Stock exchange symbol:** CAG.

MASTERFOODS USA

P.O. Box 58853, Vernon CA 90058-0853. 323/587-2727. **Physical address:** 3250 East 44th Street, Vernon CA 90058. **Contact:** Personnel Director. **World Wide Web address:** http://www.mars.com. **Description:** Manufactures pet foods. Founded in 1936. **Corporate headquarters location:** This location. **Parent company:** Mars, Inc.

MILLER BREWING COMPANY

15801 East First Street, Irwindale CA 91706. 626/969-6811. **Contact:** Personnel Department. **World Wide Web address:** http://www.millerbrewing.com. **Description:** Produces and distributes beer and other malt beverages. Principal beer brands include Miller Lite, Lite Ice, Miller Genuine Draft, Miller Genuine Draft Light, Miller High Life, Miller Reserve, Lowenbrau, Milwaukee's Best, Meister Brau, Red Dog, and Icehouse. Miller also produces Sharp's, a nonalcoholic brew. **NOTE:** Miller Brewing Company is expected to close a merger with South African Breweries in July 2002. The new company will be called SABMiller. **Common positions include:** Accountant/Auditor; Blue-Collar Worker Supervisor; Buyer; Chemist; Computer Programmer; Department Manager; Draftsperson; Electrical/Electronics Engineer; Financial Analyst; Food Scientist/Technologist; Industrial Engineer; Mechanical Engineer; Operations/Production Manager; Production/Material Planner; Public Relations Specialist; Purchasing Agent/Manager; Quality Control Supervisor; Supervisor. **Corporate headquarters location:** Milwaukee WI. **Subsidiaries include:** Jacob Leinenkugel Brewing Company (Chippewa Falls WI) brews Leinenkugel's Original Premium, Leinenkugel's Light, Leinie's Ice, Leinenkugel's Limited, Leinenkugel's Red Lager, and four seasonal beers: Leinenkugel's Genuine Bock, Leinenkugel's Honey Weiss, Leinenkugel's Autumn Gold, and Leinenkugel's Winter Lager. Molson Breweries U.S.A., Inc. (Reston VA), one of the largest beer importers in the United States, imports Molson beers from Canada, as well as Foster's

Lager and many other brands. **Operations at this facility include:** Manufacturing. **Number of employees at this location:** 1,100. **Number of employees nationwide:** 155,000.

NESTLE USA, INC.
800 North Brand Boulevard, Glendale CA 91203. 818/549-6000. **Contact:** Human Resources. **World Wide Web address:** http://www.nestle.com. **Description:** One of the largest food and beverage companies in the nation. Brand names include Nestle Crunch, Baby Ruth, and Butterfinger candy bars; Taster's Choice and Nescafe coffee; Contadina tomato and refrigerated pastas and sauces; Friskies and Fancy Feast cat food; and Beringer wines. **Common positions include:** Accountant/Auditor; Agricultural Scientist; Chemical Engineer; Computer Programmer; Electrical Engineer; Financial Analyst; Industrial Engineer; Manufacturer's/Wholesaler's Sales Representative; Marketing Specialist; Mechanical Engineer; Operations/Production Manager; Purchasing Agent/Manager; Quality Control Supervisor; Statistician; Systems Analyst; Transportation/Traffic Specialist. **Corporate headquarters location:** Vevey, Switzerland. **Parent company:** Nestle S.A.

SHAKLEE CORPORATION
4747 Willow Road, Pleasanton CA 90623. 714/670-5602. **Contact:** Roseanne Jennings, Personnel Manager. **World Wide Web address:** http://www.shaklee.com. **Description:** Manufactures and markets vitamins, minerals, protein powders, and other nutritional products.

SUNKIST GROWERS, INC.
P.O. Box 7888, Van Nuys CA 91409-7888. 818/986-4800. **Contact:** John McGovern, Director of Human Resources. **World Wide Web address:** http://www.sunkist.com. **Description:** A citrus growing and processing firm, with additional operations in confections and soft drinks. **Corporate headquarters location:** This location. **Other area locations:** Los Angeles CA. **International locations:** Ontario, Canada. **Subsidiaries include:** Fruit Growers Supply Company (also at this location).

SYSCO FOOD SERVICE OF LOS ANGELES, INC.
20701 Currier Road, Walnut CA 91789. 909/595-9595. **Contact:** Human Resources. **World Wide Web address:** http://www.syscola.com. **Description:** Markets and distributes a broad line of food products, beverages, and related supplies to restaurants, fast-food operations, schools, and hospitals.

Corporate headquarters location: Chicago IL. **Listed on:** New York Stock Exchange. **Stock exchange symbol:** SYY.

U.S. FOODSERVICE
15155 Northam Street, La Mirada CA 90638. 714/670-3500. **Fax:** 714/670-3794. **Recorded jobline:** 714/670-3500x5500. **Contact:** Human Resources Manager. **World Wide Web address:** http://www.usfoodservice.com. **Description:** U.S. Foodservice distributes food and related products to restaurants, hotels, healthcare facilities, cafeterias, and schools. **Office hours:** Monday - Friday, 8:00 a.m. - 5:00 p.m. **Corporate headquarters location:** Columbia MD. **Other U.S. locations:** Nationwide. **Parent company:** Ahold. **Listed on:** New York Stock Exchange. **Stock exchange symbol:** AHO. **Annual sales/revenues:** More than $100 million. **Number of employees at this location:** 600. **Number of employees nationwide:** 13,000.

WESTERN GROWERS ASSOCIATION
P.O. Box 2130, Newport Beach CA 92658. 949/863-1000. **Fax:** 949/863-9028. **Contact:** Diana DeWees, Vice President of Human Resources. **E-mail address:** ddewees@wga.com. **World Wide Web address:** http://www.wga.com. **Description:** An agricultural trade association providing services such as medical insurance, workers' compensation insurance, legal advice, and marketing services. Founded in 1926. **Common positions include:** Accountant/Auditor; Attorney; Claims Investigator; Clerical Supervisor; Computer Programmer; Customer Service Representative; Medical Records Technician; Public Relations Specialist; Restaurant/Food Service Manager; Sales Executive; Systems Analyst; Technical Writer/Editor; Transportation/Traffic Specialist; Typist/Word Processor; Underwriter/Assistant Underwriter. **Corporate headquarters location:** This location. **Annual sales/revenues:** $51 - $100 million. **Number of employees at this location:** 250.

YOUNG'S MARKET COMPANY, LLC
2164 North Batavia Street, Orange CA 92865. 714/283-4933. **Contact:** Naomi Buenaflor, Director of Human Resources. **World Wide Web address:** http://www.youngsmarket.com. **Description:** A beer, wine, and spirits distributor. Founded in 1888. **Corporate headquarters location:** This location. **Other U.S. locations:** AZ; CT; DC; FL; HI; MD; NY; PA; SC.

GOVERNMENT

You can expect to find the following types of agencies in this chapter:

Courts • Executive, Legislative, and General Government • Public Agencies (Firefighters, Military, Police) • United States Postal Service

THE ARBORETUM OF LOS ANGELES COUNTY
DEPARTMENT OF PARKS AND RECREATION
301 North Baldwin Avenue, Arcadia CA 91007. 626/821-3222. **Contact:** Human Resources. **World Wide Web address:** http://www.arboretum.org. **Description:** A county agency that cultivates and maintains hundreds of acres of greenery and plants at four locations open to the public throughout the year. Founded in 1949. **NOTE:** Jobseekers should send resumes to Department of Parks and Recreation, Human Resources, 433 South Vermont Avenue, Los Angeles CA 90020-1976. 213/738-2993. Please indicate area of interest.

BURBANK, CITY OF
275 East Olive Avenue, Burbank CA 91502. 818/238-5021. **Contact:** Human Resources Department. **World Wide Web address:** http://www.burbank.acityline.com. **Description:** Administrative offices for the city of Burbank. **Special programs:** Internships.

CHULA VISTA, CITY OF
276 Fourth Avenue, Chula Vista CA 91910. 619/691-5096. **Contact:** Human Resources. **World Wide Web address:** http://www.ci.chula-vista.ca.us. **Description:** Administrative offices for the city of Chula Vista. **NOTE:** Resumes and/or faxed applications may not be used in lieu of a completed city application form. Please call the phone number above to obtain an application. **Common positions include:** Accountant/Auditor; Administrative Manager; Attorney; Automotive Mechanic; Blue-Collar Worker Supervisor; Budget Analyst; Buyer; Civil Engineer; Clerical Supervisor; Computer Programmer; Construction and Building Inspector; Customer Service Representative; Economist; Electrician; Emergency Medical Technician; Financial Analyst; Human Resources Manager; Landscape Architect; Librarian; Management Analyst/Consultant; Management Trainee; Police/Law Enforcement Officer; Public Relations Specialist; Purchasing Agent/Manager; Surveyor; Systems Analyst; Urban/Regional Planner. **Corporate headquarters location:** This location.

Operations at this facility include: Administration. **Number of employees at this location:** 800.

COVINA, CITY OF
125 East College Street, Covina CA 91723. 626/858-7221. **Fax:** 626/858-7225. **Contact:** Personnel. **World Wide Web address:** http://www.ci.covina.ca.us. **Description:** Administrative offices for the city of Covina. **Common positions include:** Accountant/Auditor; Civil Engineer; Librarian; Library Technician; Management Analyst/Consultant; Management Trainee; Urban/Regional Planner. **Special programs:** Internships. **Operations at this facility include:** Administration. **Number of employees at this location:** 200.

CULVER CITY, CITY OF
9770 Culver Boulevard, Culver City CA 90232. 310/253-5640. **Recorded jobline:** 310/253-5651. **Contact:** Human Resources. **World Wide Web address:** http://www.culvercity.org. **Description:** Administrative offices for Culver City. **Common positions include:** Accountant/Auditor; Automotive Mechanic; Blue-Collar Worker Supervisor; Budget Analyst; Bus Driver; Buyer; Civil Engineer; Computer Programmer; Electrician; Management Analyst/Consultant; Purchasing Agent/Manager; Sanitary Engineer; Secretary. **Special programs:** Internships. **Corporate headquarters location:** This location. **Operations at this facility include:** Administration; Service. **Number of employees at this location:** 600.

GARDEN GROVE, CITY OF
P.O. Box 3070, Garden Grove CA 92842. 714/741-5004. **Recorded jobline:** 714/741-5016. **Contact:** Human Resources. **World Wide Web address:** http://www.ci.garden-grove.ca.us. **Description:** Administrative offices for the city of Garden Grove. **Common positions include:** Accountant/Auditor; Administrative Manager; Automotive Mechanic; Blue-Collar Worker Supervisor; Broadcast Technician; Budget Analyst; Buyer; Civil Engineer; Clerical Supervisor; Computer Programmer; Construction and Building Inspector; Human Resources Manager; Management Analyst/Consultant; Police/Law Enforcement Officer; Property and Real Estate Manager; Purchasing Agent/Manager; Systems Analyst; Transportation/Traffic Specialist; Water Transportation Specialist. **Special programs:** Internships. **Corporate headquarters location:** This location.

THE GREATER OXNARD ECONOMIC DEVELOPMENT CORPORATION

721 South A Street, Oxnard CA 93030. 805/385-7444. **Toll-free phone:** 800/422-6332. **Contact:** Human Resources. **World Wide Web address:** http://www.oxnardedc.com. **Description:** Attracts new business and improves economic conditions and development in the city of Oxnard.

REDONDO BEACH, CITY OF

415 Diamond Street, P.O. Box 270, Redondo Beach CA 90277. 310/372-1171. **Contact:** Human Resources. **World Wide Web address:** http://www.redondo.org. **Description:** Administrative offices for the city of Redondo Beach. **Common positions include:** Accountant/Auditor; Administrative Manager; Attorney; Automotive Mechanic; Blue-Collar Worker Supervisor; Budget Analyst; Buyer; Civil Engineer; Claim Representative; Clerical Supervisor; Computer Programmer; Construction and Building Inspector; Draftsperson; Electrician; Emergency Medical Technician; Human Resources Manager; Human Service Worker; Librarian; Library Technician; Management Analyst/Consultant; Paralegal; Purchasing Agent/Manager; Systems Analyst. **Corporate headquarters location:** This location. **Number of employees at this location:** 700.

U.S. FOOD AND DRUG ADMINISTRATION (FDA)

19900 MacArthur Boulevard, Suite 300, Irvine CA 92612. 949/798-7600. **Toll-free phone:** 800/INFO-FDA. **Contact:** Human Resources Department. **World Wide Web address:** http://www.fda.gov. **Description:** The FDA monitors the manufacture, import, storage, and sale of consumer products. Responsibilities include checking wharves for imports of food, drugs, cosmetics, medical devices, and radiation emitting products. **Corporate headquarters location:** Rockville MD.

VICTORVILLE, CITY OF

14343 Civic Drive, Victorville CA 92392. 760/955-5048. **Contact:** Human Resources. **World Wide Web address:** http://www.ci.victorville.ca.us.**Description:** Municipal offices for the city of Victorville. **Common positions include:** Accountant/Auditor; Administrative Manager; Architect; Attorney; Blue-Collar Worker Supervisor; Budget Analyst; Buyer; Civil Engineer; Clerical Supervisor; Computer Programmer; Construction and Building Inspector; Draftsperson; Economist; Electrician; Environmental Engineer; Financial Analyst; Human Resources Manager; Human Service Worker; Management Analyst/Consultant; Property and Real

Estate Manager; Public Relations Specialist; Purchasing Agent; Surveyor; Systems Analyst; Transportation/Traffic Specialist; Wholesale and Retail Buyer. **Special programs:** Internships. **Operations at this facility include:** Administration; Service. **Number of employees at this location:** 600.

HEALTH CARE: SERVICES, EQUIPMENT, AND PRODUCTS

You can expect to find the following types of companies in this chapter:
Dental Labs and Equipment • Home Health Care Agencies • Hospitals and Medical Centers • Medical Equipment Manufacturers and Wholesalers • Offices and Clinics of Health Practitioners • Residential Treatment Centers/Nursing Homes • Veterinary Services

ADVANCED STERILIZATION PRODUCTS
33 Technology Drive, Irvine CA 92618. 949/581-5799. **Fax:** 949/450-6889. **Contact:** Human Resources Department. **E-mail address:** resumes@aspus.jnj.com. **World Wide Web address:** http://www.sterrad.com. **Description:** Manufactures sterilization equipment that is used on surgical instruments in hospitals. **Parent company:** Johnson & Johnson (New Brunswick NJ). **International locations:** Worldwide.

ALARIS MEDICAL SYSTEMS, INC.
P.O. Box 85335, San Diego CA 92186-5335. 858/458-7000. **Physical address:** 10221 Wateridge Circle, San Diego CA 92121. **Toll-free phone:** 800/854-7128. **Fax:** 858/458-6196. **Contact:** Personnel. **E-mail address:** hr@alarismed.com. **World Wide Web address:** http://www.alarismed.com. **Description:** Designs, manufactures, and markets instruments used to monitor patients and products for intravenous infusion therapy. **Corporate headquarters location:** This location. **Other U.S. locations:** Creedmoor NC. **International locations:** Mexico; United Kingdom. **Parent company:** ALARIS Medical, Inc. **President/CEO:** William J. Mercer.

ALL-CARE ANIMAL REFERRAL CENTER
18440 Amistad Street, Fountain Valley CA 92708. 714/963-0909. **Toll-free phone:** 800/944-PETS. **Fax:** 714/962-1905. **Contact:** Human Resources. **World Wide Web address:** http://www.acarc.com. **Description:** An animal hospital with a 24-hour critical care facility.

ALLIANCE IMAGING, INC.
1065 PacifiCenter Drive, Suite 200, Anaheim CA 92806-2131. 714/688-7100. **Fax:** 714/688-3646. **Contact:** Ms. Christi Braun, Director of Human Resources. **E-mail address:** cbraun@allianceimaging.com. **World Wide Web address:**

http://www.allianceimaging.com. **Description:** Provides medical diagnostic imaging services to hospitals, physicians, and patients. Services include MRI, Open MRI, computer tomography (CT), ultrasound, and position emission tomography (PET). **Corporate headquarters location:** This location. **Other U.S. locations:** Nationwide. **Listed on:** NASDAQ. **Stock exchange symbol:** SCAN. **Chairman and CEO:** Rick Zehner.

ALPHA THERAPEUTIC CORPORATION
5555 Valley Boulevard, Los Angeles CA 90032. **Toll-free phone:** 800/421-0008. **Contact:** Human Resources. **E-mail address:** resumes@alphather.com. **World Wide Web address:** http://www.alphather.com. **Description:** Produces plasma-derived products. Product types include plasma volume expanders, for use in trauma situations; coagulation products, for treating blood clotting disorders; and immune globulin products, for treating various immune deficiencies. Founded in 1948. **Parent company:** Welfide Corporation.

AMERICAN MEDICAL RESPONSE INC.
20101 Hamilton Avenue, Suite 300, Torrance CA 90502. 310/851-7000. **Fax:** 925/454-6296. **Contact:** Jennifer Gottardy, Employment Coordinator. **World Wide Web address:** http://www.amr-inc.com. **Description:** Operates an ambulance service. **Other U.S. locations:** Nationwide.

AMERISOURCEBERGEN
4000 Metropolitan Drive, Orange CA 92868. 714/385-4000. **Fax:** 714/385-1442. **Contact:** Recruiting. **E-mail address:** techcareers@bbcjobs.com; careers@bbcjobs.com. **World Wide Web address:** http://www.amerisourcebergen.net. **Description:** Distributes pharmaceuticals and medical-surgical supplies. **Company slogan:** Our people make the difference. **Common positions include:** Accountant; Administrative Assistant; Budget Analyst; Buyer; Computer Programmer; Consultant; Data Entry Clerk; Financial Analyst; Marketing Specialist; Project Manager; Secretary; Systems Analyst; Technical Writer/Editor; Telecommunications Manager; Typist/Word Processor. **Office hours:** Monday - Friday, 7:30 a.m. - 4:30 p.m. **Corporate headquarters location:** This location. **Other U.S. locations:** Valley Forge PA. **Listed on:** New York Stock Exchange. **Stock exchange symbol:** ABC.

APRIA HEALTHCARE GROUP INC.
26220 Enterprise Court, Lake Forest CA 92630. 714/427-2000. **Toll-free phone:** 800/647-5404. **Contact:** Human Resources. **E-**

mail address: contact_us@apria.com. **World Wide Web address:** http://www.apria.com. **Description:** Provides a broad range of respiratory therapy services, home medical equipment, and infusion therapy services. Apria Healthcare Group's home health care services are provided to patients who have been discharged from hospitals, skilled nursing facilities, or convalescent homes and are being treated at home. In conjunction with medical professionals, Apria personnel deliver, install, and service medical equipment, as well as provide appropriate therapies and coordinate plans of care for their patients. Apria personnel also instruct patients and care-givers in the correct use of equipment and monitor the equipment's effectiveness. Patients and their families receive training from registered nurses and respiratory therapy professionals concerning the therapy administered including instruction in proper infusion technique and the care and use of equipment and supplies. **Common positions include:** Accountant/Auditor; Attorney; Branch Manager; Buyer; Computer Programmer; Financial Analyst; Human Resources Manager; MIS Specialist; Paralegal; Pharmacist; Registered Nurse; Respiratory Therapist; Systems Analyst; Telecommunications Manager. **Corporate headquarters location:** This location. **Other U.S. locations:** Nationwide. **International locations:** United Kingdom. **Operations at this facility include:** Administration. **Listed on:** New York Stock Exchange. **Stock exchange symbol:** AHG. **Annual sales/revenues:** More than $100 million. **Number of employees at this location:** 750. **Number of employees nationwide:** 9,000.

AXELGAARD MANUFACTURING COMPANY, LTD.
329 West Aviation Road, Fallbrook CA 92028. 760/728-3424. **Fax:** 760/728-3467. **Contact:** Human Resources. **World Wide Web address:** http://www.axelgaard.com. **Description:** Manufactures electrodes for neurostimulation. **Common positions include:** Accountant; Administrative Assistant; Applications Engineer; Blue-Collar Worker Supervisor; Chemist; Chief Financial Officer; Controller; Customer Service Representative; Database Manager; Design Engineer; Electrical/Electronics Engineer; Financial Analyst; Human Resources Manager; Manufacturing Engineer; Marketing Manager; Mechanical Engineer; MIS Specialist; Production Manager; Purchasing Agent/Manager; Sales Manager; Secretary; Transportation/Traffic Specialist.

BIOLASE TECHNOLOGY, INC.
981 Calle Amanecer, San Clemente CA 92673. 949/361-1200. **Toll-free phone:** 888/424-6527. **Fax:** 949/361-0207. **Contact:** Natalie McGregor. **E-mail address:** nmcgregor@biolase.com. **World Wide Web address:** http://www.biolase.com. **Description:** Manufactures and markets a full range of advanced dental and medical products. **Listed on:** NASDAQ. **Stock exchange symbol:** BLTI.

BIRD PRODUCTS
1100 Bird Center Drive, Palm Springs CA 92262. 760/778-7200. **Contact:** Della Adams, Human Resources. **Description:** Manufactures respiratory care and infection control products. **Common positions include:** Chemist; Electrical/Electronics Engineer; Mechanical Engineer.

BURTON MEDICAL PRODUCTS
21100 Lassen Street, Chatsworth CA 91311. 818/701-8700. **Fax:** 818/701-8725. **Contact:** Human Resources. **World Wide Web address:** http://www.burtonmedical.com. **Description:** A wholesale distributor of surgical lights. **Corporate headquarters location:** This location. **Parent company:** LUXO ASA.

CASA DE LAS CAMPANAS
18655 West Bernardo Drive, San Diego CA 92127. 858/451-9152. **Fax:** 858/592-1853. **Contact:** Jane Munson, Human Resources Manager. **World Wide Web address:** http://www.casadelascampanas.com. **Description:** A nonprofit, continuing care retirement facility with more than 500 residents. **NOTE:** Entry-level positions and second and third shifts are offered. **Common positions include:** Activity Director; Administrative Assistant; Certified Nurses Aide; Controller; Dietician/Nutritionist; Education Administrator; Emergency Medical Technician; Food Service Manager; Housekeeper; Human Resources Manager; Licensed Practical Nurse; Marketing Manager; Purchasing Agent/Manager; Registered Nurse; Sales Representative; Secretary; Social Worker. **Special programs:** Internships. **Office hours:** Monday - Thursday, 10:00 a.m. - 12:00 p.m. and 3:00 p.m. - 4:00 p.m. **Parent company:** Life Care Services LLC. **Executive Director:** Craig Wyble. **Number of employees at this location:** 300.

CEDARS-SINAI HEALTH SYSTEM
8723 Alden Drive, Room 110, Los Angeles CA 90048. 310/423-3277. **Recorded jobline:** 310/423-8230. **Contact:** Personnel. **E-mail address:** hr.web@cshs.org (for inquiries);

jobs@cshs.org (for resume submission). **World Wide Web address:** http://www.csmc.edu. **Description:** A nonprofit health care delivery system that operates through Cedar-Sinai Medical Center, as well as a network of primary care physicians. Cedars-Sinai specializes in acute, subacute, and home patient care; biomedical research; community service; and continuing medical education. **Common positions include:** Biological Scientist; Claim Representative; Clerical Supervisor; Clinical Lab Technician; Computer Programmer; Dietician/Nutritionist; EEG Technologist; Health Services Manager; Licensed Practical Nurse; Nuclear Medicine Technologist; Occupational Therapist; Pharmacist; Physical Therapist; Physician; Psychologist; Radiological Technologist; Registered Nurse; Respiratory Therapist; Speech-Language Pathologist; Surgical Technician; Systems Analyst. **Corporate headquarters location:** This location. **Operations at this facility include:** Administration; Research and Development; Service.

CHAD THERAPEUTICS, INC.
21622 Plummer Street, Chatsworth CA 91311. 818/882-0883. **Contact:** Barbara Muskin, Human Resources Manager. **E-mail address:** bmuskin@chadtherapeutics.com. **World Wide Web address:** http://www.chadtherapeutics.com. **Description:** Designs, manufactures, and markets home oxygen systems. Products names include Oxylite, Oxymatic, and Oxymizer. **Corporate headquarters location:** This location. **Listed on:** American Stock Exchange. **Stock exchange symbol:** CTU.

COASTCAST
3025 East Victoria Street, Rancho Dominguez CA 90221. 310/638-0595. **Fax:** 310/631-6820. **Contact:** Anna Leonard, Personnel Manager. **E-mail address:** careers@coastcast.com. **World Wide Web address:** http://www.coastcast.com. **Description:** Manufactures precision castings for a number of specialty products including medical implants, golf clubs, hand tools, and automotive parts. **Corporate headquarters location:** This location. **Other area locations:** Gardena CA. **Listed on:** New York Stock Exchange. **Stock exchange symbol:** PAR.

COMMUNITY HOSPITAL OF SAN BERNARDINO
1805 Medical Center Drive, San Bernardino CA 92411. 909/887-6333. **Contact:** Human Resources. **World Wide Web address:** http://www.communityhospitalsb.com. **Description:** A nonprofit, 291-bed community hospital whose facilities include a convalescent home and rehabilitation center.

CONTINUUM

10920 Via Frontera, San Diego CA 92127-1704. 858/485-0933. **Contact:** Field Recruiting. **E-mail address:** opportunities@continuumhc.com. **World Wide Web address:** http://www.continuumhc.com. **Description:** A nationwide mobile health testing service. Continuum provides health screening for unions, major corporations, public utilities, and other public and private organizations. **NOTE:** Entry-level positions are offered. **Common positions include:** Licensed Practical Nurse; Medical Assistant; Radiological Technologist; Registered Nurse. **Corporate headquarters location:** Springfield PA. **Other U.S. locations:** Wilton CT; Norcross GA. **Listed on:** Privately held. **Number of employees nationwide:** 200.

CORVAS INTERNATIONAL, INC.

3030 Science Park Road, San Diego CA 92121-1102. 858/455-9800. **Fax:** 858/455-5169. **Contact:** Human Resources. **E-mail address:** careers@corvas.com. **World Wide Web address:** http://www.corvas.com. **Description:** Designs and develops therapeutic agents for the prevention and treatment of major cardiovascular and inflammatory diseases. The company also develops drugs that block the initiation of blood clot formation (thrombosis) and white blood cell activation (inflammation). Founded in 1987. **NOTE:** Entry-level positions are offered. **Common positions include:** Accountant; Biochemist; Biological Scientist; Buyer; Chemist; Computer Programmer; Controller; Human Resources Manager; Intellectual Property Lawyer; Paralegal; Vice President. **Special programs:** Internships. **Internship information:** Summer interns are hired annually. Applicants are encouraged to send resumes beginning May 1. **Corporate headquarters location:** This location. **Operations at this facility include:** Divisional Headquarters. **Listed on:** NASDAQ. **Stock exchange symbol:** CVAS. **Annual sales/revenues:** Less than $5 million.

DEL MAR MEDICAL SYSTEMS, LLC

1621 Alton Parkway, Irvine CA 92606. 949/250-3200. **Contact:** Trish Hichten, Personnel Manager. **World Wide Web address:** http://www.delmarmedical.com. **Description:** Develops, manufactures, and markets a wide range of medical monitoring and testing equipment. Products include stress tests, ambulatory blood pressure monitors, ambulatory transesophagael testing devices, and the AVESP (Audiovisual Superimposed Electrocardiographic Presentation). **Corporate headquarters location:** This location.

EDWARDS LIFESCIENCES
One Edwards Way, Irvine CA 92614. 949/250-2500. **Toll-free phone:** 800/428-3278. **Contact:** Human Resources. **E-mail address:** eweb@edwards.com. **World Wide Web address:** http://www.edwards.com. **Description:** Designs, develops, manufactures, and markets disposable medical devices used in the handling, processing, and purifying of blood during surgical and medical procedures. **Corporate headquarters location:** This location. **International locations:** Worldwide. **Listed on:** New York Stock Exchange. **Stock exchange symbol:** EW. **Annual sales/revenues:** More than $100 million. **Number of employees at this location:** 1,400. **Number of employees worldwide:** 5,000.

EPIMMUNE INC.
5820 Nancy Ridge Drive, San Diego CA 92121-2829. 858/860-2500. **Fax:** 858/860-2600. **Contact:** Human Resources. **E-mail address:** careers@epimmune.com. **World Wide Web address:** http://www.epimmune.com. **Description:** Researches and develops vaccines to prevent and treat infectious diseases and cancer. **Corporate headquarters location:** This location. **Listed on:** NASDAQ. **Stock exchange symbol:** EPMN.

FACEY MEDICAL FOUNDATION
1211 Sepulveda Boulevard, Mission Hill CA 91345. 818/837-5655. **Fax:** 818/365-5706. **Recorded jobline:** 818/837-5695. **Contact:** Marla Adams, Human Resources Department Representative. **E-mail address:** resume@facey.com. **World Wide Web address:** http://www.facey.com. **Description:** A nonprofit, multispecialty health care clinic and medical group. Founded in 1922. **NOTE:** Entry-level positions, externships, and second and third shifts are offered. **Common positions include:** Accountant; Adjuster; Administrative Assistant; Auditor; Buyer; Chief Financial Officer; Claim Representative; Clinical Lab Technician; Computer Programmer; Controller; Dietician/Nutritionist; EKG Technician; Financial Analyst; Human Resources Manager; Licensed Vocational Nurse; Mechanical Engineer; Medical Records Technician; MIS Specialist; Physical Therapist; Physician; Project Manager; Public Relations Specialist; Purchasing Agent/Manager; Quality Control Supervisor; Radiological Technologist; Registered Nurse; Secretary; Surgical Technician; Systems Manager.

FOUNTAIN VIEW, INC.
2600 West Magnolia Boulevard, Burbank CA 91505. 818/841-8750. **Contact:** Human Resources Department. **World Wide**

Web address: http://www.seniorhousing.net/ads/fvhome. **Description:** Provides long-term care through the operation of skilled nursing centers and nursing homes. **Corporate headquarters location:** This location. **Number of employees nationwide:** 1,800.

4-D NEUROIMAGING
9727 Pacific Heights Boulevard, San Diego CA 92121. 858/453-6300. **Contact:** Human Resources Department. **World Wide Web address:** http://www.4dneuroimaging.com. **Description:** Manufactures specialized instruments for ultrasensitive magnetic field and low-temperature measurements. The company incorporates its core magnetic sensing technologies into its magnetic source imaging (MSI) system, an instrument designed to assist in the noninvasive diagnosis of a broad range of medical disorders. The MSI system developed by the company uses advanced superconducting technology to measure and locate the source of magnetic fields generated by the human body. The company is focusing the development of its technology on market applications such as brain surgery and the diagnosis and surgical planning for treatment of epilepsy and life-threatening cardiac arrhythmias. Founded in 1970. **Corporate headquarters location:** This location.

DANIEL FREEMAN MEMORIAL HOSPITAL
333 North Prairie Avenue, Inglewood CA 90301. 310/674-7050. **Contact:** Recruitment Coordinator. **World Wide Web address:** http://www.danielfreeman.org. **Description:** A nonprofit hospital that offers a variety of services including behavioral health, heart care, women's and children's services, and rehabilitation. The hospital also offers a variety of specialty programs such as the Center for Heart and Health, complimentary medicine, and emergency services. **Common positions include:** Environmental Engineer; Food Scientist/Technologist; Licensed Practical Nurse; Occupational Therapist; Pharmacist; Physical Therapist; Recreational Therapist; Registered Nurse; Respiratory Therapist; Speech-Language Pathologist; Systems Analyst. **Corporate headquarters location:** This location. **Parent company:** Tenet Healthcare Corporation. **Listed on:** New York Stock Exchange. **Stock exchange symbol:** THC. **Number of employees nationwide:** 1,500.

GARFIELD MEDICAL CENTER
525 North Garfield Avenue, Monterey Park CA 91754. 626/573-2222. **Contact:** Human Resources. **World Wide Web**

address: http://www.garfieldmedicalcenter.com. **Description:** A full-service hospital that provides acute care, emergency care, and a neonatal intensive care unit. **Parent company:** Tenet Healthcare. **Listed on:** Tenet Healthcare. **Stock exchange symbol:** THE.

GISH BIOMEDICAL, INC.
22942 Arroyo Vista, Rancho Santa Margarita CA 92688. 949/756-5485. **Toll-free phone:** 800/938-0531. **Fax:** 949/635-6291. **Contact:** Human Resources Department. **World Wide Web address:** http://www.gishbiomedical.com. **Description:** Designs, produces, and markets innovative specialty surgical devices. Gish Biomedical specializes in blood handling and fluid delivery as well as blood management systems for cardiovascular surgery, oncology, and orthopedics. **Corporate headquarters location:** This location. **Listed on:** NASDAQ. **Stock exchange symbol:** GISH.

HILLVIEW MENTAL HEALTH CENTER, INC.
11500 Eldridge Avenue, Suite 206, Lake View Terrace CA 91342. 818/896-1161. **Contact:** Human Resources Department. **Description:** An outpatient and residential mental health services facility for individuals with persistent mental disabilities. Founded in 1985. **NOTE:** Entry-level positions and second and third shifts are offered. **Common positions include:** Accountant; Administrative Assistant; Computer Operator; Counselor; Physician; Psychologist; Social Worker; Typist/Word Processor. **Corporate headquarters location:** This location. **Annual sales/revenues:** Less than $5 million. **Number of employees at this location:** 80.

INAMED CORPORATION
5540 Ekwill Street, Suite D, Santa Barbara CA 93111. 805/692-5400. **Contact:** Human Resources. **World Wide Web address:** http://www.inamed.com. **Description:** INAMED Corporation is a medical products company with 23 subsidiaries across the United States and Europe. The company develops, manufactures, and markets implantable products including mammary prostheses, tissue expanders, and facial implants; develops, produces, and distributes premium products for dermatology, wound care, and burn treatment; and packages and sterilizes medical grade components for other medical device companies. **Corporate headquarters location:** This location. **Subsidiaries include:** Bioenterics Corporation (Carpinteria CA); McGhan Medical Corporation (Santa Barbara CA); McGhan, Ltd. (Arklow, Ireland). **Listed on:** NASDAQ. **Stock exchange symbol:** IMDC.

INSIGHT HEALTH SERVICES CORPORATION

4400 MacArthur Boulevard, Suite 800, Newport Beach CA 92660. 949/476-0733. **Toll-free phone:** 800/874-8634. **Fax:** 949/476-1013. **Contact:** Human Resources. **World Wide Web address:** http://www.insighthealthcorp.com. **Description:** Engaged in the establishment and operation of outpatient diagnostic and treatment centers utilizing magnetic resonance imaging systems (MRI), computerized tomography systems (CT), multimodality radiologic imaging systems, cardiovascular diagnostic imaging systems, medical linear accelerators, and Leksell Stereotactic Gamma Units (Gamma Knife). **Common positions include:** Accountant; Administrative Assistant; Assistant Manager; Attorney; Chief Financial Officer; Finance Director; Financial Analyst; Human Resources Manager; Marketing Manager; Medical Records Technician; MIS Specialist; Nuclear Medicine Technologist; Operations Manager; Project Manager; Quality Control Supervisor; Radiological Technologist; Transportation/Traffic Specialist. **Office hours:** Monday - Friday, 8:00 a.m. - 5:00 p.m. **Corporate headquarters location:** This location. **Other U.S. locations:** Nationwide. **Listed on:** NASDAQ. **Stock exchange symbol:** IHSC. **Number of employees at this location:** 60. **Number of employees nationwide:** 800.

JENNY CRAIG INTERNATIONAL

11355 North Torrey Pines Road, La Jolla CA 92037. 858/812-7000. **Contact:** Human Resources Department. **World Wide Web address:** http://www.jennycraig.com. **Description:** Provides a comprehensive weight-loss program. Jenny Craig International sells protein- and calorie-controlled food items to program participants throughout the United States and in four other countries. **Corporate headquarters location:** This location. **Number of employees nationwide:** 5,370.

KELLY HOME CARE SERVICES

2900 Bristol Street, Suite J102, Costa Mesa CA 92626. 714/979-7413. **Fax:** 310/645-6401. **Contact:** Personnel. **World Wide Web address:** hhtp://www.kelleyhomecare.com. **Description:** Provides home health care aides for senior citizens. **Common positions include:** Home Health Aide; Supervisor. **Corporate headquarters location:** Troy MI.

KIMBERLY-CLARK CORPORATION

10509 Vista Sorrento Parkway, Suite 400, San Diego CA 92121. 858/794-8111. **Fax:** 858/314-6600. **Contact:** Human Resources. **World Wide Web address:** http://www.kimberly-clark.com. **Description:** A major manufacturer and marketer of fiber-based products for consumer and industrial customers. Kimberly-Clark does business in three primary product classes: Consumer and Service, offering a broad range of paper-based goods such as facial tissue, table napkins, and disposable gowns for medical applications; Newsprint, Pulp, and Forest Products, providing a variety of goods to industrial clients; and Paper and Specialties, producing adhesive-coated paper for commercial printing customers. **Corporate headquarters location:** Neenah WI. **Listed on:** New York Stock Exchange. **Stock exchange symbol:** KMB.

KIMBERLY-CLARK CORPORATION
2001 East Orangethorpe Avenue, Fullerton CA 92831-5396. 714/773-7500. **Contact:** Human Resources. **World Wide Web address:** http://www.kimberly-clark.com. **Description:** A major manufacturer and marketer of fiber-based products for consumer and industrial customers. Kimberly-Clark does business in three primary product classes: Consumer and Service, offering a broad range of paper-based goods such as facial tissue, table napkins, and disposable gowns for medical applications; Newsprint, Pulp, and Forest Products, providing a variety of goods to industrial clients; and Paper and Specialties, producing adhesive-coated paper for commercial printing customers. **Corporate headquarters location:** Neenah WI. **Listed on:** New York Stock Exchange. **Stock exchange symbol:** KMB.

LOGAN HEIGHTS FAMILY HEALTH CENTER
1809 National Avenue, San Diego CA 92113. 619/234-8171. **Fax:** 619/232-1360. **Contact:** Trish Beesaw, Human Resources Manager. **Description:** A nonprofit, community health center. Services include audiology, counseling, dental, dermatology, early intervention, family planning, health promotion, hearing, internal medicine, laboratory, language, OB/GYN, optometry, pediatric cardiology, pediatrics, pharmacy, radiology, social services, and speech. **Common positions include:** Accountant/Auditor; Clinical Lab Technician; Customer Service Representative; Dentist; MIS Specialist; Pharmacist; Physical Therapist; Physician; Psychologist; Systems Analyst; Typist/Word Processor. **Special programs:** Internships. **Other U.S. locations:** Mission Beach CA. **Operations at this facility include:** Administration. **Number of employees at this location:** 250.

MATRIA HEALTHCARE
17701 Cowan Avenue, Suite 150, Irvine CA 92614. 949/794-6500. **Toll-free phone:** 800/456-4060. **Contact:** Human

Resources. **E-mail address:** matriahr@matria.com. **World Wide Web address:** http://www.matria.com. **Description:** Offers medical services for pregnant women via 24-hour hotlines. Matria Healthcare is subcontracted through insurance companies. **Corporate headquarters location:** Marietta GA. **Listed on:** NASDAQ. **Stock exchange symbol:** MATR.

MAXXIM MEDICAL
43225 Business Park Drive, Temecula CA 92590. 909/699-4400. **Contact:** Human Resources. **World Wide Web address:** http://www.maxximmedical.com. **Description:** This location primarily manufactures disposable medical gloves for use in hospitals and laboratories. Overall, Maxxim Medical manufactures and sells a broad line of health care products used by hospitals, laboratories, pharmaceutical companies, medical schools, dentists, and the general public. **Common positions include:** Accountant/Auditor; Administrator; Buyer; Chemist; Mechanical Engineer; Purchasing Agent/Manager; Quality Control Supervisor. **Corporate headquarters location:** Clearwater FL. **Operations at this facility include:** Manufacturing.

MED-DESIGN CORPORATION
2810 Bunsen Avenue, Ventura CA 93003. 805/339-0375. **Contact:** Human Resources. **World Wide Web address:** http://www.med-design.com. **Description:** Designs and develops medical safety devices intended to reduce the incidence of needle accidents that primarily occur in health care settings. Products developed by the company include the retractable needle hypodermic syringe, the retractable vacuum tube phlebotomy set, and the retractable intravenous catheter insertion device. **Corporate headquarters location:** This location. **Listed on:** NASDAQ. **Stock exchange symbol:** MEDC.

MEDSEP CORPORATION
1630 Industrial Park Street, Covina CA 91722. 626/915-8219. **Toll-free phone:** 800/288-8377. **Fax:** 626/332-2518. **Contact:** Human Resources Department. **World Wide Web address:** http://www.pall.com. **Description:** Manufactures medical devices for collecting plasma and whole blood. Founded in 1946. **Company slogan:** Quality flows through our system. **Common positions include:** Accountant; Biochemist; Biological Scientist; Buyer; Chemical Engineer; Chemist; Controller; Design Engineer; Electrical/Electronics Engineer; Electrician; Environmental Engineer; Human Resources Manager; Industrial Engineer; Manufacturing Engineer;

Marketing Manager; Marketing Specialist; Mechanical Engineer; MIS Specialist; Production Manager; Quality Control Supervisor; Registered Nurse; Secretary; Vice President of Marketing; Vice President of Sales. **Corporate headquarters location:** East Hills NY. **Other U.S. locations:** FL; MA; MI. **International locations:** Asia; Canada; Europe; South America. **Parent company:** Pall Corporation. **Listed on:** New York Stock Exchange. **Stock exchange symbol:** PLL. **President:** Clarence Treppa. **Facilities Manager:** Dennis Seel. **Annual sales/revenues:** $51 - $100 million. **Number of employees at this location:** 420. **Number of employees nationwide:** 7,000. **Number of employees worldwide:** 8,000.

MEDTRONIC MINIMED
18000 Devonshire Street, Northridge CA 91325-1219. 818/362-5958. **Toll-free phone:** 800/MIN-IMED. **Fax:** 818/576-6232. **Contact:** Department of Human Resources. **E-mail address:** hr@minimed.com. **World Wide Web address:** http://www.minimed.com. **Description:** Develops and manufactures insulin pumps and other products for the treatment of diabetes. Founded in 1980. **Corporate headquarters location:** This location. **Other U.S. locations:** Hollywood FL. **International locations:** Asia; Australia; Europe; South America. **Listed on:** New York Stock Exchange. **Stock exchange symbol:** MDT. **Annual sales/revenues:** More than $100 million.

MENTOR CORPORATION
201 Mentor Drive, Santa Barbara CA 93111. 805/681-6000. **Contact:** Human Resources Department. **World Wide Web address:** http://www.mentorcorp.com. **Description:** Develops, manufactures, and markets a broad range of products for plastic and reconstructive surgery, urology, and ophthalmology. Mentor Corporation's products include surgically implantable devices, diagnostic and surgical instruments, disposable instruments, and disposable products for hospitals and home health care. **Corporate headquarters location:** This location. **Listed on:** NASDAQ. **Stock exchange symbol:** MNTR.

MERCY OCCUPATIONAL HEALTHCARE BAKERSFIELD
P.O. Box 119, Bakersfield CA 93302. 661/632-5000. **Physical address:** 2216 Truxton Avenue, Bakersfield CA 93301. **Fax:** 661/327-8061. **Contact:** Human Resources. **World Wide Web address:** http://www.mercy.org. **Description:** A hospital. **Common positions include:** Accountant/Auditor; Biomedical Engineer; Computer Programmer; Dietician/Nutritionist;

Electrical/Electronics Engineer; Financial Analyst; Licensed Practical Nurse; Medical Records Technician; Occupational Therapist; Pharmacist; Physical Therapist; Recreational Therapist; Registered Nurse; Respiratory Therapist; Social Worker; Surgical Technician; Systems Analyst. **Corporate headquarters location:** This location. **Operations at this facility include:** Administration. **Number of employees at this location:** 1,300.

METROPOLITAN STATE HOSPITAL
11401 South Bloomfield Avenue, Norwalk CA 90650. 562/863-7011. **Contact:** Human Resources. **Description:** A psychiatric hospital that is part of the California Mental Health Department.

ORMCO CORPORATION
1717 West Collins Avenue, Orange CA 92867. 714/516-7400. **Contact:** Human Resources Manager. **E-mail address:** careers@sybrondental.com. **World Wide Web address:** http://www.ormco.com. **Description:** Manufactures and markets orthodontic appliances and supplies. **Common positions include:** Accountant; Administrative Assistant; Computer Support Technician; Controller; Design Engineer; Draftsperson; Human Resources Manager; Manufacturing Engineer; Operations Manager; Production Manager; Purchasing Agent/Manager; Quality Control Supervisor. **Office hours:** Monday - Friday, 8:00 a.m. - 5:00 p.m. **Corporate headquarters location:** Orange CA. **Parent company:** Sybron Dental Specialties. **Number of employees at this location:** 110.

POMONA VALLEY HOSPITAL MEDICAL CENTER
1798 North Garey Avenue, Pomona CA 91767. **Fax:** 909/623-3253. **Recorded jobline:** 909/865-9840. **Contact:** Rolanda Bradshaw, Employment Specialist. **World Wide Web address:** http://www.pvhmc.com. **Description:** A 449-bed, nonprofit, acute care, teaching hospital. The hospital offers medical services through the Robert and Beverly Lewis Cancer Care Center; the Stead Heart Center; and the Women's Center. Founded in 1903. **Common positions include:** Clinical Lab Technician; Dietician/Nutritionist; EEG Technologist; EKG Technician; Emergency Medical Technician; Food Scientist/Technologist; Health Services Manager; Licensed Practical Nurse; Medical Records Technician; Nuclear Medicine Technologist; Occupational Therapist; Pharmacist; Physical Therapist; Physician; Radiological Technologist; Registered Nurse; Respiratory Therapist; Social Worker;

Surgical Technician; Systems Analyst. **Operations at this facility include:** Administration; Service. **Number of employees at this location:** 2,300.

PROTEIN POLYMER TECHNOLOGIES, INC.
10655 Sorrento Valley Road, San Diego CA 92121. 858/558-6064. **Fax:** 858/558-6477. **Contact:** Human Resources. **World Wide Web address:** http://www.ppti.com. **Description:** Engaged in research and development of products for surgical repair procedures including tissue adhesives and sealants, adhesion barriers, and drug delivery devices. The company also markets a line of polymer-activated cell culture products. **Corporate headquarters location:** This location.

RANCHO LOS AMIGOS NATIONAL REHABILITATION CENTER
7601 East Imperial Highway, Downey CA 90242. 562/401-7111. **Recorded jobline:** 800/970-5478. **Contact:** Human Resources. **World Wide Web address:** http://www.rancho.org. **Description:** A rehabilitation center providing care to patients who suffer from strokes, spinal cord injuries, brain injuries, or other disabling illnesses.

RESMED
14040 Danielson Street, Poway CA 92064. 858/746-2400. **Toll-free phone:** 800/424-0737. **Fax:** 858/746-5820. **Contact:** Human Resources Department Manager. **World Wide Web address:** http://www.resmed.com. **Description:** Develops, manufactures, and markets respiratory devices. ResMed specializes in respiratory products relating to sleep disordered breathing (SBD) including sleep apnea. Founded in 1989. **Corporate headquarters location:** This location. **International locations:** Worldwide. **Listed on:** New York Stock Exchange. **Stock exchange symbol:** RMD. **Annual sales/revenues:** More than $100 million.

ROBERT F. KENNEDY MEDICAL CENTER
4500 West 116th Street, Hawthorne CA 90250. 310/973-1711. **Contact:** Human Resources Department. **World Wide Web address:** http://www.dochs.org/our_community/hawthorne.asp. **Description:** An acute care hospital affiliated with the Roman Catholic Church. **Corporate headquarters location:** This location.

ST. JOHN'S HEALTH CENTER
1328 22nd Street, 6th Floor, Santa Monica CA 90404. 310/829-8633. **Toll-free phone:** 800/359-9003. **Recorded**

jobline: 310/829-8323. **Contact:** Penny Bresky, Recruitment and Retention Manager. **World Wide Web address:** http://www.stjohns.org. **Description:** A private, nonprofit, 317-bed, acute health care facility. Founded in 1939. **NOTE:** This firm does not accept unsolicited resumes. Please only respond to advertised openings. **Common positions include:** Licensed Practical Nurse; Medical Records Technician; Nuclear Medicine Technologist; Occupational Therapist; Pharmacist; Physical Therapist; Radiological Technologist; Registered Nurse; Respiratory Therapist; Surgical Technician. **Corporate headquarters location:** Leavenworth KS. **Other U.S. locations:** CO; KS; MT. **Parent company:** Sisters of Charity of Leavenworth. **Operations at this facility include:** Administration; Service. **Listed on:** Privately held. **Number of employees at this location:** 1,000.

ST. JUDE MEDICAL
15900 Valley View Court, Sylmar CA 91342. 818/362-6822. **Contact:** Human Resources. **World Wide Web address:** http://www.sjm.com. **Description:** Manufactures cardiac arrhythmia management devices including pacemakers and defibrillators. **Corporate headquarters location:** This location. **Listed on:** New York Stock Exchange. **Stock exchange symbol:** STJ.

SAN LUIS OBISPO COUNTY GENERAL HOSPITAL
1035 Palm Street, Room 384, San Luis Obispo CA 93408. 805/781-5959. **Recorded jobline:** 805/781-5958. **Contact:** Human Resources Department. **World Wide Web address:** http://www.countyofslo.org/personnel. **Description:** A hospital. **Common positions include:** Certified Nurses Aide; Pharmacist; Radiological Technologist; Registered Nurse; Respiratory Therapist. **Number of employees at this location:** 400.

SHARP HEALTHCARE
8695 Spectrum Center Boulevard, San Diego CA 92123. 858/499-4000. **Fax:** 858/499-5938. **Contact:** Human Resources Department. **E-mail address:** sharpjob@sharp.com. **World Wide Web address:** http://www.sharp.com. **Description:** A nonprofit organization consisting of six acute care hospitals, one specialty women's hospital, three medical groups, medical clinics, urgent care centers, skilled nursing facilities, and a variety of other community health education programs and related services. Founded in 1954. **NOTE:** Second and third shifts are offered. **Common positions include:** Account Representative; Accountant; Auditor; Budget Analyst; Certified Nurses Aide; Chief Financial Officer; Claim

Representative; Clerical Supervisor; Clinical Lab Technician; Computer Operator; Computer Programmer; Controller; Customer Service Representative; Dietician/Nutritionist; EEG Technologist; EKG Technician; Financial Analyst; Human Resources Manager; Licensed Practical Nurse; Medical Records Technician; Nuclear Medicine Technologist; Occupational Therapist; Pharmacist; Physical Therapist; Physician; Public Relations Specialist; Registered Nurse; Respiratory Therapist; Secretary; Social Worker; Speech-Language Pathologist; Surgical Technician; Systems Analyst; Systems Manager; Typist/Word Processor. **Office hours:** Monday - Friday, 7:00 a.m. - 7:00 p.m. **Corporate headquarters location:** This location. **Operations at this facility include:** Administration; Service. **Listed on:** Privately held. **CEO:** Michael Murphy. **Annual sales/revenues:** More than $100 million.

STAAR SURGICAL COMPANY
1911 Walker Avenue, Monrovia CA 91016. 626/303-7902. **Contact:** Human Resources Department. **E-mail address:** hrdept@staar.com. **World Wide Web address:** http://www.staar.com. **Description:** Develops, manufactures, and markets ophthalmic medical devices. The company's main product is a foldable lens used in the treatment of cataracts. Founded in 1982. **Corporate headquarters location:** This location. **Listed on:** NASDAQ. **Stock exchange symbol:** STAA.

SYNBIOTICS CORPORATION
11011 Via Frontera, San Diego CA 92127. 858/451-3771. **Contact:** Human Resources Department. **World Wide Web address:** http://www.synbiotics.com. **Description:** Develops, manufactures, and markets products and services to veterinary specialty markets. Synbiotics provides canine reproduction products and services to purebred dog breeders and their veterinarians. In addition, the company markets a line of life-stage nutritional supplements; and PennHip, a new method for the early diagnosis and evaluation of canine hip dysplasia. **Corporate headquarters location:** This location.

TENDER LOVING CARE/STAFF BUILDERS
1100 North Ventura Road, Suite 107, Oxnard CA 93030. 805/988-5890. **Contact:** Human Resources. **World Wide Web address:** http://www.staffbuilders.com. **Description:** A home health care agency. **Corporate headquarters location:** Lake Success NY. **Other U.S. locations:** Nationwide. **Number of employees nationwide:** 20,000.

TENET HEALTHCARE CORPORATION
3820 State Street, Santa Barbara CA 93105. 805/563-7000. **Contact:** Human Resources. **World Wide Web address:** http://www.tenethealth.com. **Description:** A multibillion-dollar, multihospital corporation that, in conjunction with its subsidiaries, owns or operates approximately 130 acute care facilities nationwide. **Corporate headquarters location:** This location. **Listed on:** New York Stock Exchange Stock. **Stock exchange symbol:** THC. **Number of employees nationwide:** 130,000.

TORRANCE MEMORIAL MEDICAL CENTER
3330 Lomita Boulevard, Torrance CA 90505. 310/325-9110. **Recorded jobline:** 310/517-4790. **Contact:** Michele Alarcon, Human Resources Representative. **E-mail address:** michele.alarcon@tmmc.com. **World Wide Web address:** http://www.torrancememorial.org. **Description:** A nonprofit medical center. **Corporate headquarters location:** This location.

U.S. DEPARTMENT OF VETERANS AFFAIRS
VETERANS ADMINISTRATION SAN DIEGO HEALTHCARE SYSTEM
3350 La Jolla Village Drive, San Diego CA 92161. 858/552-8585. **Contact:** Human Resources. **World Wide Web address:** http://www.san-diego.med.va.gov. **Description:** A medical center operated by the U.S. Department of Veterans Affairs. From 54 hospitals in 1930, the system has grown to include 171 medical centers; more than 364 outpatient, community and outreach clinics; 130 nursing home care units; and 37 domiciliary residences. The VA operates at least one medical center in each of the 48 contiguous states, Puerto Rico, and the District of Columbia. With approximately 76,000 medical center beds, the VA treats nearly 1 million patients in VA hospitals, 75,000 in nursing home care units, and 25,000 in domiciliary residences. The VA's outpatient clinics register approximately 24 million visits a year. The VA is affiliated with 104 medical schools, 48 dental schools, and more than 850 other schools across the country.

USC/NORRIS COMPREHENSIVE CANCER CENTER AND HOSPITAL
1441 Eastlake Avenue, Los Angeles CA 90033. 323/865-3000. **Fax:** 323/865-0118. **Contact:** Human Resources. **E-mail address:** careers@norris.hsc.usc.edu. **World Wide Web address:** http://www.uscnorris.com. **Description:** A 60-bed inpatient and outpatient tertiary care facility. USC Norris

Comprehensive Cancer Center and Hospital is a teaching and research hospital located on the Health Sciences campus of the University of Southern California. **Common positions include:** Accountant/Auditor; Budget Analyst; Buyer; Clinical Lab Technician; Computer Programmer; Financial Analyst; Medical Records Technician; Nuclear Medicine Technologist; Public Relations Specialist; Radiological Technologist; Registered Nurse; Respiratory Therapist; Systems Analyst. **Corporate headquarters location:** This location. **Operations at this facility include:** Administration; Service. **Number of employees at this location:** 400.

VILLAVIEW COMMUNITY HOSPITAL
5550 University Avenue, San Diego CA 92105. 619/582-3516. **Contact:** Human Resources. **Description:** An acute-care hospital. **Common positions include:** EEG Technologist; EKG Technician; Emergency Medical Technician; Financial Analyst; Licensed Practical Nurse; Radiological Technologist; Registered Nurse; Respiratory Therapist; Social Worker. **Number of employees at this location:** 280.

VISTA DEL MAR CHILD & FAMILY SERVICES
3200 Motor Avenue, Los Angeles CA 90034. 310/836-1223. **Contact:** Tim Hayes, Human Resources Director. **E-mail address:** jobs@vistadelmar.org. **World Wide Web address:** http://www.vistadelmar.org. **Description:** A residential treatment facility for children up to 18 years of age. Vista del Mar Child & Family Services offers a variety of programs including chemical dependency treatment, therapeutic schooling, adoption and foster care services, and counseling on both inpatient and outpatient bases. **NOTE:** Second and third shifts are offered. **Common positions include:** Daycare Worker; Education Administrator; Psychologist; Registered Nurse; Secretary; Social Worker; Teacher/Professor. **Corporate headquarters location:** http://www.vistadelmar.org. **Annual sales/revenues:** $11 - $20 million. **Number of employees at this location:** 300.

HOTELS AND RESTAURANTS

You can expect to find the following types of companies in this chapter:

Casinos • Dinner Theaters • Hotel/Motel Operators •
Resorts • Restaurants

ACAPULCO RESTAURANTS
4001 Via Oro Avenue, Suite 200, Long Beach CA 90810. 310/513-7500. **Toll-free phone:** 800/735-3501. **Contact:** Human Resources Department. **World Wide Web address:** http://www.acapulcorestaurants.com. **Description:** Operates a chain of over 40 Mexican restaurants, primarily in Southern California. **Common positions include:** General Manager; Management Trainee. **Corporate headquarters location:** This location. **Other area locations:** Statewide. **Parent company:** Restaurant Associates.

ANTHONY'S SEAFOOD GROUP
5232 Lovelock Street, San Diego CA 92110. 619/291-7254. **Contact:** Constance DeHaven, Director of Human Resources. **World Wide Web address:** http://www.gofishanthonys.com. **Description:** A family-owned restaurant chain specializing in seafood. Anthony's Fish Grotto also sells seafood to the public. **Common positions include:** General Manager; Management Trainee. **Corporate headquarters location:** This location. **Other area locations:** Chula Vista CA; Kearny Mesa CA; La Mesa CA; Mission Valley CA; Rancho Bernardo CA.

ARAMARK SPORTS AND ENTERTAINMENT SERVICES
3900 West Manchester Boulevard, Inglewood CA 90305. 310/674-2010. **Contact:** Human Resources. **World Wide Web address:** http://www.ps.aramark.com. **Description:** This location is a food service provider for the Forum. Overall, the company provides food and beverage services; operates large-format films, theaters, and casinos; and offers venue management services. **Listed on:** New York Stock Exchange. **Stock exchange symbol:** RMK.

BUFFETS, INC.
2241 Kettner Boulevard, Suite 260, San Diego CA 92101. 619/615-5390. **Recorded jobline:** 877/7BUFFET. **Contact:** Human Resources Department. **World Wide Web address:** http://www.buffet.com. **Description:** Operates and franchises buffet restaurants. The company currently operates 113 HomeTown Buffet restaurants, 245 Old Country Buffet

restaurants, and one Country Roadhouse Buffet restaurant in 34 states. The company also owns and operates four Roadhouse Grill restaurants, a Texas-style steakhouse. **NOTE:** For Human Resources, please call 651/994-8608. **Corporate headquarters location:** Eagen MN.

CALIFORNIA BEACH RESTAURANTS, INC.
17383 Sunset Boulevard, Suite 140, Pacific Palisades CA 90272. 310/459-9676. **Contact:** Human Resources Department. **Description:** Owns and operates Gladstone's 4 Fish, and RJ's - The Rib Joint. **Corporate headquarters location:** This location.

THE CHEESECAKE FACTORY INC.
26950 Agoura Road, Calabasas Hills CA 91301. 818/880-9323. **Contact:** Heidi Martin-Gilanfar, Vice President. **E-mail address:** careers@thecheesecakefactory. **World Wide Web address:** http://www.thecheesecakefactory.com. **Description:** The Cheesecake Factory operates a group of restaurants featuring an extensive menu and moderate prices. The company also operates a production facility that manufactures over 50 varieties of its signature cheesecakes and other baked goods for sale both in its restaurants and through wholesale accounts. **Corporate headquarters location:** This location. **Other area locations:** Statewide. **Other U.S. locations:** AZ; CA; CO; DC; FL; GA; IL; IN; MA; MD; MO; NJ; NV; NY; OH; PA; RI; TX; WA. **Listed on:** NASDAQ. **Stock exchange symbol:** CAKE.

COMMERCE CASINO
6131 East Telegraph Road, Commerce CA 90040. 323/721-2100. **Recorded jobline:** 323/838-3399. **Contact:** Human Resources Department. **World Wide Web address:** http://www.commercecasino.com. **Description:** A casino that hosts poker tournaments and offers a variety of gaming facilities. **NOTE:** Please apply in person.

ED DEBEVIC'S RESTAURANT
134 North La Cienega Boulevard, Beverly Hills CA 90211. 310/659-1952. **Contact:** Human Resources. **World Wide Web address:** http://www.eddebevics.com. **Description:** One location of the casual dining restaurant chain. Ed Debevic's serves American cuisine and operates a gift shop. **NOTE:** Please send resumes to: Bravo Restaurants, Inc., 600 West Jackson Boulevard, Suite 200, Chicago IL 60661. **Corporate headquarters location:** Chicago IL. **Parent company:** Debevic's Diners Ltd.

FARRELL'S ICE CREAM PARLOURS
10606 Camino Ruiz, Miramesa CA 92126. 858/578-9895.
Contact: Store Supervisor. **Description:** A restaurant franchise specializing in ice cream and ice cream products. The restaurants also sell novelties and candy. **Corporate headquarters location:** This location.

FOUR SEASONS HOTEL
300 South Doheny Drive, Los Angeles CA 90048. 310/273-2222. **Contact:** Personnel. **Fax:** 310/385-4920. **World Wide Web address:** http://www.fourseasons.com. **Description:** This location is a hotel with 285 guest rooms and two restaurants. The hotel also has a pool, whirlpool, fitness facilities, private cabanas, and approximately 10,000 square feet of meeting and function space. Overall, Four Seasons Hotels & Resorts operates approximately 50 luxury hotels and resorts in 22 countries. Founded in 1960. **Corporate headquarters location:** Toronto, Canada. **Listed on:** New York Stock Exchange. **Stock exchange symbol:** FS.

HOTEL DEL CORONADO
1500 Orange Avenue, Coronado CA 92118. 619/435-6611. **Toll-free phone:** 800/HOTELDEL. **Fax:** 619/522-8160. **Recorded jobline:** 619/522-8158. **Contact:** Employment. **E-mail address:** deljobs@hoteldel.com. **World Wide Web address:** http://www.hoteldel.com. **Description:** A 691-room oceanside resort with seven restaurants, five lounges/bars, two swimming pools, and six tennis courts. **Common positions include:** Accountant/Auditor; Attorney; Buyer; Claim Representative; Clerical Supervisor; Computer Programmer; Construction Contractor; Credit Manager; Customer Service Representative; Designer; Electrician; Financial Analyst; General Manager; Hotel Manager; Human Resources Manager; Management Trainee; Public Relations Specialist; Purchasing Agent/Manager; Restaurant/Food Service Manager; Systems Analyst; Travel Agent; Wholesale and Retail Buyer. **Special programs:** Internships. **Corporate headquarters location:** This location. **Listed on:** Privately held.

HYATT REGENCY LOS ANGELES
711 South Hope Street, Los Angeles CA 90017. 213/683-1234. **Contact:** Human Resources. **World Wide Web address:** http://www.hyatt.com. **Description:** A hotel and restaurant facility with 485 rooms. **NOTE:** Entry-level positions are offered. **Common positions include:** Accountant/Auditor; Credit Manager; General Manager; Hotel Manager; Human Resources Manager; Management Trainee; MIS Specialist;

Operations/Production Manager; Public Relations Specialist; Purchasing Agent/Manager; Quality Control Supervisor; Restaurant/Food Service Manager; Telecommunications Manager; Typist/Word Processor. **Special programs:** Internships. **Corporate headquarters location:** Chicago IL. **Other U.S. locations:** Nationwide. **International locations:** Worldwide. **Listed on:** Privately held. **Number of employees at this location:** 300. **Number of employees nationwide:** 40,000.

IHOP CORPORATION
450 North Brand Boulevard, 7th Floor, Glendale CA 91203. 818/240-6055. **Contact:** Human Resources. **E-mail address:** jobs@ihopcorp.com. **World Wide Web address:** http://www.ihop.com. **Description:** Operates the International House of Pancakes restaurant chain. **Corporate headquarters location:** This location. **Listed on:** New York Stock Exchange. **Stock exchange symbol:** IHP.

JS FOODS
4250 Executive Square, Suite 500, La Jolla CA 92037. 858/642-0064. **Contact:** Human Resources. **Description:** Manages Burger King, Tony Roma's, and Pacific Bagels franchises. **Corporate headquarters location:** This location.

JACK IN THE BOX INC.
9330 Balboa Avenue, San Diego CA 92123-1516. 858/571-2121. **Contact:** Human Resources Department. **E-mail address:** resumes@jackinthebox.com. **World Wide Web address:** http://www.jackinthebox.com. **Description:** Operates and franchises Jack in the Box restaurants, one of the nation's largest quick-serve hamburger chains. Jack in the Box restaurants are primarily located in the western and southwestern United States. International operations currently include restaurants in Hong Kong and Mexico. **Corporate headquarters location:** This location. **Listed on:** New York Stock Exchange. **Stock exchange symbol:** JBX.

CARL KARCHER ENTERPRISES INC.
P.O. Box 4349, Anaheim CA 92803-4349. 714/774-5796. **Fax:** 714/490-3630. **Recorded jobline:** 800/227-5757. **Contact:** Human Resources. **Description:** Operates Carl's Jr. restaurants. **Corporate headquarters location:** This location. **Listed on:** New York Stock Exchange. **Stock exchange symbol:** CKR.

MILLENNIUM BILTMORE HOTEL

506 South Grand Avenue, Los Angeles CA 90071. 213/624-1011. **Contact:** Human Resources. **World Wide Web address:** http://www.millennium-hotel.com. **Description:** A luxury hotel. **Common positions include:** Accountant/Auditor; Customer Service Rep.; Hotel Manager; Restaurant/Food Service Manager; Services Sales Representative. **Corporate headquarters location:** This location. **Operations at this facility include:** Administration; Sales. **Parent company:** CDL Group.

ONE PICO RESTAURANT

One Pico Boulevard, Santa Monica CA 90405-1062. 310/587-1717. **Contact:** Human Resources. **World Wide Web address:** http://www.shuttersonthebeach.com/restaurants/pico.
Description: A restaurant serving New American cuisine. The restaurant is located in Shutters Hotel.

PRANDIUM, INC.

P.O. Box 19561, Irvine CA 92623-9561. 949/863-8855 **Contact:** Ken Gowen, Department of Human Resources. **E-mail address:** careers@prandium.com. **World Wide Web address:** http://www.prandium.com. **Description:** Manages and operates several full-service Mexican restaurant chains including Casa Gallardo, Chi-Chi's, El Torito, Las Brisas, and Keystone Grill. **Common positions include:** Accountant; Administrative Assistant; Attorney; Auditor; Market Research Analyst; Marketing Manager; Marketing Specialist. **Corporate headquarters location:** This location. **Annual sales/revenues:** More than $100 million. **Number of employees at this location:** 200. **Number of employees nationwide:** 15,000.

RADISSON WILSHIRE PLAZA HOTEL

3515 Wilshire Boulevard, Los Angeles CA 90010. 213/368-3065. **Toll-free phone:** 800/333-3333. **Fax:** 213/368-3015. **Contact:** Mr. Otho Boggs, Human Resources Director. **World Wide Web address:** http://www.radisson.com. **Description:** A 393-room hotel, restaurant, and entertainment facility. **NOTE:** Entry-level positions, part-time jobs, and second and third shifts are offered. **Company slogan:** The difference is genuine. **Common positions include:** Account Manager; Account Representative; Accountant; Administrative Assistant; Administrative Manager; Assistant Manager; Auditor; Clerical Supervisor; Controller; Credit Manager; Customer Service Representative; General Manager; Human Resources Manager; Marketing Manager; Purchasing Agent/Manager; Sales Executive; Sales Manager; Sales Representative; Secretary;

Systems Manager. **Special programs:** Internships; Training; Summer Jobs. **Internship information:** Unpaid internships are available in the fields of rooms; sales and marketing; food and beverage; accounting; and human resources. **Corporate headquarters location:** Minneapolis MN. **President:** Young Sun Kim. **Facilities Manager:** Juan Narvaez. **Information Systems Manager:** Richard Kinney II. **Purchasing Manager:** Ossama El-Sherif. **Sales Manager:** Daniel D.B. Moreno.

REGENT BEVERLY WILSHIRE HOTEL
9500 Wilshire Boulevard, Beverly Hills CA 90212. 310/275-5200. **Toll-free phone:** 888/201-1806. **Fax:** 310/273-9212. **Contact:** Sharon Nixon, Director of Personnel. **World Wide Web address:** http://www.regenthotels.com. **Description:** A hotel with over 290 rooms. **Common positions include:** Buyer; Computer Operator; Credit Manager; Hotel Manager; Hotel/Motel Clerk; Human Resources Manager; Management Trainee; Payroll Clerk; Restaurant/Food Service Manager; Secretary; Systems Analyst. **Corporate headquarters location:** Hong Kong. **Parent company:** Four Seasons-Regent International. **Listed on:** New York Stock Exchange. **Stock exchange symbol:** FS. **Number of employees at this location:** 650.

SIZZLER INTERNATIONAL INC.
15301 Ventura Boulevard, Building B, #300, Sherman Oaks CA 91403. 310/568-0135. **Contact:** Human Resources. **World Wide Web address:** http://www.sizzler.com. **Description:** One of the largest franchises of the KFC Corporation and the majority stockholder for the Sizzler restaurant chain. **NOTE:** Resumes may be sent to the above e-mail address. **Common positions include:** Accountant/Auditor; Computer Programmer; Management Trainee. **Corporate headquarters location:** This location. **Operations at this facility include:** Administration.

SUTTON PLACE HOTEL
4500 MacArthur Boulevard, Newport Beach CA 92660. 949/476-2001 **Contact:** Human Resources. **World Wide Web address:** http://www.suttonplace.com. **Description:** A 435-room hotel also offering meeting space.

SYBRA INC.
9255 Town Center Drive, Suite 600, San Diego CA 92121. 858/587-8534. **Contact:** Human Resources Department. **Description:** Operates numerous locations of the restaurant chain Arby's. **Corporate headquarters location:** This location.

VAGABOND INNS CORPORATION

5933 West Century Boulevard, Suite 200, Los Angeles CA 90045. 310/410-5700. **Contact:** Personnel. **World Wide Web address:** http://www.vagabondinns.com. **Description:** Owns and operates hotels. **Common positions include:** Accountant/Auditor; Buyer; Hotel Manager; Management Trainee. **Corporate headquarters location:** This location. **Operations at this facility include:** Administration; Sales; Service.

INSURANCE

You can expect to find the following types of companies in this chapter:

Commercial and Industrial Property/Casualty Insurers • Health Maintenance Organizations (HMOs) • Medical/Life Insurance Companies

ALLIANZ INSURANCE COMPANY
3400 Riverside Drive, Suite 300, Burbank CA 91505. 818/972-8448. **Fax:** 818/972-8533. **Contact:** Human Resources Department. **E-mail address:** hr@aic-allianz.com. **World Wide Web address:** http://www.aic-allianz.com. **Description:** An insurance company specializing in commercial insurance including workers' compensation, specialty property, and casualty. **Common positions include:** Accountant/Auditor; Actuary; Claim Representative; Clerical Supervisor; Human Resources Manager; Underwriter/Assistant Underwriter. **Corporate headquarters location:** This location. **Other area locations:** Orange CA; Sacramento CA; San Francisco CA. **Other U.S. locations:** Atlanta GA; Chicago IL; New York NY. **Parent company:** Allianz (Germany). **Listed on:** Privately held. **Number of employees at this location:** 100. **Number of employees nationwide:** 325.

AMWEST SURETY INSURANCE COMPANY
5230 Las Virgenes Road, Calabasas CA 91302. 818/871-2000. **Toll-free phone:** 866/789-8119. **Fax:** 818/871-2027. **Contact:** Human Resources. **E-mail address:** info@amwest.com. **World Wide Web address:** http://www.amwest.com. **Description:** A holding company that underwrites property and casualty insurance products. Founded in 1970. **Corporate headquarters location:** This location. **Other U.S. locations:** Nationwide. **Subsidiaries include:** Amwest Surety Insurance Company; Condor Insurance Company (also at this location); Far West Bond Services; Far West Insurance Company (also at this location); Horizon Business Resources, Inc.; Raven Claims Services, Inc.; SCBS Bonding and Insurance Services, Inc.; Western States Bond Agency, Inc. **President/CEO:** John E. Savage. **Number of employees nationwide:** 500.

AURORA NATIONAL LIFE ASSURANCE COMPANY
27201 Tourney Road, Suite 225, Valencia CA 91355. 661/253-1688. **Toll-free phone:** 800/265-2652. **Contact:** Human Resources Department. **World Wide Web address:** http://www.auroralife.com. **Description:** A life insurance

provider. **Corporate headquarters location:** This location. **Other U.S. locations:** Nationwide.

AUTOMOBILE CLUB OF SOUTHERN CALIFORNIA
3333 Fairview Road, Costa Mesa 92626. 213/741-3111. **Fax:** 714/850-5058. **Contact:** Human Resources. **E-mail address:** personnel1@aaa-calif.com. **World Wide Web address:** http://www.aaa-calif.com. **Description:** Provides automotive and travel-related services and insurance to its members. **NOTE:** Please send resumes to Automobile Club of Southern California, Human Resources, 3333 Fairview Road, Costa Mesa CA 92626. **Common positions include:** Accountant/Auditor; Actuary; Adjuster; Attorney; Buyer; Claim Representative; Collector; Customer Service Representative; Economist; Financial Analyst; Investigator; Services Sales Representative; Systems Analyst; Travel Agent; Underwriter/Assistant Underwriter. **Other area locations:** Statewide. **Operations at this facility include:** Administration; Sales; Service.

BLUE SHIELD OF CALIFORNIA
6701 Center Drive West, Suite 800, Los Angeles CA 90045. 310/670-4040. **Toll-free phone:** 800/200-3242. **Contact:** Sharon Miller, Personnel Manager. **World Wide Web address:** http://www.blueshieldca.com. **Description:** A nonprofit corporation providing prepaid medical care and other health care benefits to subscribers through a variety of health care providers. The company is a member of the Blue Shield Association, an organization that provides national coordination on behalf of 69 local, autonomous Blue Shield Plans that together serve about 70 million people. **Corporate headquarters location:** San Francisco CA.

CHUBB GROUP OF INSURANCE COMPANIES
P.O. Box 30850, Los Angeles CA 90030. 213/612-0880. **Contact:** Trevor Gandy, Human Resources Manager. **World Wide Web address:** http://www.chubb.com. **Description:** A multiple-line property and casualty insurance group, serving the public through independent agents and brokers. **NOTE:** Entry-level positions are offered. **Common positions include:** Adjuster; Civil Engineer; Claim Representative; Environmental Engineer; Industrial Agent/Broker; Industrial Engineer; Management Trainee; Mining Engineer; Structural Engineer; Underwriter/Assistant Underwriter. **Special programs:** Internships; Training. **Corporate headquarters location:** Warren NJ. **Other area locations:** Fresno CA; Newport Beach CA; Pleasanton CA; Sacramento CA; San Diego CA; San

Francisco CA. **Other U.S. locations:** Nationwide. **International locations:** Worldwide. **Operations at this facility include:** Regional Headquarters. **Listed on:** New York Stock Exchange. **Stock exchange symbol:** CB. **Annual sales/revenues:** More than $100 million. **Number of employees worldwide:** 10,000.

CORVEL CORPORATION
2010 Main Street, Suite 1020, Irvine CA 92614. 949/851-1473. **Toll-free phone:** 888/7-CORVEL. **Contact:** Cathy Casil, Human Resources Manager. **World Wide Web address:** http://www.corvel.com. **Description:** CorVel Corporation manages health care delivery and provider reimbursement. Many customers contract with CorVel as an outsource vendor, while others are served by its 165 branch offices located throughout the United States. CorVel maintains over 1,000 customers and its CorCare PPO network now includes over 70,000 providers located in 26 states. **Common positions include:** Registered Nurse. **Corporate headquarters location:** This location. **Other area locations:** Statewide. **Listed on:** NASDAQ. **Stock exchange symbol:** CRVL. **Number of employees nationwide:** 1,700.

DRIVER ALLIANT INSURANCE SERVICES
1620 Fifth Avenue, San Diego CA 92101-2797. 619/238-1828. **Contact:** Director of Human Resources Department. **E-mail address:** hr@driveralliant.com. **World Wide Web address:** http://www.driveralliant.com. **Description:** Provides commercial and personal insurance including automobile, business, and homeowners. **Common positions include:** Administrative Worker/Clerk; Bond Specialist; Customer Service Representative; Employee **Corporate headquarters location:** This location. **Operations at this facility include:** Sales; Service. **Number of employees at this location:** 220.

FARMERS INSURANCE GROUP
4680 Wilshire Boulevard, Los Angeles CA 90010. 323/932-3200. **Contact:** Department of Human Resources. **E-mail address:** careers@farmersinsurance.com. **World Wide Web address:** http://www.farmersinsurance.com. **Description:** An insurance organization offering life, automobile, fire, and other forms of coverage to over 9 million property and casualty policyholders. **Common positions include:** Accountant/Auditor; Actuary; Attorney; Claim Representative. **Corporate headquarters location:** This location. **Other area locations:** Pleasanton CA; Simi Valley CA. **Other U.S. locations:** Phoenix AZ; Colorado Springs CO; Pocatello ID;

Aurora IL; Columbus OH; Oklahoma City OK; Portland OR; Austin TX. **Number of employees nationwide:** 17,000.

FIDELITY NATIONAL TITLE INSURANCE COMPANY

4050 Calle Real, Suite 100, Santa Barbara CA 93110. 805/696-9578. **Toll-free phone:** 800/815-3969. **Fax:** 805/563-8561. **Contact:** Ann Russell, Human Resources Director. **World Wide Web address:** http://www.fntic.com. **Description:** Writes title insurance policies and performs other title-related services such as escrow, collection, and trust activities in connection with real estate transactions. Founded in 1848. **Common positions include:** Accountant; Administrative Assistant; Advertising Executive; Attorney; Branch Manager; Chief Financial Officer; Clerical Supervisor; Computer Operator; Credit Manager; Finance Director; Financial Analyst; Human Resources Generalist. **Corporate headquarters location:** This location. **Other U.S. locations:** Nationwide. **Parent company:** Fidelity National Financial, Inc. **Operations at this facility include:** Regional Headquarters. **Listed on:** New York Stock Exchange. **Stock exchange symbol:** FNF. **Annual sales/revenues:** More than $100 million. **Number of employees at this location:** 150. **Number of employees nationwide:** 8,000.

THE FIRST AMERICAN CORPORATION

One First American Way, Santa Ana CA 92707-5913. 714/558-3211. **Toll-free phone:** 800/675-3505. **Contact:** Heather Smith, Personnel Director. **World Wide Web address:** http://www.firstam.com. **Description:** Offers insurance services through a nationwide network of offices and agents. **Corporate headquarters location:** This location. **Other area locations:** Bakersfield CA; Los Angeles CA; Santa Barbara CA. **Listed on:** New York Stock Exchange. **Stock exchange symbol:** FAF.

FREMONT GENERAL

2020 Santa Monica Boulevard, Suite 600, Santa Monica CA 90407. 310/315-5500. **Contact:** Human Resources Department. **Description:** A holding company with subsidiaries that conduct financial and insurance operations, primarily workers' compensation for California workers, malpractice insurance for the medical industry, life insurance, and various commercial and individual financial services. The Fremont Compensation operation deals with workmen's compensation. The medical malpractice unit offers professional liability insurance primarily for California physicians. Financial operations include asset-based lending/financing for commercial clients, thrift and loan services, and insurance. Insurance products include credit life insurance and disability coverage offered through automobile dealers, credit associations, and lending organizations. **Corporate headquarters location:** This location.

GENERAL REINSURANCE CORPORATION
550 South Hope Street, Suite 600, Los Angeles CA 90071. 213/630-1900. **Contact:** Human Resources. **Description:** Provides property and casualty reinsurance to primary insurers on a direct basis. Reinsurance is marketed and underwritten on both treaty and facultative bases. Treaty marketing efforts are focused on small to medium-sized regional and specialty property and casualty insurers. General Reinsurance does not underwrite businesses that involve aviation, ocean marine, and professional liability. **Corporate headquarters location:** Stamford CT.

GOLDEN EAGLE INSURANCE
P.O. Box 29037, Glendale CA 91209. 818/247-5001. **Contact:** Human Resources Department. **World Wide Web address:** http://www.goldeneagleins.com. **Description:** A carrier of property, casualty, and life insurance, licensed in all 50 states, with offices throughout the country. **Corporate headquarters location:** San Diego CA.

HRH INSURANCE
77-564 Country Club Drive, Suite B401, Palm Desert CA 92211. 760/360-4700. **Contact:** Human Resources. **World Wide Web address:** http://www.hrhgroup.com. **Description:** Provides all types of personal and commercial insurance including life and health.

HEALTH NET
21282 Burbank Boulevard, Woodland Hills CA 91367. 818/676-6775. **Fax:** 818/676-8544. **Contact:** Human Resources. **E-mail address:** resume@healthnet.com. **World Wide Web address:** http://www.healthnet.com. **Description:** One of California's largest health maintenance organizations. Health Net also organizes wellness programs. **Corporate headquarters location:** This location. **Parent company:** Foundation Health Systems, Inc. **Listed on:** New York Stock Exchange. **Stock exchange symbol:** HNT.

HEALTH NET
21650 Oxnard Street, Woodland Hills CA 91367. 818/676-6000. **Contact:** Department of Human Resources. **E-mail address:** resume@healthnet.com. **World Wide Web address:**

http://www.health.net. **Description:** Administers the delivery of managed care services to approximately 3.4 million individuals through its HMOs, government contracting, and specialty services managed care facilities. This location handles health plans for mid-sized companies. **Corporate headquarters location:** This location. **Listed on:** New York Stock Exchange. **Stock exchange symbol:** HNT.

HIGHLANDS INSURANCE GROUP
P.O. Box 2058, Tustin CA 92781. 714/259-5700. **Physical address:** 15621 Red Hill Avenue, Suite 280, Tustin CA 92780. **Contact:** Human Resources. **World Wide Web address:** http://www.highlandsinsurance.com. **Description:** Specializes in workers' compensation insurance. **Corporate headquarters location:** Lawrenceville NJ. **Listed on:** New York Stock Exchange. **Stock exchange symbol:** HIC.

INSURANCE COMPANY OF THE WEST
P.O. Box 85563, San Diego CA 92186-5563. 858/350-2400. **Contact:** Human Resources. **World Wide Web address:** http://www.icwgroup.com. **Description:** A commercial insurance carrier offering multirate property/casualty, workers' compensation, specialty auto, and surety lines of coverage. Founded in 1972. **Common positions include:** Adjuster; Claim Representative. **Corporate headquarters location:** This location. **Other U.S. locations:** AZ; CO; NV; NM; OR; TX; WA. **Operations at this facility include:** Service. **Number of employees at this location:** 230.

KAISER PERMANENTE
1515 North Vermont Avenue, Los Angeles CA 90027. 323/783-6900. **Fax:** 323/783-4787. **Recorded jobline:** 323/857-2615. **Contact:** Human Resources. **World Wide Web address:** http://www.kaiserpermanente.org. **Description:** A nonprofit, public-benefit, and charitable health care corporation that enrolls members and arranges for their medical services nationwide. **NOTE:** Please send all resumes to Recruiter Services, 393 East Walnut Street, LSRS #304, Pasadena CA 91188. **Common positions include:** Clinical Lab Technician; Dietician/Nutritionist; EEG Technologist; EKG Technician; Human Resources Manager; Medical Records Technician; Nuclear Medicine Technologist; Occupational Therapist; Pharmacist; Physical Therapist; Physician; Physicist; Psychologist; Public Relations Specialist; Radiological Technologist; Registered Nurse; Respiratory Therapist; Social Worker; Speech-Language Pathologist; Surgical Technician. **Special programs:** The Postgraduate Administrative Fellowship

Program is a training program for talented recent graduates pursuing health care management careers. **Corporate headquarters location:** Oakland CA. **Other U.S. locations:** Nationwide. **Listed on:** Privately held. **Number of employees nationwide:** 34,000.

KEMPER INSURANCE COMPANIES
2390 East Orangewood Avenue, Suite 400, Anaheim CA 92806. 714/935-5700. **Contact:** Personnel. **World Wide Web address:** http://www.kemperinsurance.com. **Description:** An international insurance company engaged in a wide range of insurance, financial, and related services. The company provides property, casualty, and life insurance, reinsurance, and a wide range of diversified financial services operations. **Office hours:** Monday - Friday, 8:15 a.m. - 4:30 p.m. **Corporate headquarters location:** Long Grove IL. **Other U.S. locations:** Glendale CA; San Diego CA; Santa Ana CA; West Covina CA.

LAWYERS TITLE INSURANCE CORPORATION
251 South Lake Avenue, 4th Floor, Pasadena CA 91101. 626/304-9797. **Contact:** Human Resources. **E-mail address:** corprecruiter@landam.com. **World Wide Web address:** http://www.ltic.com. **Description:** Provides title insurance and other real estate-related services on commercial and residential transactions in the United States, Canada, the Bahamas, Puerto Rico, and the U.S. Virgin Islands. Lawyers Title Insurance Corporation also provides search and examination services and closing services for a broad-based customer group that includes lenders, developers, real estate brokers, attorneys, and homebuyers. This location covers Alaska, Arizona, California, Hawaii, Nevada, Oregon, and Washington. **NOTE:** Please indicate department of interest and direct resumes to Mr. Sid Phair, 800 East Colorado Boulevard, 2nd Floor, Pasadena CA 91101. **Corporate headquarters location:** Richmond VA. **Other U.S. locations:** Tampa FL; Chicago IL; Boston MA; Troy MI; White Plains NY; Westerville OH; Memphis TN; Dallas TX. **Subsidiaries include:** Datatrace Information Services Company, Inc. (Richmond VA) markets automated public record information for public and private use; Genesis Data Systems, Inc. (Englewood CO) develops and markets computer software tailored specifically to the title industry; and Lawyers Title Exchange Company functions as an intermediary for individual and corporate investors interested in pursuing tax-free property exchanges. **Parent company:** LandAmerica. **Listed on:** New York Stock Exchange. **Stock exchange symbol:** LFG.

MARSH RISK & INSURANCE SERVICES

777 South Figueroa Street, Los Angeles CA 90017-5822. 213/624-5555. **Contact:** Employment Manager. **E-mail address:** employment.jobs@marsh.com. **World Wide Web address:** http://www.marsh.com. **Description:** A professional firm that provides advice and services worldwide through an insurance brokerage and risk management firm, reinsurance intermediary facilities, and a consulting and financial services group, to clients concerned with the management of assets and risks. **Corporate headquarters location:** New York NY. **Parent company:** Marsh & McLennan Companies, Inc.

MERCURY INSURANCE GROUP

555 West Imperial Highway, Brea CA 92821. 714/671-7305. **Recorded jobline:** 714/671-7393. **Contact:** Human Resources. **World Wide Web address:** http://www.mercuryinsurance.com. **Description:** A property and casualty insurance firm. Founded in 1962. **NOTE:** Entry-level positions are offered. **Common positions include:** Adjuster; Claim Rep.; Underwriter/Assistant Underwriter. **Special programs:** Internships; Training; Summer Jobs. **Corporate headquarters location:** This location. **Other U.S. locations:** FL; GA; IL. **Number of employees at this location:** 550. **Number of employees nationwide:** 1,800.

THE NORTHWESTERN MUTUAL LIFE INSURANCE COMPANY
THE KERRIGAN AGENCY

888 West Sixth Street, 2nd Floor, Los Angeles CA 90017. 213/243-7081. **Fax:** 213/243-7001. **Contact:** Ms. Tracy Tapp, Human Resources Department Representative. **E-mail address:** resume@northwesternmutual.com. **World Wide Web address:** http://www.northwesternmutual.com. **Description:** An insurance and investment planning company. The Northwestern Mutual Life Insurance Company specializes in individual life insurance coverage. The company's product portfolio includes permanent and term insurance, CompLife, disability income insurance, and annuity plans for the personal, business, estate, and pension planning markets. Founded in 1857. **Common positions include:** Insurance Agent/Broker. **Special programs:** Internships; Training. **Internship information:** The Kerrigan Agency offers college agent internships. These internships offer professional experience and the flexibility required for full-time students. College agents receive extensive training allowing for hands-on learning. College agents are responsible for the development of a professional practice revolving around the sale of insurance products, annuities, mutual funds, and

investments, as well as estate, retirement, education, and pension planning. Successful applicants will be independent, with strong ethics, and have a proven track record for success. Backgrounds in marketing, entrepreneurship, management, business administration, economics, finance, and liberal arts are helpful, but not required. **Corporate headquarters location:** Milwaukee WI. **Other U.S. locations:** Nationwide. **Operations at this facility include:** Sales; Service. **Annual sales/revenues:** More than $100 million. **Number of employees at this location:** 100.

PACIFIC LIFE INSURANCE
700 Newport Center Drive, Newport Beach CA 92660. 949/640-3011. **Contact:** Human Resources. **E-mail address:** plemploy@pacificlife.com. **World Wide Web address:** http://www.pacificlife.com. **Description:** Provides insurance services including group health, life, and pensions. Pacific Life Insurance also provides financial services including annuities, mutual funds, and investments. **Corporate headquarters location:** This location.

PACIFICARE HEALTH SYSTEMS, INC.
5701 Katella Avenue, Cypress CA 90630. 714/952-1121. **Contact:** Human Resources. **World Wide Web address:** http://www.pacificare.com. **Description:** A regionally focused health care company with six HMOs operating in California, Oklahoma, Oregon, Texas, Florida, and Washington. Services include PPOs, life and health insurance, Medicare risk management programs, dental care services, and pharmacy services. The company has a contract to provide health services to military personnel and their dependents in 19 states. **Corporate headquarters location:** Santa Ana CA. **Subsidiaries include:** COMPREMIER, Inc. provides workers' compensation care; Execu-Fit Health Programs, Inc.; LifeLink, Inc., is a mental health services provider; Prescription Solutions. **Listed on:** NASDAQ. **Stock exchange symbol:** PHSY.

PACIFICARE HEALTH SYSTEMS, INC.
3120 West Lake Center Drive, Santa Ana CA 92704. 714/825-5200. **Contact:** Human Resources. **World Wide Web address:** http://www.pacificare.com. **Description:** A regionally focused health care company with six HMOs operating in California, Oklahoma, Oregon, Texas, Florida, and Washington. Services include PPOs, life and health insurance, Medicare risk management programs, dental care services, and pharmacy services. The company has a contract to provide health

services to military personnel and their dependents in 19 states. **Corporate headquarters location:** This location. **Corporate headquarters location:** Santa Ana CA. **Subsidiaries include:** COMPREMIER, Inc. provides workers' compensation care; Execu-Fit Health Programs, Inc.; LifeLink, Inc., is a mental health services provider; Prescription Solutions. **Listed on:** NASDAQ. **Stock exchange symbol:** PHSY.

TALBERT MEDICAL GROUP
9930 Talbert Avenue, Fountain Valley CA 92708. 714/964-6229. **Contact:** Human Resources Department. **E-mail address:** talbert.jobs@talbertmedical.com. **Description:** An HMO that offers a full range of health care products and services to over 900,000 people in California, Nevada, Utah, Arizona, Colorado, New Mexico, and Guam. Services include third-party administrative plans, and indemnity medical, group life, and workers' compensation insurance. **Corporate headquarters location:** This location. **Number of employees nationwide:** 12,000.

21ST CENTURY INSURANCE GROUP
P.O. Box 4077, Woodland Hills CA 91365. 818/704-3700. **Fax:** 818/704-3485. **Contact:** Human Resources. **World Wide Web address:** http://www.21stcenturyinsurance.com. **Description:** Provides automobile insurance. **Common positions include:** Accountant/Auditor; Adjuster; Claim Representative; Computer Programmer; Systems Analyst. **Special programs:** Training. **Corporate headquarters location:** This location. **Listed on:** New York Stock Exchange. **Stock exchange symbol:** TW. **Number of employees at this location:** 1,400. **Number of employees nationwide:** 2,300.

WATTSHEALTH FOUNDATION, INC.
3405 West Imperial Highway, Inglewood CA 90303. 310/412-3521. **Fax:** 310/412-7129. **Recorded jobline:** 310/680-3188. **Contact:** Madria Marshall, Vice President of Personnel. **World Wide Web address:** http://www.wattshealth.org. **Description:** A health maintenance organization. **Company slogan:** A commitment to caring. **Common positions include:** Administrative Assistant; Claim Representative; Controller; Human Resources Manager; Nurse Practitioner; Physician; Radiological Technologist; Registered Nurse; Social Worker. **Corporate headquarters location:** This location. **Subsidiaries include:** UHP Healthcare (also at this location). **Parent company:** WATTSHealth Systems, Inc. **Number of employees at this location:** 600.

WAUSAU INSURANCE COMPANIES

P.O. Box 7214, Pasadena CA 91109-7314. 626/440-0444. **Physical address:** 301 North Lake Avenue, Suite 400, Pasadena CA 91101. **Contact:** Marilyn Rashka, Human Resources. **E-mail address:** marilyn.rashka.@wausau.com. **World Wide Web address:** http://www.wausau.com. **Description:** Sells casualty, property, and other commercial insurance products to medium- and large-sized companies. **Common positions include:** Attorney; Claim Representative; Services Sales Representative; Underwriter/Assistant Underwriter. **Corporate headquarters location:** Wausau WI. **Other U.S. locations:** Agoura Hills CA; Ontario CA; San Diego CA; Santa Ana CA. **Operations at this facility include:** Sales; Service.

WELLPOINT HEALTH NETWORKS INC.

One WellPoint Way, Thousand Oaks CA 91362. 818/703-4000. **Contact:** Human Resources Department. **E-mail address:** employment@wellpoint.com. **World Wide Web address:** http://www.wellpoint.com. **Description:** Provides health and life insurance through Blue Cross of California and UNICARE. **Corporate headquarters location:** This location. **Listed on:** New York Stock Exchange. **Stock exchange symbol:** WLP.

ZENITH INSURANCE COMPANY

P.O. Box 9055, Van Nuys CA 91409. 818/713-1000. **Fax:** 818/592-0265. **Contact:** Human Resources Department. **World Wide Web address:** http://www.zenithnational.com. **Description:** Provides Workers' Compensation insurance and reinsurance packages. Zenith Insurance Company also operates a homebuilding operation in Las Vegas NV andprovides workers' compensation insurance. **Common positions include:** Accountant/Auditor; Attorney; Claim Representative; Computer Programmer; Registered Nurse; Underwriter/Assistant Underwriter. **Corporate headquarters location:** This location. **Other U.S. locations:** IL; PA; TX; UT. **Parent company:** Zenith National Insurance Corp. **Listed on:** New York Stock Exchange. **Stock exchange symbol:** ZNT. **Number of employees at this location:** 500. **Number of employees nationwide:** 850.

LEGAL SERVICES

You can expect to find the following types of companies in this chapter:

Law Firms • Legal Service Agencies

BROBECK, PHLEGER & HARRISON LLP
12390 El Camino Real, Suite 1300, San Diego CA 92130. 619/234-1966. **Fax:** 858/720-2555. **Toll-free phone:** 877/621-8166. **Contact:** Robyn Kraft, Human Resources. **E-mail address:** rkraft@brobeck.com. **World Wide Web address:** http://www.brobeck.com. **Description:** A law firm practicing tax, real estate, litigation, business, technology, and financial law. Founded in 1926. **Corporate headquarters location:** San Francisco CA. **Other area locations:** Irvine CA; Los Angeles CA; Palo Alto CA. **U.S. locations:** Denver CO; Washington DC; New York NY; Austin TX; Dallas TX. **International locations:** London, England.

CARLSMITH BALL LLP
444 South Flower Street, 9th Floor, Los Angeles CA 90071. 213/955-1200. **Contact:** Human Resources. **E-mail address:** recruiting@carlsmith.com. **World Wide Web address:** http://www.carlsmith.com. **Description:** A law firm that specializes in civil law. **Special programs:** Summer associate program. **Other U.S. locations:** Washington DC; Hilo HI; Honolulu HI; Kapolei HI; Kona HI; Maui HI. **International locations:** Guam; Saipan.

DEWEY BALLANTINE
333 South Grand Street, 26th Floor, Los Angeles CA 90071. 213/626-3399. **Contact:** Human Resources. **E-mail address:** larecruitment@deweybalantine.com. **World Wide Web address:** http://www.deweyballantine.com. **Description:** An international law firm specializing in corporate, litigation, tax, ERISA/pension, bankruptcy, and real estate law. **International locations:** London, England.

GREENBERG, GLUSKER, FIELDS, CLAMAN & MACHTINGER
1900 Avenue of the Stars, Suite 2100, Los Angeles CA 90067. 310/553-3610. **Fax:** 310/553-0687. **Contact:** Patricia Patrick, Recruitment. **E-mail address:** ppatrick@ggfirm.com. **Description:** A law firm practicing bankruptcy, business and tax, entertainment, labor and employment, litigation, and probate and estate planning law.

JAMS

1920 Main Street, Suite 300, Irvine CA 92614. 949/224-1810. **Contact:** Human Resources. **World Wide Web address:** http://www.jamsadr.com. **Description:** Provides alternative dispute resolution (ADR) judicial services, which is a means of scheduling and processing cases outside the public court system. **Corporate headquarters location:** This location.

JEFFER, MANGELS, BUTLER, & MARMARO LLP

2121 Avenue of the Stars, 10th Floor, Los Angeles CA 90067. 310/203-8080. **Contact:** Hiring Partner. **World Wide Web address:** http://www.jmbm.com. **Description:** A law firm practicing litigation, corporate, entertainment, tax, bankruptcy, health, environment, and international law. **Special programs:** Summer Associate Program for law students. **Corporate headquarters location:** This location.

LATHAM & WATKINS LLP

701 B Street, Suite 2100, San Diego CA 92101. 619/236-1234. **Contact:** Cindy D. Edson, Recruitment. **E-mail address:** cindy.edson@lw.com. **World Wide Web address:** http://www.lw.com. **Description:** A law firm practicing corporate, environmental, and real estate law. **Special programs:** Public interest fellowships for recent law graduates. **International locations:** Worldwide.

LUCE, FORWARD, HAMILTON, & SCRIPPS

600 West Broadway, Suite 2400, San Diego CA 92101. 619/236-1414. **Contact:** Kathryn Kapinski, Human Resources. **E-mail address:** kkarpinski@luce.com. **World Wide Web address:** http://www.luce.com. **Description:** A law firm specializing in corporate, environmental, immigration, and real estate law. **Corporate headquarters location:** This location.

PILLSBURY WINTHROP

101 West Broadway, Suite 1800, San Diego CA 92101. 619/234-5000. **Contact:** Hiring Partner. **E-mail address:** staff_sd@pillsburywinthrop.com. **World Wide Web address:** http://www.pillsburywinthrop.com. **Description:** A law firm specializing in bankruptcy, corporate, employment, environmental, intellectual property, and real estate law. **Corporate headquarters location:** San Francisco CA.

PROCOPIO, CORY, HARGRAVES, & SAVITCH

530 B Street, Suite 2100, San Diego CA 92101-4469. 619/238-1900. **Contact:** Human Resources Manager. **E-mail address:**

bae@procopio.com. **World Wide Web address:** http://www.procopio.com. **Description:** A law firm specializing in real estate, bankruptcy, litigation, and corporate law. **Common positions include:** Administrative Manager; Attorney; Human Resources Manager; Legal Secretary; Paralegal; Purchasing Agent/Manager. **Corporate headquarters location:** This location. **Operations at this facility include:** Administration. **Listed on:** Privately held. **Number of employees at this location:** 100.

RIORDAN & McKINZIE
300 South Grand Avenue, 29th Floor, Los Angeles CA 90071. 213/629-4824. **Contact:** Hiring Partner. **World Wide Web address:** http://www.riordan.com. **Description:** A law firm specializing in corporate law. **Corporate headquarters location:** This location.

ROSENFELD, MEYER & SUSMAN
9601 Wilshire Boulevard, 4th Floor, Beverly Hills CA 90210. 310/858-7700. **Contact:** Hiring Partner. **World Wide Web address:** http://www.rmslaw.com. **Description:** A law firm specializing in litigation and entertainment law. **Corporate headquarters location:** This location.

SALTZBURG, RAY & BERGMAN
12121 Wilshire Boulevard, Suite 600, Los Angeles CA 90095. 310/481-6700. **Contact:** Hiring Partner. **Description:** A law firm specializing in bankruptcy, real estate, and corporate law. **Corporate headquarters location:** This location.

SPRAY, GOULD & BOWERS
3530 Wilshire Boulevard, Suite 1655, Los Angeles CA 90010. 213/385-3402. **Contact:** Director of Finance and Administration. **Description:** A law firm specializing in insurance, defense, and entertainment law. **Common positions include:** Accountant/Auditor; Adjuster; Attorney; Human Resources Manager; Librarian; Paralegal; Systems Analyst. **Office hours:** Monday - Friday, 8:30 a.m. - 5:00 p.m. **Corporate headquarters location:** This location. **Operations at this facility include:** Administration; Divisional Headquarters. **Listed on:** Privately held. **Number of employees at this location:** 75. **Number of employees nationwide:** 105.

STRADLING, YOCCA, CARLSON & RAUTH
660 Newport Center Drive, Suite 1600, Newport Beach CA 92660. 949/725-4000. **Contact:** Human Resources. **E-mail address:** recruiting@sycr.com. **World Wide Web address:**

http://www.sycr.com. **Description:** A law firm specializing in corporate, business, estate planning, and labor law. **Corporate headquarters location:** This location.

MANUFACTURING: MISCELLANEOUS CONSUMER

You can expect to find the following types of companies in this chapter:

Art Supplies • Batteries • Cosmetics and Related Products • Household Appliances and Audio/Video Equipment • Jewelry, Silverware, and Plated Ware• Miscellaneous Household Furniture and Fixtures • Musical Instruments• Tools • Toys and Sporting Goods

ACUSHNET COMPANY

2819 Loker Avenue East, Carlsbad CA 92008. 760/929-0377. **Toll-free phone:** 800/225-8505. **Contact:** Personnel. **E-mail address:** humanresources@acushnet.com. **World Wide Web address:** http://www.acushnet.com. **Description:** Designs, manufactures, and markets golf clubs. The company also offers a line of men's and women's golf and resort clothing, imported from Italy under the name Como Sport. **Corporate headquarters location:** New Bedford MA. **Other U.S. locations:** Nationwide. **International locations:** Hamburg, Germany.

ARDEN PARADISE MANUFACTURING COMPANY

12851 Reservoir Street, Chino CA 91710. 909/613-0998. **Contact:** Personnel Director. **Description:** Manufactures shower curtains, tablecloths, placemats, swimming pools, inflatable toys, and air mattresses.

BSH HOME APPLIANCES

5551 McFadden Avenue, Huntington Beach CA 92649. 714/901-6600. **Toll-free phone:** 800/656-9226. **Contact:** Human Resources Department. **World Wide Web address:** http://www.thermador.com. **Description:** Manufactures built-in electrical and gas kitchen appliances. **Common positions include:** Accountant/Auditor; Credit Manager; Customer Service Representative; Draftsperson; Economist; Electrical Engineer; Financial Analyst; Human Resources Manager; Industrial Engineer; Manufacturer's/Wholesaler's Sales Rep.; Marketing Specialist; Operations/Production Manager; Purchasing Agent/Manager; Quality Control Supervisor; Systems Analyst. **Corporate headquarters location:** Munich, Germany. **Parent company:** Masco. **Operations at this facility include:** Manufacturing.

BUCK KNIVES INC.
1900 Weld Boulevard, El Cajon CA 92020. 619/449-1100. **Contact:** Human Resources. **World Wide Web address:** http://www.buckknives.com. **Description:** Manufactures a variety of sport, utility, and multipurpose knives. **Chairman/CEO:** Chuck Buck.

CALLAWAY GOLF COMPANY
2180 Rutherford Road, Carlsbad CA 92008-8815. 760/931-1771. **Contact:** Human Resources Department. **E-mail address:** jobs@callawaygolf.com. **World Wide Web address:** http://www.callawaygolf.com. **Description:** Designs, develops, manufactures, and markets golf clubs. **Corporate headquarters location:** This location. **International locations:** Australia; Canada; France; Germany; Ireland; Italy; Japan; Korea; Spain, Sweden; United Kingdom. **Number of employees nationwide:** 2,225. **Listed on:** New York Stock Exchange. **Stock exchange symbol:** ELY.

CERTRON CORPORATION
1545 Sawtelle Boulevard, Los Angeles CA 90025. 310/914-0300. **Toll-free phone:** 800/854-3943. **Contact:** Human Resources Department. **World Wide Web address:** http://www.certron.com. **Description:** Certron designs, develops, manufactures, and distributes blank audiocassettes and blank videocassettes. The company is also active in the contract assembly and manufacturing of products for other firms. Its magnetic media products are sold primarily in the United States to wholesale distributors, original equipment manufacturers, mail-order companies, and major retail outlets. **Corporate headquarters location:** This location.

CORONET MANUFACTURING COMPANY INC.
P.O. Box 2065, Gardena CA 90247. 310/327-6700. **Physical address:** 16210 South Avalon Boulevard, Gardena CA 90247. **Contact:** Human Resources. **World Wide Web address:** http://www.coronetlighting.com. **Description:** Produces lamps and lighting fixtures. **Corporate headquarters location:** This location.

COSMETIC GROUP U.S.A., INC.
11312 Penrose Street, Sun Valley CA 91352. 818/767-2889. **Fax:** 818/767-4062. **Contact:** Human Resources. **Description:** Develops, formulates, and manufactures a wide range of color cosmetics and other personal care products for customers that market the products under their own brand names. **Subsidiaries include:** Arnold Zegarelli Products, Inc.

manufactures and distributes a line of hair care products. **Corporate headquarters location:** This location.

DAY RUNNER, INC.
2750 West Moore Avenue, Fullerton CA 92833. 714/680-3500. **Fax:** 714/680-3165. **Contact:** Human Resources. **E-mail address:** human.resources@dayrunner.com. **World Wide Web address:** http://www.dayrunner.com. **Description:** A leading developer, manufacturer, and marketer of paper-based organizers for the retail market. The company markets multiple lines of organizers and planners and a wide variety of refills and accessories. **Number of employees at this location:** 550.

DOUGLAS FURNITURE OF CALIFORNIA INC.
4000 Redondo Beach Avenue, Redondo Beach CA 90278. 310/643-7200. **Contact:** Mr. Steve Wilk, Director of Human Resources Department. **World Wide Web address:** http://www.douglasfurniture.com. **Description:** Manufactures a line of household cabinets for electronics and appliances. **Corporate headquarters location:** This location.

EDUCATIONAL INSIGHTS, INC.
18730 South Wilmington Avenue, Suite 100, Rancho Dominguez 90220. 310/884-2000. **Contact:** Human Resources. **World Wide Web address:** http://www.edin.com. **Description:** Designs, develops, and markets educational supplemental materials and educationally-oriented toys and games intended for use in both homes and schools. The company produces nearly 800 products including electronic teaching devices; interactive science kits; reading and language arts kits; math and geography games; and activity books. Particularly successful have been the GeoSafari interactive learning system and MathSafari, which teaches basic math concepts through fractions, decimals, and percentages to children preschool age and older. **Corporate headquarters location:** This location.

FIREPLACE MANUFACTURERS, INC.
P.O. Box 25629, Santa Ana CA 92799. 714/549-7782. **Physical address:** 2701 South Harbor Boulevard, Santa Ana CA 92704. **Contact:** Human Resources. **World Wide Web address:** http://www.fmionline.com. **Description:** Designs, manufactures, and sells energy-efficient, metal fireplace systems. **Corporate headquarters location:** This location.

GEMSTAR INTERNATIONAL GROUP LTD.
135 North Los Robles Avenue, Suite 800, Pasadena CA 91101. 626/792-5700. **Contact:** Human Resources Department. **E-mail address:** hr@tvguide.com. **World Wide Web address:** http://www.gemstartvguide.com. **Description:** Develops, manufactures, and markets videocassette recording systems. **Corporate headquarters location:** Pasadena CA. **Listed on:** NASDAQ. **Stock exchange symbol:** GMST.

JBL PROFESSIONAL MANUFACTURING
8500 Balboa Boulevard, Northridge CA 91329. 818/893-8411. **Contact:** Jean Tenuta, Supervisor of Human Resources. **World Wide Web address:** http://www.harmon.com. **Description:** Designs, manufactures, and distributes audio loudspeaker systems for professional, automotive, and home entertainment use, both domestically and internationally. **Common positions include:** Accountant/Auditor; Buyer; Chemical Engineer; Draftsperson; Human Resources Manager; Industrial Engineer; Manufacturer's/Wholesaler's Sales Rep.; Manufacturing Engineer; Purchasing Agent/Manager; Services Sales Representative; Software Engineer; Wholesale and Retail Buyer. **Corporate headquarters location:** This location. **Parent company:** Harmon International Industries Inc. **Number of employees at this location:** 2,500.

JAKKS PACIFIC, INC.
22619 Pacific Coast Highway, Suite 250, Malibu CA 90265. 310/456-7799. **Fax:** 310/317-8527. **Contact:** Department of Human Resources. **World Wide Web address:** http://www.jakkspacific.com. **Description:** Develops, manufactures, and markets toys and similar children's products including action figures and activity kits. **Corporate headquarters location:** This location. **Listed on:** NASDAQ. **Stock exchange symbol:** JAKK. **Annual sales/revenues:** More than $100 million.

LEVOLOR KIRSCH
7400 Hazard Avenue, Westminster CA 92683. 714/891-4311. **Toll-free phone:** 800/538-6567. **Contact:** Human Resources. **World Wide Web address:** http://www.levolor.com. **Description:** Manufactures various types of window coverings (metal and wood mini-blinds, pleated shades, vertical shades, and woven wood shades). **Common positions include:** Accountant/Auditor; Blue-Collar Worker Supervisor; Buyer; Computer Programmer; Credit Manager; Customer Service Representative; Department Manager; Draftsperson; General Manager; Human Resources Manager; Industrial Engineer;

Manufacturer's/Wholesaler's Sales Rep.; Marketing Specialist; Mechanical Engineer; Operations/Production Manager; Purchasing Agent/Manager; Quality Control Supervisor; Systems Analyst. **Corporate headquarters location:** High Point NC. **Parent company:** Newell Rubbermaid.

LITHONIA LIGHTING
19321 East Walnut Drive, City of Industry CA 91748. 626/965-0711. **Contact:** Sue Farrah, Personnel Director. **E-mail address:** recruiter@lithonia.com. **World Wide Web address:** http://www.lithonia.com. **Description:** Manufactures lighting and related products. **Corporate headquarters location:** Conyers GA.

MATTEL INC.
333 Continental Boulevard, El Segundo CA 90245. 310/252-2000. **Contact:** Corporate Staffing. **World Wide Web address:** http://www.mattel.com. **Description:** Produces and distributes toys, electronic products, games, books, hobby products, and family entertainment products. **Corporate headquarters location:** This location. **Other U.S. locations:** Fort Wayne IN; Mount Laurel NJ. **Listed on:** New York Stock Exchange. **Stock exchange symbol:** MAT. **Number of employees at this location:** 29,000.

MEADE INSTRUMENTS CORPORATION
6001 Oak Canyon, Irvine CA 92618. 949/451-1450. **Fax:** 949/451-1460. **Contact:** Human Resources. **World Wide Web address:** http://www.meade.com. **Description:** Manufactures telescopes, microscopes, and binoculars. Meade Instruments Corporation also manufactures a variety of accessories including photographic adapters, autoguiders, and eyepieces. Founded in 1972. **Corporate headquarters location:** This location. **Listed on:** NASDAQ. **Stock exchange symbol:** MEAD. **Annual sales/revenues:** More than $100 million.

MERLE NORMAN COSMETICS
9130 Bellanca Avenue, Los Angeles CA 90045. 310/337-2200. **Toll-free phone:** 800/421-2060. **Fax:** 310/337-2364. **Recorded jobline:** 310/337-2412. **Contact:** Monica Daigle, Recruiter. **World Wide Web address:** http://www.merlenorman.com. **Description:** Manufactures a complete line of over 500 skin care and cosmetic products sold exclusively through independently-owned studios. **Common positions include:** Administrative Assistant; Chemist; Electrician; Graphic Designer; MIS Specialist; Operations Manager; Production Manager; Secretary. **Corporate headquarters location:** This

location. **Operations at this facility include:** Administration; Manufacturing; Regional Headquarters; Research and Development. **Listed on:** Privately held. **Annual sales/revenues:** $51 - $100 million. **Number of employees at this location:** 450.

MUNCHKIN INC.
15955 Strathern, Van Nuys CA 91406-1313. 818/893-5000. **Toll-free phone:** 800/344-2229. **Contact:** Personnel. **World Wide Web address:** http://www.munchkininc.com. **Description:** Manufactures baby care products and early childhood educational and developmental toys. **Corporate headquarters location:** This location.

NEUTROGENA CORPORATION
5760 West 96th Street, Los Angeles CA 90045. 310/642-1150. **Fax:** 310/337-5537. **Recorded jobline:** 800/265-8648. **Contact:** Manager of Human Resources Department. **E-mail address:** neutrogenajobs@hiresystems.com. **World Wide Web address:** http://www.neutrogena.com. **Description:** Manufactures a variety of personal care products focusing on hair, skin, and cosmetics. **Parent company:** Johnson & Johnson (New Brunswick NJ). **Corporate headquarters location:** This location. **Listed on:** New York Stock Exchange. **Stock exchange symbol:** JNJ.

PENTAIR POOL PRODUCTS
10951 West Los Angeles Avenue, Moorpark CA 93021. 805/523-2400. **Contact:** Kim Cowles, Personnel Director. **World Wide Web address:** http://www.pentairpool.com. **Description:** Manufactures water recreation and hydrotherapy equipment. **NOTE:** Entry-level positions are offered. **Common positions include:** Accountant/Auditor; Advertising Clerk; Buyer; Computer Programmer; Design Engineer; Designer; Draftsperson; Industrial Production Manager; Management Trainee; Manufacturer's/Wholesaler's Sales Rep.; MIS Specialist; Operations/Production Manager; Systems Analyst. **Corporate headquarters location:** Sanford NC. **Other U.S. locations:** FL; NJ. **Operations at this facility include:** Administration; Manufacturing; Regional Headquarters; Research and Development; Sales; Service. **Listed on:** New York Stock Exchange. **Stock exchange symbol:** PNR. **Number of employees at this location:** 360. **Number of employees nationwide:** 380.

ROLAND CORPORATION U.S.

P.O. Box 910921, Los Angeles CA 90091-0921. 323/890-3700. **Physical address:** 5100 South Eastern Avenue, Los Angeles CA 90040. **Contact:** Debbie Parmenter, Human Resources Director. **World Wide Web address:** http://www.rolandus.com. **Description:** A distributor of electronic musical equipment including keyboards, sound modules, digital samplers, and guitar synthesizers. **Common positions include:** Administrative Assistant; Customer Service Representative. **Corporate headquarters location:** This location. **Subsidiaries include:** Rodgers Instrument; Roland Audio Development. **Listed on:** Privately held. **Annual sales/revenues:** $51 - $100 million. **Number of employees at this location:** 130. **Number of employees nationwide:** 160.

SCHWARZKOPF & DEP, INC.

2101 East Via Arado, Rancho Dominguez CA 90220-6189. 310/604-0777. **Contact:** Alexandra Konigsmann, Human Resources. **World Wide Web address:** http://www.dep.com. **Description:** A leading developer, manufacturer, and distributor of diversified personal care products. Products include Dep Styling Gel, Lavoris, Cuticura, Porcelana, Nature's Family, L.A. Looks, Agree, Halsa, Topol, and Lilt. **NOTE:** Part-time jobs are offered. **Common positions include:** Accountant; Administrative Assistant; AS400 Programmer Analyst; Auditor; Budget Analyst; Chief Financial Officer; Computer Operator; Computer Programmer; Computer Support Technician; Computer Technician; Controller; Credit Manager; Customer Service Representative; Financial Analyst; Human Resources Manager; Manufacturing Engineer; Market Research Analyst; Marketing Manager; Production Manager; Purchasing Agent/Manager; Quality Assurance Engineer; Quality Control Supervisor; Sales Manager; Secretary; Transportation/Traffic Specialist; Typist/Word Processor; Vice President of Finance; Vice President of Marketing; Vice President of Operations. **Corporate headquarters location:** This location. **Parent company:** Henkel. **Operations at this facility include:** Administration; Manufacturing; Research and Development. **President:** Robert Berglass. **Facilities Manager:** Robert Scheinholtz. **Information Systems Manager:** Oleg Debode. **Purchasing Manager:** Linda Moffat. **Sales Manager:** Dennis Gurka. **Annual sales/revenues:** More than $100 million. **Number of employees at this location:** 285.

SIMMONS COMPANY

20100 South Alameda Street, Compton CA 90220. 310/637-0101. **Fax:** 310/604-2585. **Contact:** Human Resources. **World**

Wide Web address: http://www.simmonsco.com. **Description:** A mattress and box spring manufacturer. Simmons has 15 other plants in the United States. **Common positions include:** Accountant/Auditor; Blue-Collar Worker Supervisor; Buyer; Customer Service Representative; Human Resources Manager; Purchasing Agent/Manager; Services Sales Representative. **Special programs:** Internships. **Corporate headquarters location:** Atlanta GA. **Operations at this facility include:** Administration; Divisional Headquarters; Manufacturing; Sales. **Listed on:** Privately held. **Number of employees at this location:** 220.

SYPRIS DATA SYSTEMS
605 East Huntington Drive, Monrovia CA 91016. 626/358-9500. **Contact:** Department of Human Resources. **E-mail address:** hr@syprisdatasystems.com. **World Wide Web address:** http://www.sypris.com/datasystems. **Description:** Manufacturers of analog and digital tape recorders. **Corporate headquarters location:** Louisville KY. **Parent company:** Sypris Systems. **Listed on:** NASDAQ. **Stock exchange symbol:** SYPR. **Number of employees at this location:** 120.

TDK ELECTRONICS CORPORATION
3190 East Miraloma Avenue, Anaheim CA 92806. 714/238-7900. **Contact:** Human Resources. **World Wide Web address:** http://www.tdk.com. **Description:** A manufacturer of audiocassettes and micro floppy disks. **Common positions include:** Electrical/Electronics Engineer; Mechanical Engineer. **Corporate headquarters location:** Port Washington NY. **Other U.S. locations:** Nationwide. **Operations at this facility include:** Administration; Manufacturing. **Listed on:** New York Stock Exchange. **Stock exchange symbol:** TDK. **Number of employees at this location:** 600.

THQ INC.
27001 Agoura Road, Suite 325, Calabasas Hills CA 91301. 818/871-5000. **Contact:** Human Resources Department. **E-mail address:** resume@thq.com. **World Wide Web address:** http://www.thq.com. **Description:** Develops, publishes, markets, and distributes video games for platforms that include the PlayStation, Nintendo 64, Game Boy, and PCs. **Corporate headquarters location:** This location. **Listed on:** NASDAQ. **Stock exchange symbol:** THQI. **Annual sales/revenues:** More than $100 million.

3M

6023 South Garfield Avenue, Los Angeles CA 90040. 323/726-6300. **Contact:** Human Resources. **World Wide Web address:** http://www.3m.com. **Description:** This location is an area sales office for adhesives and tapes. Overall, 3M manufactures products in three sectors: Industrial and Consumer; Information, Imaging, and Electronic; and Life Sciences. The Industrial and Consumer Sector includes a variety of products under brand names including 3M, Scotch, Post-it, Scotch-Brite, and Scotchgard. The Information, Imaging, and Electronic Sector is a leader in several high-growth global industries including telecommunications, electronics, electrical, imaging, and memory media. The Life Science Sector serves two broad market categories: health care, and traffic and personal safety. In the health care market, 3M is a leading provider of medical and surgical supplies, drug delivery systems, and dental products. In traffic and personal safety, 3M is a leader in products for transportation safety, worker protection, vehicle and sign graphics, and out-of-home advertising. **Corporate headquarters location:** St. Paul MN. **Listed on:** New York Stock Exchange. **Stock exchange symbol:** MMM.

3M

18750 Minnesota Road, Corona CA 92881. 909/737-3441. **Contact:** Human Resources. **World Wide Web address:** http://www.3m.com. **Description:** This division of 3M produces roof granules used in the manufacture of shingles. Overall, 3M manufactures products in three sectors: Industrial and Consumer; Information, Imaging, and Electronic; and Life Sciences. The Industrial and Consumer Sector includes a variety of products under brand names including 3M, Scotch, Post-it, Scotch-Brite, and Scotchgard. The Information, Imaging, and Electronic Sector is a leader in several high-growth global industries including telecommunications, electronics, electrical, imaging, and memory media. The Life Science Sector serves two broad market categories: health care, and traffic and personal safety. In the health care market, 3M is a leading provider of medical and surgical supplies, drug delivery systems, and dental products. In traffic and personal safety, 3M is a leader in products for transportation safety, worker protection, vehicle and sign graphics, and out-of-home advertising. **Corporate headquarters location:** St. Paul MN. **Listed on:** New York Stock Exchange. **Stock exchange symbol:** MMM.

VIRBAC ST. JON LABORATORIES

1656 West 240th Street, Harbor City CA 90710. 310/326-2720. **Fax:** 310/326-8026. **Contact:** Human Resources. **Description:** Develops, manufactures, and markets health care products for pets. The line includes toothpaste, toothbrushes, sprays, and enzymatic rawhide chews. The brands focus on the specialty pet retail channel with Petromalt Hairball remedy products, Petrodex dental products, Petrelief anti-itch products, Nutrimalt nutritional supplements, and Breath-eze breath mints. Founded in 1982. **NOTE:** The company expects a name change to Virbac Animal Health. Please call this location for further information.

MANUFACTURING: MISCELLANEOUS INDUSTRIAL

You can expect to find the following types of companies in this chapter:

Ball and Roller Bearings • Commercial Furniture and Fixtures • Fans, Blowers, and Purification Equipment • Industrial Machinery and Equipment • Motors and Generators/Compressors and Engine Parts • Vending Machines

ASM COMPANY, INC.

1828 West Sequoia, Orange CA 92868. 714/978-2403. **Fax:** 800/288-5104. **Contact:** Human Resources. **World Wide Web address:** http://www.asmcompany.com. **Description:** Designs, manufactures, markets, and sells engineered accessories for airless spray equipment.

AIRGUARD INDUSTRIES, INC.

1295 East Ontario Avenue, Corona CA 92881. 909/272-0708. **Fax:** 909/270-1450. **Contact:** Maria Monteon, Human Resources. **E-mail address:** maverill@airguard.com. **Description:** Manufactures commercial and industrial air filtration equipment. **Common positions include:** Accountant/Auditor; Blue-Collar Worker Supervisor; Buyer; Computer Programmer; Customer Service Representative; Human Resources Manager; Manufacturer's/Wholesaler's Sales Rep.; Operations/Production Manager; Purchasing Agent/Manager; Services Sales Representative; Systems Analyst; Transportation/Traffic Specialist; Wholesale and Retail Buyer. **Corporate headquarters location:** Louisville KY. **Other U.S. locations:** Nationwide. **Parent company:** Clarcor. **Operations at this facility include:** Administration; Divisional Headquarters; Manufacturing; Regional Headquarters; Sales. **Listed on:** New York Stock Exchange. **Number of employees at this location:** 120. **Number of employees nationwide:** 500.

AMERON INTERNATIONAL

P.O. Box 7007, Pasadena CA 91109. 626/683-4000. **Physical address:** 245 South Los Robles Avenue, Pasadena CA 91101. **Fax:** 626/683-4020. **Contact:** Human Resources Department. **World Wide Web address:** http://www.ameron.com. **Description:** Manufactures and supplies goods and services to the industrial, utility, marine, and construction markets. The business is divided into four groups: The Protective Coatings

Group develops, manufactures, and markets high-performance coatings and surface systems on a worldwide basis. These products are utilized for the preservation of major structures such as metallic and concrete facilities and equipment to prevent their decomposition by corrosion, abrasion, marine fouling, and other forms of chemical and physical attack; The Fiberglass Pipe Group develops, manufactures, and markets filament-wound and molded fiberglass pipe fittings; The Concrete and Steel Pipe Group offers products and services used in the construction of pipeline facilities for various utilities. Eight plants manufacture concrete cylinder pipe, prestressed concrete cylinder pipe, steel pipe, and reinforced concrete pipe for water transmission, and storm and industrial wastewater and sewage collection; The Construction & Allied Products Group includes the HC&D Division, which supplies ready-mix concrete, crushed and sized basaltic aggregates, dune sand, concrete pipe, and box culverts, primarily to the construction industry in Hawaii. **Corporate headquarters location:** This location. **Listed on:** New York Stock Exchange. **Stock exchange symbol:** AMN.

AMERON INTERNATIONAL

201 North Berry Street, Brea CA 92821. 714/529-1951. **Toll-free phone:** 800/9-AMERON. **Contact:** Personnel. **World Wide Web address:** http://www.ameron.com. **Description:** This location develops, manufactures, and markets proprietary, high-performance protective coatings for the offshore, chemical processing, refining, rail, power, bridge, water and waste treatment, pulp and paper, and light industrial/commercial markets. Overall, Ameron International manufactures and supplies goods and services to the industrial, utility, marine, and construction markets. The business of the company is divided into three other groups. The Fiberglass Pipe Group develops, manufactures, and markets filament-wound and molded fiberglass pipe fittings. The Construction & Allied Products Group includes the HC&D Division, which supplies ready-mix concrete, crushed and sized basaltic aggregates, dune sand, concrete pipe, and box culverts, primarily to the construction industry in Hawaii. The Concrete and Steel Pipe Group supplies products and services used in the construction of pipeline facilities for various utilities. Products include concrete cylinder pipe, prestressed concrete cylinder pipe, steel pipe, and reinforced concrete pipe for water transmission, storm and industrial wastewater, and sewage collection. **Corporate headquarters location:** Pasadena CA. **Listed on:** New York Stock Exchange. **Stock exchange symbol:** AMN.

AMISTAR CORPORATION
237 Via Vera Cruz, San Marcos CA 92069. 760/471-1700. **Fax:** 760/761-9065. **Contact:** Human Resources. **World Wide Web address:** http://www.amistar.com. **Description:** Amistar designs, develops, manufactures, markets, and services a broad variety of automatic and semi-automatic equipment for assembling electronic components to be placed in printed circuit boards. The company is also a contract assembler of printed circuit boards. **Corporate headquarters location:** This location. **Number of employees at this location:** 170. **Listed on:** NASDAQ. **Stock exchange symbol:** AMTA.

ANGELUS SANITARY CAN MACHINE COMPANY
4900 Pacific Boulevard, Los Angeles CA 90058. 323/583-2171. **Fax:** 323-587-5607. **Contact:** Mr. Wiley Fain, Director of Human Resources Department. **World Wide Web address:** http://www.angelusmachine.com. **Description:** A manufacturer and worldwide distributor of can-closing equipment. **Corporate headquarters location:** This location. **International locations:** Belgium; United Kingdom.

ASSEMBLY AND MANUFACTURING SYSTEMS CORPORATION
2222 Shasta Way, Simi Valley CA 93065. 805/583-8961. **Fax:** 805/583-0442. **Contact:** Human Resources. **Description:** Manufactures factory automation equipment. **Common positions include:** Accountant/Auditor; Designer; Draftsperson; General Manager; Industrial Production Manager; Mechanical Engineer; Purchasing Agent/Manager. **Other U.S. locations:** Columbus OH. **Operations at this facility include:** Administration; Divisional Headquarters; Manufacturing; Sales; Service. **Number of employees at this location:** 50. **Number of employees nationwide:** 125.

AVERY DENNISON CORPORATION
150 North Orange Grove Boulevard, Pasadena CA 91103. 626/304-2000. **Contact:** Human Resources Department. **World Wide Web address:** http://www.averydennison.com. **Description:** A worldwide manufacturer of self-adhesive products, pressure-sensitive base materials, label components, labeling systems, and office products. The company services a broad range of industries with products that are used in applications for marking, identifying, labeling, decorating, fastening, filing, and indexing. **Common positions include:** Accountant/Auditor; Administrator; Attorney; Chemical Engineer; Chemist; Computer Programmer; Financial Analyst; Mechanical Engineer; Secretary; Systems Analyst. **Corporate**

headquarters location: This location. **Other area locations:** Brea CA; Covina CA; Irwindale CA. **Other U.S. locations:** Framingham MA. **Listed on:** New York Stock Exchange. **Stock exchange symbol:** AVE. **Number of employees nationwide:** 16,100.

AXIOHM TRANSACTION SOLUTIONS, INC.
15070 Avenue of Science, San Diego CA 92128. 858/451-3485. **Fax:** 858/451-3573. **Contact:** Paul Gardner, Director of Human Resources. **E-mail address:** paul.gardner@axiohm.com. **World Wide Web address:** http://www.axiohm.com. **Description:** One of the world's largest designers, manufacturers, and marketers of transaction printers. Axiohm Transaction Solutions also designs and manufactures bar code printers, magstripe and smartcard readers and writers, card printers, dot matrix impact printheads, magnetic heads, print and apply labeling systems, and consumables. Founded in 1977. **Corporate headquarters location:** This location. **Other U.S. locations:** Garden Grove CA; Golden CO; Ithaca NY; Riverton WY. **International locations:** Worldwide.

BECKMAN COULTER, INC.
200 South Kraemer Boulevard, P.O. Box 8000, Brea CA 92822. 714/993-8584. **Fax:** 714/961-4113. **Contact:** Employment. **E-mail address:** breahr@beckman.com. **World Wide Web address:** http://www.beckman.com. **Description:** Sells and services a diverse range of scientific instruments, reagents, and related equipment. Products include DNA synthesizers, robotic workstations, centrifuges, electrophoresis systems, detection and measurement equipment, data processing software, and specialty chemical and automated general chemical systems. Many of the company's products are used in research and development and diagnostic analysis. **NOTE:** Second and third shifts are offered. **Common positions include:** Accountant; Administrative Assistant; Applications Engineer; Biochemist; Biological Scientist; Chemical Engineer; Computer Programmer; Computer Support Technician; Customer Service Representative; Database Administrator; Database Manager; Financial Analyst; Librarian; Marketing Specialist; Mechanical Engineer; MIS Specialist; Network/Systems Administrator; Sales Representative; Secretary; Software Engineer. **Other area locations:** Carlsbad CA; Fullerton CA; Palo Alto CA; Porterville CA; San Diego CA. **Other U.S. locations:** Nationwide. **International locations:** Worldwide. **Parent company:** Beckman Instruments, Inc. **Operations at this facility include:** Administration; Manufacturing; Research and Development. **Listed on:** New

·York Stock Exchange. **Stock exchange symbol:** BEC. **CEO:** Jack Wareham. **Annual sales/revenues:** More than $100 million. **Number of employees worldwide:** 11,000.

BECKMAN COULTER, INC.
2470 Faraday Avenue, Carlsbad CA 92008. 760/438-9151. **Fax:** 760/438-6390. **Contact:** Human Resources. **E-mail address:** clsbdhr@beckman.com. **World Wide Web address:** http://www.beckman.com. **Description:** This location develops monoclonal antibody technology for use in medical diagnostic products. Overall, Beckman Coulter sells and services a diverse range of scientific instruments, reagents, and related equipment. Products include DNA synthesizers, robotic workstations, centrifuges, electrophoresis systems, detection and measurement equipment, data processing software, and specialty chemical and automated general chemical systems. Many of the company's products are used in research and development or diagnostic analysis. **NOTE:** Second and third shifts are offered. **Common positions include:** Accountant; Administrative Assistant; Applications Engineer; Biochemist; Biological Scientist; Chemical Engineer; Computer Programmer; Computer Support Technician; Customer Service Representative; Database Administrator; Database Manager; Financial Analyst; Librarian; Marketing Specialist; Mechanical Engineer; MIS Specialist; Network/Systems Administrator; Sales Representative; Secretary; Software Engineer. **Other area locations:** Brea CA; Fullerton CA; Palo Alto CA; Porterville CA; San Diego CA. **Other U.S. locations:** Nationwide. **International locations:** Worldwide. **Parent company:** Beckman Instruments, Inc. **Listed on:** New York Stock Exchange. **Stock exchange symbol:** BEC.

CAMFIL FARR
2121 Paulhan Street, Rancho Dominguez CA 90220. 310/668-6344. **Fax:** 310/668-6313. **Contact:** Personnel. **World Wide Web address:** http://www.camfil.com. **Description:** Primarily engaged in the design, manufacture, and sale of filtration systems for use in a wide variety of industrial applications. These include heating, ventilating, and air conditioning systems, as well as gas turbines and construction equipment. Other products include noise-abatement systems and engine protection equipment. **Common positions include:** Accountant/Auditor; Administrative Manager; Buyer; Computer Programmer; Customer Service Representative; Design Engineer; Draftsperson; Mechanical Engineer; Purchasing Agent/Manager. **Corporate headquarters location:** Riverdale

NJ. **Operations at this facility include:** Administration; Research and Development; Sales.

CLAYTON INDUSTRIES

P.O. Box 5530, El Monte CA 91734-1530. 626/443-9381. **Physical address:** 4213 North Temple City Boulevard, El Monte CA 91731. **Fax:** 626/442-3787. **Contact:** Department of Human Resources. **World Wide Web address:** http://www.claytonindustries.com. **Description:** Manufactures a broad range of industrial and automotive equipment for a variety of commercial and government customers. Products include steam generators, dynamometers, and a number of automotive diagnostic components. **Common positions include:** Accountant/Auditor; Administrative Manager; Advertising Clerk; Blue-Collar Worker Supervisor; Buyer; Chemical Engineer; Computer Programmer; Customer Service Representative; Designer; Electrical/Electronics Engineer; Financial Analyst; General Manager; Industrial Engineer; Industrial Production Manager; Mechanical Engineer; Operations/Production Manager; Purchasing Agent/Manager; Quality Control Supervisor; Services Sales Representative; Software Engineer; Systems Analyst; Technical Writer/Editor; Transportation/Traffic Specialist. **Special programs:** Internships. **Corporate headquarters location:** This location. **Other U.S. locations:** Nationwide. **International locations:** Worldwide. **Operations at this facility include:** Administration; Manufacturing; Research and Development; Sales; Service. **Listed on:** Privately held. **Number of employees at this location:** 135.

DEL MAR MEDICAL SYSTEMS, LLC

1621 Alton Parkway, Irvine CA 92606. 949/250-3200. **Contact:** Trish Hichten, Personnel Manager. **World Wide Web address:** http://www.delmarmedical.com. **Description:** Develops, manufactures, and markets a wide range of medical monitoring and testing equipment. Products include stress tests, ambulatory blood pressure monitors, ambulatory transesophagael testing devices, and the AVESP (Audiovisual Superimposed Electrocardiographic Presentation). **Corporate headquarters location:** This location.

EATON AEROSPACE

4690 Colorado Boulevard, Los Angeles CA 90039. 818/409-0200. **Contact:** Rory Strahan, Personnel Manager. **World Wide Web address:** http://www.eaton.com. **Description:** Manufactures and designs actuators, servomechanisms, AC/DC motors, solenoids, and gears. **Corporate headquarters**

location: Cleveland OH. **Listed on:** New York Stock Exchange. **Stock exchange symbol:** ETN.

EATON AEROSPACE

4520 Electronics Place, Los Angeles CA 90039. 818/550-4200. **Contact:** Human Resources. **World Wide Web address:** http://www.eaton.com. **Description:** Manufactures and designs actuators, servomechanisms, AC/DC motors, solenoids, and gears. **Common positions include:** Accountant/Auditor; Aerospace Engineer; Buyer; Designer; Draftsperson; Electrical/Electronics Engineer; General Manager; Human Resources Manager; Mechanical Engineer; Purchasing Agent/Manager; Quality Control Supervisor. **Corporate headquarters location:** Cleveland OH. **Operations at this facility include:** Manufacturing; Research and Development. **Listed on:** New York Stock Exchange. **Stock exchange symbol:** ETN.

ELECTRA-GEAR

1110 Anaheim Boulevard, Anaheim CA 92801. 714/535-6061. **Toll-free phone:** 800/877-4327. **Fax:** 714/535-2489. **Contact:** April Price, Human Resources Department Administrator. **E-mail address:** humanresources@electragear.com. **World Wide Web address:** http://www.electragear.com. **Description:** Manufactures a wide variety of motors, gear boxes, and speed reducers. **Common positions include:** Accountant/Auditor; Adjuster; Blue-Collar Worker Supervisor; Computer Operator; Customer Service Representative; Department Manager; Electrical/Electronics Engineer; Human Resources Manager; Industrial Engineer; Inspector/Tester/Grader; Machinist; Manufacturer's/Wholesaler's Sales Representative; Mechanical Engineer; Receptionist; Secretary. **Corporate headquarters location:** Beloit WI. **Parent company:** Regal-Beloit Corporation. **Listed on:** New York Stock Exchange. **Number of employees at this location:** 130.

ELECTRO SCIENTIFIC INDUSTRIES

2310 Aldergrove Avenue, Escondido CA 92029. 714/541-4818. **Fax:** 760/741-8245. **Contact:** Human Resources. **World Wide Web address:** http://www.elcsci.com. **Description:** Develops, manufactures, and sells a line of computer-controlled drilling machines, used to produce large volumes of accurately positioned holes in PCBs, and routers, used to cut and shape PCBs during the manufacturing process. **Common positions include:** Account Manager; Accountant; Administrative Assistant; Administrative Manager; Applications Engineer; Blue-Collar Worker Supervisor; Buyer; Chief

Financial Officer; Computer Operator; Computer Programmer; Controller; Customer Service Representative; Database Manager; Design Engineer; Draftsperson; Electrical/Electronics Engineer; Electrician; General Manager; Human Resources Manager; Industrial Engineer; Manufacturing Engineer; MIS Specialist; Operations Manager; Production Manager; Project Manager; Sales Engineer; Sales Manager; Sales Representative; Secretary; Software Engineer; Systems Analyst; Vice President. **Corporate headquarters location:** Portland OR. **Other U.S. locations:** Palomar CA; San Diego CA; Santa Ana CA; Chicago IL. **International locations:** China; Hong Kong; Japan; Korea; Taiwan; United Kingdom. **Listed on:** NASDAQ. **Stock exchange symbol:** ESIO. **President/CEO:** Donald Van Luvanee. **Facilities Manager:** Brian Meehan. **Annual sales/revenues:** $21 - $50 million. **Number of employees at this location:** 900.

EXCELLON AUTOMATION
24751 Crenshaw Boulevard, Torrance CA 90505. 310/534-6300. **Fax:** 310/534-6771. **Contact:** Human Resources Director. **E-mail address:** hr@excellon.com. **World Wide Web address:** http://www.excellon.com. **Description:** Manufactures machine tools including routers, laser drilling equipment, and high-precision drilling systems. **Common positions include:** Accountant/Auditor; Buyer; Electrical/Electronics Engineer; Mechanical Engineer; Purchasing Agent/Manager; Software Engineer. **Corporate headquarters location:** Bellevue WA. **Parent company:** Esterline Technologies. **Operations at this facility include:** Manufacturing. **Listed on:** New York Stock Exchange. **Stock exchange symbol:** ESL. **Number of employees at this location:** 225. **Number of employees nationwide:** 300.

FAIRCHILD FASTENERS - U.S.
800 South State College Boulevard, Fullerton CA 92831. 714/871-1550. **Contact:** Personnel Manager. **World Wide Web address:** http://www.fairchildfasteners.com. **Description:** Manufactures and supplies precision fastening systems and components and latching devices for aerospace and industrial applications. Fairchild Fasteners - U.S. was established to collectively manage all of Fairchild's fastener operations in the United States. Fairchild Fasteners - Europe (Germany) is its sister company. **Common positions include:** Aerospace Engineer; Computer Programmer; Customer Service Representative; Draftsperson; Industrial Engineer; Machinist; Mechanical Engineer; Metallurgical Engineer. **Corporate headquarters location:** Dulles VA. **Parent company:** The Fairchild Corporation. **Operations at this facility include:**

Administration; Manufacturing; Research and Development; Sales; Service. **Listed on:** New York Stock Exchange. **Stock exchange symbol:** FA. **President/CEO:** Eric Steiner. **Number of employees at this location:** 600.

FAIRCHILD FASTENERS - U.S.

3000 West Lomita Boulevard, Torrance CA 90505. 310/530-2220. **Contact:** Human Resources Manager. **World Wide Web address:** http://www.fairchildfasteners.com. **Description:** Manufactures and supplies precision fastening systems and components and latching devices for aerospace and industrial applications. Fairchild Fasteners - U.S. was established to collectively manage all of Fairchild's fastener operations in the United States. Fairchild Fasteners - Europe (Germany) is its sister company. **Corporate headquarters location:** Dulles VA. **Listed on:** New York Stock Exchange. **Stock exchange symbol:** FA. **Parent company:** The Fairchild Corporation.

FLOWSERVE CORPORATION

1909 East Cashden Street, Rancho Dominguez CA 90220. 310/669-9023. **Contact:** Human Resources Department. **World Wide Web address:** http://www.flowserve.com. **Description:** Manufactures fluid control systems. **Common positions include:** Design Engineer; Electrical/Electronics Engineer; Manufacturing Engineer; Mechanical Engineer. **Corporate headquarters location:** Dallas TX. **Listed on:** New York Stock Exchange. **Stock exchange symbol:** FLS.

GOULD'S PUMPS INC.

P.O. Box 1254, City of Industry CA 91749-1254. 562/949-2113. **Contact:** Karen Perez, Personnel Manager. **World Wide Web address:** http://www.itt.com. **Description:** Engineers, manufactures, and sells centrifugal pumps and component parts with related drivers and accessories. Gould's serves a broad variety of industries including petrochemical and refining, pulp and paper, mining, and marine. The company maintains manufacturing facilities in a number of states, as well as production and sales locations overseas. **Corporate headquarters location:** Seneca Falls NY. **Parent company:** ITT Industries. **Listed on:** New York Stock Exchange. **Stock exchange symbol:** ITT.

GRENEKER

3100 East 12th Street, Los Angeles CA 90023. 323/263-9000. **Fax:** 323/263-9543. **Contact:** Personnel Director. **World Wide Web address:** http://www.greneker.com. **Description:** Designs and manufactures mannequins and custom crafts utilizing a number of materials including fiberglass, concrete, wood and metal. **Common positions include:** Accountant/Auditor; Buyer; Computer Programmer; Cost Estimator; Credit Manager; Customer Service Representative; Designer; General Manager; Human Resources Manager; Manufacturer's/Wholesaler's Sales Rep.; Purchasing Agent/Manager; Services Sales Representative; Systems Analyst; Wholesale and Retail Buyer. **Corporate headquarters location:** This location. **Other U.S. locations:** NY; TX. **Operations at this facility include:** Administration; Manufacturing; Research and Development; Sales. **Number of employees at this location:** 285.

HASKEL INTERNATIONAL, INC.

100 East Graham Place, Burbank CA 91502. 818/843-4000. **Fax:** 818/556-2526. **Contact:** Human Resources Department. **World Wide Web address:** http://www.haskel.com. **Description:** Manufactures pneumatically driven, high-pressure liquid pumps and gas boosters for industrial, commercial, aerospace, and military applications. The company sells and distributes its own pneumatically driven pumps, gas boosters, air amplifiers, and high-pressure valves, as well as third-party valves, cylinders and actuators, and other hydraulic and pneumatic devices. The company's high-pressure pumps and systems are used worldwide in manufacturing processes for industrial pressure testing and controls, fluid storage and containment, and a wide variety of other applications. Haskel International also specializes in the trading of electronic components. Founded in 1946. **Corporate headquarters location:** This location.

HILL PHOENIX

3601 Walnut Avenue, Chino CA 91710. 909/590-4432. **Contact:** Becky Luman, Payroll. **World Wide Web address:** http://www.hillphoenix.com. **Description:** Manufactures refrigerated merchandisers, refrigeration systems, and electrical distribution centers for commercial and industrial companies. **Corporate headquarters location:** Conyers GA.

HOBART CORPORATION

5584 Bandini Boulevard, Bell CA 90201. 323/260-7321. **Contact:** Human Resources. **World Wide Web address:** http://www.hobartcorp.com. **Description:** This location is a sales office. Overall, Hobart Corporation manufactures restaurant equipment including mixers, slicers, cooking equipment, and refrigeration devices. **Corporate headquarters location:** Troy OH. **Parent company:** Premark International.

HUNTER INDUSTRIES
1940 Diamond Street, San Marcos CA 92069. 760/744-5240.
Contact: Human Resources Department. **E-mail address:**
hr@hunterindustries.com. **World Wide Web address:**
http://www.hunterindustries.com. **Description:** Manufactures
irrigation equipment. **Corporate headquarters location:** This
location.

HUTCHINSON SEAL CORPORATION
NATIONAL O-RING DIVISION
11634 Patton Road, Downey CA 90241-5295. 562/862-8163.
Fax: 562/862-4596. **Contact:** Personnel. **World Wide Web**
address: http://www.hutchinsonrubber.com. **Description:**
Engaged in various distribution and manufacturing operations.
Corporate headquarters location: This location. **Subsidiaries**
include: National O-Ring, which manufactures and distributes
a full-range of standard-size, low-cost, synthetic rubber o-ring
sealing devices for use in automotive and industrial
applications.

ITT JABSCO
1485 Dale Way, Costa Mesa CA 92626-2158. 714/545-8251.
Contact: Steve Cibull, Human Resources Director. **World**
Wide Web address: http://www.jabsco.com. **Description:**
Manufactures pumps for marine craft, RVs, and industrial
usage. ITT Jabsco is an operating unit of ITT Fluid Technology
Corporation. **Common positions include:** Accountant/Auditor;
Administrator; Advertising Clerk; Blue-Collar Worker
Supervisor; Buyer; Chemist; Commercial Artist; Computer
Programmer; Credit Manager; Customer Service
Representative; Department Manager; Draftsperson; Financial
Analyst; General Manager; Human Resources Manager;
Industrial Engineer; Manufacturer's/Wholesaler's Sales Rep.;
Marketing Specialist; Mechanical Engineer; Public Relations
Specialist; Purchasing Agent/Manager; Quality Control
Supervisor; Systems Analyst. **Corporate headquarters location:**
This location. **Parent company:** ITT Corporation is a
diversified, global enterprise engaged in three major business
areas: Financial and Business Services, which includes ITT
Hartford, ITT Financial Corporation, and ITT Communications
and Information Services, Inc.; Manufactured Products, which
includes ITT Automotive, ITT Defense & Electronics, Inc., and
ITT Fluid Technology Corporation; and Sheraton Hotels (ITT
Sheraton Corporation). **Operations at this facility include:**
Administration; Manufacturing; Research and Development;
Sales; Service. **Listed on:** New York Stock Exchange. **Stock**
exchange symbol: ITT.

JOHNSON LIFT/HYSTER

P.O. Box 60007, City of Industry CA 91716-9600. 562/692-9311. **Contact:** Human Resources Director. **World Wide Web address:** http://www.johnson-lift.com. **Description:** Engaged in marketing material-handling equipment (industrial truck lifts and personnel lifts) and related parts and service. **Common positions include:** Accountant/Auditor; Credit Manager; Manufacturer's/Wholesaler's Sales Rep. **Parent company:** Hyster-Yale Material Handling, Inc. **Operations at this facility include:** Administration; Sales.

LASCO BATHWARE, INC.

8101 East Kaiser Boulevard, Suite 130, Anaheim CA 92808. 714/993-1220. **Toll-free phone:** 800/877-2205. **Contact:** Human Resources Department. **World Wide Web address:** http://www.lascobathware.com. **Description:** Manufactures bath fixtures. Products include acrylic and fiberglass bathtubs, whirlpools, showers, and shower tubs. LASCO Bathware also manufactures shower doors and steam generators. Founded in 1947. **Corporate headquarters location:** This location.

LUFKIN INDUSTRIES INC.

30011 Ivy Glenn Drive, Suite 222, Laguna Niguel CA 92677-5017. 949/249-7850. **Contact:** Human Resources. **E-mail address:** vbarbay@lufkin.com. **World Wide Web address:** http://www.lufkin.com. **NOTE:** Please submit resumes to Human Resources, Lufkin Industries, P.O. Box 849, Lufkin TX 75902. **Description:** This location manufactures gearboxes as part of the company's power transmission division. Overall, Lufkin Industries manufactures and markets products to global industrial, energy, and transportation companies through its four divisions: Oilfield, Foundry, Trailer, and Power Transmission. **Corporate headquarters location:** Lufkin TX. **Listed on:** NASDAQ. **Stock exchange symbol:** LUFK.

MERIT ABRASIVE PRODUCTS INC.

7301 Orangewood Avenue, Garden Grove CA 92841. 310/639-4242. **Toll-free phone:** 800/421-1936. **Contact:** Human Resources Department. **World Wide Web address:** http://www.meritabr.com. **Description:** Manufactures coated abrasive tools. **Corporate headquarters location:** This location.

MILLER DIAL CORPORATION

P.O. Box 5868, El Monte CA 91731. 626/444-4555. **Physical address:** 4400 North Temple City Boulevard, El Monte CA 91731. **Fax:** 626/443-3267. **Contact:** Personnel Department. **World Wide Web address:** http://www.millerdial.com.

Description: One of the world's largest manufacturers of nameplates and other function identification products including panels, dials, membrane switches, and labels. **Corporate headquarters location:** This location.

PACO JOHNSTON PUMP COMPANY
3215 Producer Way, Pomona CA 91768. 909/594-9959. **Contact:** Human Resources Department. **E-mail address:** jphr@flow-products.com. **World Wide Web address:** http://www.johnston-pump.com. **Description:** Manufactures, markets, and services engineered centrifugal pumps to the commercial, construction, industrial, municipal, and irrigation markets. The company's product line includes end suction, double suction split case, in-lines, and booster systems, as well as sump and sewage pumps. **NOTE:** All hiring is conducted by the parent company. Please direct resumes to Paco Johnston Pump Company, Human Resources, 800 Koomey Road, Brookshire TX 77423. 281/934-6014. **Common positions include:** Customer Service Representative; Manufacturer's/Wholesaler's Sales Rep.; Mechanical Engineer. **Other U.S. locations:** Oakland CA; Portland OR; Dallas TX; Seattle WA. **Operations at this facility include:** Manufacturing; Sales; Service. **Number of employees at this location:** 20. **Number of employees nationwide:** 250.

PHILADELPHIA GEAR CORPORATION
P.O. Box 700, Lynwood CA 90262. 310/605-2600. **Physical address:** 2600 East Imperial Highway, Lynwood CA 90262. **Fax:** 310/898-3594. **Contact:** Human Resources. **E-mail address:** westcoast@philagear.com. **World Wide Web address:** http://www.philagear.com. **Description:** Manufactures heavy machinery gear and cable equipment. **Corporate headquarters location:** Norristown PA.

POWER-SONIC CORPORATION
9163 Siempre Viva Road, Suite A, San Diego CA 92154. 619/661-2020. **Fax:** 619/661-3650. **Contact:** Ms. Kim Tran, Personnel Manager. **E-mail address:** jobs@power-sonic.com. **Description:** Manufactures rechargeable batteries for original equipment manufacturers. **Corporate headquarters location:** This location. **International locations:** Mexicali, Mexico. **Parent company:** Eldon Industries.

REHRIG PACIFIC COMPANY
4010 East 26th Street, Los Angeles CA 90023. 323/262-5145. **Contact:** Jim Drew, Chief Financial Officer. **World Wide Web address:** http://www.rehrigpacific.com. **Description:**

Manufactures plastic shipping containers. **Corporate headquarters location:** This location.

REULAND ELECTRIC
17969 East Railroad Street, City of Industry CA 91749. 626/964-6411. **Contact:** Employee Relations. **E-mail address:** hr-ca@reuland.com. **World Wide Web address:** http://www.reuland.com. **Description:** Manufactures custom-designed motors, brakes, and controls for industrial clients. **Common positions include:** Accountant/Auditor; Administrator; Blue-Collar Worker Supervisor; Buyer; Claim Representative; Computer Programmer; Credit Manager; Customer Service Representative; Draftsperson; Economist; Electrical/Electronics Engineer; General Manager; Human Resources Manager; Industrial Designer; Industrial Engineer; Management Trainee; Manufacturer's/Wholesaler's Sales Rep.; Marketing Specialist; Mechanical Engineer; Operations/Production Manager; Public Relations Specialist; Quality Control Supervisor; Systems Analyst. **Corporate headquarters location:** This location. **Operations at this facility include:** Administration; Manufacturing; Motor Division.

SI TECHNOLOGIES
14192 Franklin Avenue, Tustin CA 92780. 714/505-6483. **Fax:** 714/573-3843. **Contact:** Human Resources Department. **World Wide Web address:** http://www.sitechnologies.com. **Description:** Designs, manufactures, and markets industrial sensors, and weighing and factory automation systems. **Corporate headquarters location:** This location. **Other U.S. locations:** Chicago IL; Cumberland MD; Detroit MI; Mooresville NC; Eugene OR; Lynnwood WA; Seattle WA. **International locations:** Canada; France; Germany; the Netherlands; United Kingdom. **Listed on:** NASDAQ. **Stock exchange symbol:** SISI. **President/CEO:** Rick A. Beets. **Annual sales/revenues:** $21 - $50 million. **Number of employees worldwide:** 400.

SAINT-GOBAIN CALMAR INC.
333 South Turnbull Canyon Road, City of Industry CA 91745. 626/330-3161. **Toll-free phone:** 800/599-2124. **Contact:** Human Resources Manager. **World Wide Web address:** http://www.calmar.com. **Description:** A leading producer of high-performance mechanical (nonaerosol) dispensing systems. Saint-Gobain Calmar Inc. also develops child-resistant and tamper-evident caps that are used by pharmaceutical firms. **Common positions include:** Accountant/Auditor; Design

Engineer; Mechanical Engineer. **Corporate headquarters location:** Watchung NJ. **Other area locations:** Cerritos CA; San Leandro CA; Union City CA. **Other U.S. locations:** Nationwide. **International locations:** Worldwide.

SEMICONDUCTOR PROCESS EQUIPMENT CORPORATION
25145 Anza Drive, Valencia CA 91355. 661/257-0934. **Fax:** 661/257-1083. **Contact:** Dede Long, Recruiter. **World Wide Web address:** http://www.team-spec.com. **Description:** A leading manufacturer of specialized processing equipment used by semiconductor manufacturers. Founded in 1986. **Common positions include:** Electrical/Electronics Engineer; Electrician; Mechanical Engineer; Project Manager; Sales Engineer; Software Engineer; Technical Writer/Editor. **Office hours:** Monday - Friday, 8:00 a.m. - 5:00 p.m. **Corporate headquarters location:** This location. **Listed on:** Privately held. **Annual sales/revenues:** $11 - $20 million. **Number of employees at this location:** 125.

STRUCTURAL COMPOSITES INDUSTRIES
325 Enterprise Place, Pomona CA 91768. **Contact:** Human Resources Department. **World Wide Web address:** http://www.scicomposites.com. **Description:** Specializes in OSHA-approved powered-air and supplied-air systems and self-contained breathing apparatus (SCBA). Products include gas mask filters, industrial air and respiratory protection filters, Airstream helmets, the Powerflow full-facepiece respirator with a motor and filter, and the Delta line of disposable particulate respirators. The company also produces fully overwrapped composite pressure vessels used in firefighting. **Corporate headquarters location:** This location. **Parent company:** Harsco Corporation Gas and Fluid Control Group.

TAB PRODUCTS COMPANY
12501 East Imperial Highway, Norwalk CA 90650. 562/868-1585. **Fax:** 562/868-1575. **Contact:** Human Resources Department. **E-mail address:** staffing@tab.com. **World Wide Web address:** http://www.tab.com. **Description:** A document management company specializing in managing paper-based through electronic documents. Products and services include lateral color-coding filing supplies, storage and mobile systems, document management software, imaging services, and professional services. **Common positions include:** Accountant/Auditor; Adjuster; Budget Analyst; Buyer; Computer Programmer; Credit Manager; Customer Service Representative; Economist; Financial Analyst; Services Sales Representative; Software Engineer; Systems Analyst; Technical

Writer/Editor. **Corporate headquarters location:** Vernon Hills IL. **Other U.S. locations:** Nationwide. **Operations at this facility include:** Administration; Research and Development; Sales; Service. **Listed on:** American Stock Exchange. **Stock exchange symbol:** TBP. **Number of employees at this location:** 120. **Number of employees nationwide:** 1,000.

TELEDYNE TECHNOLOGIES INC.
12333 West Olympic Boulevard, Los Angeles CA 90064. 310/893-1600. **Contact:** Human Resources. **World Wide Web address:** http://www.teledynetechnologies.com. **Description:** Manufactures avionics systems, broadband communications subsystems, and engines for the aerospace, defense, and manufacturing industries. The company also provides engineering and information technology services to corporate and government clients. **Corporate headquarters location:** This location. **Listed on:** New York Stock Exchange. **Stock exchange symbol:** TDY.

3-D SYSTEMS INC.
26081 Avenue Hall, Valencia CA 91355. 661/295-5600. **Contact:** Personnel. **E-mail address:** jobs@3dsystems.com. **World Wide Web address:** http://www.3dsystems.com. **Description:** Manufactures stereolithography equipment. Founded in 1986. **Corporate headquarters location:** This location. **International locations:** China; France; Germany; Italy; United Kingdom. **Listed on:** NASDAQ. **Stock exchange symbol:** TDSC.

THYSSENKRUPP ELEVATOR COMPANY
6048 Triangle Drive, Commerce CA 90040. 909/594-5747. **Contact:** Human Resources Department. **World Wide Web address:** http://www.thyssenelevator.com. **Description:** Provides elevator and escalator products, services, and technology. **Corporate headquarters location:** Salt Lake City UT.

USFILTER
40-004 Cook Street, Palm Desert CA 92211. 760/340-0098. **Contact:** Human Resources Department. **E-mail address:** corpstaff@usfilter.com. **World Wide Web address:** http://www.usfilter.com. **Description:** Manufactures and services water purification and treatment equipment. Primary customers are the electronic, utility, and pharmaceutical industries. **Corporate headquarters location:** This location. **Parent company:** Vivendi. **Listed on:** New York Stock Exchange. **Stock exchange symbol:** V.

VACCO INDUSTRIES

10350 VACCO Street, South El Monte CA 91733-3399. 626/443-7121. **Fax:** 626/442-6943. **Contact:** Jim Cumbie, Director of Human Resources. **E-mail address:** hr@vacco.com. **World Wide Web address:** http://www.vacco.com. **Description:** Manufactures high-technology valves and screens used on submarines. **Parent company:** ESCO Electronics Corporation is a diversified producer of defense systems and commercial products sold to a variety of customers worldwide. ESCO's products are broadly defined as electronic products, valves and filters, mobile tactical systems, armament systems, automatic test equipment, utility load management equipment, and anechoic/shielding systems. ESCO's other operating subsidiaries include Distribution Control Systems, Inc., EMC Test Systems. L.P., PTI Technologies, Inc., Rantec Microwave & Electronics, Comtrak Technologies, Inc., Filtertek Inc., and Lindgren RF Enclosures. **Corporate headquarters location:** St. Louis MO. **Listed on:** New York Stock Exchange. **Stock exchange symbol:** ESE.

VIRCO MANUFACTURING CORPORATION

2027 Harpers Way, Torrance CA 90501. 310/533-0474. **Contact:** Anjelica Gamble, Personnel Director. **World Wide Web address:** http://www.virco-mfg.com. **Description:** Manufactures school and office furniture. **Corporate headquarters location:** This location. **Listed on:** American Stock Exchange. **Stock exchange symbol:** VIR.

ZURN-WILKINS

1747 Commerce Way, Paso Robles CA 93446. 805/238-7100. **Contact:** Department of Human Resources. **E-mail address:** human.resources@zurn.com. **World Wide Web address:** http://www.zurn.com. **Description:** Manufactures backflow prevention devices and residential, commercial, and industrial pressure-reducing and regulating valves and equipment as part of the Water Control segment of Zurn Industries. **Parent company:** Zurn Industries operates in three other industry segments as well. The Power Systems segment designs, constructs, and operates small to medium-sized alternate energy and combined-cycle power plants; designs steam generators and waste heat energy recovery and incineration systems; and produces equipment and fans to control emissions of solid particulate and gaseous pollutants. The Mechanical Power Transmission segment manufactures and markets clutches, couplings, and universal joints in the United States and Europe. The last segment, Lynx Golf, manufactures golf clubs in Nevada, which are finished and assembled in

California, Mexico, and Scotland for distribution worldwide. **Corporate headquarters location:** Erie PA.

MINING/GAS/PETROLEUM/ENERGY RELATED

You can expect to find the following types of companies in this chapter:

Anthracite, Coal, and Ore Mining • Mining Machinery and Equipment • Oil and Gas Field Services • Petroleum and Natural Gas

BP AMOCO
1801 East Sepulveda Boulevard, Carson CA 90745. 310/549-6204. **Contact:** Human Resources. **World Wide Web address:** http://www.bpamoco.com. **Description:** Engaged in all phases of the petroleum energy business. The company also manufactures and markets petrochemicals; has interests in coal, copper, molybdenum, and other minerals; and produces a wide range of metal products and solar energy devices. **Corporate headquarters location:** This location. **Other U.S. locations:** AL; AK; CA; GA; IL; MD; OH; OK; SC; TX; VA. **International locations:** Worldwide. **Listed on:** New York Stock Exchange. **Stock exchange symbol:** BP.

BARTON INSTRUMENT SYSTEMS, LLC
900 South Turnbull Canyon Road, City of Industry CA 91745. 626/961-2547. **Fax:** 626/937-0422. **Contact:** Human Resources. **E-mail address:** hr@barton-instruments.com. **World Wide Web address:** http://www.barton-instruments.com. **Description:** Develops and manufactures measurement information systems. Products are used for inventory management, flow measurement, and process monitoring control for the oil, gas, power, and chemical and petrochemical process industries. **Corporate headquarters location:** This location. **Other U.S. locations:** Nationwide. **International locations:** Worldwide. **Parent company:** American Commercial Holdings (Lexington KY).

BERRY PETROLEUM COMPANY
5201 Truxtun Avenue, Suite 300, Bakersfield CA 93309. **Contact:** Human Resources. **E-mail address:** ree@bry.com. **World Wide Web address:** http://www.bry.com. **Description:** Engaged in the production, development, exploration, blending, and marketing of crude oil and natural gas. Founded in 1909. **Corporate headquarters location:** This location. **Listed on:** New York Stock Exchange. **Stock exchange symbol:** BRY. **CEO/President:** Jerry Hoffman. **Annual sales/revenues:** $51 - $100 million. **Number of employees at this location:** 100.

CHEVRONTEXACO
1546 Chinagrade Loop, Bakersfield CA 93308. 661/392-2200. **Contact:** Human Resources Department. **World Wide Web address:** http://www.chevrontexaco.com. **Description:** An international oil firm with operations in more than 90 countries. ChevronTexaco is engaged in worldwide integrated petroleum operations including the exploration and production of crude oil and natural gas reserves; the transportation of crude oil, natural gas, and petroleum products by pipeline, tanker, and motor equipment; the operation of oil-refining complexes; and the wholesale and retail marketing of petroleum products. **Common positions include:** Accountant/Auditor; Chemical Engineer; Chemist; Computer Programmer; Geologist/Geophysicist; Mechanical Engineer; Petroleum Engineer; Systems Analyst. **Special programs:** Internships. **Corporate headquarters location:** San Francisco CA. **Listed on:** New York Stock Exchange. **Stock exchange symbol:** CVX.

EXXONMOBIL CORPORATION
3700 West 190th Street, Torrance CA 90504. 310/212-2800. **Contact:** Human Resources. **World Wide Web address:** http://www.exxonmobil.com. **Description:** A refinery facility for the energy developer, producer, and distributor. **Corporate headquarters location:** Irving TX. **Listed on:** New York Stock Exchange. **Stock exchange symbol:** XOM.

GENERAL ATOMICS
P.O. Box 85608, San Diego CA 92186-5608. 858/455-3000. **Fax:** 858/455-2232. **Recorded jobline:** 858/455-4545. **Contact:** Personnel. **World Wide Web address:** http://www.ga.com. **Description:** Provides a broad range of energy research and development programs including gas-cooled nuclear reactors, thermonuclear fusion, defense systems, hazardous and nuclear wastes, electronic instrumentation, control systems, and research reactors, as well as uranium mining, milling, and conversion. **NOTE:** Positions are filled primarily through attrition. **Common positions include:** Chemical Engineer; Civil Engineer; Computer Programmer; Electrical/Electronics Engineer; Mechanical Engineer; Nuclear Engineer; Physicist. **Corporate headquarters location:** This location. **Other U.S. locations:** Gore OK. **Operations at this facility include:** Administration; Research and Development. **Number of employees at this location:** 1,800.

MATHESON TRI GAS
6775 Central Avenue, Newark CA 94560. 909/987-4611. **Contact:** Human Resources Department. **E-mail address:** hr-recruitment@matheson-trigas.com. **World Wide Web address:** http://www.mathesontrigas.com. **Description:** Distributes regulators, valves, and gas mixtures to gas companies. **Corporate headquarters location:** Parsippany NJ.

OCCIDENTAL OF ELK HILLS, INC.
P.O. Box 1001, Tupman CA 93276. 661/763-6000. **Physical address:** 28590 Highway 119, Tupman CA 93276. **Contact:** Human Resources Department. **World Wide Web address:** http://www.oxy.com. **Description:** Produces oil, gas, and natural gas for the Naval Petroleum Reserve in Elk Hills CA. **Corporate headquarters location:** Los Angeles CA. **Listed on:** New York Stock Exchange. **Stock exchange symbol:** OXY. **Number of employees at this location:** 500.

OCCIDENTAL PETROLEUM CORPORATION
10889 Wilshire Boulevard, Los Angeles CA 90024. 310/208-8800. **Contact:** Human Resources. **World Wide Web address:** http://www.oxy.com. **Description:** One of the world's leading oil and natural gas exploration companies. **Corporate headquarters location:** This location. **Listed on:** New York Stock Exchange. **Stock exchange symbol:** OXY.

SEMPRA ENERGY
101 Ash Street, San Diego CA 92101. 619/696-2000. **Fax:** 619/696-4463. **Contact:** Human Resources Department. **E-mail address:** careers@sempra.com. **World Wide Web address:** http://www.sempra.com. **Description:** Provides electric and natural gas products. **Common positions include:** Policy Analyst. **Special programs:** Internships. **Corporate headquarters location:** This location. **Other U.S. locations:** Nationwide. **International locations:** Worldwide. **Subsidiaries include:** Southern California Gas Co.; San Diego Gas and Electric; Sempra Energy Trading; Sempra Energy International; Sempra Energy Solutions; Sempra Energy Resources; Sempra Energy Utility Ventures. **Listed on:** New York Stock Exchange. **Stock exchange symbol:** SRE. **Annual sales/revenues:** More than $100 million. **Number of employees worldwide:** 12,000.

SHELL SOLAR
4650 Adohr Lane, Camarillo CA 93012. 805/482-6800. **Fax:** 805/388-6394. **Contact:** Lita Rigonan, Human Resources Manager. **World Wide Web address:** http://www.shell-solar-piz.de.com. **Description:** A manufacturer of solar cells.

Founded in 1975. **Common positions include:** Marketing Manager. **Corporate headquarters location:** This location. **Other U.S. locations:** Vancouver WA. **Number of employees at this location:** 230.

UNOCAL
2141 Rosecrans Avenue, El Segundo CA 90245. 310/726-7600. **Contact:** Annette Martin, Human Resources. **World Wide Web address:** http://www.unocal.com. **Description:** Explores, produces, refines, and markets petroleum and natural gas products; produces geothermal energy; manufactures gasoline, lubricant, asphalt, chemicals, and waxes; and mines minerals. **Common positions include:** Accountant/Auditor; Attorney; Chemical Engineer; Chemist; Computer Programmer; Management Trainee; Mechanical Engineer; Paralegal; Petroleum Engineer. **Corporate headquarters location:** This location. **Operations at this facility include:** Administration; Divisional Headquarters; Regional Headquarters. **Listed on:** New York Stock Exchange. **Stock exchange symbol:** UCL.

WYNN OIL COMPANY
1050 West Fifth Street, Azusa CA 91702-9510. 626/334-0231. **Contact:** Lynn Levoy, Manager of Human Resources Department. **E-mail address:** wynns_humanre@wynnsusa.com. **World Wide Web address:** http://www.wynnsusa.com. **Description:** Manufactures oil and gas additives. **Common positions include:** Accountant/Auditor; Adjuster; Automotive Mechanic; Chemist; Claim Representative; Computer Programmer; Credit Manager; Human Resources Manager; Manufacturer's/Wholesaler's Sales Rep.; Market Research Analyst; Receptionist; Secretary; Typist/Word Processor. **Corporate headquarters location:** This location. **Parent company:** Wynn's International. **Operations at this facility include:** Administration; Manufacturing; Sales; Service.

PAPER AND WOOD PRODUCTS

You can expect to find the following types of companies in this chapter:

Forest and Wood Products and Services • Lumber and Wood Wholesale• Millwork, Plywood, and Structural Members • Paper and Wood Mills

ADVANCE PAPER BOX COMPANY
6100 South Gramercy Place, Los Angeles CA 90047. 323/750-2550. **Contact:** Bernie Konig, Personnel Manager. **Description:** Manufactures folding cartons, set-up boxes, record jackets, and other packaging products.

DIXIELINE LUMBER COMPANY
P.O. Box 85307, San Diego CA 92110. 619/224-4120. **Physical address:** 3250 Sports Arena Boulevard, San Diego CA 92110. **Fax:** 619/222-2762. **Contact:** Human Resources. **World Wide Web address:** http://www.dixieline.com. **Description:** A lumber distributor. The company also operates 10 lumber and home center retail outlets throughout Southern California. **Common positions include:** Accountant/Auditor; Branch Manager; Computer Programmer; Credit Manager; Customer Service Representative; Human Resources Manager; Systems Analyst. **Corporate headquarters location:** This location. **Operations at this facility include:** Administration; Divisional Headquarters; Sales; Service. **Listed on:** Privately held. **Number of employees at this location:** 100.

FORTIFIBER CORPORATION
4489 Bandini Boulevard, Los Angeles CA 90023. 323/268-6783. **Toll-free phone:** 800/332-5727. **Contact:** Human Resources Department. **World Wide Web address:** http://www.fortifiber.com. **Description:** Manufactures and markets single-ply, saturated kraft paper for use in the construction industry. **Common positions include:** Accountant/Auditor; Administrator; Blue-Collar Worker Supervisor; Branch Manager; Buyer; Computer Programmer; Credit Manager; Customer Service Representative; Department Manager; Draftsperson; Electrical/Electronics Engineer; Financial Analyst; General Manager; Human Resources Manager; Industrial Engineer; Management Trainee; Manufacturer's/Wholesaler's Sales Rep.; Marketing Specialist; Mechanical Engineer; Operations/Production Manager; Production Manager; Purchasing Agent/Manager; Quality Control Supervisor. **Corporate headquarters location:** Incline

Village NV. **Other area locations:** Portland CA; Tracy CA. **Other U.S. locations:** Attleboro MA; Howard MI. **Operations at this facility include:** Administration; Manufacturing; Research and Development; Sales; Service.

GENERAL VENEER MANUFACTURING COMPANY

P.O. Box 1607, South Gate CA 90280. 323/564-2661. **Physical address:** 8652 Otis Street, South Gate CA 90280. **Contact:** Doug S. DeWitt, Personnel Director. **World Wide Web address:** http://www.generalveneer.com. **Description:** Manufactures doors and plywood products for home, commercial, and industrial use. **Corporate headquarters location:** This location. **Other U.S. locations:** Compton CA.

KIMBERLY-CLARK CORPORATION

10509 Vista Sorrento Parkway, Suite 400, San Diego CA 92121. 858/794-8111. **Fax:** 858/314-6600. **Contact:** Human Resources. **World Wide Web address:** http://www.kimberly-clark.com. **Description:** A major manufacturer and marketer of fiber-based products for consumer and industrial customers. Kimberly-Clark does business in three primary product classes: Consumer and Service, offering a broad range of paper-based goods such as facial tissue, table napkins, and disposable gowns for medical applications; Newsprint, Pulp, and Forest Products, providing a variety of goods to industrial clients; and Paper and Specialties, producing adhesive-coated paper for commercial printing customers. **Corporate headquarters location:** Neenah WI. **Listed on:** New York Stock Exchange. **Stock exchange symbol:** KMB.

KIMBERLY-CLARK CORPORATION

2001 East Orangethorpe Avenue, Fullerton CA 92831-5396. 714/773-7500. **Contact:** Human Resources. **World Wide Web address:** http://www.kimberly-clark.com. **Description:** A major manufacturer and marketer of fiber-based products for consumer and industrial customers. Kimberly-Clark does business in three primary product classes: Consumer and Service, offering a broad range of paper-based goods such as facial tissue, table napkins, and disposable gowns for medical applications; Newsprint, Pulp, and Forest Products, providing a variety of goods to industrial clients; and Paper and Specialties, producing adhesive-coated paper for commercial printing customers. **Corporate headquarters location:** Neenah WI. **Listed on:** New York Stock Exchange. **Stock exchange symbol:** KMB.

PRINTING AND PUBLISHING

You can expect to find the following types of companies in this chapter:
Book, Newspaper, and Periodical Publishers • Commercial Photographers• Commercial Printing Services • Graphic Designers

ADVANCED MARKETING SERVICES, INC. (AMS)
5880 Oberlin Drive, Suite 400, San Diego CA 92121-9653. 858/457-2500. **Fax:** 858/452-2237. **Contact:** Molly Wood, Human Resources Representative. **World Wide Web address:** http://www.admsweb.com. **Description:** A leading distributor of general interest, computer, and business books to membership warehouse clubs and office product superstores. Advanced Marketing Services works with leading publishers and focuses on a limited number of titles. **NOTE:** Entry-level positions are offered. **Common positions include:** Account Manager; Accountant; Advertising Clerk; Buyer; Computer Programmer; Customer Service Representative; Financial Analyst; Graphic Artist; Marketing Specialist; Sales Executive. **Corporate headquarters location:** This location. **Listed on:** New York Stock Exchange. **Stock exchange symbol:** MKT. **Annual sales/revenues:** More than $100 million. **Number of employees at this location:** 400. **Number of employees nationwide:** 500.

AMERICAN BANK NOTE COMPANY
3500 West Olive Avenue, Suite 300, Burbank CA 91505. 818/972-1700. **Contact:** Human Resources. **Description:** This location is a national sales office. Overall, the company is a printer of counterfeit-resistant documents and one of the largest security printers in the world. American Bank Note Company creates secure documents for governments and corporations worldwide. Products include currencies; passports; stock and bond certificates; and bank, corporate, government, and traveler's checks; as well as food coupons, gift vouchers and certificates, driver's licenses, product authentication labels, and vital documents. **Corporate headquarters location:** New York NY. **Other area locations:** Burbank CA; Long Beach CA; San Francisco CA. **Other U.S. locations:** Washington DC; Atlanta GA; Needham MA; St. Louis MO; Horsham PA; Huntington Valley PA; Philadelphia PA; Pittsburgh PA; Dallas TX. **Parent company:** American Bank Note Corporation also operates two other subsidiaries: American Bank Note Holographics, Inc., one of the world's

largest producers of the laser-generated, three-dimensional images that appear on credit cards and products requiring proof of authenticity; and American Bank Note Company Brazil, one of Brazil's largest private security printers and a provider of personalized checks, financial transaction cards, and prepaid telephone cards. **Listed on:** New York Stock Exchange.

ANDERSON NEWS COMPANY
2970 North Ontario Street, Burbank CA 91504. 818/845-8347. **Contact:** Human Resources. **World Wide Web address:** http://www.andersonnews.com. **Description:** Distributes books and magazines to airports, bookstores, convenience stores, military installations, newsstands, and supermarkets. **Corporate headquarters location:** Knoxville TN.

ANTELOPE VALLEY PRESS
P.O. Box 4050, Palmdale CA 93590-4050. 661/273-2700. **Toll-free phone:** 877/729-7946. **Physical address:** 37404 Sierra Highway, Palmdale CA 93550. **Contact:** Personnel. **World Wide Web address:** http://www.avpress.com. **Description:** Publishers of the *Antelope Valley Press,* a daily newspaper with a weekday circulation of 32,000.

APPERSON PRINT MANAGEMENT
6855 East Gage Avenue, City of Commerce CA 90040. 562/927-4718. **Contact:** Human Resources Department. **E-mail address:** agarcia@appersonprint.com. **World Wide Web address:** http://www.appersonprint.com. **Description:** Manufactures business forms. **Common positions include:** Manufacturer's/Wholesaler's Sales Representative. **Corporate headquarters location:** This location. **Other area locations:** Fresno CA; San Francisco CA. **Other U.S. locations:** Miami FL; Atlanta GA; Chicago IL; Bridgewater NJ; Charlotte NC; Dallas TX; Houston TX; Seattle WA. **Number of employees at this location:** 150. **Number of employees nationwide:** 400.

THE BAKERSFIELD CALIFORNIAN INC.
1707 Eye Street, Bakersfield CA 93301. 661/395-7482. **Fax:** 661/395-7484. **Contact:** Human Resources Department. **E-mail address:** jobs@bakersfield.com. **World Wide Web address:** http://www.bakersfield.com. **Description:** The *Bakersfield Californian* is a mid-sized, family-owned newspaper with a daily circulation of 84,000 and a Sunday circulation of 93,000. **Common positions include:** Advertising Clerk; Management Trainee; Manufacturer's/Wholesaler's Sales Rep.; Reporter. **Special programs:** Internships. **Corporate headquarters**

location: This location. **Number of employees at this location:** 500.

BANK PRINTING COMPANY INC.
P.O. Box 296, Downey CA 90241-0296. 562/862-7001. **Physical address:** 9102 Firestone Boulevard, Unit J, Downey CA 90241. **Contact:** Human Resources. **Description:** Prints bank checks and a variety of other banking papers. **Corporate headquarters location:** This location. **Other area locations:** Cerritos CA.

BOWNE OF LOS ANGELES, INC.
633 West Fifth Street, Suite 1400, Los Angeles CA 90071. 213/627-2200. **Fax:** 213/532-3103. **Contact:** Human Resources Department. **World Wide Web address:** http://www.bowne.com. **Description:** Engaged in financial and corporate printing services. **NOTE:** Please send resumes to Human Resources, Bowne of Los Angeles, Inc., 2103 East University Drive, Dominguez Hills CA 90220. **Corporate headquarters location:** New York NY. **Other U.S. locations:** Nationwide. **International locations:** Worldwide. **Parent company:** Bowne & Company, Inc. **Listed on:** New York Stock Exchange. **Stock exchange symbol:** BNE.

BROWNTROUT PUBLISHERS INC.
P.O. Box 280070, San Francisco CA 94128-0070. 310/316-4480. **Toll-free phone:** 800/777-7812. **Fax:** 310/316-1138. **Contact:** Human Resources. **World Wide Web address:** http://www.browntrout.com. **Description:** Publishes desk calendars and gift books on subjects including art, history, animals, sports, and travel. The company also customizes calendars for corporations and private businesses. **Corporate headquarters location:** This location. **International locations:** Australia; Canada; Mexico; United Kingdom.

CONTINENTAL GRAPHICS GROUP
101 South La Brea Avenue, Los Angeles CA 90036. 323/938-2511. **Contact:** Department of Human Resources. **E-mail address:** employment@cgxpress.com. **World Wide Web address:** http://www.cgxpress.com. **Description:** A commercial printer offering a wide variety of services including technical documentation, reproduction, creation, and manufacture of displays, type composition, and typesetting. Continental Graphics is also engaged in xerography, microfilming, and all operations leading to camera-ready art. **Corporate headquarters location:** This location. **Other area locations:**

Cypress CA; Rancho Cucamonga CA. **Parent company:** Republic Corporation.

DAILY JOURNAL CORPORATION
P.O. Box 54026, Los Angeles CA 90054-0026. 213/229-5300. **Physical address:** 915 East First Street, Los Angeles CA 90012. **Contact:** Human Resources. **World Wide Web address:** http://www.dailyjournal.com. **Description:** Publishes the *Los Angeles Daily Journal, Daily Commerce, California Real Estate Journal,* and *Nevada Journal,* each based in Los Angeles; *San Francisco Daily Journal* in San Francisco; the *Daily Recorder* in Sacramento; the *Inter-City Express* in Oakland; *Marin County Court Reporter* in San Rafael; *Orange County Reporter* in Santa Ana; *San Jose Post-Record* in San Jose; *Sonoma County Daily Herald-Recorder* in Santa Rosa; *San Diego Commerce* in San Diego; *Business Journal* in Riverside; and *Washington Journal* in Seattle. The company also serves as a newspaper representative specializing in public notice advertising. **Corporate headquarters location:** This location.

DAILY NEWS
P.O. Box 4200, Woodland Hills CA 91365-4200. 818/713-3000. **Contact:** Human Resources. **World Wide Web address:** http://www.dailynews.com. **Description:** A daily newspaper. **Parent company:** Los Angeles Newspaper Group.

FREEDOM COMMUNICATIONS INC.
P.O. Box 19549, Irvine CA 92623. 949/553-9292. **Physical address:** 17666 Fitch, Irvine CA 92614. **Contact:** Human Resources Department. **World Wide Web address:** http://www.freedom.com. **Description:** Owns the *Orange County Register* and 26 other daily newspapers, as well as 25 weekly newspapers and five television stations.

IN A WORD
811 West Seventh Street, Suite 204, Los Angeles CA 90017. 213/688-6200. **Toll-free phone:** 800/805-WORD. **Fax:** 213/688-6201. **Contact:** Stella Fridman Hayes, Director of Language Services. **E-mail address:** stellaf@inaword.net. **World Wide Web address:** http://www.inaword.net. **Description:** Offers language translation services on documents including patents, legal documents, product labels, manuals and user guides, advertising copy, and Web material. The company also provides interpreters for meetings and training seminars and electronic publishing services. **Corporate headquarters location:** This location.

LOS ANGELES MAGAZINE

5900 Wilshire Boulevard, 10th Floor, Los Angeles CA 90036. 323/801-0040. **Contact:** Human Resources. **World Wide Web address:** http://www.lamag.com. **Description:** A city magazine that focuses on local issues, people, trends, events, and lifestyles. *Los Angeles Magazine* also includes options and opportunities available throughout the Southern California area. Founded in 1960. **NOTE:** Entry-level positions are offered. **Common positions include:** Advertising Clerk; Advertising Executive; Editor; Editorial Assistant; Graphic Artist; Graphic Designer. **Special programs:** Internships. **Corporate headquarters location:** This location. **Parent company:** Emmis Communications Inc. **Listed on:** NASDAQ. **Stock exchange symbol:** EMMS. **Number of employees at this location:** 50.

LOS ANGELES TIMES

202 West First Street, Los Angeles CA 90012. 213/237-3700. **Contact:** Human Resources. **World Wide Web address:** http://www.latimes.com. **Description:** Publishes a daily newspaper with a circulation of over 1 million. **Parent company:** The Tribune Company (Chicago IL). **Listed on:** New York Stock Exchange. **Stock exchange symbol:** TRB.

McGRAW-HILL COMPANY

1333 South Mayflower Avenue, 3rd Floor, Monrovia CA 91016-4066. 626/305-4000. **Contact:** Human Resources. **E-mail address:** career_ops@mcgraw-hill.com. **World Wide Web address:** http://www.mcgraw-hill.com. **Description:** One of the nation's largest book and magazine publishers. McGraw-Hill is a provider of information and services through books, magazines, newsletters, software, CD-ROMs, and online data, fax, and TV broadcasting services. The company operates four network-affiliated TV stations and also publishes *Business Week* magazine and books for college, medical, international, legal, and professional markets. McGraw-Hill also offers financial services including Standard & Poor's, commodity items, and international and logistics management products and services. **Corporate headquarters location:** NewYork NY. **Listed on:** New York Stock Exchange. **Stock exchange symbol:** MHP.

MITCHELL INTERNATIONAL

9889 Willow Creek Road, San Diego CA 92131. 858/578-6550. **Toll-free phone:** 800/854-7030. **Fax:** 858/530-4636. **Contact:** Department of Human Resources. **E-mail address:** web.resume@mitchell.com. **World Wide Web address:**

http://www.mitchell.com. **Description:** Provides printed information and electronic software products for the automotive industry. **Common positions include:** Accountant/Auditor; Administrative Manager; Automotive Mechanic; Budget Analyst; Computer Programmer; Construction and Building Inspector; Construction Contractor; Credit Manager; Customer Service Representative; Economist; Editor; Financial Analyst; Human Resources Manager; Human Service Worker; Insurance Agent/Broker; Librarian; Public Relations Specialist; Purchasing Agent/Manager; Quality Control Supervisor; Services Sales Representative; Software Engineer; Systems Analyst; Technical Writer/Editor. **Special programs:** Internships. **Corporate headquarters location:** Stamford CT. **Other U.S. locations:** Chicago IL; Detroit MI; McLean VA; Milwaukee WI. **Subsidiaries include:** EH Boeckh (Milwaukee WI); Mitchell-Medical (VA); NAG's (Detroit MI). **Parent company:** Thomson Corporation. **Number of employees at this location:** 500. **Number of employees nationwide:** 730.

PHOTOBITION LOS ANGELES
1919 Empire Avenue, Burbank CA 91504. 213/380-2980. **Fax:** 818/840-8384. **Contact:** Personnel. **World Wide Web address:** http://www.customcolorservices.com. **Description:** A custom photographic lab also specializing in digital reproductions on film, inkjet, and other large format media.

PRIMEDIA
33046 Calle Aviador, San Juan Capistrano CA 92675. 949/496-5922. **Contact:** Human Resources. **World Wide Web address:** http://www.primedia.com. **Description:** Publishes *Skin Diver, Gravity Games, Surfer, Powder, Snowboarder,* and *Bike* magazines. The company also produces cable television and home video programs. **Listed on:** New York Stock Exchange. **Stock exchange symbol:** PRM.

GEORGE RICE & SONS
2001 North Soto Street, Los Angeles CA 90032. 323/223-2020. **Contact:** Jan Miller, Human Resources Manager. **World Wide Web address:** http://wwww.quebecor.com. **Description:** Provides commercial lithography and printing services. **Corporate headquarters location:** Greenwich CT. **Parent company:** Quebecor Inc. **Listed on:** New York Stock Exchange. **Stock exchange symbol:** IQW.

SAGE PUBLICATIONS, INC.

2455 Teller Road, Thousand Oaks CA 91320. 805/499-0721. **Fax:** 805/375-1720. **Contact:** Roberta Isaef, Director of Human Resources. **E-mail address:** hr.resume@sagepub.com. **World Wide Web address:** http://www.sagepub.com. **Description:** Publishes academic journals and textbooks for graduate and upper-level college courses in various disciplines including political science and psychology. **NOTE:** Entry-level positions and second and third shifts are offered. **Common positions include:** Accountant; Administrative Assistant; Advertising Executive; Auditor; Claim Representative; Clerical Supervisor; Computer Programmer; Computer Support Technician; Customer Service Representative; Database Administrator; Database Manager; Desktop Publishing Specialist; Editor; Editorial Assistant; Graphic Artist; Graphic Designer; Marketing Manager; Network/Systems Administrator; Secretary. **Special programs:** Internships; Training. **Corporate headquarters location:** This location.

SCENIC ART

43176 Business Park Drive, Suite 103, Temecula CA 92590-3622. 909/587-6602. **Contact:** Mr. D.J. Sanders, Director of Operations. **Description:** Provides printing services. Founded in 1989. **Common positions include:** Account Representative; Accountant; Graphic Artist; Graphic Designer; Operations Manager; Sales Executive. **Corporate headquarters location:** This location. **Annual sales/revenues:** Less than $5 million.

VARIETY, INC.

5700 Wilshire Boulevard, Suite 120, Los Angeles CA 90036. 323/857-6600. **Contact:** Human Resources. **E-mail address:** hrlosangeles@cahners.com. **World Wide Web address:** http://www.variety.com. **Description:** Publishes a magazine that focuses on the entertainment and film industries. **Corporate headquarters location:** Newton MA. **Parent company:** Reed Business Information. **Listed on:** New York Stock Exchange. **Stock exchange symbol:** ENL.

REAL ESTATE

You can expect to find the following types of companies in this chapter:

Land Subdividers and Developers • Real Estate Agents, Managers, and Operators • Real Estate Investment Trusts

BURNHAM REAL ESTATE SERVICE
P.O. Box 122910, San Diego CA 92112. 619/236-1555. **Contact:** Human Resources Department. **World Wide Web address:** http://www.johnburnham.com. **E-mail address:** job@johnburnham.com. **Description:** A real estate investor and syndicate. The firm serves as the general partner or investor in a number of real estate ventures including two public partnerships. **NOTE:** Please send resume to: Human Resources Department, 750 B Street, Suite 2400, San Diego CA 92101-2476. **Corporate headquarters location:** This location.

CASTLE AND COOKE REALTY, INC.
10900 Wilshire Boulevard, Suite 1600, Los Angeles CA 90024. 310/208-6055. **Contact:** Human Resources. **E-mail address:** human-resources@castle-cooke.com. **World Wide Web address:** http://www.castlecookerealty.com. **Description:** A holding company for firms involved in construction and real estate. Castle and Cooke also owns country clubs, private membership clubs, and a horse farm. **Corporate headquarters location:** Mililani HI.

CENTERTRUST RETAIL PROPERTIES, INC.
P.O. Box 10010, Manhattan Beach CA 90266. 310/546-4520. **Physical address:** 3500 Sepulveda Boulevard, Manhattan Beach CA 90266. **Fax:** 310/546-6798. **Contact:** Human Resources. **Description:** A real estate investment trust that develops, owns, and manages retail shopping centers throughout Southern California. Over 60 properties are owned or controlled by the company. **Corporate headquarters location:** This location. **Listed on:** New York Stock Exchange. **Stock exchange symbol:** CTA. **President/CEO:** Edward Fox.

CENTURY 21 AWARD
5640 Baltimore Drive, La Mesa CA 91942. 619/463-5000. **Toll-free phone:** 800/293-1657. **Contact:** Human Resources Department Representative. **World Wide Web address:** http://www.century21award.com. **Description:** A real estate agency. **Special programs:** Career seminars held weekly for

potential agents. **Other area locations:** Bonita CA; Carlsbad CA; Del Mar CA; El Cajon CA; Escondido CA; Fallbrook CA; San Diego CA.

COLDWELL BANKER
27271 Las Ramblas, Mission Viejo CA 92691. 949/367-1800. **Contact:** Human Resources Department. **World Wide Web address:** http://www.coldwellbanker.com. **Description:** A full-service real estate company focusing on commercial and residential real estate, as well as luxury home and resort sales. **Corporate headquarters location:** Parsippany NJ. **Other U.S. locations:** Nationwide. **International locations:** Canada. **Parent company:** Cendant Corporation. **Listed on:** New York Stock Exchange. **Stock exchange symbol:** CD.

E&Y KENNETH LEVENTHAL REAL ESTATE GROUP
2049 Century Park East, Suite 1800, Los Angeles CA 90067. 310/277-0880. **Contact:** Human Resources. **World Wide Web address:** http://www.ey.com. **Description:** A full-service real estate agency providing real estate, tax, and audit advice to developers, builders, lenders, owners, and users of real estate. **Parent company:** Ernst & Young.

FOUNTAINGLEN PROPERTIES LLC
4220 Von Karman Avenue, 2nd Floor, Newport Beach CA 92660-2002. 949/223-5000. **Fax:** 949/223-5043. **Contact:** Pam Laipple, Human Resources. **World Wide Web address:** http://www.fountainglen.com. **Description:** A real estate agency specializing in residential and industrial properties. Pacific Gulf also owns apartment buildings. **Corporate headquarters location:** This location.

KAUFMAN & BROAD HOME CORPORATION
10990 Wilshire Boulevard, 7th Floor, Los Angeles CA 90024. 310/231-4000. **Contact:** Gary Ray, Vice President of Human Resources Department. **World Wide Web address:** http://www.kaufmanandbroad.com. **Description:** Kaufman & Broad builds and markets single-family homes; provides mortgage banking services; develops commercial projects and high-density residential properties; and acquires and develops land. **Corporate headquarters location:** This location. **Listed on:** New York Stock Exchange. **Stock exchange symbol:** KBH.

KOLL COMPANY
4343 Von Karman Avenue, Newport Beach CA 92660. 949/833-3030. **Contact:** Corporate Recruiting. **World Wide Web address:** http://www.koll.com. **Description:** A real estate

development, acquisition, management, and construction firm. The company leases and manages property, operating regional divisions along the West Coast. **Corporate headquarters location:** This location.

WILLIAM LYON COMPANY
4490 Von Karman Avenue, Newport Beach CA 92660. 949/833-3600. **Contact:** Personnel. **World Wide Web address:** http://www.lyonhomes.com. **Description:** Engaged in home building, financing, and land development. Assets include apartments and commercial real estate that the Hughes Investment Company and Koll Company assist in developing. Lyon also finances residential development through companies such as Warmington Homes, the Aikens Development Company, and the Lusk Company. **Corporate headquarters location:** This location. **Listed on:** New York Stock Exchange. **Stock exchange symbol:** WLS.

TRIZEC PROPERTIES
4350 La Jolla Village Drive, Suite 700, San Diego CA 92122. 858/546-1001. **Contact:** Nancy Wilk, Director of Human Resources Department. **World Wide Web address:** http://www.trz.com. **Description:** Trizec is a real estate development/property management company focusing on office buildings and technology complexes with properties across the United States, Canada, and Europe. **Corporate headquarters location:** New York NY. **Listed:** New York Stock Exchange. **Stock exchange symbol:** TRZ.

RETAIL

You can expect to find the following types of companies in this chapter:

Catalog Retailers • Department Stores; Specialty Stores •
Retail Bakeries • Supermarkets

ALBERTSON'S
6931 La Palma Avenue, Buena Park CA 90620-1158. 714/522-1054. **Contact:** Department of Human Resources. **E-mail address:** employment@albertsons.com. **World Wide Web address:** http://www.albertsons.com. **Description:** Operates a nationwide chain of food stores. The company also operates fabric, automotive supplies, and department stores; warehouses; distribution facilities; and manufacturing plants. **Corporate headquarters location:** Boise ID. **Parent company:** American Stores. **Listed on:** New York Stock Exchange. **Stock exchange symbol:** ABS.

ARDEN GROUP, INC.
P.O. Box 512256, Los Angeles CA 90051-2256. 310/638-2842. **Physical address:** 2020 South Central Avenue, Compton CA 90220. **Fax:** 310/604-4896. **Contact:** Human Resources. **E-mail address:** personnel@gelsons.com. **World Wide Web address:** http://www.gelsons.com. **Description:** A holding company for Gelson's Markets, which operates 13 Gelson's and two Mayfair supermarkets in the greater Los Angeles area. **Corporate headquarters location:** This location. **Listed on:** NASDAQ. **Stock exchange symbol:** ARDNA. **Number of employees nationwide:** 1,900.

ARNOLDS ACQUISITIONS
4750 Kearny Mesa Road, San Diego CA 92111. 858/549-6000. **Contact:** Personnel. **Description:** A furniture retailer operating stores under the name Arnolds Home Furnishings. **Common positions include:** Attorney; Buyer; Credit Manager; Customer Service Representative; Financial Analyst; Marketing Specialist; Services Sales Representative. **Corporate headquarters location:** This location. **Operations at this facility include:** Administration; Regional Headquarters; Service.

AVON PRODUCTS INC.
2940 East Foothill Boulevard, Pasadena CA 91121. 626/578-8000. **Contact:** Personnel. **E-mail address:** jobs@avon.com. **World Wide Web address:** http://www.avoncareers.com. **Description:** This location is a distribution center for the West

322/The Los Angeles JobBank

Coast. Overall, Avon Products Inc. is a direct seller of beauty care products, fashion jewelry, gifts, fragrances, and decorative products. Avon, a *Fortune* 500 company, markets its products through a network of 2.8 million independent sales representatives in 135 countries worldwide. **NOTE:** Salespeople are considered independent contractors or dealers and most work part-time. If you are interested in becoming a sales representative, please call 800/FOR-AVON, or visit the company's Website for more information. **Corporate headquarters location:** New York NY. **Other U.S. locations:** Newark DE; Atlanta GA; Morton Grove NY; Rye NY; Suffern NY; Springdale OH.

BARNES & NOBLE BOOKSTORES
6326 East Pacific Coast Highway, Long Beach CA 90803. 562/431-2253. **Contact:** Manager. **World Wide Web address:** http://www.bn.com. **Description:** A bookstore chain operating nationwide. This location has a cafe and a music department in addition to its book departments. **Corporate headquarters location:** New York NY. **Listed on:** NASDAQ. **Stock exchange symbol:** BKS.

BARNES & NOBLE BOOKSTORES
1201 Third Street Promenade, Santa Monica CA 90401. 310/260-9110. **Contact:** Manager. **World Wide Web address:** http://www.bn.com. **Description:** A bookstore chain operating nationwide. This location has a cafe and a music department in addition to its book departments. **Corporate headquarters location:** New York NY. **Listed on:** NASDAQ. **Stock exchange symbol:** BKS.

BASKIN-ROBBINS, INC.
600 North Brand Boulevard, 6th Floor, Glendale CA 91203. 818/956-0031. **Contact:** Director of Human Resources. **Description:** An ice cream manufacturer that also operates retail locations. **NOTE:** Please send resumes to: Human Resources Department, 14 Pacella Park Drive, Randolph MA 02368. **Corporate headquarters location:** Randolph MA. **International locations:** Worldwide. **Parent company:** Allied Domecq Quick Service Restaurants. **Number of employees nationwide:** 875.

BENO'S FAMILY FASHIONS
1512 Santee Street, Los Angeles CA 90015. 213/748-2222. **Contact:** Personnel. **Description:** Operates a chain of retail stores in California and Nevada selling a wide variety of merchandise, with emphasis on apparel for men, women, and

children. More than 55 stores are operated under the name of Beno's. **Common positions include:** Accountant/Auditor; Advertising Clerk; Branch Manager; Buyer; Retail Sales Worker. **Corporate headquarters location:** This location. **Number of employees nationwide:** 550.

BRIDGESTONE/FIRESTONE, INC.

24031 El Toro Road, Suite 250, Laguna Hills CA 92656. 949/951-4616. **Contact:** Human Resources Department. **World Wide Web address:** http://www.bridgestone-firestone.com. **Description:** This location sells a broad line of tires and wheels for the automotive aftermarket and services and maintains automobiles at its retail service centers. Overall, Bridgestone/Firestone is engaged in the development, manufacture, and sale of a broad line of tires for the original equipment and replacement markets worldwide. **Common positions include:** Automotive Mechanic; Customer Service Representative; Management Trainee; Services Sales Representative. **Corporate headquarters location:** Nashville TN. **Other U.S. locations:** AR; IA; IN; MI; NC; OH; OK; SC. **International locations:** Argentina; Brazil; Canada; Chile; Columbia; Costa Rica; Mexico; Venezuela. **Operations at this facility include:** Sales; Service. **Number of employees nationwide:** 60,000.

CITY CHEVROLET/GEO/VOLKSWAGEN

P.O. Box 85345, San Diego CA 92186. 619/276-6171. **Physical address:** 12111 Morena Boulevard, San Diego CA 92110. **Contact:** John Nieman, General Manager. **World Wide Web address:** http://www.perfectpages.com/city.html. **Description:** Sells new and used automobiles. **Corporate headquarters location:** This location.

CLOTHESTIME, INC.

5325 East Hunter Avenue, Anaheim CA 92807. 714/779-5881. **Fax:** 714/693-7402. **Contact:** Human Resources. **World Wide Web address:** http://www.clothestime.com. **Description:** Operates a chain of women's apparel stores offering value-priced, fashionable sportswear, dresses, and accessories. **Corporate headquarters location:** This location. **Operations at this facility include:** Administration. **Number of employees at this location:** 400. **Number of employees nationwide:** 4,200.

DEARDEN'S

700 South Main Street, Los Angeles CA 90014. 213/362-9600. **Contact:** Raquel Bensimon, President. **Description:** A retailer

of furniture, appliances, televisions, and audio equipment. **Corporate headquarters location:** This location.

FACTORY 2-U STORES, INC.

4000 Ruffin Road, San Diego CA 92123-1866. 858/627-1800. **Fax:** 858/637-4196. **Contact:** Human Resources. **E-mail address:** mailus@factory2-u.com. **World Wide Web address:** http://www.factory2-u.com. **Description:** Operates over 200 Factory 2-U and Family Bargain Center stores, which primarily sell in-season family apparel and housewares at discounted prices. **NOTE:** Entry-level positions are offered. **Common positions include:** Administrative Manager; Computer Programmer; Financial Analyst; Human Resources Manager; Market Research Analyst; Systems Analyst. **Corporate headquarters location:** This location. **Other U.S. locations:** AZ; LA; NV; NM; OK; OR; TX; WA. **Operations at this facility include:** Administration; Divisional Headquarters; Manufacturing; Sales; Service. **Listed on:** NASDAQ. **Stock exchange symbol:** FTUS. **Chairman and CEO:** Mike Searles. **Annual sales/revenues:** More than $100 million. **Number of employees at this location:** 250. **Number of employees nationwide:** 3,700.

49ER SHOPS, INC.

6049 East Seventh Street, Long Beach CA 90840. 562/985-7854. **Contact:** Nancy Green, Personnel Director. **E-mail address:** jobs@mail.bks.csulb.edu. **World Wide Web address:** http://www.csulb.edu/aux/49ershops. **Description:** Operates the bookstore, copy center, and food services on California State University's Long Beach campus. **Corporate headquarters location:** This location. **Number of employees at this location:** 450.

FREDERICK'S OF HOLLYWOOD

6608 Hollywood Boulevard, Hollywood CA 90028. 323/466-5151. **Contact:** Department of Human Resources. **E-mail address:** jobs@fredericks.com. **World Wide Web address:** http://www.fredericks.com. **Description:** A specialty retailer operating a chain of women's intimate-apparel stores throughout the United States. The company also has a national mail-order apparel business selling lingerie, bras, dresses, sportswear, leisurewear, swimwear, hosiery, specialty men's wear, and accessories. Frederick's of Hollywood purchases its merchandise from a variety of manufacturers. **Corporate headquarters location:** This location.

HARRIS AND FRANK INC.
17629 Ventura Boulevard, Encino CA 91316. 818/783-3125. **Contact:** Personnel Department. **Description:** A specialty fashion store chain of men's and women's clothing including a tuxedo rental department. Harris and Frank operates 19 store locations. **Operations at this facility include:** Regional Headquarters.

HOT TOPIC
18305 East San Jose Avenue, City of Industry CA 91748. 626/839-4681. **Fax:** 626/581-9263. **Contact:** Personnel. **World Wide Web address:** http://www.hottopic.com. **Description:** Operates a chain of mall-based retail outlets. Hot Topic's product line features clothing and accessories relating to various alternative music-related lifestyles. Founded in 1988. **Corporate headquarters location:** This location. **Other U.S. locations:** Nationwide. **Listed on:** NASDAQ. **Stock exchange symbol:** HOTT. **Annual sales/revenues:** More than $100 million.

MAIL BOXES ETC.
6060 Cornerstone Court West, San Diego CA 92121. 858/455-8800. **Fax:** 858/625-3159. **Contact:** Human Resources. **World Wide Web address:** http://www.mbe.com. **Description:** Operates through two wholly-owned subsidiaries. Mail Boxes Etc. provides franchisees with a system of business training, site location, marketing, advertising programs, and management support designed to assist the franchisee in opening and operating MBE Centers. **Corporate headquarters location:** This location. **Subsidiaries include:** Mail Boxes Etc. USA grants territorial franchise rights for the operation or sale of service centers specializing in postal, packaging, business, and communications services. MBE Service Corp. offers electronic tax filing services. **Parent company:** UPS. **Listed on:** New York Stock Exchange. **Stock exchange symbol:** UPS.

MELISSA DATA
22382 Avenida Empressa, Rancho Santa Margarita CA 92688-2112. **Toll-free phone:** 800/800-MAIL. **Contact:** Human Resources. **E-mail address:** hr@melissadata.com. **World Wide Web address:** http://www.melissadata.com. **Description:** A catalog retailer of direct mail software. **Corporate headquarters location:** This location.

PACIFIC SUNWEAR
2450 East Miraloma Avenue, Anaheim CA 92806. 714/414-4000. **Fax:** 714/701-4294. **Contact:** Human Resources. **E-mail**

address: careers@pacificsunwear.com. **World Wide Web address:** http://www.pacsun.com. **Description:** A surf- and skateboard-style clothing retailer. **Corporate headquarters location:** This location. **Other U.S. locations:** Nationwide. **Listed on:** NASDAQ. **Stock exchange symbol:** PSUN. **Annual sales/revenues:** More than $100 million.

RALPHS GROCERY COMPANY
P.O. Box 54143, Los Angeles CA 90054. 310/884-9000. **Physical address:** 1100 West Artesia Boulevard, Compton CA 90200. **Recorded jobline:** 310/884-4642. **Contact:** Personnel. **World Wide Web address:** http://www.ralphs.com. **Description:** Operates a chain of grocery stores throughout California. **Corporate headquarters location:** This location. **Parent company:** The Kroger Company (Cincinnati OH). **Listed on:** New York Stock Exchange. **Stock exchange symbol:** KR.

ROBINSONS-MAY COMPANY
6160 Laurel Canyon Boulevard, North Hollywood CA 91606. 818/508-5226. **Contact:** Employment Office. **World Wide Web address:** http://www.maycompany.com. **Description:** One of the nation's largest retailing organizations. Robinsons-May owns and operates a chain of department stores serving California, Arizona, and Nevada. **Corporate headquarters location:** This location. **Parent company:** May Department Stores Company. **Listed on:** New York Stock Exchange. **Stock exchange symbol:** MAY.

SMART & FINAL, INC.
600 Citadel Drive, Commerce CA 90040. 323/869-7500. **Contact:** Department of Human Resources. **E-mail address:** hr@smartandfinal.com. **World Wide Web address:** http://www.smartandfinal.com. **Description:** One of the largest, nonmember, warehouse, grocery chains in the United States. Smart and Final operates 218 nonmembership stores and two food service distribution businesses located in southern Florida (Henry Lee Company) and Northern California (Port Stockton Food Distributors). Founded in 1871. **Common positions include:** Computer Programmer; Editor; Human Resources Manager; Internet Services Manager; MIS Specialist; Multimedia Designer; Purchasing Agent/Manager; Software Engineer; Systems Analyst; Technical Writer/Editor. **Corporate headquarters location:** This location. **Other U.S. locations:** AZ; CA; FL; NV. **International locations:** Mexico. **Operations at this facility include:** Administration; Divisional Headquarters; Regional Headquarters. **Listed on:** New York Stock Exchange. **Stock exchange symbol:** SMF. **Annual**

sales/revenues: More than $100 million. **Number of employees at this location:** 600. **Number of employees nationwide:** 5,000.

VIKING OFFICE PRODUCTS
P.O. Box 61144, Los Angeles CA 90061. 323/321-4493. **Physical address:** 950 West 190th Street, Torrance CA 90502. **Contact:** Human Resources. **World Wide Web address:** http://www.vikingop.com. **Description:** One of the largest direct marketing companies selling office products to small and medium-sized businesses. **Corporate headquarters location:** This location. **Parent company:** Office Depot. **Listed on:** New York Stock Exchange. **Stock exchange symbol:** ODP. **Number of employees nationwide:** 1,065.

THE VONS COMPANIES, INC.
P.O. Box 513338, Los Angeles CA 90051-1338. 626/821-7000. **Physical address:** 618 South Michillinda Avenue, Arcadia CA 91007. **Contact:** Human Resources. **World Wide Web address:** http://www.vons.com. **Description:** One of the largest operators of supermarkets and drugstores in Southern California. Vons's Super Combo stores offer video rental, dry cleaning, and photo development services in addition to traditional grocery store and drugstore products. Vons owns five EXPO stores that offer discount drugs and warehouse foods; operates a milk-processing plant; and manages ice cream, delicatessen, meat-processing, and baking facilities. **Corporate headquarters location:** This location. **Parent company:** Safeway, Inc. **Listed on:** New York Stock Exchange. **Stock exchange symbol:** SWY.

WHEREHOUSE ENTERTAINMENT
19701 Hamilton Avenue, Torrance CA 90502. 310/538-2314. **Contact:** Rachel Centeno, Human Resources Manager. **World Wide Web address:** http://www.wherehousemusic.com. **Description:** A retailer of prerecorded music and videos. **Common positions include:** Accountant/Auditor; Administrative Manager; Advertising Clerk; Budget Analyst; Buyer; Claim Representative; Computer Programmer; Construction Contractor; Customer Service Representative; Designer; Financial Analyst; General Manager; Human Resources Manager; Management Trainee; Property and Real Estate Manager; Purchasing Agent/Manager; Software Engineer; Systems Analyst; Technical Writer/Editor; Wholesale and Retail Buyer. **Special programs:** Internships. **Corporate headquarters location:** This location. **Subsidiaries include:** Leopolos; Odyssey; Paradise Music; Record Shop; Rocky Mountain

Records. **Parent company:** One Capitol Partners. **Operations at this facility include:** Administration; Divisional Headquarters. **Listed on:** Privately held. **Number of employees at this location:** 230. **Number of employees nationwide:** 8,000.

STONE, CLAY, GLASS, AND CONCRETE PRODUCTS

You can expect to find the following types of companies in this chapter:

Cement, Tile, Sand, and Gravel • Crushed and Broken Stone • Glass and Glass Products • Mineral Products

AFG INDUSTRIES, INC.
17300 Silica Drive, Victorville CA 92392. 760/241-2237. **Contact:** Human Resources. **World Wide Web address:** http://www.afg.com. **Description:** Manufactures, distributes, and packages flat glass. **Corporate headquarters location:** Kingsport TN. **Other U.S. locations:** Nationwide.

ALDILA, INC.
12140 Community Road, Poway CA 92064-6871. 858/513-1801. **Contact:** Human Resources Department. **E-mail address:** hradmin@aldila.com. **World Wide Web address:** http://www.aldila.com. **Description:** ALDILA is a leading manufacturer of graphite golf shafts. Founded in 1972. **Corporate headquarters location:** This location. **Other U.S. locations:** Evanston NY. **International locations:** China; Mexico. **Listed on:** NASDAQ. **Stock exchange symbol:** ALDA.

CERADYNE, INC.
3169 Red Hill Avenue, Costa Mesa CA 92626. 714/549-0421. **Fax:** 714/549-8573. **Contact:** Human Resources. **World Wide Web address:** http://www.ceradyne.com. **Description:** A nationwide manufacturer specializing in high-tech ceramics for armor and commercial applications. **Common positions include:** Accountant/Auditor; Blue-Collar Worker Supervisor; Customer Service Representative; Human Resources Manager; Mechanical Engineer; Purchasing Agent/Manager; Quality Assurance Engineer. **Corporate headquarters location:** This location. **Other U.S. locations:** Scottsdale GA; Lexington KY. **Operations at this facility include:** Administration; Manufacturing; Research and Development; Sales. **Listed on:** NASDAQ. **Stock exchange symbol:** CRDN. **Number of employees at this location:** 110. **Number of employees nationwide:** 230.

DAYTON/RICHMOND
9415 Sorenson Avenue, Santa Fe Springs CA 90670. 562/946-5504. **Toll-free phone:** 800/745-3701. **Contact:** Personnel. **World Wide Web address:** http://www.daytonsuperior.com.

Description: Manufactures concrete lifting systems, concrete modular forms, concrete accessories, and metal accessories for the construction industry. **Corporate headquarters location:** Dayton OH. **Operations at this facility include:** Sales Service Center; Technical Services; Western Division Offices. **Parent company:** Dayton Superior Company. **Listed on:** Privately held.

GLADDING McBEAN
4301 East Firestone Boulevard, South Gate CA 90280. 323/564-5654. **Contact:** Human Resources Department. **World Wide Web address:** http://www.gladdingmcbean.com. **Description:** Manufactures clay pipe, tile, garden pottery, and architectural terra cotta. **Corporate headquarters location:** Sacramento CA. **Number of employees at this location:** 250.

LAGUNA CLAY COMPANY
14400 Lomitas Avenue, City of Industry CA 91746. 626/330-0631. **Toll-free phone:** 800/452-4862. **Contact:** Human Resources Department. **World Wide Web address:** http://www.lagunaclay.com. **Description:** Manufactures clay and ceramic materials. **Corporate headquarters location:** This location.

NATIONAL GYPSUM COMPANY
1850 Pier B Street, Long Beach CA 90813. 562/435-4465. **Fax:** 562/495-3922. **Contact:** Caroline Dixon, Human Resources. **World Wide Web address:** http://www.national-gypsum.com. **Description:** Manufactures gypsum wallboard and joint compounds. National Gypsum is an integrated, diversified manufacturer of products for building, construction, and shelter markets. **NOTE:** Entry-level positions and second and third shifts are offered. **Common positions include:** Account Manager; Accountant; Administrative Manager; Assistant Manager; Blue-Collar Worker Supervisor; Clerical Supervisor; Electrician; Environmental Engineer; Human Resources Manager; Industrial Engineer; Management Trainee; Manufacturing Engineer; Production Manager; Purchasing Agent/Manager; Quality Control Supervisor. **Special programs:** Training. **Corporate headquarters location:** Charlotte NC. **Other U.S. locations:** Nationwide. **Listed on:** Privately held. **Number of employees at this location:** 100. **Number of employees nationwide:** 3,000.

NEWBASIS
2626 Kansas Avenue, Riverside CA 92057. 909/787-0600. **Toll-free phone:** 888/NEW-BASIS. **Contact:** Human Resources.

World Wide Web address: http://www.newbasis.com. **Description:** Manufactures concrete, lumber, and other related building materials. **Other area locations:** Auburn CA. **Other U.S. locations:** AR; FL; TX. **International locations:** Chile; Mexico.

SAINT-GOBAIN CONTAINER CORPORATION

P.O. Box 5238, El Monte CA 91734. 626/448-9831. **Physical address:** 4000 North Arden Drive, El Monte CA 91731. **Contact:** Human Resources. **World Wide Web address:** http://www.saint-gobain.com. **Description:** Manufactures glass containers, such as bottles and jars for the beverage and food industries. **Corporate headquarters location:** Muncie IL. **Other U.S. locations:** Nationwide. **Parent company:** Saint-Gobain Group.

TXI RIVERSIDE CEMENT COMPANY

P.O. Box 51479, Ontario CA 91761-0079. 909/635-1800. **Fax:** 909/635-1897. **Contact:** Human Resources Department. **World Wide Web address:** http://www.txi.com/cement. **Description:** Manufactures cement. **Corporate headquarters location:** This location. **Listed on:** New York Stock Exchange. **Stock exchange symbol:** TXI.

VULCAN MATERIALS COMPANY

P.O. Box 2950, Los Angeles CA 90051. 323/258-2777. **Physical address:** 3200 San Fernando Road, Los Angeles CA 90065. **Contact:** Human Resources Department. **World Wide Web address:** http://www.vulcanmaterials.com. **E-mail address:** careers_ca@vmcmail.com. **Description:** Engaged in the business of extracting, processing, and selling rock, sand, and gravel, either in aggregate form, as ready-mixed concrete, or as asphaltic concrete. **Corporate headquarters location:** Birmingham AL. **Other area locations:** San Francisco CA; Ventura CA. **Listed on:** New York Stock Exchange. **Stock exchange symbol:** VMC.

TRANSPORTATION/TRAVEL

You can expect to find the following types of companies in this chapter:

Air, Railroad, and Water Transportation Services • Courier Services • Local and Interurban Passenger Transit • Ship Building and Repair • Transportation Equipment Travel Agencies • Trucking • Warehousing and Storage

ANCRA INTERNATIONAL LLC
4880 West Rosecrans Avenue, Hawthorne CA 90250. 310/973-5000. **Toll-free phone:** 800/973-5092. **Contact:** Tammy Carson, Human Resources. **World Wide Web address:** http://www.ancra-llc.com. **Description:** Manufactures cargo restraint equipment for the trucking and aircraft industries including aircraft fittings, winches, cam buckles, o/c buckles, shoring beams, cargo systems, and track. Ancra also maintains off-road and marine divisions. **Common positions include:** Accountant/Auditor; Customer Service Representative; Manufacturer's/Wholesaler's Sales Rep.; Manufacturing Engineer; Marketing Specialist; Operations/Production Manager; Purchasing Agent/Manager; Quality Control Supervisor. **Corporate headquarters location:** This location. **Other U.S. locations:** Erlanger KY.

CALIFORNIA CARTAGE COMPANY
P.O. Box 92829, Long Beach CA 90809-2829. 562/427-1143. **Contact:** Personnel Director. **World Wide Web address:** http://www.calcartage.com. **Description:** A trucking company that provides freight handling, warehousing, and container freight station operations. **Corporate headquarters location:** This location. **Other area locations:** Carson CA; City of Industry CA; Compton CA; Fontana CA; National City CA; Oakland CA; Vernon CA; Wilmington CA. **Other U.S. locations:** Nationwide.

CATALINA YACHTS INC.
21200 Victory Boulevard, Woodland Hills CA 91367-2522. 818/884-7700. **Fax:** 818/884-3810. **Contact:** Personnel. **World Wide Web address:** http://www.catalinayachts.com. **Description:** Manufactures yachts. **Corporate headquarters location:** This location. **Other U.S. locations:** Largo FL.

GLOBAL VAN LINES
150 Paularino Avenue, Costa Mesa CA 92626. 714/921-1200. **Physical address:** 810 West Taft Street, Orange CA 92865. **Contact:** Manager/Administration. **World Wide Web address:** http://www.globalvanlines.com. **Description:** Provides shipping and storage services for the general public. **Corporate headquarters location:** This location.

LAIDLAW TRANSIT, INC.
4337 Rowland Avenue, El Monte CA 91731. 626/448-9446. **Contact:** Human Resources Director. **World Wide Web address:** http://ww.laidlawtransit.com. **Description:** Provides bus service for many districts of Los Angeles County and charter bus service to private customers. The company is also a school bus contractor. **Other area locations:** Culver City CA; Los Angeles CA. **Parent company:** Laidlaw, Inc. provides solid waste collection, compaction, transportation, treatment, transfer and disposal services; provides hazardous waste services; operates hazardous waste facilities and wastewater treatment plants; and operates passenger and school buses, transit system buses, and tour and charter buses. **Corporate headquarters location:** Kansas City KS. **Listed on:** American Stock Exchange. **Stock exchange symbol:** GLL.

THAI AIRWAYS INTERNATIONAL PUBLIC COMPANY LIMITED
222 North Sepulveda Boulevard, Suite 1950, El Segundo CA 90245. 310/640-0097x202. **Fax:** 310/640-7675. **Contact:** Janet Mazon, Personnel Coordinator. **Description:** An international passenger and freight air carrier. **NOTE:** Flight crews are only hired through the Bangkok, Thailand location. **Common positions include:** Services Sales Representative; Ticket Agent. **Corporate headquarters location:** Bangkok, Thailand. **Other U.S. locations:** Nationwide. **Operations at this facility include:** Regional Headquarters. **Number of employees at this location:** 50. **Number of employees nationwide:** 100.

UTILITIES: ELECTRIC/GAS/WATER

You can expect to find the following types of companies in this chapter:
Gas, Electric, and Fuel Companies; Other Energy-Producing Companies • Public Utility Holding Companies • Water Utilities

---

CALIFORNIA WATER SERVICE COMPANY

2632 West 237th Street, Torrance CA 90505. 310/257-1400. **Contact:** Human Resources Department. **E-mail address:** employment@calwater.com. **World Wide Web address:** http://www.calwater.com. **Description:** A public utility providing water service. **Subsidiaries include:** CWS Utility Services; Washington Water Service Company. **Listed on:** New York Stock Exchange. **Stock exchange symbol:** CWT.

EDISON INTERNATIONAL

2244 Walnut Grove Avenue, Rosemead CA 91770. 626/302-1212. **Contact:** Personnel. **E-mail address:** employ@sce.com. **World Wide Web address:** http://www.edison.com. **Description:** A holding company. **Corporate headquarters location:** This location. **Subsidiaries include:** Southern California Edison Company. **Listed on:** New York Stock Exchange. **Stock exchange symbol:** EIX.

SAN DIEGO GAS AND ELECTRIC COMPANY

101 Ash Street, San Diego CA 92101. 619/696-2000. **Recorded jobline:** 858/654-1600. **Contact:** Human Resources. **E-mail address:** jobs@sdge.com. **World Wide Web address:** http://www.sdge.com. **Description:** Provides gas and electricity to residential and commercial customers. **Corporate headquarters location:** This location. **Parent company:** Sempra Energy. **Listed on:** American Stock Exchange. **Stock exchange symbol:** SDO.

SOUTHERN CALIFORNIA GAS COMPANY

555 West Fifth Street, Los Angeles CA 90013. 213/244-1200. **Contact:** Human Resources. **E-mail address:** jobs@sdge.com. **World Wide Web address:** http://www.socalgas.com. **Description:** Transports and distributes natural gas. **NOTE:** This company does not accept resumes through postal mail. Please be sure to include job code in the subject line of your e-mail. **Corporate headquarters location:** This location. **Parent company:** Sempra Energy is the result of the June 1998 merger between Pacific Enterprises and Enova Corporation. **Number**

of employees at this location: 1,000. **Number of employees nationwide:** 8,400.

MISCELLANEOUS WHOLESALING

You can expect to find the following types of companies in this chapter:

Exporters and Importers • General Wholesale Distribution Companies

A-MARK PRECIOUS METALS INC.
100 Wilshire Boulevard, 3rd Floor, Santa Monica CA 90401. 310/319-0200. **Fax:** 310/319-0279. **Contact:** Human Resources Department. **E-mail address:** hr@amark.com. **World Wide Web address:** http://www.amark.com. **Description:** A precious metals wholesaler that buys and sells gold, silver, and platinum coins. Clients include banks, brokerage houses, refiners, jewelers, investment advisors, coin dealers, and government mint officials. **Number of employees at this location:** 25.

McJUNKIN CORPORATION
2064 East University Drive, Rancho Dominguez CA 90220-6419. 310/605-5392. **Contact:** Human Resources Department. **World Wide Web address:** http://www.mcjunkin.com. **Description:** A distributor of pipe, valves, fittings, power transmission products, and general industrial products. **Common positions include:** Accountant/Auditor; Branch Manager; Buyer; Computer Programmer; Credit Manager; Customer Service Representative; Department Manager; General Manager; Human Resources Manager; Management Trainee; Manufacturer's/Wholesaler's Sales Representative; Operations/Production Manager; Quality Control Supervisor; Systems Analyst. **Corporate headquarters location:** This location. **Operations at this facility include:** Sales.

McMASTER-CARR SUPPLY COMPANY
9630 Norwalk Boulevard, Santa Fe Springs CA 90670. 562/695-2449. **Contact:** Human Resources Department. **E-mail address:** recruiting@mcmaster.com. **World Wide Web address:** http://www.mcmaster.com. **Description:** A distributor of industrial products and supplies including a complete line of products for maintaining a manufacturing facility. The company's broad customer base includes most major manufacturers in North America, as well as many major industrial firms in South and Central America, the Middle and Far East, and Africa. **Common positions include:** Customer Service Rep.; Management Trainee; Operations/Production Manager. **Corporate headquarters location:** Elmhurst IL. **Other**

U.S. locations: Atlanta GA; Dayton NJ; Cleveland OH. **Listed on:** Privately held.

INDEX OF PRIMARY EMPLOYERS

ACCOUNTING & MANAGEMENT CONSULTING

Arthur Andersen/50
AON Consulting/50
Deloitte & Touche/51
Mercer Human Resource
    Consulting/51, 52
PricewaterhouseCoopers/52

ADVERTISING, MARKETING, AND PUBLIC RELATIONS

BBDO West/53
BDS Marketing/53
Cerrell Associates, Inc./53
DDB Needham Worldwide, Inc./53
Dailey & Associates Advertising/54
DavisElen/54
Ogilvy & Mather/54
Saatchi & Saatchi Advertising/54
Viacom Outdoor/54
Western Initiative Media
    Corporation/55

AEROSPACE

The Aerospace Corporation/56
Ametek Aerospace/56
B/E Aerospace/57
The Boeing Company/57
C&D Aerospace, Inc./57
J.C. Carter Company, Inc./58
Embee Inc./58
Fairchild Fasteners - U.S./58
Garrett Aviation Services/59
Goodrich Aerostructures Group/59
Hamilton Sunstrand Power Systems/59
Hamilton Sunstrand Sensor Systems/60
Hi-Shear Technology Corporation/60
Hydro-Aire, Inc./61
ITT Industries/Gilfillan Division/61
Meggitt PLC/62
Mercury Air Group, Inc./62
Monogram Systems/63
Northrop Grumman Corporation/63
Northop Grumman Information
    Technology/63, 64
PTI Technologies, Inc./64
Pacific Scientific Company/65
Phaostron Instrument and Electronic
    Company/65
Senior Aerospace/65
Smith Aerospace/65
TRW Space & Electronics Group/66
H.R. Textron, Inc./66
Thales In-Flight Systems/66

APPAREL, FASHION, AND TEXTILES

Action Embroidery/68
Ashworth, Inc./68
Authentic Fitness Corporation/68
Barco of California/68
Beach Patrol Inc./69
Byer California/69
Chambers Belt/69
Deckers Outdoor Corporation/69
Guess? Inc./69
K-Swiss Inc./70
L.A. Gear, Inc./70
Leggett & Platt, Inc./70
Workrite Uniform Company, Inc./70

ARCHITECTURE/ CONSTRUCTION/ ENGINEERING (MISC.)

ABS Consulting/72
Advanced Foam/72
Air Conditioning Company, Inc./72
Amelco Corporation/73
Anthony and Sylvan Pools/73
Boyle Engineering Corporation/73
Calprop Corporation/73
Capital Pacific Holding/74
Coast Foundry & Manufacturing
    Company/74
Daniel, Mann, Johnson &
    Mendenhall/74
Elixir Industries/74
Exponent, Inc./74
FM Global/75
Ferguson Enterprises, Inc./75
Fluor Corporation/75
Holmes and Narver Inc./76
Hunter Douglas/76
Jacobs Engineering Group Inc./77
Jensen Industries, Inc./77
Matich Corporation/78
McElroy Metal Inc./78
Nielsen Dillingham Builders/78
Roel Construction Company/79
The Ryland Group, Inc./79
Southdown Concrete Products, Inc./79
Standard Pacific Homes/80
Trans-Pacific Consultants/80

ARTS, ENTERTAINMENT, SPORTS, AND RECREATION

AIMS Multimedia/81
Artisan Entertainment/81
Bally Total Fitness/81
Castle Rock Entertainment/82
Composite Image Systems/82
Creative Artists Agency, Inc. (CAA)/82
Del Mar Thoroughbred Club/82
Deluxe Laboratories, Inc./82

AUTOMOTIVE

BANKING/SAVINGS & LOANS/ OTHER DEPOSITORY INSTITUTIONS (MISC.)

BIOTECHNOLOGY/ PHARMACEUTICALS/ SCIENTIFIC R&D (MISC.)

La Jolla Pharmaceutical Company
(LJP)/119
Laboratory Corporation of America
(LabCorp)/119
Ligand Pharmaceuticals Inc./119
Merck Research Laboratories/119
Nexell Therapeutics/120
Psychemedics Corporation/120
Quest Diagnostics/120
Quest Diagnostics at Nichols
Institute/120
Questcor Pharmaceuticals
Corporation/121
QUIDEL Corporation/121
Shaklee Corporation/121
SkyePharma/122
Syncor International Corporation/122
Tanabe Research Laboratories USA,
Inc./122
Unilab Corporation/122
Vical Inc./123
Watson Pharmaceuticals, Inc./123

BUSINESS SERVICES/ NON-SCIENTIFIC RESEARCH

ABM Industries Incorporated/124
ADT Security Services/124
Academy Tent & Canvas/124
ARAMARK Uniform Services/125
Automatic Data Processing (ADP)/125
Burns International Security
Services/126
Computer Horizons Corporation/126
Electro Rent Corporation/126
Electronic Clearing House, Inc.
(ECHO)/126
In A Word/127
Pinkerton Security & Investigation
Services/127
Pitney Bowes Management
Services/127
Prudential Overall Supply/128
Sourcecorp/128
Western Oilfields Supply Company/dba
Rain for Rent/129

CHARITIES/SOCIAL SERVICES

American Cancer Society/130
American Red Cross/130
Bienvenidos Children's Center/131
Exceptional Children's Foundation/131
Goodwill Industries of Southern
California/131
Orange County Association for
Retarded Citizens/131
Regional Center of Orange County/131

CHEMICALS/RUBBER AND PLASTICS

American Vanguard Corporation/133
Ameron International/133, 134
Arrk Product Development Group/134
Calbiochem-Novabiochem/134
Coast Packaging//135
Goodyear Tire & Rubber Company/135
Henkel Inc./135
Honeywell/136
Hutchinson Seal Corporation/ National
O-Ring Division/136
InteSys Technologies/136
Pactiv Corporation/137
Plastic Dress-Up Company/137
Ropak Corporation/137
Shipley Ronal/137
Summa Industries/138
Tricor Refining LLC/138
U.S. Borax Inc./138
United Plastics Group/139
WD-40 Company/139

COMMUNICATIONS: TELECOMMUNICATIONS/ BROADCASTING

ABC Family/140
ABC, Inc./140
ADC Telecommunications, Inc./
Wireline Systems Division/140
Adaptive Broadband/141
CBS Corporation/141
Cox Communications, Inc./141
DMX Music LLC/141
Discovery Communications Inc./142
Fox Television/KTTV-Fox 11/142
Freedom Communications Inc./142
Harris Corporation/142
L3 Communications, Inc./143
Nlynx Systems/143
QUALCOMM Incorporated/143
Unisys Pulsepoint
Communications/144
Verizon Communications/144
Westwood One Inc./145

COMPUTERS (MISC.)

ASD Software/146
Accenture/146
Acma Computers/146
Acom Solutions Inc./146
Actel Corporation/147
Advanced Computer Solutions/147
Ajilon Services Inc./147
Amdahl Corporation/147
Anacomp, Inc./148
Aonix/148
Auto-Graphics, Inc./148

EDUCATIONAL SERVICES

ELECTRONIC/INDUSTRIAL ELECTRICAL EQUIPMENT AND COMPONENTS

Advanced Photonix, Inc./185
Amistar Corporation/185
Astec America/185
Avnet, Inc./186
BAE SYSTEMS/186
BEI Technologies/186
Babcock, Inc./186
Bourns, Inc./187
California Amplifier Inc./187
Cohu, Inc./187
Conexant Systems Inc./188
Cubic Corporation/188
Custom Control Sensors, Inc./189
DPAC Technologies/189
Diodes Inc./189
Elgar Electronics Corporation/190
Elpac Electronics Inc./190
Endevco Corporation/190
Enovation Graphic Systems Inc./191
Glenair Inc./191
Graybar Electric Inc./191
HRL Laboratories, LLC/191
Hewlett-Packard Company/192
Hirose Electric USA, Inc./193
Honeywell/193
ITT Cannon/193
Interlink Electronics/194
Interstate Electronics Corporation/194
Invensys Climate Controls/194
JMAR Precision Systems, Inc./195
JMAR Technologies, Inc./195
Joslyn Sunbank Company, LLC/196
Kimball Microelectronics, Inc./196
Kyocera America, Inc./197
L3 Communications, Inc./197
Laser Power Optics/197
Leach International/198
Litton Industries, Inc./198
Lockheed Martin/198
Meggitt PLC/198
Micron Imaging Design Center/199
ORINCON Industries/199
Power-One, Inc./199
Pulse Engineering Inc./200
Pyxis Corporation/200
Racal Instruments/200
Raytheon Systems Company/201
Remec, Inc./201
Rexel Calcon/201
Sanmina-SCI Corporation/201
Scantron Corporation/202
Semicoa Semiconductors, Inc./202
Square D Company/203
Taitron Components Inc./203
Teradyne, Inc./Semiconductor Test
   Division/203
Trikon Technologies, Inc./204
TriPoint Global/204

Universal Electronics Inc./204
Vishay Intertechnology/205
WEMS Electronics Inc./205
Western Digital Corporation/205
Xontech, Inc./205

ENVIRONMENTAL & WASTE MANAGEMENT SERVICES

ARCADIS/207
Browning-Ferris Industries, Inc.
   (BFI)/207
ENSR International/207
ENVIRON Corporation/208
International Technology Corporation
   (IT)/208
Montgomery Watson/208
Parsons Corporation/209
Safety-Kleen Corporation/209
Severn Trent Laboratories, Inc./209
J.F. Shea Company, Inc./210
Smith-Emery Company/210
Tetra Tech, Inc./210
URS Corporation/211
USA Biomass Corporation/211
Waste Management, Inc./212

FABRICATED METAL PRODUCTS AND PRIMARY METALS

AGI (Athanor Group, Inc.)/213
Accuride International Inc./213
Carpenter Special Products
   Corporation/213
A.M. Castle & Company/214
Cerro Metal Products/214
Crown City Plating Company/214
Davis Wire Corporation/214
E.M.J./215
General Dynamics Ordnance and
   Tactical Systems/215
A.L. Johnson Company/215
Madison Industries, Inc./216
P.A.C. Foundries/216
Reliance Steel & Aluminum
   Company/216
TW Metals/216

FINANCIAL SERVICES (MISC.)

AFSA Data Corporation/218
Aames Financial Corporation/218
American General Finance/218
Bear, Stearns & Company, Inc./218
California First Leasing Corporation/219
The Capital Group Companies/
   American Funds Distributors/219
Commonwealth Financial
   Corporation/220
Consumer Portfolio Services, Inc./220
Countrywide Credit Industries/220, 221

San Luis Obispo County General Hospital/251
Sharp HealthCare/251
STAAR Surgical Company/252
Synbiotics Corporation/252
Tender Loving Care/Staff Builders/252
Tenet Healthcare Corporation/253
Torrance Memorial Medical Center/253
U.S. Department of Veterans Affairs Veterans Administration San Diego Healthcare System/253
USC/Norris Comprehensive Cancer Center and Hospital/253
Villaview Community Hospital/254
Vista del Mar Child & Family Services/254

HOTELS AND RESTAURANTS

Acapulco Restaurants/255
Anthony's Seafood Group/255
ARAMARK Sports and Entertainment Services/255
Buffets, Inc./255
California Beach Restaurants, Inc./256
The Cheesecake Factory Inc./256
Commerce Casino/256
Ed Debevic's Restaurant/256
Farrell's Ice Cream Parlours/257
Four Seasons Hotel/257
Hotel Del Coronado/257
Hyatt Regency Los Angeles/257
IHOP Corporation/258
JS Foods/258
Jack In The Box Inc./258
Carl Karcher Enterprises Inc./258
Millennium Biltmore Hotel/259
One Pico Restaurant/259
Prandium, Inc./259
Radisson Wilshire Plaza Hotel/259
Regent Beverly Wilshire Hotel/260
Sizzler International Inc./260
Sutton Place Hotel/260
Sybra Inc./260
Vagabond Inns Corporation/261

INSURANCE

Allianz Insurance Company/262
Amwest Surety Insurance Company/262
Aurora National Life Assurance Company/262
Automobile Club of Southern California/263
Blue Shield of California/263
Chubb Group of Insurance Companies/263
CorVel Corporation/264
Driver Alliant Insurance Services/264
Farmers Insurance Group/264

Fidelity National Title Insurance Company/265
The First American Corporation/265
Fremont General/265
General Reinsurance Corporation/266
Golden Eagle Insurance/266
HRH Insurance/266
Health Net/266
Highlands Insurance Group/267
Insurance Company of the West/267
Kaiser Permanente/267
Kemper Insurance Companies/268
Lawyers Title Insurance Corporation/268
Marsh Risk & Insurance Services/269
Mercury Insurance Group/269
The Northwestern Mutual Life Insurance Company/The Kerrigan Agency/269
Pacific Life Insurance/270
PacifiCare Health Systems, Inc./270
Talbert Medical Group/271
21st Century Insurance Group/271
WATTSHealth Foundation, Inc./271
Wausau Insurance Companies/272
WellPoint Health Networks Inc./272
Zenith Insurance Company/272

LEGAL SERVICES

Brobeck, Phleger & Harrison LLP/273
Carlsmith Ball LLP/273
Dewey Ballantine/273
Greenberg, Glusker, Fields, Claman & Machtinger/273
JAMS/274
Jeffer, Mangels, Butler, & Marmaro LLP/274
Latham & Watkins LLP/274
Luce, Forward, Hamilton, & Scripps/274
Pillsbury Winthrop/274
Procopio, Cory, Hargraves, & Savitch/274
Riordan & McKinzie/275
Rosenfeld, Meyer & Susman/275
Saltzburg, Ray & Bergman/275
Spray, Gould & Bowers/275
Stradling, Yocca, Carlson & Rauth/275

MANUFACTURING: MISCELLANEOUS CONSUMER

Acushnet Company/277
Arden Paradise Manufacturing Company/277
BSH Home Appliances/277
Buck Knives Inc./278
Callaway Golf Company/278
Certron Corporation/278
Coronet Manufacturing Company Inc./278

MANUFACTURING: MISCELLANEOUS INDUSTRIAL

MINING/GAS/PETROLEUM/ ENERGY RELATED

PAPER AND WOOD PRODUCTS

PRINTING AND PUBLISHING

Your Job Hunt
Your Feedback

Comments, questions, or suggestions? We want to hear from you!
Please complete this questionnaire and mail it to:

The JobBank Staff
Adams Media Corporation
57 Littlefield Street
Avon, MA 02322

Did this book provide helpful advice and valuable information which you used in your job search? What did you like about it?

How could we improve this book to help you in your job search? Is there a specific company we left out or an industry you'd like to see more of in a future edition? No suggestion is too small or too large.

Would you recommend this book to a friend beginning a job hunt?

Name:

Occupation:

Which JobBank did you use?

Mailing address:

E-mail address:

Daytime phone: